Thank You for Visiting

ESSAYS ON ALICE MUNRO'S WORKS III

ESSENTIAL WRITERS SERIES 60

Canada

ONTARIO ARTS COUNCIL
CONSEIL DES ARTS DE L'ONTARIO
an Ontario government agency
un organisme du gouvernement de l'Ontario

Ontario

Canada Council for the Arts
Conseil des arts du Canada

Guernica Editions Inc. acknowledges the support of the Canada Council for the Arts and the Ontario Arts Council. The Ontario Arts Council is an agency of the Government of Ontario. We acknowledge the financial support of the Government of Canada.

Thank You for Visiting

ESSAYS ON ALICE MUNRO'S WORKS III

Edited by J.R. (Tim) Struthers

GUERNICA EDITIONS
TORONTO • CHICAGO • BUFFALO • LANCASTER (U.K.)
2025

Guernica Founder: Antonio D'Alfonso

J.R. (Tim) Struthers, editor
Michael Mirolla, general editor
Joseph Pivato, series editor
Cover and Interior Design: Rafael Chimicatti
Front Cover Image: Catherine Sheldrick Ross

Guernica Editions Inc.
1241 Marble Rock Rd., Gananoque (ON), Canada K7G 2V4
2250 Military Road, Tonawanda, N.Y. 14150-6000 U.S.A.
www.guernicaeditions.com

Distributors:
Independent Publishers Group (IPG)
600 North Pulaski Road, Chicago IL 60624
University of Toronto Press Distribution (UTP)
5201 Dufferin Street, Toronto (ON), Canada M3H 5T8

First edition.
Printed in Canada.

Legal Deposit—First Quarter
Library of Congress Catalog Card Number: 2024945147
Library and Archives Canada Cataloguing in Publication
Title: Thank you for visiting : essays on Alice Munro's works III /
edited by J.R. (Tim) Struthers.
Names: Struthers, J. R. Tim, 1950- editor.
Series: Essential writers series ; 60.
Description: Series statement: Essentials writers series ; 60
Includes bibliographical references.
Identifiers: Canadiana (print) 20240452186 | Canadiana (ebook) 20240454774
ISBN 9781771839891 (softcover) | ISBN 9781771839907 (EPUB)
Subjects: LCSH: Munro, Alice, 1931-2024—Criticism and interpretation.
CSH: Canadian literature (English)—20th century—History and criticism.
CSH: Canadian literature (English)—21st century— History and criticism.
LCGFT: Literary criticism.
Classification: LCC PS8576.U57 Z886 2025 | DDC C813/.54—dc23

Like
Alice Munro Country: Essays on Her Works I
and
Alice Munro Everlasting: Essays on Her Works II
this volume
Thank You for Visiting: Essays on Alice Munro's Works III
is dedicated to Alice Munro
with admiration, with gratitude, and with love
for a lifetime spent working so ardently
in devotion to the form of the short story

And in honour of her enduring work on Alice Munro
this volume is also dedicated to Catherine Sheldrick Ross
of whom the editor of this book continued to say admiringly
to their ever-increasing amusement as they both got older,
"When I grow up, I want to *be* Catherine Sheldrick Ross."

Contents

Celebrating Alice Munro

J.R. (Tim) Struthers

Continuously. From the time, back in 1975, when I published the first two scholarly articles worldwide on her work. In 2013, when she was awarded the Nobel Prize in Literature for her short stories. Now in 2025, with the publication of this book. And for years and years in the future.

1. "What Are You Writing Now?"

From 2016 to 2020 I worked ardently on preparing two massive companion volumes, each containing twenty contributions, in honour of Alice Munro, the pair published under the titles *Alice Munro Country* and *Alice Munro Everlasting* by Guernica Editions of Toronto in the Spring of 2020 and including three items of my own. First, a new bibliography of 401 items (that number merrily chosen by way of an allusion to the major highway that runs through Alice Munro's and my home region of Southwestern Ontario): a bibliography designed to draw attention to a range of cultural and critical resources, including various studies of the short story, that I consider beneficial for understanding Munro, designed to document important past research on Munro not only in North America but also throughout Europe, and designed to facilitate further research on Munro. Second, a previously unpublished interview conducted by me with Munro here in Guelph, Ontario on Remembrance Day 1988. And, third, a new critical essay on her novella "Powers" – thereby bringing the total number of scholarly pieces about Munro that I produced over my final decade teaching full-time at the University of Guelph to ten.

Plus two more commentaries commenced during the last two years of that period and now published in *Reading Alice Munro's Breakthrough*

Books: A Suite in Four Voices (2024) and here. Including amongst these dozen studies a revised version, expanded from an original twenty typed pages by some forty-five typed pages, of my essay "Alice Munro and the American South," first published in 1975, as was an essay of mine discussing Munro's *künstlerroman*, what I think a publisher would now call her novel-in-stories rather than her novel, *Lives of Girls and Women*, in the context of Joyce's *A Portrait of the Artist as a Young Man*. These two essays, by good fortune for me, representing the first two scholarly articles, I claim, in the history of Munro criticism. And here we are a half-century later, with Alice Munro the enthusiastically celebrated winner back in 2013 of the Nobel Prize in Literature and the author, as I record in the bibliography "Book by Book," of 148 collected stories to be found in fourteen books of new work published over a forty-five-year span from *Dance of the Happy Shades* in 1968 to *Dear Life* in 2012.

"What are you writing now?" the gifted fiction writer and editor and critic John Metcalf asked me, probably when I phoned him on 12 November 2019 to wish him a happy 81st birthday, some months after John had read and responded very favourably to a draft of my essay on Munro's novella "Powers." It was a question that I came to appreciate as the highest compliment John had ever given, or could ever give, me. Thinking of me not as a university teacher, not as the publisher of Red Kite Press which issued two of his books, not as a co-editor with him of *Canadian Classics: An Anthology of Stories* and of the short story theory collection *How Stories Mean*, or more recently of Clark Blaise's *Selected Essays*, not as an interviewer or as a bibliographer, but as a writer.

"What are you writing now?"

What did I have left to say about Alice Munro, the first Canadian writer, the first short story writer, and only the thirteenth woman to win the Nobel Prize in Literature? Perhaps that on the very morning which marked the 455th anniversary of the birth of William Shakespeare, I awoke joyfully from a dream of meeting her for the first time in many years – Alice now in old age yet continuing to look so radiant. I had been wondering what I could possibly write about her and thinking that I would like to adapt a line deeply entrenched in my mind but remaining just out of reach: a line beginning with a question something like "What could I say about...?" From what author did that derive, I wondered.

Then, just as I arrived downstairs to prepare breakfast, I remembered the source. Alice Munro, of course. It's the thought that goes through the mind of the actress Rose in the last sentence of the final, title story of *Who Do You Think You Are?* – a book to which, now more than forty years ago, I had devoted a long chapter of my PhD dissertation on the Canadian story cycle. Rose has seen a story in her hometown newspaper reporting the death in middle age of her childhood schoolmate, the mimic Ralph Gillespie, and responds, "What could she say about herself and Ralph Gillespie, except that she felt his life, close, closer than the lives of men she'd loved, one slot over from her own?" I cannot think of a declaration more fitting to describe the feelings of so many remarkable readers about the ever-mesmerizing work of Alice Munro.

"What are you writing now?"

Well ...

This, "Celebrating Alice Munro."

2. The Only Voice

It is important for us, even on an occasion such as this one that invites us to focus so very deservedly on one extraordinary writer's accomplishments, to take account of, to celebrate, as Alice Munro would have us do, all those other writers comprising the rich and diverse traditions of writing – past, present, and future – that flow into and next to and onward from her own work. Writing, first, in every genre, right here in short story writer Alice Munro's and poet/playwright James Reaney's and critic Catherine Sheldrick Ross's and my own region of Souwesto. And, second, the short story, throughout Canada. Still, reading an Alice Munro story is such an absolutely unique, energizing, transcendent experience. It is also an extremely intimate experience. And in that process – to adapt the phrase that Frank O'Connor made famous in his classic study of the short story – her voice becomes for so many of us, reading her in how many different languages, "the only voice." That has held true for me in many ways, decade after decade now for a full fifty years, however powerfully various contemporaries of Munro's, predecessors of her, and others following her have gotten into my mind and blood.

3. Epic Questions

Here, before I proceed any further, I will interrupt myself to ask: Does not Alice Munro, by so profoundly and so magnificently developing, enlarging, freeing up the possibilities of the art form, the short story, that *she* practises, urge and perhaps compel those who would write about her work to imagine their own ways of developing, enlarging, freeing up the possibilities of the art form, the critical essay, that *they* practise? Indeed, could not certain critical essays, as I view stories by Alice Munro such as "Meneseteung," be considered instances of the "brief epic" form, involving epic subjects, epic tasks, epic catalogues, epic questions, and suchlike matters?

4. The Souwesto Renaissance

As I said earlier, it is important for us, even when highlighting one extraordinary writer's accomplishments, to take account of, to celebrate, as Alice Munro would have us do, all those other writers comprising the rich and diverse traditions of writing that flow into and next to and onward from her own work. Writing, first, in every genre, right here in our own region of Souwesto. And, second, the short story, throughout Canada. Thus it would not be inappropriate to cite the name of Alice Munro not as "the only voice" but as "one voice" in at least two different and wide-ranging lists of, first, important Souwesto writers in every genre, and, second, important Canadian writers of the short story. Individuals mainly of Alice Munro's generation whose writing, along with hers, has enriched – and to a very large extent *defined* – the imaginative lives of so many of us. Hence, if asked, first, to provide in, say, two paragraphs, a description of various highlights for me of Souwesto writing (and if permitted to give a nod to work in the visual arts and in music by other favourite Souwesto artists) I would offer this brief account ...

Following earlier important Southwestern Ontario writers such as Queenston, Upper Canada-born novelist, poet, and journalist John Richardson (1796-1852) and, later, Brantford, Canada West-born novelist and journalist Sara Jeannette Duncan (1861-1922) and Six Nations Indian Reserve-born poet, performer, and prose writer E. Pauline Johnson

(1861-1913), there emerged in the early and middle twentieth century a number of significant Southwestern Ontario writers. These include: Ruscomb, Ontario-born poet, short story writer, novelist, critic, and anthologist Raymond Knister (1899-1932), six of whose best stories were collected in *Selected Stories of Raymond Knister* (1972); Thamesville, Ontario-born novelist, ghost story writer, playwright, and journalist Robertson Davies (1913-1995), author of the set of novels, starting with *Fifth Business* (1970), known as The Deptford Trilogy; and London, Ontario-born George Elliott (1923-1996), author of four story cycles including *The Kissing Man* (1962) and *The bittersweet man* (1994) and *Crazy Water Boys* (1995) and *Sand gardens on First Beach* (2010). Another writer of special note is Cape Croker Indian Reserve-born ethnologist, mythographer, essayist, and linguist Basil Johnston (1929-2015), author of *Ojibway Heritage* (1976) and other very significant works, among them his *Anishinaube Thesaurus* (2007), where readers interested in sources for the title of Munro's story "Meneseteung" will be intrigued to find on the very first page the following English definition of the Ojibway words *ministik* and *ministikoowun*: "island(s) in or at the mouth of a river, usually formed by silt." (Hence, as I have argued in the essay "'Meneseteung': The Dynamics of Co-Creation," "Meneseteung" means "place of little islands.") And of course, Sarnia, Ontario-born, Point Edward, Ontario-raised poet, novelist, and nonfiction writer Don Gutteridge (1937-2023), author, amongst a great many titles, of the poem sequence *A True History of Lambton County* (1977).

Together with Alice Munro, the most important Southwestern Ontario writer is the poet, short story writer, playwright, little magazine editor, and critic James Reaney (1926-2008), native of the Stratford, Ontario area, for the final forty-eight years of his life a resident of London, Ontario, and long-time crusader for regionalism. Reaney was the author of a great many works, amongst them most importantly the epic trilogy of plays, beginning with *Sticks & Stones* (1975), entitled *The Donnellys*, about the nineteenth-century Irish-Canadian family of that name. As well, Souwesto is or was the birthplace and the imaginative "Home" – to echo the title of an Alice Munro story first published in *74: New Canadian Stories* then rewritten for publication in her family history/herstory *The View from Castle Rock* (2006) – of a younger generation of fine writers. Among them: poet, short story writer, and critic Len Gasparini; poet and playwright Penn Kemp, my first cousin and the first poet laureate for the City of London; short story writer and novelist Bonnie Burnard; critic Catherine Sheldrick Ross; poet, journalist, nonfiction writer, and small press publisher Marty Gervais; playwright and essayist William Butt; fiction writer, nonfiction writer, anthologist, and on-line literary magazine editor Douglas Glover; poet and nonfiction writer Christopher Dewdney; poet, nonfiction writer, and anthologist John B. Lee; poet and playwright Daniel David Moses; short story writer and novelist Terry Griggs; poet and nonfiction writer John Terpstra, and novelist Nino Ricci. And, too, Souwesto is or was the birthplace and the imaginative "Home" of many distinguished visual artists, such as painters Jack Chambers, Tony Urquhart, Greg Curnoe, and cartoonist Seth. Along with many distinguished musicians, among them four of five members of The Band, Rick Danko, Garth Hudson, Richard Manuel, and (culturally, at least) Robbie Robertson, as well as individual singer/songwriters Winston George and Scott Merritt and Jessy Bell Smith. Speaking in an interview with Graeme Gibson, Alice Munro declared of her own region and of its significance as a source of imaginative material for her fellow Souwesto artists: "I can think of several writers now who are working out of Southwestern Ontario. It is rich in possibilities in this way. I mean the part of the country I come from is absolutely Gothic. You can't get it all down."

5. The Canadian Renaissance

And second, my list of – I'll start with thirty – recommended Canadian short story writers: "The Canadian Renaissance," I like to term them ...

Mavis Gallant, George Elliott, Norman Levine, Margaret Laurence, James Reaney, Hugh Hood, Alice Munro, Jane Rule, Leon Rooke, Rudy Wiebe, George Bowering, Carol Shields, Audrey Thomas, Elisabeth Harvor, Alistair MacLeod, Kent Thompson, Jack Hodgins, John Metcalf, Margaret Atwood, Clark Blaise, Raymond Fraser, Len Gasparini, Olive Senior, Ray Smith, Thomas King, Marianne Micros, Keath Fraser, Douglas Glover, Terry Griggs, Diane Schoemperlen ...

And of course more.

Many many more.

6. And

Did I say we could cite Alice Munro in two key lists? I should have identified a third, even broader category. For Alice Munro stands amongst the greatest of world writers, I would argue, ever.

7. Epilogue

I'd like to finish with three quotations.

First, by Joseph Campbell, from Chapter 1, "Metaphor and Religious Mystery," in his book *Thou Art That: Transforming Religious Metaphor*. I quote this passage because it strikes me as a perfect description of Alice Munro's achievement and importance:

> How, in the contemporary period, can we evoke the imagery that communicates the most profound and most richly developed sense of experiencing life? These images must point past themselves to that ultimate truth which must be told: that life does not have any one absolutely fixed meaning. These images must point past all meanings given, beyond all definitions and relationships, to that really ineffable mystery that is just the existence, the being of ourselves and of our world. If we give that mystery an exact meaning we diminish the experience of its real depth. But when a poet [or we might say a lyric short story writer] carries the mind into a context of meanings and then pitches it past those, one knows that marvelous rapture that comes from going past all categories of definition. Here we sense the function of metaphor that allows us to make a journey we could not otherwise make, past all categories of definition.

Second, by Wendell Berry, from his lecture "It All Turns on Affection" in his book *It All Turns on Affection: The Jefferson Lecture & Other Essays*. A volume which I gave to my good friend the painter, educator, and now-retired Ontario College of Art and Design President Ron Shuebrook at an event held in Guelph to celebrate his preceding 70th birthday back on 29 July 2013 and most especially to honour his life-long accomplishments, his inspiring creativity, his enduring friendship. The statement by Berry positing encouragingly: "We do not have to live as if we are alone."

And last, essayed by me: Whenever you hold an Alice Munro story in your hand or mind, you will not feel alone.

8. "What Are You Writing Now?"

Well ...

Well ...

Truth be told, I've got three new essays on Alice Munro underway.

Perhaps I could tantalize you by briefly outlining them ...

No? There isn't room to mention even one more?

Some other time, then. I'll look forward to the pleasure of our visit.

Editing Alice Munro

Ann Close

Generally speaking, the book editor's job is to insure the text of the book the author is writing is as strong as possible, always keeping in mind that it is the author's book and being sure that it remains so. Each sort of writing has its own editorial demands and, in the case of short fiction, helping to order the stories or mold them into a collection is one of them. A lot of editorial work is intuitive. To a large extent, it's just being a good reader and being able to get so far inside a piece of writing that you can feel the places where things go a little – or a lot – wrong. Alice Munro had a clown's car full of editors, myself among them, but by all our accounts she needed very little editing, although she was always gracious about receiving suggestions and occasionally sought them.

The best things in life come about by luck and/or hard work. I have to say that I became Alice Munro's editor mostly by luck. Her agent, Virginia (Ginger) Barber, and I both attended the same Virginia college and were friends. I was already an editor at Alfred A. Knopf, Publishers, when Ginger decided to become an agent. An agent friend of hers suggested that she might find some interesting clients in Canada, and of course she did. She came back from her first trip with some stories from the book Alice Munro was working on, two of which Ginger placed with *The New Yorker*, where they were published to much excitement and welcoming of a "new" writer. I put the quotation marks there because Alice had already published three books in Canada, one of which had won Canada's prized Governor General's Award. Ginger then sent the stories around to several editors, and it was my great good fortune that Knopf became her U.S. publisher, and I her editor, for all her future publications.

The first of Alice's books was published in the States in 1979, and we called it *The Beggar Maid*, the name of one of those two stories that Ginger sold to *The New Yorker* and that had caused such a stir. The same collection was published in Canada as *Who Do You Think You Are?*. Two different titles, the same book. Something her Canadian editor, Douglas Gibson, and I decided never to do again. People, even Munro scholars, still think that there's another, mysteriously unavailable, book out there somewhere.

In 1979, when *The Beggar Maid* came out in the States, publishing books of stories was not easy. There was a decided notion that they had lesser publishing oomph than novels, a notion unfortunately borne out by the sales figures. Of course, there was Eudora Welty, whose stories were beloved; Katherine Anne Porter, who was not publishing that much anymore but whose story "Pale Horse, Pale Rider" was in every college anthology; and Canada's own Mavis Gallant, also published by *The New Yorker*. But the pressure for novels was great.

Alice's stories were, of course, never lesser pieces of writing, although she felt that same pressure, and for half her career she would say to me, "I think I've started a novel!" Fortunately those efforts always ended up as stories, stories that by all standards were as rich and complicated and fulfilling as any novel, with amazing time shifts, rounded characters with complete lives, set in particular landscapes, and were a different, fuller kind of story than was generally being published in 1979. Eventually she came around to the idea that she was probably never going to write a novel, even saying to me more than once that she'd come to think there was "too much extraneous material" in most novels. But she hadn't gotten there yet when we published *The Beggar Maid*.

All the stories in *The Beggar Maid* were connected, however, so much so that somebody had tried to make the book into a novel by chopping the ends off all the stories, even moving the final section of the story "The Beggar Maid" to the end of the book. Alice, Doug, and I all vehemently agreed this was a disaster, and we restored the endings or put them in their proper place and published the book as "connected stories" – with the subtitle in the States *Stories of Flo and Rose* – giving, along with John Updike's Maples stories, published the same year, fresh life to that now popular form.

From that first book, Munro was beloved by U.S. critics. Through the publication of eleven new collections and various volumes of *Selected Stories* there was only a scant handful of negative reviews, and even those were almost apologetically so. John Gardner, the well-known critic and novelist, said: "Whether Alice Munro's *The Beggar Maid* is a collection of stories or a new kind of novel, I'm not quite sure, but whatever it is, it's wonderful. The psychological precision, even when Munro is dealing with the most minor characters, is a delight, and the startling twists – for instance the unexpected leaps in time, the transformation of familiar characters – they make the book what books ought to be, a little wild, a little mysterious. All things considered – wonderful!"

Looking back at Alice Munro's career, it's easy to see certain things that have made it so successful. Of course, it's all in the stories themselves. As with every major writer, it is impossible to figure out exactly what they're doing that makes the work what it is. Stories have their own exigencies of form, a form halfway between poetry and novels. So much to express in such a short space. So much between the lines. So much not visible, hidden under the waterline, in Hemingway's famous analogy of good writing's being like an iceberg, very little on top and a lot down below, unseen. So many times I've thought there was something expressed outright in one of Alice's stories, but upon rereading I could never find it in actual words. The inexplicable magic of a great writer.

Being Alice Munro's editor has certainly been one of the great things that has happened in my life. Can you imagine what it has been like to open your mail and have a new Alice Munro story fall out of the package? All the hundred ten or twenty times this happened I felt exactly the same way Caroline See in a review of *Runaway* (2004) in *The Washington Post* described herself feeling: like there was "a big dish of Beluga caviar [that] sails in on a sparkling bed of ice, with a mother-of-pearl spoon. You remember: This is why you eat, read, make love, whatever – to be left silly with admiration and delight." At the office, I always meant to put the stories aside to read at home, but without fail started them as soon as I got them. As all her readers know, you just sort of slide into the world they create without any conscious effort and leave with the greatest regret.

The truth is Alice had many editors, with Virginia (Ginger) Barber, her agent, usually her first reader. We each had our roles to play, although those roles changed from book to book and story to story. The first stories at *The New Yorker* were bought and edited by Charles (Chip) McGrath who, after he left, was followed in turn by Daniel Menaker, Alice Quinn, and Deborah Treisman. In Canada Douglas Gibson published her first at Macmillan of Canada and afterwards at McClelland & Stewart, where he established Douglas Gibson Books and was later publisher and president. Since Knopf became the house that did the copyediting and proofreading and set the type we all used to print from, after the first couple of books I became the editor always of her final version. But as we would all tell you, I'm sure, being Alice's editor was easy, because Alice did most of the work. As Deborah Treisman notably said about the process: "Editing Alice Munro's stories is sometimes a lesson in feeling extraneous."

I didn't line edit the stories much. Most came in almost perfect shape. Other times we would have a conversation about something that wasn't quite working. Sometimes she would change the voice from one version to another. The story "The Progress of Love," for instance, arrived originally in the first person, but she tried it in the third person for *The New Yorker*, then we changed it back to the first person for the book. Sometimes a story went to everyone involved at the same time. As the shifts of time and place for which she became so well known appeared more regularly in the stories, Alice often sought editorial opinions about whether the shifts were in the right place. I remember one story, "Vandals," which was giving her a very hard time and, at her request, Ginger, Dan Menaker, and I all offered possible ways to fix it. That time, I believe it was Dan who came up with an idea that led her to something she was comfortable with.

Alice took risks as a writer and did so right from the beginning. This is why each collection is miraculously always better than the one before it. For example, in "Royal Beatings" (from *The Beggar Maid* and the first of her stories to appear in *The New Yorker*), the very idea of the story – parents and child engaged in a ritual of punishment and forgiveness that brings misery but ultimately certain satisfactions to them all – is risky. And in the much later "Runaway," the use of a vivid but could-be-obvious image of a tiny goat crashing precipitously into the story is a risk that works its magic brilliantly. In general in *Runaway*, Alice used more aggressive symbols than she had in past collections.

Runaway is particularly interesting to me because often the women in the stories seem to be in situations that Alice's characters have occupied in past stories, but they make different choices. For example, in "Passion," Grace, the main character, does not run away with the object of her passion as many Munro characters do. She passes up the chance. In the story "Runaway," Carla doesn't leave her husband; she gets off the bus she is taking and comes back home. *Runaway* is lighter in some ways than Alice's previous collection, *Hateship, Friendship, Courtship, Loveship, Marriage* (2001), and it is very much about younger women. Even when the stories are recalled by women further along in life, the action takes place when they are younger. In *Hateship*, there is a lot about illness and dying, and so the characters are older.

Alice's collections are always held together by certain elements she was interested in at the time. So much so that when we were putting a collection together, it was easy to think a story didn't "fit." This happened over and over to one story called, simply, "Wood." It probably got weeded out of five or six collections, although she would rewrite it every time, so much so that when it finally appeared in *Too Much Happiness* (2009) it had become a major story. Alice never stopped challenging herself, which kept her writing in top form for over fifty years.

By the time Alice, Doug, and I were putting a collection together, Alice was usually still rewriting, often fiddling, in particular with the endings. In the early days when Mr. Shawn was still at *The New Yorker*, he would edit out phrases or sentences that he thought were sexually suggestive or indelicate in some way. We loved trying to figure out what he thought was meant by what was deleted, since it wasn't always obvious. Mostly we restored it. Whatever she did, it was a gift to watch the stories emerge into their final form.

Like many writers, Alice never wanted to be obvious about the endings of her stories. As her editor, sometimes I would push her a little on that, because there might be no resolution at all to a story. I might ask her to put a hint of what was coming in the body of the story so that the ending wouldn't be too abrupt. Or maybe I'd say, "The ending isn't quite clear," or, "Not quite working." Some of what she always worked on was having the right "beat" to an ending, so that it sat right in the story, easing you into another thought or out of the story. At some point she would stop, or I would stop her. We used to laugh and say that my most important job as her editor was telling her when to stop. When I asked her once while we were still working on something in proof if she wanted to read the galleys one more time, she said, "No, because I'll just rewrite everything."

The three endings we worked on the hardest in *Runaway*, for example, were "Silence," "Powers," and "Tricks." On her own Alice did eight revisions of "Powers." It was hard to finish off the story part of it and still give Nancy her due. Alice also went through many revisions of the ending for "The Bear Came Over the Mountain" (from *Hateship*). And she worked hard and long on the exact words that end "Amundsen" in *Dear Life* (2012).

Alice also wrote stories with historical settings – such as "Meneseteung," from *Friend of My Youth* (1990), "Carried Away," "The Albanian Virgin," "A Wilderness Station," all from *Open Secrets* (1994), and "Too Much Happiness," from *Too Much Happiness*. And in *The View from Castle Rock* (2006) she worked what little she knew of her family's history into a group of stories that follow her father's family from Scotland in the early 1800s up through her own girlhood. When I read them I was bowled over. Although she was working with so little that she actually knew, she was able to make absolutely real and believable characters come alive in such different times and places. While you don't follow the same people from story to story – you sort of drop in on different folks in succeeding generations – the collection has a saga-like feel. There is a large focus on fathers, which is interesting since Alice has said she considers her mother to have provided her major material. But stories about her father begin in *The Moons of Jupiter* (1982), and appear throughout the collections, including here, with the masterful "Working for a Living," "Fathers," and the lovingly lovely "Home."

As a person, Alice was interesting, and she enjoyed enjoying herself. But early on she had let me know that she didn't want to do much publicity. Since she was published simultaneously in Canada, the U.S., and England, with many foreign countries not far behind, she didn't want her life to get swamped with publicity. She also had never figured out how to have a "persona" that answered all the publicity questions much the same way. She took each question seriously and as if she had never heard it before, answering each one with full attention. She did do readings and some interviews with *The Paris Review* and *The New York Times*, but no television or people poking around her house or interviewing her family. She didn't like the idea of going on the road alone, so I went with her on two long reading trips, and we had some grand times out on the road together. She was growing more and more beloved here in the States, attracting bigger and more adoring audiences. I also visited her quite a few times in Clinton, Ontario, and saw the house in Wingham, where she grew up. Ginger Barber and I were both Southerners, and I think it was no surprise that we understood Alice's people so well, since many of the same English, Irish, and Scottish folks settled the South.

Publishing Alice for as long as I have, I've thought hard about what it was that made the stories resonate so strongly for me and for so many others. The very last four stories of her very last book unexpectedly led me to some interesting thoughts on that subject. The first story of the group, "The Eye," in particular. The story is about a little six-year-old girl and the older teenager who comes to help out a mother having a third baby. The older girl, a little wild, a little sassy, sings popular songs over the local radio station. Just the sort of girl the mother disapproves of but the little girl is fascinated by. And sure enough, the older girl is killed one night coming home by herself from a dance hall. Despite what the mother thinks of the girl, she goes to the girl's house to pay her respects, and she takes the little girl with her, insisting she walk by the body in the open casket. The child, of course, doesn't want to see her friend dead, but finally she walks by the body and, to her amazement and immense relief, the corpse gives her a big wink. An event she holds onto until she is an older girl herself.

I knew immediately who this girl was: a sort of girl that your mother never approves of, but whom a little girl thinks is fascinating. Already at six or seven you know that one day you will have some of what this girl has – curled hair and lipstick and something you don't quite understand. You may not have the sass, but you wouldn't mind. Your parents would never let you do the amazing things she's doing – going dancing by herself, singing songs on the radio, but there's a siren call to the teen you will be. It also has something to do with the magic of childhood, when fairies, Santa Claus, and other amazing things populate your universe, and reality is still an unclear thing. It's a wonderful story, and it makes large something that would pass almost unnoticed in a novel, a minor incident, part of describing who the girl becomes, but in a short story it is all.

So I'm happy that Alice stuck to stories, and investigated so beautifully, and with such precision, the lives of girls and women. And eternally grateful that I had the chance to work so closely on them.

Alice Munro and Robertson Davies and the Scottish Borders

Douglas Gibson

The View from Castle Rock is the 2006 book by Alice Munro that I was exceptionally proud to publish. Exceptionally, because it was dedicated in Alice's words, "to Douglas Gibson, who has sustained me through many travails, and whose enthusiasm for this particular book has even sent him prowling through the graveyard of Ettrick kirk, probably in the rain."

I have a very happy history (not always in the rain) with Alice. It began with our very first meeting, in London (the Ontario one). With the help of an introduction by our mutual friend, Harry J. Boyle, I went to lunch with her there in 1974. I planned to sit worshipfully at her feet. But I soon learned to my horror that Alice was so "blocked" that she was no longer writing. Many, many people – friends, booksellers, other writers, and even publishers – were telling her that it was foolish to try to make a career out of writing short stories. She should stop that and become a novelist. Impressed by their unanimous conviction – which was indeed unanimous, and very confident – she was trying to write a novel. But it wasn't working. In fact, things were so bad that she found herself unable to write at all.

I was horrified. "But, Alice, you're a great short story writer. That's what you must do!"

I went on to say that as a publisher I would always be proud to publish her short stories, and that she could forget about writing novels, because I would never ask her for one. The advice caught her ear. And in 1986, as we became professionally closer, I published *The Progress of*

Love, and after that I went on to publish all of her short story collections, all the way to the Nobel Prize.

Which brings us to *The View from Castle Rock*, her 2006 collection. It is, of course, a superb book, and it tells us a lot about the Scotland that Alice got to know, both in her travels and her reading, and above all in her tracking down of great stories about her Laidlaw ancestors in the Scottish Borders, in the Ettrick Valley.

For almost all of us, the most interesting of Alice's relatives is the remarkable William Laidlaw, who was born around 1700. His remote farm was at the very western end of the Ettrick River, and was sourly but realistically called "Far Hope." In the local Scots this became "Phaup," and our man was known as "Will o' Phaup."

The small town of Ettrick lies on the river of that name. In the midst of the Ettrick Kirkyard, Will's tombstone grandly declares: "Here lyeth William Laidlaw, the far-famed Will o' Phaup, who for feats of frolic, agility and strength, had no equal in his day...." His agility and strength soon showed. He leaped over rivers. On land, as a young shepherd he sprinted about the hills, herding surprised sheep. Once he headed west over the hills to Moffat – remember that name – where on a whim he entered the public race that was the feature of the local Fair. During the race, in Alice's words of what we might call running commentary, "his country breeches fall down. He lets them fall, kicks his way out of them, and continues running in nothing but a shirt, and he wins." Scandal! All this in front of the delightedly shocked "leddies."

He marries in due course and produces children, who two hundred years later gave us Alice Laidlaw, who went on to marry a bookseller named James Munro. But as we investigate the Laidlaw family history, we learn more about Will. That he's not only a great athlete, he's a bootlegger and a heavy drinker, and a troublemaker. Above all, he has a mystical side to him. He meets with fairies and evil spirits. He has to protect his children from ghosts. And he sponsors wide-ranging discussion groups at his far-away farm.

One of the free-thinkers who sparkle in these outspoken philosophical and political groups is the man who wrote his "frolic, agility and strength" obituary, his son-in-law James Hogg. I could write a whole book about this man, "The Ettrick Shepherd." In fact, many whole books have indeed been written about him, this self-educated shepherd lad from Ettrickhall Farm in the Ettrick Forest, who became a major literary figure. As his fame grew as a writer, in the days when Edinburgh and its magazines in effect ran the English-speaking world of literature, this rough figure from the hills met everyone. He met John Galt (the Scottish novelist and far-travelling Canadian immigration organizer), William Wordsworth, Lord Byron, and Sir Walter Scott, everyone. Over time he became hugely successful, as the Edinburgh-based author of many articles and book reviews. He was also a well-known poet. His poem "Charlie Is My Darling" actually became a popular Jacobite song, long after Bonnie Prince Charlie was safely gone. But his most lasting achievement was the 1824 novel, *The Private Memoirs and Confessions of a Justified Sinner*. It continues to attract readers of all sorts, and its popularity continues to grow, to this day. The memorable title certainly helps.

A word now about old Scottish farming practices. *The Oxford Dictionary* defines the word "bothy" as a "Hut, cottage." More helpfully it goes on, "one-roomed building in which workmen are lodged." On small farms, such as the one where Robert Burns grew up (visited now by millions at Alloway, in my home county of Ayrshire), the family simply huddled together, squeezing the livestock behind the nearest wall, so that the heat of the horses and cows could help to warm the chilly thatched farm buildings.

On larger farms, when unattached workmen became part of the farm team, they were lodged in a separate building called a "bothy." It was in no way luxurious. But it produced its own bachelor lifestyle, often mildly scandalous. It also created a new form of literature called "Bothy Ballads." By an amazing stroke of luck, we now all have the opportunity to visit an old bothy, in real life.

Read on.

The Southern Upland Way is a coast-to-coast walking trail across Scotland. It winds through the Borders from the North Sea all the way west to the coast, ending near the ferry that splashes its way across to Larne in Northern Ireland. Right in the middle lies a place that should now be a famous attraction. It is the bothy on the Way, at Over Phawhope (map reference NT 182082).

The reason for its fame is that it was occupied by the Laidlaw family for many generations. Then in 1818 James Laidlaw (1763-1829), the grandson of Will o' Phaup, sailed with his family from Leith to Canada. From Quebec City they travelled by boat upstream to what is now Ontario. Many generations later, Alice Ann Laidlaw was born in rural Wingham, in Huron County, Ontario, on July 10, 1931. On her marriage she became Alice Munro. In 2013 the much-admired writer won the Nobel Prize in Literature.

Details of her writing life are given in the excellent biography *Alice Munro: Writing Her Lives* by Robert Thacker published in an updated edition by Emblem in 2011, with a daring final reference in the copy (that, modest cough, was written by me) at the back of the book. "We also follow the slow but steady upward trajectory of her triumphant writing career as, story by story, book by book, prize by prize, she gains fame around the world, until rumours of a Nobel Prize begin to circulate ..."

Many Canadian admirers of this world-famous figure have been attracted to visit the old Laidlaw farm in the Scottish Borders, where the ancient sheep farm can still be visited. In my book *Stories about Storytellers*, I give specific directions to anyone in Scotland who might be interested in this chance to visit the past. After speaking admiringly of my patient wife Jane, I note that

> we interrupted a visit to Scotland to explore the setting for Alice's then-forthcoming book, *The View from Castle Rock*. We knew that Alice's ancestors, the Laidlaws, came to Canada in 1818 from the Scottish Borders. We had also learned from the first version of the manuscript that the earliest known Laidlaw relatives, born around 1700, lived at the very end of the Ettrick Valley, at a farm named Far Hope. We were sure that we could find it.

My book goes on to give precise directions:

> The Ettrick River flows roughly from west to east into the North Sea about halfway between Edinburgh and the English border. From the town of Peebles we drove south until we met the Ettrick Valley. On the way we

passed Tushielaw (Alice, I remembered from the manuscript, on her own exploration had caught a bus from Tushielaw – not a name to forget).

Following the river west we were among wild, lonely, bare hills, sheep country for many generations, ever since the medieval forest that once sheltered William "Braveheart" Wallace's guerillas was felled. It left no trace among the hills but the name "Ettrick Forest." The only place that had even a cluster of houses, and a small grey school, and a church, was Ettrick itself. There, in the graveyard by the Kirk, we found the grave of William Laidlaw of Far Hope, locally called "Phaup." The tombstone of course memorably declares: "Here lyeth William Laidlaw, the far-fam'd Will o' Phaup who for feats of frolic, agility and strength, had no equal in his day."

Beside it lay the grave of the man who wrote the epitaph, Will's grandson, James Hogg. I copied the wording down carefully for Alice's book. Inside the spare Presbyterian Kirk I noted that the first man from the parish to die in the First World War was a Robert Laidlaw, who shared a name – and no doubt, bloodlines – with Alice's Canadian father.

Jane and I returned to the car and headed west with mounting excitement. Now the Ettrick River was narrowing to the point that we could imagine Will o' Phaup trying one of his legendary leaps across it. Soon the farms were falling away, the road becoming a track. We parked the car and started to walk in to Potburn, the farm that lies before Far Hope. To our relief, Potburn proved to be deserted, occupied only by sparrows and finches, although the curtains in the windows hinted at recent occupancy. Now the buildings of Far Hope were in plain sight.

"Far Hope" indeed. It was supposedly the highest farm in Scotland, a designation that held no prospect of rich land. Our map told us that the hills that rose right behind the low stone house were the spine of Scotland. Just over their tops the rainwater drained west into the Solway, and the Atlantic, a fact that I was able to pass on to Alice. Photographs of Far Hope show the bothy on the walking trail known as the Southern Upland Way.

The old farm buildings were to us a surprise and a delight. Usually a visit to a 300-year-old farm site will produce either a heap of rubble showing only bare outlines or, perhaps worse, a working farm, where literary intruders are not routinely welcomed, by man or dog. Miraculously, Far Hope is preserved in something close to its original state, and is unoccupied, yet at the same time open to all comers as a "bothy" (a rough sleeping hostel) on the walking trail.

Inside, a literary tourist can pace the rough stone floor, seeing the original kitchen layout around the fireplace, and can easily imagine the old family's straw bedding in place. A stroll around the silent outbuildings reveals where the horse was stabled, and the milk-providing cow. Sheep pens, the farm's raison d'être, are prominent, and the Ettrick provides running water at the door.

Before we left, I wrote in the visitor's book an account of Alice Munro's career, and its links to this small, humble place. I hope that many Canadians – and Americans, and other world visitors familiar with Alice's work, especially *The View from Castle Rock* – will tear themselves away from the fleshpots of Edinburgh and make the pilgrimage to Far Hope.

So now we must spread the word that this fine ancient stone farmhouse associated with a great writer with links to Scotland is open to visitors. It may not be another Alloway, for Burns admirers. Or another Abbotsford, for lovers of Sir Walter Scott. But it will never be forgotten by the countless Alice Munro fans around the world who learn about it, and who excitedly visit the Ettrick Valley.

But there is more.

At the ancient Laidlaw farm right beside the Ettrick, we know that one of the most historic literary sites in Scotland lies there, because of its link with Alice Munro. Amazingly, another site linked with a great Canadian author lies immediately to the west. For just over these hills – right there – near Moffat, is the territory that in the 18th century was home to the family of Robertson Davies.

I had the good fortune to edit and publish many of the magnificently bearded Davies' varied works, although I was too late to publish *Fifth Business*, the 1970 novel that created a sensation and made this Toronto man a figure of world renown. I also missed *The Manticore* (1972), his next novel, but I did edit and publish the third novel in The Deptford Trilogy, *World of Wonders*, in 1975. That title neatly summarizes what it was like to enter the world of this great literary figure, who was also the founding Master of Massey College at the University of Toronto.

I knew him well, worked on all of his later books, carried his coffin on a cold December day in 1995, and spoke at the memorable funeral celebration that was televised right across Canada. I sometimes visit his grave in Toronto's Mount Pleasant Cemetery, a fifteen-minute walk from our house. (Anyone keen to visit his grave will find it near the centre of the half of the Cemetery that lies east of Mount Pleasant Road, in Section 35, Lot 76, right beside his father's stone, which is large and appropriately impressive for Senator Rupert Davies.)

But we must turn back to his family, and its roots in the Scottish Borders. Amazingly, these Border ancestors had nothing to do with the great novelist's Scottish-descended MacKay mother. No, it is on the Welsh Davies side that the Marchbanks appear, providing us with a name to remember. From Davies family records we know that James Marchbank (mentioned as marrying Janet Mitchell) "was born at Nether Fenton, but his forefathers belonged to Kilpatrick Juxta, near Moffat. There is Marchbank Wood and Marchbank Farm." We will learn much more about these ancient places.

My Scottish-born friend Patricia Main has researched this area very thoroughly. Near Moffat is astonishing territory. It is surrounded by mountains. To the east we have Ettrick Pen (690 feet) just above the stream we know well. To the north stands Hart Fell (868 feet). To the west, just beyond Beattock is the Queensberry range at 697 feet.

A fascinating old road (now labelled the A708) runs north-east from Moffat towards Selkirk, Peebles, and eventually Edinburgh. It runs along what is called Moffat Water Valley. The dramatic geography here is indicated by the fact that the Grey Mare's Tail Waterfall foams alongside it. The sword-clanging history is demonstrated by the fact that along the valley lies the famous hidden pass named "The Devil's Beef Tub," where stolen herds were hidden away by the Border Reivers. These were the armoured men who for centuries made their living by secretly riding, in the dark, to steal their neighbours' cattle. Preferably English cattle, but not always.

We know that Robertson Davies was very aware of the importance of his ancestors. In her expert biography, *Robertson Davies: Man of Myth* (1994), Judith Skelton Grant gives detailed ancient charts of his ancestors, including "James Marchbank 1778-1848 of the hilly districts near

Moffat, Tweedside, Yarrow and Ettrick." Very significantly, she writes that "For Davies these great-aunts and uncles are larger-than-life figures, struck sharply into his imagination by his father's tales, and their personalities and lives are vigorously present in his mind, even though he met them only briefly or not at all."

So we can only imagine the extent of his pleasure in making much of his Marchbanks ancestors. We know without a doubt that they were important to him. Astonishingly, he wrote newspaper columns – even books! – under the carefully chosen pen name "Samuel Marchbanks."

Elizabeth Marchbank (1822-1877), a young farm girl, played a central role here by marrying William Robertson, bringing that name into the writer's family in the middle of the 19th century. And we all know how vital the name "Robertson" was to become.

We know a little about the name Marchbanks; another version is "Marjoribanks." We also know that farmers routinely took the name of their farm as the surname for the whole family. Boys in my class in Dunlop were often known by their farm names, "Big Bourock," or his young brother "Wee Bourock." The records tell us that the Marchbanks who concern us lived near Moffat. Pat Main's tireless researches have found, with the aid of records from the Scottish National Library, mentions of Marchbank farmers in the census, and a collection of farm buildings on the southwest side of Moffat. Even an old Marchbank school.

A kind Scottish authority who works for Dumfries and Galloway gives even more precise directions to the original Marchbanks farm. It lies just southwest of Moffat, on the southern outskirts of Beattock. It is an old farm, with a number of ancient buildings attached, and even a smaller farm, Upper Marchbank, just to the north.

And here we turn with gratified amazement to the research done by my old St. Andrews roommate, Keith, and his wife, Cynthia, who prefer to remain officially anonymous. From their base in the Borders they have travelled the country near Moffat and Beattock, and have taken many fascinating photographs, including one which catches the setting of this ancient farm, carefully preserved over the centuries, its views sweeping away to the west.

The little road where the tourist can find the original Marchbank, or Marchbanks, Farm, lies just opposite the historic sign to "Kilpatrick

Juxta Church." This ancient local church is very suitable for a literary tourist to explore.

To be precise, this old farm, with its important link to Canadian Literature, lies very near Beattock, between the farms of Biggarts and Cauldholm. Just as our Ettrick Valley Laidlaw site takes us very near the Southern Upland Way walking trail, so this farm lies close to the Annandale Way trail, and the sign for Marchbank is owned by "Crown Estate Scotland."

The literary nostrils start to quiver when we learn that this farm lies near Beattock. Because the superb poet W.H. Auden made Beattock the centrepiece of his classic poem from the 1930s called "Night Mail." It includes the famous lines:

> Pulling up Beattock, a steady climb:
> The gradient's against her, but she's on time.
> Past cotton-grass and moorland boulder
> Shovelling white steam over her shoulder,
> Snorting noisily as she passes
> Silent miles of wind-bent grasses.

To find where the old Marchbank farm lies today, after many generations, and many mapping changes, is fascinating. Thanks to Keith and Cynthia and their photographing the old territory that has remained open farmland over the centuries, we can all roam around there today as literary tourists. And it is a fascinating coincidence that these Marchbank ancestors of Robertson Davies lived near Moffat, just over the hill from the Alice Munro Laidlaw bothy at Ettrick.

That forbiddingly steep hill is less forbidding when we remember that Will o' Phaup scaled it before winning his near-naked race at Moffat. And there are rumours of smugglers using those very slopes.

Never underestimate the importance of Scottish smugglers. They are often central figures in Scottish history, as records of battles on the beaches of Troon reveal. In his 1999 book *The Scottish Nation*, T.M. Devine flatly states: "Where the Scots excelled was in undercutting their English rivals by developing smuggling on a grand scale. Indeed, smuggling was by no means confined to the American trades but became the great growth industry in Scotland during the decades after 1707." So don't allow anyone to say that the Scots got nothing out of the Union with England.

We know too that Robert Burns himself spent the last years of his life working as an exciseman, based in nearby Dumfries. His role there, which included leading troops that exchanged musket fire with smugglers as they captured the *Rosamond* of Plymouth in the Solway (the smugglers escaping from the captured ship by wading away across the flat Solway sands), meant that he was in the region, not far from Moffat. Knowing the history of Will o' Phaup we are struck by the stories of smugglers swooping over those same hills from Moffat with their cargo of choice, which might have been brandy, or even tea. Anything on which taxes were due, taxes that Scots were notably reluctant to pay.

I had hoped to work up to an astounding climax with a story about W.O. Mitchell and his family's farm just outside my village of Dunlop. Certainly readers of his most famous book, *Who Has Seen the Wind*, will recall the moment after young Brian's father dies. The grieving Scottish granny takes down the family Bible and reads, "This is Maggie Biggart's book. It was given to her on her wedding day in Dunlop, Scotland – May – 1832."

When I, born in 1943, was growing up there, Dunlop was a small place of around 700 people, and I knew every farmer, including some Biggarts. But W.O.'s people left for Canada, eventually Saskatchewan, so completely and finally that even the books by his son Orm and his daughter-in-law Barbara have not been able to solve the mystery of the exact location of the old Dunlop family farm.

So we are left without a dramatic climax. But we do have the delightful news that two of Canada's greatest all-time literary figures – Alice Munro and Robertson Davies – have links with ancient family farms in the Scottish Borders only about twenty miles apart. You might say, within hearty hiking distance of each other.

Connections

Isla Duncan

It was not until the late 1980s that I discovered Alice Munro's fiction, when I borrowed *Lives of Girls and Women* from my local public library. At the time I was teaching English at a tough comprehensive school in Ayrshire, in the west of Scotland. A few years later, after working part-time for a PhD at Strathclyde University, in Glasgow, I managed to secure a lecturing post there and gradually made Canadian Women's Writings my research subject, focusing on Alice Munro and Margaret Laurence.

I can identify the exact time when I decided I wanted to pursue an academic career, beyond the classroom: it was in 1990, on a miserable, *dreich* October evening in Waterstone's Bookstore, Sauchiehall Street, Glasgow, where I had gone to hear Munro read from her latest collection, *Friend of My Youth* (1990). She read passages from "Wigtime," enthralling everyone in the packed basement, patiently answering questions, and courteously signing copies of her book afterwards. I thought to myself then: it is not enough for me to read and love her stories; I want to study them, and understand *why* they are so memorable.

Munro's public reading in Glasgow, in October 1990, followed by several months the period at the start of that year when the writer stayed much longer in Scotland, specifically in its border country. There she identified the farm in the Ettrick Valley her Laidlaw ancestors had emigrated from, and conducted research on her Scottish heritage. Munro writes in the Foreword to *The View from Castle Rock*: "About ten or twelve years ago I began to take more than a random interest in the history of one side of my family" (2006: [ix]). She tells of having once lived for a few months close to the Ettrick Valley, uncovering the details of what, in "No Advantages," she calls her family's "long history" (2006: 7) that she would use in the stories forming Part One of that collection.

It pleases me that Alice Munro traces her connections to my homeland, a country I am very proud of. Scotland means more to me now because I no longer live there, having moved to southern England over twenty years ago, for work. But my partner and I stay in Dumfries and Galloway at least four times a year, when I can try to assuage my homesickness. It is a further source of pleasure to me that this region could be regarded as Alice Munro Country in Scotland, for here you would find most of the significant places Munro mentions in "No Advantages" – the Ettrick Valley, Far-Hope (pronounced *Phaw*-Hope), Moffat, the Solway Firth (but not Selkirk, which is in the Scottish Borders).

The writer's connection with Scotland is important to me as a reader and as a student of Munro's work. There are other reasons for my patriotic affection, and one of these was, at one time, and perhaps still is, quite a personal one. In Munro's stories there are recurrent references to qualities such as self-effacement, humility, and self-consciousness: particularly in her earlier work, female narrators and protagonists are encouraged to shy away from display, from pretensions. Del Jordan in *Lives of Girls and Women* explains that her aunts' searing, "final condemnation" of showing off is "*Don't they think they're somebody*" (1990: 32; emphasis in orig.); the narrator in "Half a Grapefruit," from *The Beggar Maid*, to use the book's British title, recounts how the adolescent Rose, having rashly confessed in class to eating this exotic fruit at breakfast, encounters her classmates' consequent ridicule, enduring it long afterwards. Rose would hear the quietly mocking call "Half-a-grapefruit!" as she walked home, never letting on she heard, but acknowledging painfully that "We sweat for our pretensions" (1980: 41). Rose, of course, is set for future struggles with other people's expectations of what is appropriate, or dutifully decorous, for her: hence, in "The Beggar Maid," the man she eventually marries, the patrician Patrick, lives in the hope that Rose's "accent could be eliminated, her friends could be discredited and removed, her vulgarity could be discouraged" (1980: 85).

In "Chaddeleys and Flemings," from *The Moons of Jupiter*, when the narrator throws a Pyrex dish at her husband, Richard, in outrage at his cruel and derisive dismissal of her aunt Iris as "'a pathetic old tart'" (1986: 17) I always clench my fist in gleeful, comradely appreciation. Such an act I would love to have had the courage to commit: I wish I could have challenged the person who imitated my father's rural accent, confronted the teaching colleague who made snide remarks about the cheap car I drove (a Yugo). I similarly admire Rose's stance in "The Beggar Maid" when, in response to Patrick's urbane snobbery, she acknowledges a hardening "loyalty" to her own upbringing and to "the store and the town, the flat, somewhat scrubby unremarkable countryside" that he so disparages (1980: 91).

I grew up in a prefab in the northeast Scottish town of Blairgowrie, and was encouraged throughout my childhood to be mindful and proud of my lowly origins. The adults I knew, and knew about, were like my parents: they served in local shops and garages; they worked in the foundry, the laundry, on the fruit farms, or in the factory that processed the fruit; they were not lawyers, dentists, accountants, doctors. My siblings and I were constantly taught humility – not genuflecting subservience but a self-effacing courtesy which could sometimes border on withdrawal.

My father's motto, for instance, was *Flee laich, flee lang* (Fly low, fly long): when he was offered advancement in his naval career at the end of the Second World War, he refused it, because he didn't think he could cope with the responsibility. And when my mum was encouraged to take on the job of manager in the bakery where she worked, she declined, maintaining *Wha'd listen tae me?* Both my parents preferred to remain in the background; they disliked showiness, ostentation, and so do I. But at times a reluctance to come forward can thwart and impede your progress, as I learned in academia when I felt too awkward to present conference papers, always anxious about condescension, rejection, and failure. Modest publications in Canadian Women's Writings are triumphs over a fragile self-belief that I addressed only in later years, nearing the end of my working life.

It was never easy for me to forge an academic career in my chosen subject. In the two universities where I have taught, I was employed principally as a language specialist, and had to fight to introduce a module in Contemporary Canadian Fiction. A Shakespeare colleague in the department was adamant Alice Munro had written *The Color Purple*; most of my early students had heard of only Margaret Atwood, the American writer, and always misspelled Margaret Laurence's surname, no doubt thinking of the canonical English author. But a couple of years after my retirement, the university did ask me to mark the launch of my book, *Alice Munro's Narrative Art* (2011), with a public lecture; I found there were numerous titles by Munro in the library; former students wrote telling me that the story "The Love of a Good Woman" was the best literary work they had studied at university; and one shelf in my bookcase could be filled with copies of my published essays.

Studies in literary linguistics at Strathclyde gave me the confidence, the metalanguage, and the discipline to start writing about Munro's fiction, and hope that what I wrote might be published. With greater authority and precision I could explore aspects such as the richness of her many narrative voices; the complexity in the stories' structures; the lushness of temporal and narrative layering; the sheer stylistic flair which characterizes her work. And all the time I was teaching and working on Munro's fiction, I remembered the pupils I had left behind in the Ayrshire comprehensive school: I thought of how some of the older pupils, studying for their Highers, had responded to the extracts from *The Beggar Maid* I used in class, how they puzzled over the indeterminate endings, struggled with the incongruities, disliked characters like the snobbish Patrick, but laughed at the antics of Milton Homer, and heartily appreciated Flo's fondness for vulgarity. Their responses kept me mindful of the *primacy* of pleasure in reading. I remembered how they, like me, enjoyed learning about another country they had never visited.

The strong sense of "Canadianness" in Alice Munro's stories was another reason I was drawn to them – it still is. I love how she affectionately delineates the distinctive Southwestern Ontario landscape, how she draws attention to the ways her characters speak, with their regional idiolects, how they furnish their homes with items and furniture that seem to me peculiarly Canadian. I like identifying on my map those authentic places she mentions, like Goderich, London, Grey County, distinguishing them from the fictional Tuppertown, Hanratty, and Dalgleish.[1] There are regular references to things I hadn't read of until I encountered them in Munro's fiction: woodlots, townships, chesterfields, tongue-in-groove boards, wispy tamarack, swamp roads, sidewalks cracked by maple-tree roots. These phenomena set my imagination alight, making me picture settings far from my small-town Scottish world, in distance, but somehow near it in the *couthy* quality, the homeliness.

Munro pays homage to her beloved Southwestern Ontario landscape in a statement I think best encapsulates her affection:

> The reason I write so often about the country to the east of Lake Huron is just that I love it. It means something to me that no other country can[...]. I am intoxicated by this particular landscape, by the almost flat fields, the swamps, the hardwood bush lots, by the continental climate with its extravagant winters. I am at home with the brick houses, the falling-down barns, the occasional farms that have swimming pools and airplanes, the trailer parks, burdensome old churches, Wal-Mart, and Canadian Tire. I speak the language. (*A Wilderness Station*, 2015: xv)

That love of a landscape and the rich knowledge of lives lived on it, over time, were enthralling to me. In a less exalted way, perhaps, I too am devoted to my patch of land, the Strathmore Valley, between the southern Grampian Mountains and the Sidlaw Hills, in the counties of Perth and Angus. I cherish, and desperately miss, its purple heather moors, vast barley fields in autumn, farm byres deep in straw, lochs edged with reed and meadowsweet, rivers rushing down through glens.

It was not long after I began my studies of Munro's work that I managed to save enough for a holiday in Canada. I desperately wanted to see the landscape that will be forever associated with her fiction. A Canadian friend I knew from work invited me to stay at her home in Toronto, and from there we drove to Huron County. I will never forget my first sight of Lake Huron, that immense expanse of glistening blue water, nor would images of landmarks like Turnberry Plain, the Maitland River, Wingham Town Hall, with its exotic cupola, be dislodged from my memory. The short trip to Huron County will stay in my mind all my days.

Visiting Canada, and more specifically the land in which most of Munro's stories are set, profoundly enriched my teaching and my studies. The whole experience afforded me greater authority about my subject: I could talk about and show slides of Wingham, for instance, explain the history of certain townships, the geography of certain Southwestern Ontario counties, land that Munro describes as "a record of ancient events [...] formed by the advancing, stationary, and retreating ice" (2006: 318); I now understood more about the people who settled in that part of Ontario, and who would be the foundations of Munro's characters: the housewives in the small towns "who belonged to the Flora Simpson Club" (*Family Furnishings*, 2015: 211); "farmers [who] came into town with some money in their pockets [when] the stores had brightened up after the Depression doldrums" (2006: 203); the "Scotch Presbyterians, Congregationalists, Methodists from the north of England" who built up the churches described in *Lives of Girls and Women* (1990: 79).

To these characters, who feature with some regularity in Munro's stories, I would ascribe a particular *Scottish* significance, because the images they conjured up were so familiar to me, when I was young. The "Flora Simpson Club" which the narrator's Aunt Alfrida, in "Family Furnishings," attracts with the advice page, "Round and About Town," reminds me of stalwart Scottish papers like *The Sunday Post* and *The People's Friend*, which have been in print for well over a century. (At one time, in the 1960s, *The Sunday Post* was read by 80% of the Scottish population.) Both these papers contained, and still have, popular columns such as "The Doc Replies," where readers write in with innocent queries about health, and "Raw Deals," where the columnist exposes poor trading practices. The young narrator's description, in "Lying Under the Apple Tree," of the brightly lit, busy main street stores on a Saturday night makes me instantly think of my hometown, especially at the height of the fruit growing season, when berry pickers from the neighbouring farms would throng the streets with their newly earned cash. And any mention of church goers in a Munro story brings to mind my Presbyterian upbringing. Del Jordan's awareness of the various faiths in Jubilee has me recall a similar wealth of churches in my childhood, and her offhand, but clamorous observation that "Doctors, lawyers, merchants passed the plate" (1990: 79) always makes me smile.

These are some of the close associations that my own idiosyncratic Scottishness helps me to make with Alice Munro's stories. I now read, study, and enjoy Munro's fiction *again and again*, with not necessarily any need or desire to discern an argument, a particular avenue for exploration, a lens through which to view the narrative. This freedom allows me to value and to celebrate the personal connections I've described above.

Note

1. "Dalgleish" is a very Scottish name. As David Dorward explains in his book *Scottish Surnames*, the surname derives from Gaelic *dal glas*, meaning "green field," and first occurs in the lands near Selkirk, in the Scottish Borders (2003: 63). The surname is most frequent on Scotland's east coast.

Works Cited

Dorward, David. *Scottish Surnames*. 1995. Edinburgh: Mercat, 2003.

Munro, Alice. *The Beggar Maid: Stories of Flo and Rose*. 1980. London: Penguin, 1980.

---. *Family Furnishings: Selected Stories 1995-2014*. 2014. Fwd. Jane Smiley. New York: Vintage International, 2015.

---. *Friend of My Youth*. London: Chatto & Windus, 1990.

---. *Lives of Girls and Women*. 1971. Toronto: Penguin, 1990.

---. *The Moons of Jupiter*. 1982. Introd. Alice Munro. Markham, ON: Penguin, 1986.

---. *The View from Castle Rock*. Toronto: McClelland & Stewart, 2006.

---. *A Wilderness Station: Selected Stories 1968-1994*. Introd. Alice Munro. New York: Vintage International, 2015.

The Change of Seasons: Once Upon a Time with Alice Munro

Reg Thompson

At ten o'clock on a fine morning in late September 2013, I arrived at Alice Munro's house in Clinton, to pick up Alice and her friend Sally Gregson. We were taking a day trip to Grey County.

This excursion came about from a request Alice made a few weeks earlier. She asked if I would take her to visit the Mannerow Cemetery again. This was a trip she and her late husband Gerry had done several times. I had not been there before, though I had meant to go for years, ever since they had first told me about it.

Alice does not drive. All their years together it was the team of Gerald Fremlin the geographer, driving, and Alice Munro the writer, riding shotgun, and from that vantage point free to observe and remark and absorb as they explored the countryside. And what has come out of that exploration of the landscape and the life on it is well-known to the world now in the works of Munro.

Alice and Gerry used to travel around with a set of maps that showed in great detail the landforms of southern Ontario. She wrote a fine essay called "What Do You Want To Know For?" about their exploration of Grey County and its varied and interesting terrain, and their chance discovery of the Mannerow Cemetery, object of our day's quest. Drumlins, eskers, moraines, glacial till. The evidence of the ice age is easy to spot on the face of Grey County. That essay was published in 1994 in the PEN Canada travel anthology called *Writing Away*. It is one of my all-time favourite Munro pieces. It was published again in 2006 in a modified version in the collection *The View from Castle Rock*.

I drove north and east through the counties of Huron, Bruce, and Grey. A warm day, some harvest still going on, just the edge of autumn so far, the beginnings of fall colours. We discussed the evolving countryside, the changes in buildings, how rare it is to see a big elm now.

We detoured and explored in the towns along the way. In Wingham – the old Lower Town road, Alice's childhood house, the sites of various old remembered neighbours, the fairgrounds with the metal banner over the gate: TO THE FALLEN HEROES OF TURNBERRY TWP 1914-18 1939-45.

Alice asked me stop a minute beside the overgrown empty lot where the school used to stand. "The kids beat me up at that school," she said, and I heard the six-year-old girl and the hurt that has lasted forever.

On to Teeswater, where we saw interesting spires in the skyline, and followed side streets to see the impressive churches they mark. You can tell a lot about a town's culture and the commitment of its founders and fortunes by the churches they built, and how they stand now.

Then on through Mildmay and Neustadt. The territory becomes noticeably Lutheran. Alice spotted a small cemetery by the roadside and asked if we could stop, so we did, and spent a good half-hour walking among the monuments and history of St. John's Lutheran. These people, names, stones utterly unknown to us, yet we could see the community, the heritage, the family connections between repeated surnames on monuments, the progression of the generations. And as always in an old cemetery, the short lives and early deaths that mark the tragedies and sadnesses of another time.

There were half a dozen stones here of a peculiar design I have not seen anywhere else. Stones marking the graves of children often have a lamb in profile lying on the top. These had a lamb, but cut from the upper front of the stone, resting on a sort of curved shelf just below the top, over the inscription. I have not noticed this technique before, but I'll be watching for them from now on. Maybe it was the style of one local carver.

Then we drove ahead to the very busy town of Hanover. We stopped and lingered over a late lunch. Leaving Hanover I misread a road sign and mistakenly headed east. It was some time before I discovered the error. We then had to go north, but now were in unanticipated territory. I became pressingly aware of the shrinking afternoon. I was now racing to catch up for meandering time.

Eventually we got to the right area, Sullivan Township, the road to McCullough Lake. We must now be very near the cemetery. But the road wound through a wooded area, around the south end of the lake, an old cottage settlement. Away from the lake – several miles of increasingly heavy bush, no sign of a cemetery – I concluded this was a mistake. A loop east around on another road, to approach from the extreme north end of the road we already did the south section of. Concession 4. The cemetery's geographical location is Lot 19, Concession 4. This is Concession 4. Now where is this cemetery?

Alice didn't think the lay of the land matched her memory of previous visits, but that was years ago. Fields have grown up in trees, buildings have disappeared. There are a lot of new houses, Amish farmhouses, white frame, because this is a heavily Amish area now, a new social development. The landscape is changed.

We passed a driveway sign advertising ACCOUNTANT SERVICES, and I realized we saw it a while ago. So we had covered the whole length of the concession. What cemetery?

In frustration, I turned west onto a sideroad, which I knew was not the right direction. Over a small hill there was a bend, and near the road, a bungalow. There was a man working at a utility trailer beside the garage. I parked, walked over to him. I explained we were looking for an old cemetery, a small cemetery, called Cedardale. He said he's from Cambridge, so he does not really know this area, but he'd ask his mom.

He fetched mother. I said it's a small cemetery, called Cedardale, used to be called Mannerows. Mother – God bless her! – said, yes, there's a cemetery, she's not sure of the name, but it's just back down that hill, and around to the right, cross a little bridge, then another right turn, and cross another bridge, and that's where the cemetery is.

So we did that, and within three minutes we crossed the second bridge, up a slight rise past creek-side cedar trees (hence Cedardale) and there it was. The little cemetery, surrounded by a chain-link fence. The famous earth-mound tomb in the middle. I have had the picture of it in my head nearly twenty years, and here it is. Like a giant barrel lying on its side in the middle of the cemetery, covered in long grass. No gravestones near it.

Alice was overcome with joy. "Oh, I didn't think we were going to find it," she said. "I thought it was getting too late, we were going to have to go home." And I said, "We came to see the cemetery. It's not *dark* yet, Alice; we were not going home without finding it."

We got out of the car. I grabbed the camera. This was a once-in-a-lifetime moment. I asked Alice to go over to the fence and stand under the iron arch that says CEDARDALE, and I took her picture. The proof. Then I undid the fastener chain and opened the gate.

We explored the cemetery. I took pictures of the grassy tomb, the big cedar in front of it. Almost identical to the photo of years ago. Maybe the tree is a little bigger? The strange mound is about twenty feet long, seven high at the arc of the rounded top. No names, no dates. Stone blocks supporting the rising curve of the mound, and a stone arch in the east end filled and sealed with bricks at ground level. So the burial chamber must be nearly as deep below ground as the rounded mound rises above it. Think of opening it for a funeral, another occupant, every few years, until it was full. Then sealed up permanently. Never to be opened again. And unlike graves with tombstones, no names, dates, nothing to say who is spending eternity in there.

This was the Mannerow farm. This is a Mannerow family tomb. There is a similar smaller tomb in a corner of the cemetery, more Mannerows, no names or marker there either.

Was this an idea the first Mannerows brought from their native Germany? The rest of the cemetery looks as old cemeteries usually look – a variety of styles of monuments, the changing eras in fashion. Many here have German inscriptions, showing the origins of the community.

There's a low spot in the middle of the cemetery. I stood there, sighting pictures. The late afternoon sun was slanting and very bright, washing out the subjects. Near the west end stand two rows of old white gravestones, forming a large cross in the turf. Many years ago they were removed from original grave locations and rearranged here. They stand like dominoes, one behind the other, just enough space left to let you read the inscriptions.

I took a picture as Alice walked among them, reading the ages, the years, the German words. And I had this thought, as I sometimes do in her company: many people would give anything to be in my shoes right now, to be spending time with Alice Munro. Fans who would be beside themselves with joy at being in the presence of this famous writer. But I am never stunned into amazement; Alice and I have been friends too long for that.

This was sixteen days before she won the Nobel Prize. In one of the interviews after the award was announced, she said, "I am a straightforward Canadian woman."

It was a full day. As we drove home across this ordinary wonderful landscape that Alice has made quietly famous to the world, we were appropriately driving into the sunset. Deceptive ordinariness. When Alice wrote her piece twenty years earlier about their discovery of the cemetery and unravelling its history, she ended it by saying "Back where nothing seems to be happening, beyond the change of seasons."

It turned out, when I checked the old Grey County atlas from 1880, what the problem was about the 4th Concession location. Lot 19 is a *corner* lot, so it happens that the access to it is not from the concession road along the front, as you would expect, but from the sideroad that runs along the south side. So the cemetery is not even visible from the 4th Concession. That view is bush.

There was a funny aspect to our difficulty in finding the cemetery. Alice and Gerry had first discovered it by chance, just driving by on the road. When they tried to find it again over a year later, they drove around and could not locate it. They made several visits to the area but without success. A frustrating puzzle.

Alice happened to be in the Clinton library checking the Grey County atlas for church and cemetery locations when I dropped in. She explained the problem to me. Well, she had forgotten that they had told me about this cemetery with the strange tomb when I was visiting them shortly after the original discovery. And they had given me some directions how to find the cemetery – the names of small places nearby. I had written down a few key words on a piece of paper that I thought I could find in my papers at home. I went home and found it. The words were *Peabody, Scone, McCullough Lake.*

That was all it took. They realized they had been fixated on an area just south of the right terrain. So they found the cemetery again, with the help of their own directions that they had intended for my future use. After that, Alice was able to write her marvelous essay – "What Do You Want To Know For?." And then on this fine fall day twenty years on, we lost the cemetery and had to rediscover it all over again.

Two days later Alice came to see me at work. She told me what a wonderful day it was, how much she and Sally had enjoyed it. "Can we go again?" she asked, and I said "Of course we can" and she told me she was leaving in a few days for Victoria for the winter, and I thought: Come, Spring.

***

The next year – post-Nobel award – when Alice was settled back in her house in Clinton, we started going on countryside rambles. It became a regular routine, usually Tuesdays. Driving the back roads, exploring bypassed hamlets, remnants of ancient swamps and forests, tiny pioneer cemeteries. We did return to visit the Mannerow Cemetery again, a number of times. We kept up those country drives for several years, until Alice left Huron County. They were interesting adventures, fine days. Good times.

This first visit to Mannerows was the beginning, and remains very special in memory.

Alive to Herself: The Achievement of Alice Munro

Margaret Atwood

Alice Munro is among the major writers of English fiction of our time. She's been accorded armfuls of super-superlatives by critics in both North America and the United Kingdom, she's won many awards, and she has a devoted international readership. Among writers themselves, her name is spoken in hushed tones. Most recently she's been used as a stick to flog the enemy with, in various inter-writerly combats. "You call this writing?" the floggers say, in effect. "Alice Munro! Now *that's* writing!" She's the kind of writer about whom it is often said – no matter how well-known she becomes – that she ought to be better known.

None of this happened overnight. Alice Munro has been writing since the 1950s, and her first collection – *Dance of the Happy Shades* – appeared in 1968. In total she has published fourteen volumes of new work, typically averaging nine or ten stories each. Though her fiction has been a regular feature of *The New Yorker* since the 1970s, her recent elevation to international literary sainthood took as long as it did partly because of the form in which she writes. She is a writer of stories – "short stories," as they used to be called, or "short fiction," which is now more common. Though many American and British and Canadian writers of the first rank have practised this form, there is still a widespread but false tendency to equate length with importance.

Thus Alice Munro has been among those writers subject to periodic rediscovery, at least outside Canada. It's as if she jumps out of a cake – *Surprise!* – and then has to jump out of it again, and then again. Readers don't see her name in lights on every billboard. They come across her as if by accident or fate, and are drawn in, and then there is an outbreak of wonder and excitement, and incredulity – *Where did Alice Munro come from? Why didn't anybody tell me? How can such excellence have sprung from nowhere?*

***

But Alice Munro did not spring from nowhere. She sprang – though it's a verb her characters would find overly sprightly, and indeed pretentious – from Huron County, in Southwestern Ontario.

Ontario is the large province of Canada that stretches from the Ottawa River to the western end of Lake Superior. This is a huge and varied space, but Southwestern Ontario is a distinct part of it. It was called Souwesto by the painter Greg Curnoe, a name that has stuck. Curnoe's view was that Souwesto was an area of considerable interest, but also of considerable psychic murkiness and oddity, a view shared by many. Robertson Davies, also from Souwesto, used to say, "I know the dark folkways of my people," and Alice Munro knows them, too. You are likely to run into quite a few signs in Souwesto wheat fields telling you to be prepared to meet your God, or else your doom – felt to be much the same thing.

Lake Huron lies at the western edge of Souwesto, Lake Erie to the south. The country is mostly flat farmland, cut by several wide, winding rivers prone to flooding, and on the rivers – because of the available boat transport, and the power provided by water-driven mills – a number of smaller and larger towns grew up in the nineteenth century. Each has its red-brick town hall (usually with a tower), each its post-office building and its handful of churches of various denominations, each its main street and its residential section of gracious homes, and its other residential section on the wrong side of the tracks. Each has its families with long memories and stashes of bones in the closets.

Souwesto contains the site of the famous Donnelly Massacre of the nineteenth century, when a large family was slaughtered and their home burnt as a result of political resentments carried over from Ireland. Lush nature, repressed emotions, respectable fronts, hidden sexual excesses, outbreaks of violence, lurid crimes, long-held grudges, strange rumours – none are ever far away in Munro's Souwesto, partly because all have been provided by the real life of the region itself.

Oddly enough, a number of writers have come from Souwesto. Oddly, because when Alice Munro was growing up in the 1930s and '40s, the idea of a person from Canada – but especially one from small town Southwestern Ontario – thinking they could be a writer to be taken seriously in the world at large was laughable. Even by the '50s and '60s there were very few publishers in Canada, and even they were mostly textbook publishers who imported whatever so-called literature was to be had from England and the United States. There might be some amateur theatre – high-school performances, Little Theatre groups. There was, however, the radio, and in the '50s and '60s Alice Munro got her start through CBC programmes produced by Robert Weaver.

But very few Canadian writers of any sort were known to an international readership, and it was taken for granted that if you had hankerings of that kind – hankerings about which you would of course feel defensive and ashamed, because art was not something a grown-up morally credible person would fool around with – it would be best for you if you left the country. Everyone knew that writing was not a thing you could ever expect to make your living at.

It might be marginally acceptable to dabble around the edges of water-colour painting or poetry if you were a certain kind of man, described by Munro in "The Turkey Season":

> There were homosexuals in town, and we knew who they were: an elegant, light-voiced, wavy-haired paperhanger who called himself an interior decorator; the minister's widow's fat, spoiled only son, who went so far as to enter baking contests and had crocheted a tablecloth; a hypochondriacal church organist and music teacher who kept the choir and his pupils in line with screaming tantrums.

Or you could do art as a hobby, if you were a woman with time on your hands, or you could scrape out a living at some poorly paid quasi-artistic job. Munro's stories are sprinkled with women like this. They go in for piano-playing, or write chatty newspaper columns. Or – more tragically – they have a real though small talent, like Almeda Joynt Roth in "Meneseteung," but there is no context for them. Almeda produces one volume of minor verse, published in 1873, called *Offerings*:

> The local paper, the *Vidette*, referred to her as "our poetess." There seems to be a mixture of respect and contempt, both for her calling and for her sex – or for their predictable conjuncture.

At the beginning of the story Almeda is a maiden lady whose family has died. She lives alone, preserves her good name, and does charitable works. But by the end, the dammed-up river of art has overflowed – helped on by hefty doses of laudanum-laced painkiller – and it sweeps her rational self away:

> Poems, even. Yes, again, poems. Or one poem. Isn't that the idea – one very great poem that will contain everything and, oh, that will make all the other poems, the poems she has written, inconsequential, mere trial and error, mere rags? ... The name of the poem is the name of the river. No, in fact it is the river, the Meneseteung, that is the poem ... Almeda looks deep, deep into the river of her mind and into the tablecloth, and she sees the crocheted roses floating.

This seemed to be the fate of an artist – of necessity, a minor artist – in the small Souwesto towns of yore: silence enforced by the need for respectability, or else an eccentricity verging on madness.

If you moved to a larger Canadian city, you might at least find a few others of your ilk, but in the small towns of Souwesto you'd be on your own. Nevertheless, John Kenneth Galbraith, Robertson Davies, Marian Engel, Graeme Gibson, and James Reaney all came out of Souwesto, and Alice Munro herself – after a spell on the West Coast – moved back there, and for decades lived not far from her birthplace of Wingham, the prototype of the various Jubilees and Hanrattys and Dalglieshes in her stories.

Through Munro's fiction, Souwesto's Huron County has joined Faulkner's Yoknapatawpha County as a slice of land made legendary by the excellence of the writer who has celebrated it, though in both cases "celebrated" is not quite the right word. "Anatomized" might be closer to what goes on in the work of Munro, though even that term is too clinical. What should we call the combination of obsessive scrutiny, archeological unearthing, precise and detailed recollection, wallowing in the seamier and meaner and more vengeful undersides of human nature, telling of erotic secrets, nostalgia for vanished miseries, and rejoicing in the fullness and variety of life, stirred all together?

At the end of Munro's *Lives of Girls and Women* (1971), her only novel and a *bildungsroman* – a novel of development, in this case a portrait of the artist as a young girl – there's a telling passage. Del Jordan of Jubilee, who has by now – true to her last name – crossed over into the promised land of womanhood and also of writerhood, says of her adolescence:

> It did not occur to me then that one day I would be so greedy for Jubilee. Voracious and misguided as Uncle Craig out at Jenkin's Bend, writing his History, I would want to write things down.
>
> I would try to make lists. A list of all the stores and businesses going up and down the main street and who owned them, a list of family names, names on the tombstones in the Cemetery and any inscriptions underneath ...
>
> The hope of accuracy we bring to such tasks is crazy, heartbreaking.
>
> And no list could hold what I wanted, for what I wanted was every last thing, every layer of speech and thought, stroke of light on bark or walls, every smell, pothole, pain, crack, delusion, held still and held together – radiant, everlasting.

As a programme for a life's work this is daunting. Nevertheless it's a programme Alice Munro was to follow over the next forty years with remarkable fidelity.

***

Alice Munro was born Alice Laidlaw, in 1931, which means that she was a small child during the Depression. She was eight in 1939, the year Canada entered the Second World War, and she attended university – The University of Western Ontario, in London – in the postwar years. She was twenty-five and a young mother when Elvis Presley first became famous, and thirty-eight at the time of the flower-child revolution and the advent of the women's movement in 1968-69, a moment in time that saw the publication of her first book. In 1981 she was fifty. Her stories are set mainly over these years – the '30s to the '80s – or even before then, in the time of ancestral memory.

Her own ancestry was partly Scotch Presbyterian: she can trace her family back to James Hogg, the Ettrick Shepherd, friend of Robert Burns and the Edinburgh literati of the late eighteenth century and author of *The Private Memoirs and Confessions of a Justified Sinner*, which could itself be a Munro title. On the other side of the family there were Anglicans, for whom the worst sin is said to consist of using the wrong fork at dinner. Munro's acute consciousness of social class, and of the minutiae and sneers separating one level from the next, is honestly come by, as is – from the Presbyterians – her characters' habit of rigorously examining their own deeds, emotions, motives, and consciences, and finding them wanting. In a traditional Protestant culture, such as that of small-town Souwesto, forgiveness is not easily come by, punishments are frequent and harsh, potential humiliation and shame lurk around every corner, and nobody gets away with much.

But this tradition also contains the doctrine of justification by faith alone: grace descends upon us without any action on our part. In Munro's work, grace abounds, but it is strangely disguised: nothing can be predicted. Emotions erupt. Preconceptions crumble. Surprises proliferate. Astonishments leap out. Malicious acts can have positive consequences. Salvation arrives when least expected, and in peculiar forms.

However, as soon as you make such a pronouncement about Munro's writing – or any other such analysis, inference, or generalization about it – you're aware of that mocking commentator so often present in a Munro story – the one who says, in essence, *Who do you think you are? What gives you the right to think you know anything about me, or about anyone else for that matter?* Or, to quote from *Lives of Girls and Women* again, "People's lives ... were dull, simple, amazing and unfathomable – deep caves paved with kitchen linoleum." The key word here is "unfathomable."

***

The first two stories, "Royal Beatings" and "The Beggar Maid," in the selection of Munro's work published in the United States as *Carried Away* and in Canada as *Alice Munro's Best* are from a book with two different titles. In Canada it was called – after a term of peevish accusation used to let the air out of somebody else's puffed-up head – *Who Do You Think You Are?*. In the United States and England it was called, romantically, *The Beggar Maid*. The stories in this enigmatically-titled book have a common protagonist – Rose, who grows up in a poorer section of a town called Hanratty with her father and her stepmother Flo, then goes to university on scholarship, marries a man from a social level far above hers and later runs away from him, and then, later still, becomes an actress – a cardinal sin and cause for shame in the Hanratty still inhabited by Flo. *Who Do You Think You Are?* is thus another *bildungsroman* – an account of the formation of its heroine – and another portrait of the artist.

What is fakery, what is authenticity? Which emotions and modes of behaviour and speech are honest and true, which pretended or pretentious? Or can they be separated? Munro's characters think frequently about such matters.

As in art, so in life. Hanratty society is divided in two by the river that flows through the town:

> In Hanratty the social structure ran from doctors and dentists and lawyers down to foundry workers and factory workers and draymen; in West Hanratty it ran from factory workers and foundry workers down to large improvident families of casual bootleggers and prostitutes and unsuccessful thieves.

Each half of the town claims jeering rights against the other. Flo goes across to Hanratty, the better part of town, to shop, but also to

> see people, and listen to them. Among the people she listened to were Mrs. Lawyer Davies, Mrs. Anglican Rector Henley-Smith, and Mrs. Horse-Doctor McKay. She came home and imitated them at supper: their high-flown remarks, their flibberty voices. Monsters, she made them seem; of foolishness, and showiness, and self-approbation.

But when Rose goes to college and boards with a lady professor and becomes engaged to Patrick, son of a West Coast department-store tycoon, and gets a look at upper-middle-class surroundings, Flo in turn becomes monstrous in Rose's eyes, and Rose is divided against herself. Patrick's visit to Rose's hometown is a disaster for Rose:

> She felt ashamed on more levels than she could count. She was ashamed of the food and the swan and the plastic tablecloth; ashamed for Patrick,

> the gloomy snob, who made a startled grimace when Flo passed him the toothpick-holder; ashamed for Flo with her timidity and hypocrisy and pretensions; most of all ashamed for herself. She didn't even have any way that she could talk, and sound natural.

Yet as soon as Patrick begins to criticize her town and family, Rose feels "a layer of loyalty and protectiveness ... hardening around every memory she had...."

This state of divided allegiance applies to Munro's vocation as well as to considerations of social status. Her fictional world is peopled with secondary characters who despise art and artifice, and any kind of pretentiousness or showing off. It's against these attitudes and the self-mistrust they inspire that her central characters must struggle in order to free themselves enough to create anything at all.

At the same time her protagonists share this scorn of the artificial side of art, and the distrust of it. What should be written about? How should one write? How much of art is genuine, how much just a bag of cheap tricks – imitating people, manipulating their emotions, making faces? How can one affirm anything about another person – even a made-up person – without presumption? Above all, how should a story end? (Munro often provides one ending, then questions or revises it. Or else she simply distrusts it, as in the final paragraph of "Meneseteung" where the narrator says, "I may have got it wrong.") Isn't the very act of writing an act of arrogance, isn't the pen a broken reed? A number of stories – "Friend of My Youth," "Carried Away," "Wilderness Station," Hateship, Friendship, Courtship, Loveship, Marriage" – contain letters that display the vanity or falsity or even the malice of their writers. If the writing of letters can be so devious, what about writing itself?

This tension has remained with her: as in "The Moons of Jupiter," Munro's artistic characters are punished for not succeeding, but they are punished also for success. The woman writer, Janet, thinking about her father, says:

> I could hear him saying, Well, I didn't see anything about you in *Maclean's*. And if he had read something about me he would say, Well, I didn't think too much of that writeup. His tone would be humorous and indulgent but would produce in me a familiar dreariness of spirit.

The message I got from him was simple: Fame must be striven for, then apologized for. Getting or not getting it, you will be to blame.

***

"Dreariness of spirit" is one of the great Munro enemies. Her characters do battle with it in every way they can, fighting against stifling mores and other people's deadening expectations and imposed rules of behaviour, and every possible kind of muffling and spiritual smothering. Given a choice between being a person who does good works but has inauthentic feelings and is numb at heart and one who behaves badly but is true to what she really feels and is thus alive to herself, a Munro woman is likely to choose the latter; or, if she chooses the former, she will then comment on her own slipperiness, guile, wiliness, slyness, and perversity. Honesty, in Munro's work, is not the best policy: it is not a policy at all, but an essential element, like air. The characters must get hold of at least some of it, by means fair or foul, or – they feel – they will go under.

The battle for authenticity is waged most significantly in the field of sex. The Munro social world – like most societies in which silence and secrecy are the norm in sexual matters – carries a high erotic charge, and this charge extends like a neon penumbra around each character, illuminating landscapes, rooms, and objects – a rumpled bed says more, in the hands of Munro, than any graphic in-out, in-out depiction of genitalia ever could. Even if a story is not primarily about a love affair or sexual encounter, men and women are always aware of one another as men and women, positively or negatively, recognizing sexual attraction and curiosity or else sexual revulsion. Women are immediately attuned to the sexual power of other women, and are wary of it, or envious. Men show off and preen and flirt and seduce and compete.

Munro's characters are as alert as dogs in a perfume store to the sexual chemistry in a gathering – the chemistry among others, as well as their own visceral responses. Falling in love, falling in lust, sneaking around on spouses and enjoying it, telling sexual lies, doing shameful things they feel compelled to do out of irresistible desire, making sexual calculations based on social desperation – few writers have explored such processes more thoroughly, and more ruthlessly. Pushing the sexual boundaries is distinctly thrilling for many a Munro woman; but in order to trespass you have to know exactly where the fence is, and Munro's universe is criss-crossed with meticulously defined borders. Hands, chairs, glances – all are part of an intricate inner map strewn with barbed wire and booby traps, and secret paths through the shrubbery.

For women of Munro's generation, sexual expression was a liberation and a way out. But out of what? Out of the denial and limiting scorn she describes so well in "The Turkey Season":

> Lily said she never let her husband come near her if he had been drinking. Marjorie said since the time she nearly died with a hemorrhage she never let her husband come near her, period. Lily said quickly that it was only when he'd been drinking that he tried anything. I could see that it was a matter of pride not to let your husband come near you, but I couldn't quite believe that "come near" meant "have sex."

For older women like Lily and Marjorie, to enjoy sex would have been a humiliating defeat. For women like Rose, in "The Beggar Maid," it's a matter for pride and celebration, a victory. For later generations of women – post Sexual Revolution – enjoying sex was to become simply a duty, the perfect orgasm yet another thing to add to their list of required accomplishments; and when enjoyment becomes a duty, we're back in the land of "dreariness of spirit." But for a Munro character in the throes of sexual exploration, the spirit may be confused and ashamed and tormented, even cruel and sadistic – some of the couples in her stories get pleasure out of torturing each other emotionally, just like some real people – but it is never dreary.

In some of the later stories, sex can be less impetuous, more calculated. For example, Grant, in "The Bear Came Over the Mountain," uses it as the decisive element in an astonishing feat of emotional commodities-trading. His beloved wife Fiona has dementia, and has become attached to a similarly-afflicted man in her care facility. When this man is taken home by his hard-bitten, practical wife Marian, Fiona pines. Grant wants to persuade Marian to put her husband back in the institution, but Marian refuses: it would cost too much. However, Grant detects that Marian is lonely and sexually available. She has a wrinkled-up face, but her body is still attractive. Like an adroit salesman, Grant moves in to close the deal. Munro knows full well that sex can be a glory and a torment, but it can also be a bargaining chip.

***

The society Munro writes about is a Christian one. This Christianity is not often overt; it's merely the general background. Flo in "The Beggar Maid" decorates the "walls with a number of admonitions, pious and cheerful and mildly bawdy":

> THE LORD IS MY SHEPHERD
> BELIEVE IN THE LORD JESUS CHRIST AND THOU SHALT BE SAVED
>
> Why did Flo have those, when she wasn't even religious? They were what people had, common as calendars.
>
> THIS IS MY KITCHEN AND I WILL DO AS I DARNED PLEASE
> MORE THAN TWO PERSONS TO A BED IS DANGEROUS AND UNLAWFUL

Christianity is "what people had" – and in Canada, church and state were never separated along the lines laid down in the United States. Prayers and Bible readings were daily fare in publicly funded schools. This cultural Christianity has provided ample material for Munro, but it is also connected with one of the most distinctive patterns in her image-making and storytelling.

The central Christian tenet is that two disparate and mutually exclusive elements – divinity and humanity – got jammed together in Christ, neither annihilating the other. The result was not a demi-god, or a God in disguise: God became totally a human being while remaining at the same time totally divine. To believe that Christ was only a man or to believe he was simply God were both declared heretical by the early Christian church. Christianity thus depends on a denial of either/or classifying logic and an acceptance of both-at-once mystery. Logic says that A cannot be both itself and non-A at the same time, Christianity says it can. The formulation "A but also non-A" is indispensable to it.

Many of Munro's stories resolve themselves – or fail to resolve themselves – in precisely this way. The example that first comes to mind – though there are many – is from *Lives of Girls and Women*, in which the teacher who'd staged the high school's airy and joyful operettas drowns herself in the river.

> Miss Farris in her velvet skating costume ... Miss Farris *con brio* ... Miss Farris floating face down, unprotesting, in the Wawanash River, six days before she was found. Though there is no plausible way of hanging those pictures together – if the last one is true then must it not alter the others? – they are going to have to stay together now.

For Munro, a thing can be true, but not true, but true nonetheless. "It is real and dishonest," thinks Georgia, of her remorse, in "Differently." "How hard it is for me to believe that I made that up," says the narrator, Fame, of "The Progress of Love." "It seems so much the truth it is the truth; it's what I believe about them. I haven't stopped believing it." The world is profane *and* sacred. It must be swallowed whole. There's always more to be known about it than you can ever know.

***

In a story called "Something I've Been Meaning To Tell You," jealous Et describes her sister's former lover – a promiscuous ladies' man – and the look he gives to every woman, a look "that made him seem to want to be a deep-sea diver diving down, down through all the emptiness and cold and wreckage to discover the one thing he had set his heart on, something small and precious, hard to locate, as a ruby maybe on the ocean floor."

Munro's stories abound in such questionable seekers and well-fingered ploys. But they abound also in such insights: within any story, within any human being, there may be a dangerous treasure, a priceless ruby. A heart's desire.

The Past, the Future, and the Myths of the Modern Rural Souwesto: An Essay of Concern

Noah Kozicki

The past was in him, never to be forgotten nor ignored. But he didn't know whether he was to forgive. He wanted only to keep what was good and pass it on.
– George Elliott, "An act of piety," *The Kissing Man* (12)

Their words and my words, a curious re-creation of lives, in a given setting that was as truthful as our notion of the past can ever be.
– Alice Munro, Foreword, *The View from Castle Rock* ([x])

This essay is about the past and death. It is also about resurrection. This essay is about the past, the future, and their intersection. It is also about the father, the child, and what is passed between. It is about discerning what is good and carrying it on, which lives we choose to re-create. Through an approach focusing on archetypal criticism informed by Northrop Frye, Mircea Eliade, Carl Jung, and personal reference, I will seek to articulate the mythical resonances lying beneath the rural and small-town Souwesto experience. The legacy of these histories will be traced temporally from early Ontarian exploration and settlement to contemporary concerns of agribusiness, rural bedroom communities, and artificial rusticity. Along the way, the myths I identify will be those which have informed my own life. Those which have been carried by my parents, their parents. The mythical subtexts beneath each aphorism half-said on the farm in Norfolk County that I grew up on.

In *The Critical Path*, Frye tells us that "there is no private symbolism" (22). This assertion is fundamental to my analysis. It is with this idea that I can begin to approach and examine the literary tradition of Southwestern Ontario. It is through such thinking that I can find the same symbols and their associated meanings in pre-confederation poetry through to Munro. Indeed, Frye understands "the immense importance of certain structural elements in the literary tradition, such as conventions, genres, and the recurring use of certain images or image-clusters, which [he] came to call archetypes" (*Critical Path* 23). Because this understanding will continually inform the body of my argument, it makes sense to start with a preamble about archetypal criticism to get the basic framework in our heads before going forward. Then we can start connecting the dots and hope to experience a revelatory appreciation. Frye writes that "[a] fully developed or encyclopaedic myth comprises everything that it most concerns its society to know, ... a myth of concern" (*Critical Path* 36). The westernized myth of concern in Southwestern Ontario descends from an inheritance of the Judaeo-Christian myth found in the Bible which arrived with European settlers. Yes, we continue to grow increasingly diverse and secular as a region, but Jung finds that "[s]ince the stars have fallen from heaven and our highest symbols have paled, a secret life holds sway in the unconscious" (*Archetypes* 23). Most of us may no longer acknowledge such symbols consciously, but many of us are still the inheritors of a range of biblical ideas, symbols, and archetypes.

In the rural Souwesto I call home, where country-churches sporadically mark the steady concessions, we may still think in that language even if we don't necessarily speak it. Jung names the unconscious as the inheritor of this language but perhaps these "highest symbols" are most readily recognized in what Frye calls "[t]he world of imagination, ... partly a holiday or Sabbath world where we rest from belief and commitment" (*Critical Path* 169) which is why it may be easier to recognize such symbols in works of poetry and other literature. Furthermore, Frye formulates his own theory regarding these fallen stars when writing that "[o]n Earth and in history, Christianity destroyed the belief in the Classical gods, but the Classical gods promptly went to the imaginative heaven of poetry" (*Critical Path* 169). I will later examine how Romantic writers revived the old gods through poetry, but I think it's fair to contend that in our current postmodern climate each succeeding generation is becoming increasingly separated from a consciousness of Judaeo-Christian symbols. If Frye contends that Christianity destroyed the classical gods and that they retreated into poetry, then I contend that this cycle has continued and that the postmodern's renouncement of traditional values has slain Christian symbology. Yet I think I can indicate the retreat of such symbology into literature, particularly in the simultaneously sacred and profane portrayal of the pastoral in Souwesto texts.

I believe that Alice Munro concentrates on the heritage of formal symbolism in *The View from Castle Rock* as she traces her lineage from the myth of Will O'Phaup to the modern Souwesto. Munro feels that Will O'Phaup's "life was lived in a world still remote and self-contained, still harboring its own mythology and local wonders. And he was one of them" (*Castle Rock* 8-9). Perhaps it is this desire for a self-contained mythology which urges Munro to carve out her own local wonders, however unexceptional they may seem to the unappreciative eye. I believe this desire for mythologization aligns with Del Jordan's mission in *Lives of Girls and Women* where what she "wanted was every last thing, every layer of speech and thought, stroke of light on bark or walls, every smell, pothole, pain, crack, delusion, held still and held together – radiant, everlasting" (Munro, *Lives* 253), her own self-contained mythology like that belonging to Will O'Phaup.

Furthermore, Munro writes in *Castle Rock* how the poetry of L.M. Montgomery moved her in her youth toward a deeper consideration of the natural world surrounding her; she longs to lie under the canopy of an apple tree and watch the sky above, finding that "[t]here was a formality about this idea that I longed for. It was almost like kneeling down in church, which in our church we didn't do" (*Castle Rock* 199). We perceive the desire for a return to a formal faith (stimulated by the poetry and other literature which retains its symbols) which is deeper than contemporary religion, yet in this search Munro finds that she "was not quite swept into the state of mind, of worship, that [she] had been hoping for" (*Castle Rock* 200). Faith mingles with doubt when the postmodern reaches toward formal values of faith and its mythological symbology. Myself, I carved my grandfather's name into a tree after he died, a grave on his own land, some bizarre search for formal meaning and reverence – carved in a tree (probably ash and itself dead now) like some sweetheart's name. Indeed, the mythical in the modern age is no longer as large as Will O'Phaup, but rather Munro finds that transcendent resonances lie in the "dull, simple, amazing and unfathomable" (*Lives* 253) lives of small-town residents. When faith *is* achieved in the rural Souwesto texts I'll be examining, it is usually through some cohabitation of both formal teachings or symbolism and a personally possessed truth.

In response to Kierkegaard's notions of such ideas, Frye writes that Kierkegaard "speaks of the personal as in itself a subversive and revolutionary force.... For him the highest form of truth is personally possessed truth" (*Critical Path* 130). This idea informs notions of rural piety in Souwesto texts where formal religion has become impersonal or even totalitarian. Regarding this totalitarianism, consider the Bishop in James Reaney's dramatic trilogy *The Donnellys* who urges Father Girard to influence his Parish into voting for a Liberal candidate, stressing that "the Donnellys must change their voting pattern" (Reaney 210). Or we can recall that it is Father Connolly who proposes the secret society which will persecute the Donnellys, declaring "I propose to form a Peace Society. ... I want all the men who are interested in preserving peace and order in the parish of St. Patrick's, Biddulph, to sign their names. All those who do not sign I shall consider backsliders, blacklegs and sympathizers with this gang of evildoers" (Reaney 219). The Donnellys alone stand against this totalitarian combination of church, state, and scapegoat violence. The aforementioned sort of revolutionary rural piety will be examined later in James Reaney's *The Donnellys* and in George Elliott's story cycle *The Kissing Man* where an individualistic faith grounded in the symbology of the natural world, or the natural world itself, is pitted against an impersonal doubt.

Indeed, those that attain personally possessed truth in Elliott are admirable models of self-fulfillment. In "An act of piety," Honey Salkald addresses the memory of his grandfather Mayhew: "[y]ou worked hard and felt that all the things you did were essential, so you created your own comforts that were like bowing to the strength of the land. You were very much like a Christian, but you were Mayhew Salkald first" (Elliott 11). My father's own agnostic piety, his humility, the pride in his work, helping his neighbours, seems similar. He says something about how those up in the front pews at church are "the worst ones." I think this brand of rural piety informs the structural conventions of the examined texts where formal symbolism is invoked but tinged with doubt and self-consciousness – consider again the reverent mythologizing of the apple tree in *Castle Rock* or the mythologizing of the seemingly banal in *Lives*. Munro's reverence involves a personal appraisal of what others cannot fully see or value. The apple tree is mythologized when it is imbued with the meaning implied by Munro's choice to give the experience its own story ("Lying Under the Apple Tree") in which she must undergo a trial to secure the sought meaning. Munro must trespass and remain unseen if she wishes to experience the formality which she imagines in the apple tree – a heightened sense of adventure for a heightened sense of meaning. In this same story, Munro writes that she "went rampaging through [her] school texts to uncover them before they could be read and despised in class" (*Castle Rock* 198). It is in such a quest for personally possessed truth and the ensuing reverent mythologization that we find a desire for the type of meaning which is lost when we do not consider the past.

I should acknowledge that it's not just Judaeo-Christian ideas which Souwesto has inherited either, for the Bible is descendent of Greco-Roman and Near-Eastern mythologies. Rather, there is some formal and universal symbolism being striven toward which is more complex than what an organized religion can account for. Accordingly, Jung finds that

> [t]he forms we use for assigning meaning are historical categories that reach back into the mists of time – a fact we do not take sufficiently into account. Interpretations make use of certain linguistic matrices that are themselves derived from primordial images. From whatever side we approach this question, everywhere we find ourselves confronted with the history of language, with images and motifs that lead straight back to the primitive wonder-world. (*Archetypes* 32-33)

Such ideas will lend themselves to the arguments which follow. We will see how various ideas and actions in Souwesto history and literature recreate a traditional, and even ancient, model. At that point, we can see how the model is made more complex by the postmodern in its contemporary literary resuscitation and examine the permanence and value of such rural myths. Now, it is time to go back in time to see where these Souwesto myths originated.

Let us begin then with the slaying of the Ontarian giant, since Eliade writes that "in certain archaic cosmogonies, the world was given existence through the sacrifice of a primordial monster, symbolizing chaos…, or through that of a cosmic giant" (*Cosmos and History* 20). I'm considering the vastness of Ontario with its hinterlands, pre-Cambrian shield, and dead winters as such a giant of chaos. Like Zeus slaying Typhon or Apollo who slayed the Earth's serpent-daughter Python, the first European explorers were operating within the same context, albeit under different semantics. Just as the origin of the cosmos begins with the separation of order from chaos, so too must all human settling re-enact this tradition. Every human mode of destruction and construction follows some mythical model of this kind, except for uncultivated nature. Or as Eliade writes, "everything in the world that surrounds us does not have a prototype of this kind. … They correspond to a mythical model, but of another nature: all these wild, uncultivated regions and the like are assimilated to chaos; they still participate in the undifferentiated, formless modality of pre-Creation" (*Cosmos and History* 9).

We can find an according literary example in the larger Ontarian context. Romantic Ontarian poetry focused on the period of early French exploration throughout the 1600s and emboldened this order-chaos relationship, as in the case of Charles Sangster. Poet, sometime resident of Essex County, and briefly the editor of the Amherstburg *Courier*, Sangster writes in *The St. Lawrence and the Saguenay*, "Long years ago the early Voyageurs / Gladdened these wilds with some romantic air; / The moonlight, dancing on their dripping oars, / Showed the slow batteaux passing by with care" (Sangster in Gustafson 43). This theme of humanity imprinting itself onto nature is bolstered with the lines, "This rugged wilderness which we survey / Extends in wild, magnificent array, / To regions rarely trod by mortal feet" (Sangster in Gustafson 44). Today I might only find this type of primeval chaos while on Lake Erie. Watching the same old stones be beaten by the same ancient black waters, dipping my hands to feel the cool history.

This particular past radiated with ripe motifs for the Ontarian Romantic poet of the 1800s to capture and convey in verse. First, the imperial monotheism of the French and then the British dialectically produced conceptions of false gods. In his essay "Canada: New World without Revolution" Frye summarizes these imposed ideas which found "that there were no gods in nature; that nature was a fellow creature of man, and that all the gods that had been discovered in it were devils" (437). Secondly, we discern the idea of human consciousness or order encountering the unconsciousness of chaotic nature (which we saw in Sangster). Lastly, the poet's focus is on the first nomads or explorers who chronicled the chaos. Such motifs align with Frye's articulation of the Romantic thematic mode where Gods are no longer found in nature, or have "retreated to the sky" (*Anatomy* 53) since the mythic mode; we encounter "the theme of the boundary of consciousness, the sense of the poetic mind as passing from one world to another, or as simultaneously aware of both" (*Anatomy* 54); and we observe the portrayal of romantic heroes who belong to a "nomadic" age (*Anatomy* 54).

However, this Romantic model of Ontarian poetry, which reflects the pre-Confederation settler's mindset and champions the imposition of order onto chaos, encounters a problem. The problem being that the Europeans were not the first to order the Ontarian chaos. Indeed, in "The Mystery of the Neutral Indians" Abraham Rotstein writes that "increasing contact with the white man brought an expansion in the range and character of trade goods, particularly firearms, and a change in the source of their goods. Hence it disrupted the basic political balance that had existed among the Indians" (Rotstein 26). The problems revolving around imposed European systems are articulated in Ontarian Charles Mair's "Tecumseh" where Tecumseh is the speaker and asserts that "... Once we were strong. / Once all this mighty continent was ours, / And the Great Spirit made it for our use. / He knew no boundaries, so had we peace / In the vast shelter of His handiwork" (Mair in Gustafson 47). Furthermore, he found "No greed of gold, no quarrels over God" (Mair in Gustafson 47), which seem to be the two primary destabilizers of Indigenous ways of life. When the Europeans meet and clash with Indigenous peoples, they are again re-enacting an archetypal model explicated by Eliade: "[s]truggles, conflicts, and wars for the most part have a ritual cause and function. They are a stimulating opposition between the two halves of a clan, or a struggle between the representatives of two divinities" (*Cosmos and History* 29).

The Indigenous Peoples are a frequent subject in early Romantic Ontarian poetry. They seem to represent something like gods harbouring their own mythologies and appear as romantic heroes belonging to the kind of nomadic age which Romantic poetry venerates (*Anatomy* 54). When these mythologies were swallowed by imperial monotheism, Ontarian poets attempted to preserve them in their writing where they juxtaposed the profane industry of the Western man with the sacred and ostensibly primeval life of the Indigenous. As classical gods retreated into Romantic texts, so too were Indigenous Peoples (broadly) sublimated into Ontarian writing as their cultures were sussed out by monotheistic conversion. Charles Sangster captures such ideas in *The St. Lawrence and the Saguenay* where he first identifies the absence of the old Western mythological figures, "... No nymphic trains appear, / To charm the pale Ideal Worshipper / Of Beauty; nor Neriads from the deeps below; / Nor hideous Gnomes, to fill the breast with fear" (Sangster in Smith 14). Rather, the "legendary lore" of the land surrounds the Indigenous Peoples as Sangster writes, "... The feet / Of the Red Man have pressed each wave-zoned shore, / And many an eye of beauty oft did greet / The painted warriors and their birchen fleet, / As they returned with trophies of the slain. / That race has passed away; their fair retreat / In its primeval loneness smiles again" (Sangster in Smith 15). The image of the feet in particular recalls a freedom of movement according to the Romantic poet's interest in the nomad. Yet Sangster continues to write that this aforementioned smile fades with "the echo of the huntsman's gun," where the baying of his hounds "Rouses the lounging student from his book," where "A pic-nic party, resting in the shade" rise to watch "the strong steamer ... like a huge serpent" (Sangster in Smith 15). Sangster articulates the disappearance of culture and lore in the name of industry and pleasure, particularly condemning industry where the beauty of the Indigenous "birchen fleet" has given way to the corrupting and mythic serpentine connotation of "the strong steamer" (Sangster in Smith 15). Why else might Romantic poets of this period be intrigued by the symbols of a different culture?

Perhaps it is the same reason why today so many who are uninterested in Western faiths have turned to the East to better themselves. Jung writes that "[t]he gods of Greece and Rome perished from the same disease as did our Christian symbols: people discovered then, as today, that they had no thoughts whatever on the subject. On the other hand, the gods of the strangers still had unexhausted mana" (*Archetypes* 14). "[T]he gods of the strangers" retain that sense of mystery and intrigue which arouses the mystic and primeval perceptions which charm the

Romantic poet with an idealized world. This shifting landscape of early Ontario was what the poet witnessed: the imposition of European consciousness onto what was conceived as basically an uncultivated chaos (because Indigenous Peoples lived *with* nature rather than against it) and a divine battlefield set for ritual domination where the defeated party might retreat into literary veneration. It is important to keep these ideas in mind going forward as we'll see the effects of the European notions of godlessness in nature and the consequential cultural desecration later. Yet at the same time, those desecrated cultures would find some semblance of reverence in Ontarian poetry – but it was too little too late to alter perceptions in 'the real world.' In Sangster we find a preference for the primeval over industry and we will later find that this dichotomy between an earnest natural world and an exploitative serpentine industry permeates those texts which articulate the distinctions among the urban, the small town, and the rural country. For now, let's refer back to Frye and articulate what the primary concerns of this early period were and what myths they established (or re-established) as these will provide us with an idea of what was desired of uncultivated Ontario.

Frye writes that our "[p]rimary concerns may be considered in four main areas: food and drink, along with related bodily needs; sex; property (i.e. money, possessions, shelter, clothing, and everything that constitutes property in the sense of what is 'proper' to one's life); liberty of movement. The general object of primary concern is expressed in the Biblical phrase 'life more abundantly'" (*Words with Power* 42), says Frye, echoing the Gospel of John 10.10. As demonstrated by what has been discussed thus far, we find that an imperial monotheism was the rationalization for the acquisition of property in the name of empire. We can also contend, based on Frye's understanding, that the Romantic poet's interest in the nomadic must have something to do with the metaphorical relationship between liberty of movement and an artistic liberty of thought. In an industrial sense, a liberty of movement manifested in the establishment of communication lines in early Ontario which led to a Quebec terminus. Yet the roads of Southwestern Ontario would not see effective execution until much later. In *Twenty-Seven Years in Canada West* Samuel Strickland, first coming to the Huron Tract in the summer of 1825, struggled with movement until reflecting in 1852 on the progress made:

> behold what the energies and good management of the Canada Company have effected. Stage-coaches travel with safety and dispatch along the same tract where formerly I had the utmost difficulty to make my way on horseback without the chance of being swept from the saddle by the limbs of trees and tangled brushwood. A continuous settlement of the finest farms now skirts both sides of this road, from the southern boundary-line of this district to Goderich. (I: 196-97)

Expansion, passage, and other such imperial objectives evidently reveal themselves as the primary Western concerns of the period which would have been rationalized by secondary concerns.

Frye describes secondary concerns as those which "arise from the social contract, and include patriotic and other attachments of loyalty, religious beliefs, and class-conditioned attitudes and behavior" (*Words with Power* 42). Thus, secondary concerns can rationalize the ascendancy of primary concerns and myth or even supersede primary concerns in cases where ideology overrules our own determinations, such as in war where death for the state overrules our life-drive. What we find in the imperial secondary concerns of early Canadian settlers is a Baroque sense of self, which Frye articulates by discussing the Baroque age:

> an age of intense belief in the supremacy of human consciousness over nature. It had discovered something of the technological potential of mathematics, once mathematics had become attached to a powerful social organization. It was not an age of individualism, as is often said, but an age of relatively enlightened despotism, and in some ways very like the dawn of civilization in the Near East, when the pyramids of Egypt and the ziggurats of Babylon emerged as dramatic witness to what men could do when united under a sufficiently strong social will. ("Canada" 436)

Accordingly, we can read the settlers' imperial path through nature as a Baroque act which championed the human consciousness and felled any gods in the forests – an act which began cutting communication lines through nature to establish a productive colony in the New World.

Domination of the wilds of Ontario would certainly brandish an admirable social will to the other nations of the Atlantic seaboard. The stage was being set for cultivation and the imposition of European values or myths. Mircea Eliade finds that

> [s]ettlement in a new, unknown, uncultivated country is equivalent to an act of Creation. When the Scandinavian colonists took possession of Iceland, ... [t]heir enterprise was for them only the repetition of a primordial act: the transformation of chaos into cosmos by the divine act of Creation. By cultivating the desert soil, they in fact repeated the act of the gods, who organized chaos by giving it forms and norms. Better still, a territorial conquest does not become real until after ... the ritual of taking possession, which is only a copy of the primordial act of the Creation of the World. (*Cosmos and History* 10)

The British flowed in alongside Loyalists seeking refuge following the American Revolution; as J.K. Johnson finds, many of the latter "had also lost their property and most of their possessions" and "were allowed by the colonial government at Quebec to take up land along the north shore of the St. Lawrence River.... So began the process of land distribution in Upper Canada" (11). Accordingly, Ontario becomes an archetypal land of hope where industry will reveal the treasures of the wild landscape. Strickland argued that "[n]othing, indeed, but industry and enterprise is needed to change the waste and solitary places of Upper Canada into a garden of Eden, which it is designed by the Supreme Architect to become" (*Twenty-Seven Years* I: 65). Where industry promises to make an "Eden" of "the waste and solitary places," the land of Ontario becomes emblematic, paradoxically, of both chaos and hope.

Consequently, this hopeful chaos becomes the property of a vast working class where fresh starts for immigrants are founded in co-operative cultivating efforts. In this early period, we see a general anti-administration ethos emerge which still permeates rural literature and was introduced earlier as a binary opposition between the natural world and industry in Sangster. However, Johnson writes that settlers found solace in successfully petitioning for land because they "went immediately from being nobodies to possessors of official documents" (16). These documents were often improvised and encouraged swift development of the land which would ideally be upgraded to a deed.

Yet "[a] deed to land had no immediate practical value. It did not hasten the task of clearing the land or make it more productive" (Johnson 17). Nonetheless, while the British government tried to establish a landed aristocracy and entertained absentee speculators with their Crown and Clergy reserves, they were simultaneously asking settlers to develop and farm the land. Already we find tensions between rural industry and urban administration developing – a battle between practicality and paperwork. Today I've seen this myth continue as the translation of farm paperwork into e-forms befuddles and demeans an older generation of once proud farmers made inarticulate by unnecessary technologies.

Frye writes that "[myths] play a leading role in defining a society, in giving it a shared possession of knowledge, or what is assumed to be knowledge, peculiar to it. Its proclamation is not so much 'This is true' as 'This is what you must know'" (*Words with Power* 31). What exactly did these early settlers have to know? That co-operation was better than total self-sufficiency and cultivation was more important than administrative permissions; Upper Canada was a land of hope – glory and industry hiding somewhere in the trees. Christian myth and the exclusion of paganism then made the clearing of the trees easier. Whereas secondary concerns usually come to take over primary ones, we may consider this time as neo-primitive enough that immigrants and the pioneer working class were concerned more with primary needs than secondary concerns of social authority. We find a preference for the natural and self-reliant over administration. If we follow along with Frye's thoughts it may be fair to imagine these historical figures as having become pseudo-gods by being more myth than reality, since "literature is always and everywhere polytheistic, however far its characters may have modulated from what we ordinarily think of as gods" (*Words with Power* 71). So we may be apt to consider them the first gods, the creators, reckoning order from chaos (from a Western standpoint).

For Frye "a mythology creates in the midst of its society the verbal equivalent of a *temenos* or sacred ground, a limited and sacrosanct area" (*Words with Power* 31); therefore it's important to discuss what principles these 'gods' brought with them from their emigrated nations to form this *temenos*. Of the peculiarly cruel physical examination of neighbours in eighteenth-century Scotland, Munro writes in *The View from Castle Rock*,

"The Elders went from house to house to see that no cooking was in progress on a Sunday and at times their harsh hands were employed in severely squeezing the breasts of any woman suspected of having borne an illegitimate child, so that a drop of milk might betray her. But the very fact that such vigilance was thought necessary shows how these believers were waylaid by Nature in their lives, as people always are" (*Castle Rock* 18). The same volume later focuses on the Souwesto small-town's intimate yet distant observations as Munro reflects on a comparable yet more subtle attitude, noting that if her mother had known of her visiting farmhand Russell Craik for dinner, she "would have found a way to say to me that once you went into certain houses as an equal and a friend ... you showed that the value you put on yourself was not very high, and after that others would value you accordingly" (*Castle Rock* 214). In such examples we are reminded that the expressions of our 'principles' may change, but the urges characterized by one's being "waylaid by Nature" (*Castle Rock* 18) remain. What else was brought here? What misshapen attitudes and practices, however progressively acclimated, still tend to our *temenos* or sacred ground?

Frye writes about these kinds of imported ideas in "Canada: New World without Revolution" and how their legacy continues to affect us: a legacy which asks us to reconsider our societal championing of 'progress.' Concerning the emigration of ideas, Frye argues that "[w]hat is important is not nationality but cultural assumptions. The Baroque age was an age of intense belief in the supremacy of human consciousness over nature" ("Canada" 436). Returning to Munro's Scottish elders, isn't the deeming of a child's 'illegitimacy' itself the application of cultural reason to a natural act? We've already discussed at some length the effect of such assumptions, but here we're going to keep pulling this thread as it weaves itself beyond cultural ritual and into an industrial Ontarian tapestry.

In "Canada: New World without Revolution" Frye is chiefly concerned with human consciousness in its relation to nature, dialectical mental habits, and the effect of technology on cultural heritage. Just as early settlers roughly drew communication lines across the province, so too with mathematical precision did the British government. Paths turned to roads, to highways, to railways, and finally to airways. Such communications improvement, to Frye, "always means a wider and straighter path through nature, and a corresponding decline of interest in it" ("Canada" 436). Consciousness separates from nature and makes it object. Such thinking provides little nuance and favours a binary dialectic. A similar dialectic pervades the imperial monotheism previously discussed, which ripped the gods from nature in order to educate the 'pagan' Indigenous Peoples in the dogma of the Christian 'truth.' This attitude taught us, as Frye writes, "to assume that nature, not being inhabited or protected by gods or potentially dangerous spirits, was simply something available for human exploitation" ("Canada" 437). Indeed, it was a glorious war for the victors who, as Samuel Strickland wrote, may ask themselves "[w]hat were the red battle-fields of Napoleon, in comparison to this bloodless victory, won over the forests of the Huron! The sight of that first sheaf, cut by the gentle hand of woman, was one that angels rejoiced to see" (Strickland I: 310).

We may wonder how soon these pioneers regretted the greedy taste of this battle, and perhaps first, for Munro's lineage at least, this remorse was of a monetary tang. Munro's ancestor, Big Rob, writes in his journal that "[o]n the 5th of November, 1852, I cut down the first tree on my lot, and if I had the trees on it now, which were on it then, I would be the richest man in Morris Township" (*Castle Rock* 116). One might say we'd all be the richer for an earlier recognition of cultural- and bio-diversity. Frye notes that the Cartesian separation from nature developed from a Christian view which condemned idols in nature; thus the idol became "human consciousness itself, separated from nature" ("Canada" 437). Desecrated Indigenous cultures were treated with vitriolic irreverence by Christian teachers in the name of imperial progress and now what culture remains is being surpassed by technological and economic 'progress'; Frye writes that in 1975 "[t]he skyline of Toronto sixty years ago was dominated by the spires of the great churches: now the churches are points of depression" ("Canada" 439). One culture was erased in favour of another which is now being forgotten itself. First the old gods retreated into poetry, then Indigenous cultures fought evaporation into Christian industry, and now Christian symbology pales in the postmodern. We have felled our first trees, and we are doomed to fell what cultural saplings are left if we refuse to recognize our irreverence. What then will we have but a monoculture of both soil and thought? Let's continue by examining the blooming agricultural colony which Southwestern

Ontario once was and what cultural seeds were sown amongst the same earth which continues to provide for so many Ontarians.

The ordering principle would decide what Souwesto would become. Cultural and literary critic John Riddell finds this principle is that which "controls the re-creation of fact" (45). As Riddell observes, "to make visible, or audible, or tactile the welding of the physical world with the world of idea is primarily the need of mythopoeic man to quantify (desperately, one feels at times) existence in the face of possible negation. It is an act of survival as relevant as any of a purely biological nature" (45). A Souwesto resident's survival depended on two assumptions: farming as the foundation of progress and a myth of utilitarianism. The land was the great equalizer of class which forced co-operation and self-sufficiency simultaneously. The Souwesto labourer was an autodidactic one; the inaccessibility of his hinterland home necessitated each family to become their own craftsmen. As noted above, the primary concerns took precedence over the secondary; disparate peoples of various religions and backgrounds were united under the labouring *religio*, which Frye calls the "common body of acts and beliefs for the community" (*Critical Path* 106) associated with cultivation and construction.

Men co-operated in 'bees' to fell trees and raise buildings. Strickland describes a bee as "a neighbourly gathering for any industrious purpose – a friendly clubbing of labour, assisted by an abundance of good cheer" (*Twenty-Seven Years* I: 35). Interestingly, Frye finds that "a building, at least one requiring so immense an organization of labour, is the most socially concerned response that it is possible to make to the order of nature" (*Critical Path* 44). Through construction, settlers invoked the ordering principle. The autodidactic craftsmanship of the early nineteenth century is shown in Strickland's observation that "[i]ndustry in man, woman, or child, gentle or simple, is necessary in Canada. Therefore the idle, luxurious, and dissipated must not leave their homes, unless they resolve to work either with willing hands or clever heads – they will find employment for both in a colony" (*Twenty-Seven Years* II: 319).

Where labour, co-operation, and industry shape the primary concerns and form the tethering *religio* of the society, it may be argued that secondary concerns of religious denomination are of a lesser social importance. Arguments over 'which version of whose god said what' did no good for the development of the land. While travelling to what we now call Ontario in the story "Illinois" in *The View from Castle Rock*, Mary Laidlaw observes a similarly grounded approach to dogma at the inn outside Joliet. Munro writes that there were "[n]o fierce arguments about doctrine. No mention either of ghosts or weird visitors, as in the old days in Ettrick. Here it was all down-to-earth, it was all about what you could find and do and understand about the real world under your feet, and she supposed that Will would have approved" (*Castle Rock* 99). Although the example is imagined as American, Munro presents the inn as a hub for all kinds of immigrants and travellers harbouring their own distinct cultural backgrounds and according beliefs. It seems there was a will of the people stronger than the divisions amongst its ranks. Yet of course, these amorphous ideas of god and rural piety were still Westernized. We'll see later how a similarly grounded and earthly faith engenders ideas of rural piety in George Elliott's *The Kissing Man*, James Reaney's *The Donnellys*, and John B. Lee's *The Farm on the Hill He Calls Home*. For now, we may note that these were the concerns of this period of cultivation and before reaching for the contemporary era, it would be prudent to develop a system through which to analyze its myths and concerns.

Let's begin with an explication of the matrixes of mythology which Frye is drawing from. Here we will navigate the myths of concern and freedom which informed the literary developments of Southwestern Ontario. Our primary and secondary concerns, discussed above, connect the body and the mind. For instance, the primary bodily concern for "freedom of movement" logically extends into "freedom of thought" (*Words with Power* 45) and here we may recall my earlier examination of this relationship in the Romantic poet's veneration of the nomad. Frye writes that these extensions are expressed through "*logos* idioms" (*Words with Power* 45). In this sense, a concern for life leads to a concern regarding immortality and legacy. I think this concern becomes apparent in texts interrogating culture and heritage, especially those which deal with inheritance. Consider John B. Lee's meditations on this subject in *The Farm on the Hill He Calls Home*. Lee finds that "[m]any of the words I write are ancestor worship" (*The Farm* 14); or he considers the history of the farm and those on it as "stories it was given me to tell"

(*The Farm* 17). Furthermore, Lee writes that the "duty to honour the past and consider the future, these are my inheritance" (*The Farm* 18).

This view of culture has an ancient origin in the poet for Frye, who thinks of the poet "as being at the center of a cross.... The horizontal bar forms the social and ideological conditioning.... The vertical bar is the mythological line of descent from previous poets back to Homer" (*Words with Power* 47). Soon we'll see how James Reaney in *The Donnellys* situated himself upon the cross by adhering to a historical line and a mythological line of descent while introducing his own satirical flair through an ironic and postmodern mode. The Romantic period of Ontarian literature also emphasizes this 'poet-cross' idea by way of its classical idolization and allusion. In Souwesto rural literature this mythological dimension is found in notions of the opposing abhorred and desired worlds where, as Frye observes, "the model world is most directly expressed in idyl and pastoral and idealized romance" (*Critical Path* 55). This world is typically characterized by its location in imaginative space as an idealized vision of life and higher consciousness; it is that which becomes available in Frye's "world of imagination" (*Critical Path* 169).

The Biblical model world to which derivative Western literature reaches would be Eden before the Fall; the abhorred world would then be the fallen and earthly kingdom of sin, vice, and shame. Where do we see this in rural literature? The pastoral and bucolic have (perhaps begrudgingly in Souwesto texts) remained as derivations of the Edenic scene and the abhorred world has been symbolically exiled to urbanized spaces. However, modern writers like Munro provide nuance within this dichotomy as mentioned in the apple tree example with her postmodern sense of the inability to return to formal symbols. In less nuanced texts, like rustic advertising for example, the rural country is envisioned as simple, honest, hardworking, and pious while the city takes on the weight of excess, guile, sloth, and sin. In his book *You Can't Get There from Here: The Past as Present in Small-Town Ontario Fiction*, Ryan Porter writes that "[t]hese ads allude to an idyllic myth as old as pastoral literature: that outside the urban centre exist ease and escape" (7). Fortunately, this line can be blurred in literature to create more complex tensions than the dichotomy allows, but the basic formula still persists.

The (sometimes abhorred) cities we have today developed out of what Frye calls the truth of correspondence, which contends that "each age of science stands on the shoulders of its predecessors" (*Critical Path* 83). Poetry, however, does not. Frye finds that poetry arises from recurrence, not progress. Accordingly, the rural is a site of poetic inspiration where one can praise the recurrence of that Edenic vision in its pastoral frame while vilifying the 'progress' of the abhorred urban world. The truth of correspondence, that each new scientific and technological development corresponds with and develops from the last, leaves us with what Frye calls "[t]he bourgeois progressive myth" (*Critical Path* 87). This is a myth which makes us believe that our 'progress' is moving toward an ideal or "benevolent future," but which gradually "began to break down under the shocks of twentieth-century disasters" (*Critical Path* 87). Frye finds that a further problem with the bourgeois and Marxist progressive myths is that they "project an ideal into the future; both can rationalize the most atrocious present acts as leading to a future good" (*Critical Path* 88). The rationalization of the horrific is engendered by the notion of progress which according to Frye decides that "[i]f two cultures collide, the one that gets enslaved or exterminated is the primitive one. The victorious one was more progressive because it had better weapons and armies" (*Critical Path* 85). Or, as Major John Richardson – for a time an Essex County resident and during the War of 1812 a volunteer at Amherstburg's Fort Malden – writes in his early long poem *Tecumseh* (1828), "their engines vomit through the air / Fresh streams of carnage, while a new command / Bids yet to fiercer warmth the furious war, / And Murder's breath, which desolates the land, / Falls hotly mingling with the crimson tide / Which stains each deck and oozes thro' each side" (Canto First, XIV.3-8).

This invariable desolation is the fundamental problem with the 'progress' which desecrated the cultures that were here before the arrival of Europeans. The Europeans imperially forced their Baroque consciousness and monotheism onto the Indigenous Peoples; European gods had long since retreated into obscurity and so it was required that the gods in the Souwesto forests were similarly evicted. This 'progress' is the sort which characterizes the abhorred urban world. Conversely, Frye finds that the poetic is free of the contemporary ascendant ideology of progress; poetry lies in the recurrence of the primitive, in the revitalization of myth. Frye writes that "[n]o matter what compromises or social arrangements may be made, poetry speaks the language of myth and not the language of reason or fact: further, it represents something primitive in society, not something that progressively improves or refines itself" (*Critical Path* 84).

Consider again why Eden is the model world of poetic thought and why the pastoral setting becomes receptive to Edenic imagery and connotation – it is in the natural world where recurrence reigns and progress remains hidden within its potential for exploitation. To be in the pastoral is to be in Eden, to observe what Mircea Eliade calls mythical or sacred time (*Cosmos and History* 35) – to experience the very same world and rituals which ancients did. Settling, building, hunting, agriculture, the arts – these practices are sacred because they are based in an archetypal model or mythical origin. In contrast, Eliade writes that "profane activities are those which have no mythical meaning, that is, which lack exemplary models" (*Cosmos and History* 28). Regarding both sacred time and profane time, Eliade writes: "[t]he abolition of profane time and the individual's projection into mythical time do not occur, of course, except at essential periods – those, that is, when the individual is truly himself: on the occasion of rituals or of important acts (alimentation, generation, ceremonies, hunting, fishing, war, work). The rest of his life is passed in profane time, which is without meaning: in the state of 'becoming'" (*Cosmos and History* 35).

I think I saw my grandfather slip into mythical time when he was dying, laid out beneath the bay window, watching the snow-dusted field. Sliding through time, myself becoming someone else in his eyes. Reliving sacred experiences and ignoring the profane. The cell-phone tower which had been in that window's view since the house was built became strange. My grandfather didn't recognize the blinking red light which he must have seen every night of his life, some profane symbol of 'progress' becoming nothing. I've wondered at that episode for years and I am glad I can find some understanding of it, or at least pretend to know what it meant. With Eliade, we learn that art is able to project one into mythical time because the creation or witnessing of it are sacred actions – visual art and poetry are fundamental to our humanity and reach back into our most primitive states. The arts speak to us like Munro's seashell as "a messenger from near and far, because I could hold it to my ear – when nobody was there to stop me – and discover the tremendous pounding of my own blood, and of the sea" (*Castle Rock* 349). The occupations of the rural sphere also pass in mythical time – farming, as John B. Lee affirms in his poem "Burning Land," has been sacred since long before Virgil's *Georgics*.

Both poetry and the pastoral are sacred because they adhere to archetypal models, so perhaps it should be unsurprising that a rural writer would be able to articulate such ideas here discussed. Someone who knew both the recurring sacred acts of farming and poetry, as well as the urban employment of the world of progress. In a letter to Alfred Harcourt, Raymond Knister seeks to articulate 'truth' and in doing so touches on the ideas of poetic recurrence and abhorred progress here discussed. Knister writes that "the truth of poetry needs to be revealed universally. It is at the base of religion, and is one of the very few still accessible sources of religion. Our casting away of false gods has up to now resulted in the acceptance of a faith more grotesquely false – faith in civilization and betterment of conditions and mechanical adjustment" ("This truth ..." 179). It is the poetry of laying down beneath an apple tree with its pastoral and Edenic implications which Munro believes in, even if the ideal image is unreachable.

Kent County-born poet Archibald Lampman similarly voices his concern with "mechanical adjustment" in his eschatological "The City of the End of Things" where the titular city has become so autonomously mechanized that man cannot exist within it else "His soul would shrivel" (Lampman in Smith 80). Lampman imagines ceaseless machine production where "The inhuman music lifts and falls" and "clanking hands / Obey a hideous routine" (Lampman in Smith 79). This inhuman autonomy seems to be the ultimate destination of 'progress' which began optimistically enough. Lampman writes: "Once there were multitudes of men, / That built that city in their pride, / Until its might was made, and then / They withered age by age and died" (Lampman in Smith 80). Lampman envisions the judgment day of that grotesque faith which Knister warns us of. The death of the gods and an irreverence toward the past has us putting our faith in an ideal world which can only be revealed through 'progress.' If we follow Frye's outlines of narrative modes in *Anatomy of Criticism* then we can consider the periods of god-death (whether Indigenous or Judaeo-Christian) which were rationalized by 'progress,' these moments where spirits passed out of nature, as a Romantic tragedy (*Anatomy* 34-35). That initial narrative mode which shaped Souwesto literature and history.

Logically then, by identifying the common myths and archetypal narratives which rural literature subscribes to, we should be able to proceed forward and observe how Souwesto history and literature continued to develop. The Romantic thematic mode of retreating gods and the Romantic tragedy of dying gods have been noted, but we can also identify elements of the Romantic comedy during the late eighteenth century. The Romantic comedy is idyllic, and Frye writes that it uses the pastoral as a vehicle for "the theme of escape from society to the extent of idealizing a simplified life in the country or on the frontier" (*Anatomy* 40-41). So far, we've seen this idealization in Strickland and the hopeful history of an uncultivated Southwestern Ontario; the imagery of the Romantic comedy in its Edenic pastoral qualities therefore equates itself, as Frye explains, with the same imagery used in the Bible to signify "the theme of salvation" (*Anatomy* 41). Pastoral Ontario was just that, a salvation for those who sought it. As the initial cultivation was completed, the secondary concerns of the society began to take precedence over the primary. Symbolically, the work gives way to supposedly idle hands and minds.

This shift from labour to idleness is symbolically manifested in the life and writing of Raymond Knister and of John B. Lee. The value placed on prideful labour in the rural context haunts the writing of these authors; Lee puts it poignantly with his statement that "[w]riting isn't real work. Not on the farm" (*The Farm* 97). Similarly, in Knister's novel *White Narcissus*, Richard Milne remarks that writing is a tiresome occupation to which farmer Hymerson replies, "'Get you fellows out in the hayfield'" – in short, Milne "had forgotten the terms of intercourse in the country, ... that he should be able to 'give as good as was sent'" (Knister, *White Narcissus* 29). I myself have often experienced some difficulty in giving voice to my tiring attempts at painting or writing when I could just as well be shovelling chicken shit. I am reminded of Rose's consideration of the difference between her father and herself in "Half a Grapefruit" from Munro's *Who Do You Think You Are?* where Rose reflects that "[a]ll the things he had beaten down, successfully submerged, in himself, had surfaced again in her, and she was showing no will to combat them. She mooned and daydreamed, she was vain and eager to show off; her whole life was in her head. She had not inherited the thing he took pride in, and counted on – his skill with his hands, his thoroughness and conscientiousness at any work" (*Who* 45-46). The best I may hope for is the honest application of that work ethic and conscientiousness characteristic of farming to my own daydreamed occupations.

As we continue to discuss this relationship between labour and idleness, we may note that the period of early urbanization which arose following the preliminary cultivation of Southwestern Ontario presents the problem of a society no longer obligated by labour to co-operate; instead, tribalism founded in distinct beliefs emerges. The finest example of this period is found in James Reaney's dramatic trilogy *The Donnellys* where the titular nineteenth-century family faces the dangers of idle administration and tribalism head-on. Frye writes that the high mimetic narrative imagines a society of established courts and cities which engender a gaze tending toward a central point and are emblematic of nationalism "unified by patriotic and religious ideas" (*Anatomy* 54). *The Donnellys* imagines such a society as it locates the family under the constant gaze of legal administration and the pseudo-nationalistic Whitefeet society, thus placing them under the pressures of secondary concerns which are beginning to take precedence over the primary in the developing region. Seeing that the Donnellys were regularly cast under their "Black" moniker and depicted as monstrous, Reaney inversely portrays the family as deeply human through their fierce loyalties to one another and their near-powerlessness in the face of administrative forces. For example, Reaney writes about how the Donnellys lost half of the farm along with the wheat they had sown which, Mr. Donnelly states, "was harvested by a piece of paper" (*The Donnellys* 43). Here we see again that Souwesto theme which takes subjects grounded in the natural world and confronts them with administration. By showing the Donnellys' valour and vulnerability, Reaney sheds the black myth and indicates their humanity.

Furthermore, the devout resistance of the Donnellys in the face of clerical injustice sees them as champions of a higher church, more reverential than their adversaries – as having attained the personally possessed truth of rural piety. As a result, the Donnellys' religious persecution incites divine transcendence through Reaney and thus he takes a thematically ironic return to myth and evokes ancient Egyptian writings. In *Man and the Sacred*, Eliade cites the ancient Egyptian "Coffin Texts" to articulate the connection of the soul with nature: "*The gods are living in me for I live and grow in the corn that sustains the Honoured Ones. / I cover the earth,*

/ whether I live or die I am Barley, / I am not destroyed. / I have entered the Order" (41). This same theme is revitalized in Reaney when the harvesting and processing of barley recalls the persecution of the Donnellys. Reaney lets the barley speak for itself regarding its harvesting and it tells us that "they sold me to the brewer / And he brewed me on the pan / But, when I got into the jug / I was the strongest man" (*The Donnellys* 14). The humble resilience and maintenance of personal truth in the face of impersonal administration makes the Donnellys "the strongest man"; it is what allows them into "the Order." Again, rural piety and personally possessed truth belong to those who are connected to the land and its symbols. Again my grandfather appears, with his funeral-wreaths woven of wheat, himself meeting harvest. I myself connecting him to the land through tree-carving; a name travelling down through the roots to the muddy earth. Consider again the monoculture of both soil and thought.

Perhaps these thoughts are too structuralist-sounding or too reliant on what may seem like basic assumptions. But what I'm doing is using these archetypal recurrences as a tool, like a level, to maintain a straight line from the past until now. "You never drop a level" is something my dad says whenever we're using one – it should be obvious enough, you drop the thing or throw it into a toolbox too hard and you're liable to knock the whole thing off kilter. Well, look, I'm not dropping it. Through the straight level which a structuralist approach provides, I am able to observe those values in the Souwesto which are sacred – why? Because they belong to the past and because they recur, and I want to recognize these things so that I can "keep what was good and pass it on" (Elliot 12). We just saw an example of such recurrence in Reaney's Egyptian recollection. After I'm finished my levelling here, I'm going to lay the level delicately back down and show you what these things are – but you can probably already guess they're tied up in recurrence, rural piety, personal truth, and their associated myths.

Moving along the level and being careful not to knock the vial, let's examine how as society has continued to develop in Southwestern Ontario, we arrive at a literature marked by individualism. Such an attitude, together with the contrast between the objective and the subjective or even the body and the mind, is an essential characteristic of such texts (Frye, *Anatomy* 56-57). Accordingly, rural literature suits these characteristics when protagonists operate outside of urban society or feel out of place. Munro's writing occupies this mode insofar as her characters are regularly *just* out of place due to their beliefs or find themselves out of place through class and gender distinctions. Evoking the recurrence of tragic modes, these concerns over one's belonging are manifested through themes of exclusion. Munro shows us that even the most banal facts of life can force us to reconsider our social status and question our belonging.

In Munro's *Who Do You Think You Are?* Rose enters high school to find that "Differences soon became evident, between town and country" (*Who* 38), simply in the components of their school lunches. Desperate to escape the subtle ridicule of her teacher, Rose lies about having brought half a grapefruit. This bisected fruit and the social intricacies it symbolizes are significant enough that the phrase "Half a Grapefruit" titles this section of *Who Do You Think You Are?*. The isolating condition of generational gender distinctions also arises in the text when Flo and Rose's father rebuke her scholarly pursuits. Seeing that "Rose brought a pile of books home every night[,] ... Flo expressed hostility to them as she did toward all books" (*Who* 44). Such hostility tinges the condescension of Rose's father, his attitude that a woman, in addition to being "energetic, practical, clever at making and saving" as well as "shrewd," needed to "be naive intellectually, childlike, contemptuous of maps and long words and anything in books, full of charming jumbled notions, superstitions, traditional beliefs" (*Who* 45). As such, Rose's sense of belonging is mitigated by a household that insults her own beliefs and pursuits. Tragically, she cannot achieve insider status in her own home; perhaps this is why she would create such an exotic lie during her school lunch. Half a grapefruit shines as a status symbol which betrays her Hanratty home and store with its offering of "[a] few spotty bananas, small unpromising oranges" (*Who* 39).

In comic modes the action inversely deals with the incorporation of an ordinary person into a desired group. I think such an incorporation can be found in the "Baptizing" section of *Lives of Girls and Women*. Del, who has been struggling with her mother's proprieties and obsession with cultural enrichment, finds Garnet French whose messy family isn't self-conscious or concerned with appearances. Like a baptism or a pilgrimage, her time with the French family represents a kind of return to that Edenic innocence of pastoral play Del enjoyed during her childhood on the Flats Road. The similar 'improprieties' and indecorous freedoms found with the French family make Del declare that "[t]here is no denying [she] was happy in that house" (Munro, *Lives* 226). Instead of choosing her bookish schoolmate Jerry whose pretensions identify him with Del's mother, Del chooses Garnet, the messy signifier of men like her father and Uncle Benny.

For Jung, the father (or King) is the passer of wisdom to the child or the translator of heritage; this idea manifests in ancient motifs of lost treasures where the treasure is the wisdom lost by the inheritor who must regain it. Or, as Jung explains, "the son is sent forth by his parents to seek the pearl that fell from the King's crown" (*Archetypes* 18). Furthermore, the treasure may be lost in the water – Jung's symbol for the unconscious. Thus both Munro and the argument of this essay are seeking to return to the lost heritage or what we saw Jung call the fallen stars (*Archetypes* 23). I'd like to explicate this idea by noting it in another Souwesto writer. This notion of lost wisdom, or returning to heritage, seems to be the primary concern in George Elliott's story from *The Kissing Man* called "A leaf for everything good." In this story an old man passes on his knowledge of the fish occupying a pond which is seemingly void of life. The perquisite for catching these unlikely and mythical fish seems to be faith or simply an adherence to the teachings of the old man (heritage).

Interestingly, Jung uses the metaphor of the fisherman to discuss the probing of the unconscious waters from an anchored standpoint in reality (*Archetypes* 24). In Elliott, the lost treasure lies within the fish, signifying something like a personally possessed truth which can be retrieved through faith where the crowd sees doubt. The crowd or the urban abhorred world of the town signifies a progressive culture which is irreverent toward past myth and heritage (heritage being signified by Munro's father in "Working for a Living" from *The View from Castle Rock* and the old man in "A leaf for everything good"). Munro's father remarks of his immigrant ancestors, "'To think what their ancestors did,' he said. 'The nerve it took, to pick up and cross the ocean. What was it squashed their spirits? So soon'" (*Castle Rock* 126). We find that personally possessed truth and the faith of rural piety is opposed to impersonal groupthink and doubt. In Elliott's story the boy Finn does eventually catch the fish but when he does, he skips town to escape its irreverence and doubt.

In the Jubilee of Munro's *Lives of Girls and Women*, things may seem above-board but beneath the veneer there is a lacking integrity engendering its inhabitants' duplicity and a subtextual inclination toward dishonesty. The primary men whom Del is concerned with in Jubilee – Jerry, Mr. Chamberlain, and Garnet French – are all show. Jerry locks Del away naked and Mr. Chamberlain takes sexual advantage of her. Tragedy and comedy meet where protagonists are rural-urban mediators, always outsiders who *just* don't quite belong. Del fits this archetype particularly well as she signifies both the integrity of the rural and a humble cultural intelligence of the urban – an assessment that is also true of Rose in *Who Do You Think You Are?*. Richard Milne in Knister's *White Narcissus* faces a similar predicament because his city-dwelling makes his home a foreign place where he is reminded of the rules of the rural which prescribe him as outsider. Knister also identifies with "The Wind" as a mediating presence which "noses through barn-yards and flower-beds. / He makes one of bays and the black flats of skyscrapers" (Knister, *After Exile* 15). Dynamic, the wind knows both the barn-yards and the skyscrapers; its freedom of movement is ascribed with a similar freedom of thought. This symbol is reinforced in "Wind's Way" where Knister writes, "I shall sing with the whoop of the wind [...] // For the way of the wind with city smoke [...] // For its way with field-scent, voices, road-dust" (Knister, *After Exile* 93). Thus the texts of Elliott, Munro, and Knister are aligned with notions of exclusion and incorporation.

Now we'll see how these ideas are expressed in the postmodern and contemporary – which is not to say that any of the Souwesto texts examined are explicitly postmodern, just that it is the moniker employed to describe our ironic, existential, and self-contemptuous culture. Like the postmodernist who renounces existing values, the ironic thematic mode is strongly individualist and opposes moral judgments decreed by the tribe. This repudiation usually manifests in rural literature as a turning away from the urban sphere. The tragedy of the nineteenth century deals with an isolation without impetus – the protagonists aren't necessarily to blame; they simply don't fit. The outsider may be blameless but is target of a scapegoat ritual. The black comedic savagery of the Donnellys' persecution pertains to this area and reminds us of how the contemporary circumstance of the author, Reaney, affects the body of the historical text. Again, we find that Reaney occupies the position of the poet on the cross noted by Frye; Reaney aligns historical, mythical, and literary descendance with his postmodern and contemporary social conditioning which gives him a satirical edge.

So what are the key myths and conventions which we find from the pioneers to the postmodernists in the rural Souwesto literary scene? What did my level find? First, notions of pastoral salvation. This myth began with the first European settlers and continues into Munro where at times the rural invites a return to innocence and integrity. Building on this, we encounter the idea of the urban sphere as the abhorred world of progress which separates consciousness from nature and thus devalues our humanity. Thirdly, we find ideas of imperial monotheism sublimating into a bloody tribalism which is manifested in the form of clique gossip in the contemporary small town. If we consider this imperial monotheism as a myth of concern, then the corresponding myth of freedom would consist of notions of rural piety. We find this rural piety oftentimes connected with a personally possessed truth which develops out of a reverence for the past.

What do these myths and values I've examined mean for contemporary Souwesto? What do they mean for our future? To answer these questions, we first need to look at what myths and values are more readily observable in contemporary Souwesto. By examining Ryan Porter's *You Can't Get There from Here*, I think we can gain a sense of what aspects of the rural are being valued today (perhaps detrimentally). It seems to me what we praise and take from rural contexts is intensely superficial – I don't blame anyone for this kind of reductivism (and I'm hesitant even to call it that); after all, we can't all be farm-kid English majors with the prerequisite time and interest to bother looking into the rural myths of Southwestern Ontario. I suppose the primary problem with the presentation of rural values lies in their commodification which holds up a funhouse mirror to exaggerate those marketable aspects of the rural ethos. I like to think of it as an artificial rustic insemination. Let's explore this sense of commodification in Porter so that I can place my own hometown of Waterford (the closest town to our farm) under scrutiny and examine how this exaggerated rusticity has a sense of self-deception to it. So why the lack of depth? I think it's because the rural has let itself become defined and characterized by the urban voice, or that its values can only be those which directly juxtapose the urban sphere. This relationship is a sort of contrived courtship in which the rural identity construes itself only as what the urban suitor wants of it. Why? Because Porter finds that small towns "are generally part of a fabric of communities and ... exist within close proximity to an urban centre, close enough to be within a sphere of economic and cultural influence" (11).

The survival of the small town in this fabric requires its adherence to the economic and cultural influence of the urban sphere – the small town seeks to attract the urban identity with slowed-down life in "bedroom communities" or with "aesthetically 'traditional' heritage shopping destinations" (Porter 7). The superficial values survive because they are economically viable. It's why in my hometown you can sell a brand-new piece of plywood, painted and scraped down to look worn and rustic, with some trite aphoristic rural-speak painted across it. Somehow the 'authenticity' of the rural sphere is supposed to make up for the sale of an inauthentic product. Worse, when it's not sold to urban out-of-towners, it's sold right to the rural populace who let their identities be categorized and sold to them for forty dollars so they can assert their pride with a faux-rustic sign reading 'Farmhouse.' Whether us rural folk (perhaps the use of 'folk' is itself faux authenticity) construe our identities in spite of the urban sphere or in accordance with its perception of us, we are still articulating ourselves in the language of the urban voice. In *The View from Castle Rock*, Munro poignantly sums up the relationship between the marketable idea and the reality of rural life with a meditation on footwear: "I am wearing open sandals, cheap water-buffalo sandals. This type of footwear is worn by a lot of women I know and it is seen to indicate a preference for country life, a belief in what is simple and natural. It is not practical when you are doing the sort of job I am doing now. Bits of hay and sheep pellets, which are like big black raisins, get squashed between my toes" (*Castle Rock* 311).

Regarding the literary mythos of small-town Ontario (and I contend the cultural mythos as well), Porter writes that this mythos "is most often created by urban voices who speak at a remove from their subjects, across a distance that can be spatial, temporal, or even cultural. This distance allows urban narrators to shape these communities into something they need them to be, to see what they want to see, and to remember those past places not as they were, but in a way determined by the present" (9). The rural today is trying to be something we are ostensibly needed to be and, in this struggle, we have forgotten our own language, and again, are articulating ourselves in an urban voice. Of course, this is not always true. There are older generations which seem to be maintaining a true authenticity and rural piety which ambivalently neither adheres to, nor acts in spite of, the urban sphere. But that group of farmers (to which my grandfather belonged) that met every morning in the Cockshutt diner are dying one by one, the diner itself having become yet another boutique for handmade home décor and tchotchkes. This aesthetic commodification of the rural is why Munro's nuanced appreciation of small-town life is so important, at least to my argument.

I have to agree with Porter when he writes that "the nature of experience in a small town, Munro's texts reveal, can be as complex and sophisticated as anything gained through urban life" (Porter 19). Munro's reverent mythologizing of the small town and the rural sphere is based in recurrence, in formal symbolism, and in deeply considered articulations of the depths and the distinctions of various rural groups. Part of this recurrence comes from an adherence to her heritage. A rural Souwesto woman winning a Nobel Prize? In the most estimable sense she is a "bumpkin genius" (*Castle Rock* 20) like her ancestor James Hogg. Hell, she's a hero just like Will O'Phaup. She took the rural landscape and the lives therein and showed that they were worth looking at, that there was meaning as nuanced as the mythical world of O'Phaup. Like Will, she asserted her "own mythology and local wonders" (*Castle Rock* 9).

Poetic recurrence, paying mind to the past, that's the answer to this identity problem. We've seen the effects of 'progress' on culture, so why would we ever want to sell ourselves for the sake of urbanizing economic progress? I have no way of telling how different my hometown will be once the under-construction subdivisions are finished and we meet the population influx, but I know it will not be the same. The view of the field which I saw every morning on the school bus (which was my own Mariposan train into the small town) will no longer exist and even my sight of the old mill will be obscured. How do we solve the rural identity crisis? What can the myths which I've examined in Souwesto historical and literary writings provide in the face of this self-deception? How do we regain a voice?

Munro has something to do with the answer; so do Knister and Elliott and Reaney and Lee. These are the nuanced mediators between the urban and the rural spheres – they can recognize what is good in both worlds, what is worth carrying. Perhaps they see all the meaning of the past disappearing too quickly, like what Munro sees in her father's home, "this peculiar house – the kitchen part of it built in the eighteen-sixties – can be dissolved, in a way, and lost, inside an ordinary comfortable house of the present time" (*Castle Rock* 289). These writers are familiar both with pastoral recurrence and urban progress. Their subtle responses offer an alternative to the reductive perceptions of both sides. Jung puts forward his ideas regarding dichotomies such as this when he writes that "the tendency to relativize opposites is a notable peculiarity of the unconscious. One must immediately add, however, that this is true only in cases of exaggerated moral sensibility; in other cases the unconscious can insist just as inexorably on the irreconcilability of the opposites" (*Archetypes* 36). We are reminded of this irreconcilability by Munro in *The View from Castle Rock* when she recalls that "people in town did generally look upon the people from the country as more apt to be slow-witted, tongue-tied, uncivilized, than themselves, and somewhat more docile in spite of their strength. And farmers saw people who lived in towns as having an easy life and being unlikely to survive in situations calling for fortitude, self-reliance, hard work" (*Castle Rock* 128-29).

I think it's fair to contend that there is a moral sensibility which is engendered by having a hand in both worlds, by being able to empathize with and to articulate the limitations of each. We can consider this sensibility in Lee when he writes, "I may not have chosen a career in agriculture, nor a life in the country, but agriculture has played an important role in forming my values and in defining my concerns" (*The Farm* 43). Similarly, Richard Milne in *White Narcissus* "knew that he could never be freed from the hold of this soil, however far from it he had travelled" (Knister, *White Narcissus* 21). Recall too the rural-urban mediating characterization of the wind in Knister's poems. The significance of these mediators, as an answer to the problem of the rural voice, also lies in their maintenance of personally possessed truth. This personally possessed truth is an aspirational myth of the literature I've been examining, and it seems that it is produced in the mediation between the urban and the rural, in the mediator's discernment of which aspects to adhere to and borrow from the different worlds. I also think it is fair to say that what Kierkegaard calls the 'revolutionary' aspect of personally possessed truth and the nuance which it requires has implications larger than my rural subject. The whole world could learn from rural piety, from individually wrought truth, and from nuanced mediation. I believe such knowledge would undercut what I think is the rampant tribalism of today – an observation which I don't think necessitates evidence. We see in the previously examined texts how personally possessed truth offers an alternative to impersonal truths, religions, and administrations.

These rural mediators represent the reconciliation of different worlds and provide a hopeful answer to tribalism, which Reaney explores in the fierce neo-primitive state of nature facing The Donnellys. The writings of such mediators and their precarious position also entrenches them in the previously examined myths of recurrence and progress. Munro with reverent mythologizing, Elliott with his recovering of lost meaning, Knister with his meditations on poetic truth and technological progress, and Lee with his considerations of agriculture facing the rise of agribusiness. Lee is concerned with ecology and the idea that culture is produced in the interaction between humans and their environment – thus an agribusiness which endangers our ecology also endangers our culture. Lee writes that "[c]ivilization depends upon the availability of food. Culture comes from cultivation. Culture depends upon leisure and abundance. The great achievements of civilization are entirely rooted in the success of agriculture" (*The Farm* 103). Following the same thought, "[i]t seems quite a natural evolution to connect the cultivation of acres to the cultivation of the mind and to see a strong connection between agriculture and high culture, between the tilling of the earth and the literary arts in particular" (*The Farm* 101); or, put more poignantly, "[p]oetry is the fruit of wheat" (*The Farm* 103). Time will tell if poetry can be cultivated from the practices of agribusiness.

These writers and these myths urge us to reconsider 'progress'; to me, they urge us to stop and ask if the small town really needs another rustic boutique. We must keep such considerations in mind alongside Frye's articulations of progress in order to maintain a nuanced position in time. We must stop here in the present to consider our past before deciding on the future. In *The View from Castle Rock,* Munro warns us of an irreverence toward the past: "there was something about all this rushing away, loosing oneself entirely from family and past, there was something rash and self-trusting about it that might not help a man, that might put him more in the way of such an accident, such a fate" (*Castle Rock* 110). We must recall the Cartesian consciousness which desecrated Indigenous cultures, which separated us from nature and thus our past therein. What is our 'progress' doing for remote or nondominant cultures? What is it doing for our ecology? Souwesto is a rich land; like novelist, short story writer, and essayist Douglas Glover, I'm from Norfolk County which is endearingly named "Ontario's Garden." But what do we do when the soil dies? Perhaps we need to reconsider the myth of progress and stop using a projected ideal world to rationalize our industry. Perhaps what we need is reverence for the sake of reverence. A respect which does not ask for recompense. A reverence like Munro's which finds the mythical and the beautiful in everything, a reverence for the present which could save our future – like Lee, upholding the "duty to honour the past and consider the future" (*The Farm* 18).

Already we struggle to return to the pastoral and an Edenic imaginative space and I fear we will never be able to return if 'progress' continues. As long as we continue to erase those parts of us which are based in recurrence, which are based in myth, we lose our sacred acts and in doing so lose the meaning in our lives. Remember, Eliade finds that "the only profane activities are those which have no mythical meaning" (*Cosmos and History* 28). Already agribusiness is supplanting the sacred heritage of farming as it moves the farmer further from the land and from direct husbandry. This progress not only has cultural ramifications but ecological ones as well; Lee writes that "[w]ith the passing away of agriculture, with its evolution into agribusiness, comes the death of the soil" (*The Farm* 101). The great diminution of culture and ecology by 'progress' continues. Similarly the heritage of the rural and small-town is being sold to survive in an increasingly urban world. I do not wish to speak as a luddite or some conservative champion of a myth of concern, but I think that our 'progress' needs to be re-evaluated just as Souwesto writers have urged us to do for so long – from Richardson, Sangster, Lampman, and Knister to Elliott, Reaney, Munro, and Lee.

It may be time to remember that progress has more to offer than technological development and mechanizations which ease our lives into a submissive passivity. Socio-cultural progress needs to rise above conventional notions of 'progress' – but I think this will require a reverence for the past. The reverence in Munro and Lee is a hopeful sign. Maybe this postmodern, ironic narrative mode which is daily life will circle us back to the start – to a mythic mode. This cyclical return is what Munro's reverent mythologizing of the everyday does for me and it seems to align somehow with New Sincerity and post-postmodernism. We also saw this amalgamation of the ironic and the mythic in Reaney's *The Donnellys*. In *The Farm on the Hill He Calls Home*, Lee's grandfather tells him that "[t]he land is more than the grave of the father. It is also the soil of the son" (105). I am afraid that our fathers' graves are growing unkempt, necrotic even. In recognizing our fathers' pasts and their own meditations on progress and recurrence, maybe we can develop the kind of personal truth necessary for survival in the nihilist postmodern climate; maybe we can restore our stars and find meaning in them. Perhaps we can lay our heads down against the roots of an apple tree and screw our eyes upward, like Munro, and struggle for meaning. I would rather struggle for meaning than renounce it; I would rather mythologize the banal than nothing at all.

Why does it feel right to hang off the tractor-pulled planter with pale dust spinning up to settle in your hair? To ensure that every seed is twisting down the hopper and neatly meeting the earth? Though the industrial additions to the perennial work diminish its sacredness, there is still a reprieve from the profane. A reprieve from passivity and idleness. It's probably why my dad is so industrious. Ready and waiting for meaning – meaning in the coldest January morning and on the hottest day of August. Meaning ready to be met and reset with the frost or the dew. If you don't want to call it meaning, if you want to scoff at the sacred pretense, then call it occupation, call it distraction even. Maybe it's distraction from the sheer profane monotony of everything – it's why I practise art; my father and I both seek distraction, to activate the sacred through productive acts. Farming, writing, painting. The same desire satisfied through distinct actions. Moments of participation in what Eliade calls 'mythical time.' Meaning. For a moment, meaning.

So we have come to see the immense scope of these Souwesto texts which originate in such a seemingly small region. By examining the myths which generated our current environment and continue to shape it, we see that these myths are greater than Southwestern Ontario. Like a whole world of meaning struggling inside an apple tree, these rural texts are a microcosm representing the whole of our contemporary struggle with postmodern culture. These myths, these texts, entertain the idea of fulfillment based in the striving toward meaning despite the encroachment of the profane and impersonal. Something like the humble piety of Mayhew Salkald in George Elliott's story "An act of piety." Honey addresses his dead grandfather Mayhew, his teachings: "[y]ou never said it, but what you meant was that barns are necessary, and men to build good ones are necessary and worth something" (Elliott 11). Honey continues, "[y]ou knew about permanence the day you moved onto your own property" (Elliott 11). In the face of a 'progress' which has left quiet those red barns now dull and shattered along the sides of freeways, drill a deep well, raise high the roof beams, build now with the future in mind, with permanence in mind, and we can continue to carry the good.

Works Consulted

Crawford, Isabella Valancy. "From *Malcolm's Katie*." *The Oxford Book of Canadian Verse in English and French.* Ed and introd. A.J.M. Smith. Toronto: Oxford UP, 1960. 46-53.

Eliade, Mircea. *Cosmos and History: The Myth of the Eternal Return.* Trans. Willard R. Trask. New York: Harper & Row, 1959.

---. *Man and the Sacred: A Thematic Source Book of the History of Religions.* New York: Harper & Row, 1974.

Elliott, George. *The Kissing Man.* Toronto: Macmillan, 1962.

Frye, Northrop. *Anatomy of Criticism: Four Essays.* Ed. Robert D. Denham. Toronto: U of Toronto P, 2006. Vol. 22 of The Collected Works of Northrop Frye. 30 vols.

---. "Canada: New World without Revolution." *Northrop Frye on Canada.* Ed. Jean O'Grady and David Staines. Toronto: U of Toronto P, 2016. 435-47. Vol. 12 of The Collected Works of Northrop Frye. 30 vols.

---. *The Critical Path: An Essay on the Social Context of Literary Criticism.* Bloomington, IN: Indiana UP, 1971.

---. "Haunted by Lack of Ghosts." *Northrop Frye on Canada.* Ed. Jean O'Grady and David Staines. Toronto: U of Toronto P, 2016. 472-92. Vol. 12 of The Collected Works of Northrop Frye. 30 vols.

---. "The Narrative Tradition in English Canadian Poetry." *Northrop Frye on Canada*. Ed. Jean O'Grady and David Staines. Toronto: U of Toronto P, 2016. 55-63. Vol. 12 of The Collected Works of Northrop Frye. 30 vols.

---. "Silence in the Sea." *Northrop Frye on Canada*. Ed. Jean O'Grady and David Staines. Toronto: U of Toronto P, 2016. 383-97. Vol. 12 of The Collected Works of Northrop Frye. 30 vols.

---. *Words with Power: Being a Second Study of "The Bible and Literature"*. San Diego, CA: Harcourt Brace Jovanovich, 1990.

Gill, Glen Robert. *Northrop Frye and the Phenomenology of Myth*. Toronto: U of Toronto P, 2006.

Glover, Douglas. "The Familiar Dead." *Notes Home from a Prodigal Son*. Ottawa: Oberon, 1999. 147-71.

Griggs, Terry. *Quickening*. Erin, ON: The Porcupine's Quill, 1990.

Hall, Roger, William Westfall, and Laurel Sefton MacDowell, eds. *Patterns of the Past: Interpreting Ontario's History*. Toronto: Dundurn, 1988.

Jaenen, Cornelius J., ed. and introd. *The French Regime in the Upper Country of Canada During the Seventeenth Century*. Toronto: Champlain Society, 1996.

Johnson, E. Pauline. *Flint and Feather; The Complete Poems of E. Pauline Johnson (Tekahionwake)*. Introd. Theodore Watts-Dunton. Don Mills, ON: Paperjacks, 1972.

Johnson, J.K. *In Duty Bound: Men, Women, and the State in Upper Canada, 1783-1841*. Montreal, QC and Kingston, ON: McGill-Queen's UP, 2014.

Johnston, Basil. *Ojibway Heritage*. Toronto: McClelland and Stewart, 1976.

Jung, C.G. *The Archetypes and the Collective Unconscious*. 2nd ed. Princeton, NJ: Princeton UP, 1968. Bollingen Ser. XX.

Keith, W.J. *Literary Images of Ontario*. Toronto: U of Toronto P, 1992.

---. *The Rural Tradition: A Study of the Non-Fiction Prose Writers of the English Countryside*. Toronto: U of Toronto P, 1974.

King, Thomas. *The Truth about Stories: A Native Narrative*. Toronto: House of Anansi, 2003. The Massey Lectures Ser.

Klinck, Carl F., gen. ed. *Literary History of Canada: Canadian Literature in English*. 2nd ed. 3 vols. Toronto: U of Toronto P, 1976.

Knister, Raymond. "This truth...." *After Exile: A Raymond Knister Poetry Reader*. Ed. Gregory Betts. Toronto: Exile Editions, 2003. 179.

---. *White Narcissus.* Introd. Philip Child. Toronto: McClelland and Stewart, 1962. New Canadian Library 32.

---. "The Wind." *After Exile: A Raymond Knister Poetry Reader.* Ed. Gregory Betts. Toronto: Exile Editions, 2003. 15.

---. "Wind's Way." *After Exile: A Raymond Knister Poetry Reader.* Ed. Gregory Betts. Toronto: Exile Editions, 2003. 93.

Lampman, Archibald. "The City of the End of Things." *The Oxford Book of Canadian Verse in English and French.* Ed. and introd. A.J.M. Smith, Toronto: Oxford UP, 1960. 78-81.

Leacock, Stephen. *Sunshine Sketches of a Little Town.* Ed. Gerald Lynch. Ottawa: Tecumseh, 1996. Canadian Critical Editions.

Lee, John B. "Burning Land: Poem." *Numéro Cinq.* 4 May 2010. <http://numerocinqmagazine.com/2010/05/21/burning-land-a-poem-by-john-b-lee/>.

---. *The Farm on the Hill He Calls Home.* Windsor, ON: Black Moss, 2004. Settlements Ser. 1.

Lemire, Jeff. *Essex County.* Atlanta: Top Shelf, 2009.

Mair, Charles. "From *Tecumseh.*" *The Penguin Book of Canadian Verse.* Ed. and introd. Ralph Gustafson. Rev. ed. Harmondsworth, Eng.: Penguin, 1967. 47-48.

Munro, Alice. *Dance of the Happy Shades.* Fwd. Hugh Garner. Toronto: Ryerson, 1968.

---. *Lives of Girls and Women.* Toronto: McGraw-Hill Ryerson, 1971.

---. *The View from Castle Rock.* Toronto: McClelland & Stewart, 2006.

---. *Who Do You Think You Are?* Toronto: Macmillan of Canada, 1978.

O'Grady, Jean. Introduction. *Northrop Frye on Canada.* Ed. Jean O'Grady and David Staines. Toronto: U of Toronto P, 2016. xxi-xlviii. Vol. 12 of The Collected Works of Northrop Frye. 30 vols.

Porter, Ryan. *You Can't Get There from Here: The Past as Present in Small-Town Ontario Fiction.* Toronto: U of Toronto P, 2019.

Reaney, James. *The Donnellys.* With Scholarly Apparatus by James Noonan. Victoria: Porcépic, 1983.

Richardson, John. *Tecumseh, a Poem in Four Cantos.* Ed. Douglas Daymond and Leslie Monkman. London, ON: Canadian Poetry, 1992.

Riddell, John. "'This Northern Mouth': Ideas of Myth and Regionalism in Modern Canadian Poetry." *Northrop Frye's Canadian Literary Criticism and Its Influence.* Ed. Branko Gorjup. Toronto: U of Toronto P, 2009. 44-60.

Rotstein, Abraham. "The Mystery of the Neutral Indians." *Patterns of the Past: Interpreting Ontario's History*. Ed. Roger Hall, William Westfall, and Laurel Sefton MacDowell. Toronto: Dundurn, 1988. 11-36.

Sangster, Charles. "From *The St. Lawrence and the Saguenay*." *The Penguin Book of Canadian Verse*. Ed. and introd. Ralph Gustafson. Rev. ed. Harmondsworth, Eng.: Penguin, 1967. 43.

---. "From *The St. Lawrence and the Saguenay*: [The Thousand Islands]." *The Oxford Book of Canadian Verse in English and French*. Ed. and introd. A.J.M. Smith. Toronto: Oxford UP, 1960. 13-15.

Soper, Ella, and Nicholas Bradley, eds. *Greening the Maple: Canadian Ecocriticism in Context*. Calgary, AB: U of Calgary P, 2013. Energy, Ecology, and the Environment Ser. 7.

Strickland, Samuel. *Twenty-Seven Years in Canada West; Or, The Experience of an Early Settler*. Ed. Agnes Strickland. Introd. Carl F. Klinck. Edmonton: M.G. Hurtig, 1972.

Struthers, J.R. (Tim), ed. *Alice Munro Country: Essays on Her Works 1*. Toronto: Guernica Editions, 2020. Essential Writers Ser. 51.

Traill, Catherine Parr. *The Backwoods of Canada*. Introd. Clara Thomas. Toronto: McClelland and Stewart, 1971. New Canadian Library 51.

Weaver, John. "Society and Culture in Rural and Small-Town Ontario: Alice Munro's Testimony on the Forty Years from 1945 to 1985." *Alice Munro Country: Essays on Her Works 1*. Ed. J.R. (Tim) Struthers. Toronto: Guernica Editions, 2020. 155-80. Essential Writers Ser. 51.

Performing Munro in Huron County

Taylor Marie Graham

"Dear Life"

At the end of her final collection of short stories, *Dear Life*, Nobel laureate Alice Munro includes four pieces which she calls "*not quite stories ... autobiographical in feeling, though not, sometimes, entirely so in fact ... the first and last – and the closest – things I have to say about my own life*" (255; emphasis in orig.). Towards the end of the fourth and last of the "*not quite stories*" in this collection, Munro discusses an instance when she was reading her hometown newspaper from Wingham, Ontario. This incident may or may not have actually occurred, according to the previous statement, yet whether it happened in fact or not this described incident aligns with a feeling or emotional truth of Munro's experience of life.

In "Dear Life" Munro explains that after getting married and moving to Vancouver,

> I still got the weekly paper that was published in the town where I grew up. I think somebody, maybe my father and his second wife, made sure that I had a subscription. Often I barely looked at it, but one time, when I did, I saw [that someone with] the [maiden] name Netterfield . . . had written a letter to the paper. (316)

Included with the letter was a poem written by this woman who, like Munro, did not live in Huron County any longer, but "still had a subscription to her hometown paper" (316). As Munro read through the poem, she made a startling discovery: this woman had lived in

Munro's childhood home before Munro's family had moved in! The poem described the newspaper poet's memories and experiences of her own childhood in Munro's childhood home.

This occurrence is significant not only because it's certainly interesting for anyone to find out who else has occupied a space which is as intimate to our sense of self as our childhood home. Specifically for Munro, this discovery was compounded by the fact that her own writing is often focused on this same place, this farm house in Huron County. Munro has written various stories set in versions of this house and the surrounding area, so much so it became a writerly obsession of hers which a number of critics have noted over the years. In his biography of Munro, Robert Thacker makes this point in his prologue. He describes Munro's home as a "mysterious, touchable place," a place that from Vancouver and later Victoria she "recalled, imagined, and detailed" in her stories and, when she returned home years later, "confront[ed] it anew with its surfaces and depths still there, resonant" (12). The area has even been named "Alice Munro Country," further demonstrating not only the region's stamp on Munro, but Munro's stamp on the region in return. This moniker is used freely by writers and scholars alike, as exemplified by a short story by Madeleine Thien and an essay collection edited by J.R. (Tim) Struthers both using "Alice Munro Country" as their title.

In her short story "Dear Life," Munro discusses the poem by the previous occupant of her often re-imagined home over a couple pages and it is perhaps unsurprising that she provides a few notes. Munro corrects the poet's misremembering of the trees. "I believe she was remembering it wrong – they were elms, which had all died of Dutch elm disease by now" (317). She is more generous with the poet's omissions, however. Munro recognizes that the writer makes some editing choices similar to the ones she would have made. "She had left out, just as I would have done, the way the spring got muddied up and soiled all around by horses' hooves. And of course left out the manure" (317).

This seemingly small interchange between Munro and this poet, perhaps not entirely factual in its retelling, has fascinated me since I first read it in the summer of 2020. I have so many questions. Did the newspaper poet know she lived in the house of Alice Munro, who by that time was garnering vast literary praise for her writing? What did the poet think of Munro's versions of the house and the area if she did indeed read her work? Is there more in the poem Munro is not saying that aligns or misaligns with her view of this place, perhaps coloured by a generational divide between herself and the poet? What did Munro think of other writers trying to write about her home? How might these versions connect or collide in their renditions of this place many different people call home? I found myself obsessing over these questions that arose after reading this passage in "Dear Life."

Growing Up in Alice Munro Country

The reason behind this obsession no doubt had something to do with growing up in "Alice Munro Country" myself. No, I did not grow up in Alice Munro's old farmhouse, and in fact I spent very little of my childhood in Wingham, Ontario, but to this day I consider other Huron County staples such as Goderich, Clinton, and Port Albert my home.

If you'll indulge me, I'll share a little about my version of "Alice Munro Country" with you. When I was nearly six years old, in July of 1992, my mother got a job teaching math and science at the high school in Goderich. This prompted a move with her and my stepfather to the area and, after renting a few houses, eventually we settled in the lakeside hamlet community of Port Albert. As a result, unlike many Huron County residents including Munro, I did not spend my very first years in Huron County. The rest of my family was in Windsor where I spent my very early years, so throughout my childhood I travelled quite regularly to see friends and family a few hours away in the border city to Detroit.

I did not have six degrees of separation with the other Huron County children and the fact that my father was Italian did give me a certain mild exoticism to the predominantly Dutch, English, Irish, and Scotch families who occupied this area. I was a bit of an outsider as a child, spending most of my elementary school time playing by myself in our spacious country backyard making up stories or convincing myself I could control the wind. I also lived right near the Port Albert beach and spent a lot of summers swimming in Lake Huron for hours, long after sunset.

My experience of high school in the region was highly charged. Everything felt like it was moving swiftly. I played every sport you could. I read every book in front of me. I went to every party. I acted in every school play and remember mostly feeling like anything was possible for my future if I wanted it hard enough. Unfortunately, I also knew a lot of young people, especially my girlfriends, who had experienced sexual violence of some kind at quite a young age. I think back to one friend I had in Grade 9 whose parents inexplicably let a twenty-two-year-old man call himself her boyfriend. Another instance that hung over me for much of my life was when I was in Grade 4. At the end of May 1995, a teenager named Mistie Murray went missing from the high school where my mother taught in Goderich and while it's still a mystery, some believe she ended up in sex trafficking.

I do want to mention too that it wasn't until more recently that I started to understand the difficult colonial history of the area. Throughout my childhood as a privileged White settler, I was blind to the fact that Port Albert is situated on part of the Huron Tract, Treaty 29, the ancestral lands of the Haudenosaunee, Anishinaabe, and Neutral Indigenous Peoples. According to the Huron County Museum, Treaty 29 "ceded 99% of the [Indigenous] communities' remaining lands to the British Crown, and designated four reserves" (Duern) within an hour's drive from my childhood home. I've been very fortunate to have been able to learn more about this important and complex history from Indigenous leaders and story keepers including Randall Kahgee who is the former four consecutive term Chief of the Saugeen First Nation and Senior Counsel with Olthuis Kleer Townshend LLP. "We are all treaty people," Kahgee explained in a 2021 talk, "and we all have an obligation to hold up the treaties which are supposed to be predicated on mutual respect, a nation to nation relationship" (Kahgee, "What Does It Mean"). Working continually to understand and enact my treaty obligations is an important part of my relationship with Indigenous lands and peoples today.

I don't know when I first started to hear about Alice Munro because most of my family being from Windsor and Detroit were more interested in American media and novelists. I gobbled up books by John Irving, watched a lot of *Seinfeld*, and my family often had the Talking Heads on repeat in the living room. I remember knowing there was a famous writer who lived in the area, but mostly people ended their sentences with "and she probably thinks she's great" or something else equally sarcastic. I'm sure there were many devoted fans of Munro in Huron County in the Nineties, but I didn't run into any of them. Instead my general feeling was that folks who spoke about Munro thought it was strange that someone would want to write about this place we were all from.

Thankfully, my mother and stepfather were exceptions to that rule because both were always deep readers and loved seeing folks like themselves represented on screens and pages. I think it was my Mom's copy of *The Progress of Love* which eventually introduced me to Munro. I remember laughing and being surprised to see something of myself and people I knew in the stories, not to mention the bizarre joy at seeing the names of nearby towns and landmarks on the page. I think something akin to Munro's shock at recognizing her house in Netterfield's poem hit me then as I read through Munro's work set in Huron County for the first time. I'm almost certain it was *Open Secrets* I read next, not at all aware of how much this book would make its impact on me in the next years ahead. I remember being both disturbed by the violence against women and even children in certain stories, as well as feeling a difficult sense of validation of experience considering the many hidden (and not so hidden) truths I knew about girls and women close to me at the time. Similar to Munro's experience with the newspaper poet, I've been thinking about how this text and others by Munro aligned or misaligned with my own versions of Huron County since then.

As so many artists do, I left home to head to the big city, Toronto in my case, to study theatre at York University. There I wrote some generally urban works, but it's safe to say that as I became a playwright I also became obsessed with Huron County, with re-examining my childhood there. While living in Toronto, I wrote a play called *Cottage Radio* about a tornado which hit Goderich in 2011 and another play called *White Wedding* about being on the outskirts of a rural wedding in an old high school.

Blyth Festival

My recently completed PhD work was also Huron County focused. My dissertation involved looking at the Blyth Festival Theatre which is a professional theatre located in Huron County. Since 1975, they have been producing new Canadian works including adaptations of Munro's short stories as well as other stage versions of Huron County by different artists. My dissertation asks: Who is Canada according to Blyth? Who are rural Canadians according to Blyth and who gets to occupy rural spaces?

For this work I chose to dig into a few decolonial theories including one by the influential Canadian theatre historian and theorist Alan Filewod, who was inspired by postcolonial theorist Benedict Anderson's work. Filewod asserts that the Canada performed on stages across this country represents an imagined community. Filewod has written extensively on the application of the performed imagined Canada on stages across this landmass now called Canada and he has inspired many studies along the same line of questioning. In *Performing Canada: The Nation Enacted in the Imagined Theatre* Filewod explains:

> I paraphrase Benedict Anderson's celebrated argument to suggest that the theatre as it is imagined, formally (through policy, canonization, spectacle, and critical discourse) and informally (through polemics, noncanonical textualities, pageants, literary closet dramas, and failed aspirations), is a legitimizing performance of the imagined community that is the nation. (1)

Because the Blyth Festival Theatre is found in a Huron County town with fewer than 1,000 people, it's perhaps unsurprising that their performed version of Canada is often set in the countryside. In this way, Blyth Festival performs an imaginary narrative of Canadian rural life on their stage. Imaginary rurals performed on stages like Blyth's have real affects on the real rural people and places in Canada. This conceptual rural is reinforced by others' imaginary ideals of rurality which makes the ability to see the actual rural much more difficult, especially if it doesn't fit with the imaginary view of who and what occupies these spaces. In this way it's easy to become blind to any aspect of the rural which doesn't fit with the imagined because it complicates the dominant notion of rural. It can also be potentially uncomfortable and can generate conflict when something or someone occupies an imagined space in which they are not thought by others to belong.

In a lot of ways, the goal of my dissertation was to complicate imaginary depictions of rural Canada and point to important complications that have been performed on the Blyth Festival Stage throughout its fifty-year history. Within this history are productions by artists of colour, Indigenous artists, White settler Canadians, and other communities. What became clear to me throughout this research was that each version of Huron County and other Canadian rural places is impacted deeply by the author's own identity and experience. Also important are the difficult negotiations theatres like Blyth make when considering and confronting past performed imaginary rurals on their stages.

Play Adaptations of Munro at Blyth

One of the quotations that you can find on many of Munro's book covers is from Cynthia Ozick. "She is our Chekhov," Ozick declares, connecting Munro's work with that of one of the most famous playwrights and short story writers who has ever lived. As a playwright myself, I've often found it puzzling that the Blyth Festival Theatre has only produced two play adaptations of Munro's short stories on their stage.

The first play, *How I Met My Husband*, was adapted by Munro and the Blyth company players at the time during the second year of the festival in 1976 from Alice Munro's short story of the same name collected in her preceding book, *Something I've Been Meaning To Tell You* (1974). It's also worth mentioning that this story was also a television drama by Munro collected in *The Play's the Thing: Four Original Television Dramas* edited by Tony Gifford. Based on some key similarities and differences in the scripts and on anecdotal stories of the play's development conveyed by artists associated with Blyth today, it seems likely to me that the creative team behind the play version may have used this television drama as a tool while developing the play script, but that ultimately the play was adapted in the rehearsal room by Munro and the team specifically with the stage in mind.

While every other play in the first couple of years of the festival was later reproduced, this one play was not despite the short story author's ever-increasing fame. While researching, I was under the assumption that the lack of a remount may have been due to a poor adaptation or production with low box office sales as a result. But after reading the play myself, it's my opinion that the script is well crafted, staying true to the original short story in many ways, yet allowing the interior elements of the story room in successful scene work. I wondered then if perhaps the production was not very successful in staging the script. After looking at box office reports I saw that this theory wasn't accurate either because *How I Met My Husband* met comparable numbers to the other shows that summer and was not the lowest earner out of the bunch ("Performance File").

What Munro's play does is push against a utopian portrayal of rural Canada and demonstrate complications for settler women including sexual desire, class, and discontent. Edie, the play's protagonist, is a hired girl paid to help with daily chores for a well-to-do family for a summer. Edie is clearly not content with this position in the house as the audience hears through monologues including her criticisms of her employers. She also pursues her sexual desire for an engaged pilot, pushing against a pious ideal of rural women as chaste and happy to wait patiently for the men to pursue their passions. In this way both the play and the short story actively resist utopian ideals of rural life for settler women.

The decision not to remount this dramatic adaptation of Munro's depiction of the inner lives of girls and women from the region would seem to suggest a patriarchal influence on this theatre's production history. It wasn't until 2020 that Artistic Director Gil Garratt picked a full season of women's work to be performed on Blyth's stage including *How I Met My Husband*: "I found an old hand-typed manuscript in a drawer at the theatre," he said, "and when I read it, I knew we had to make it part of our 46th season. Alice means so much to our country and to this community" (Garratt as qtd. in Tomasek). Of the actual play, Garrett declared: "This play is a lost jewel in Canadian theatre" (Garratt as qtd. in Tomasek). The COVID-19 pandemic which closed the doors of all theatres across Canada for much of 2020 put a stop to this season of course, and the play has not been reprogrammed since reopening.

The only other play based on an Alice Munro short story to make it to Blyth Festival Theatre's stage was written by a playwright I deeply admire. *Courting Johanna* by Marcia Johnson was produced in the summer of 2008. In an essay by Shelley Scott about this adaptation, the genesis for this play is described:

> Marcia Johnson ... was working at Blyth as a playwright in residence when she met Munro at a public event. In the course of a conversation

> about what Johnson liked about each of Munro's stories in her most recent collection and how they could work as plays, Munro offered "Hateship, Friendship, Courtship, Loveship, Marriage" for adaptation. The generous offer was both unprecedented and unexpected; according to Johnson, Blyth's artistic directors had been asking for permission to adapt an Alice Munro story "for thirty years." (108)

This chance meeting between Johnson and Munro ended the three decades' long hiatus of Munro's work on the Blyth stage.

The published play *Courting Johanna* begins with a playwright's note where Marcia Johnson writes about her development process. She mentions that she was trying to play with the structure of the original story in order to find the most suitable way to take the narrative from the page to the stage. She mentions that Kate Lynch, her director, ended up convincing her to stick to the original structure of the story. While Johnson does not clearly state this, it seems as though she had other plans – though it's unclear what exactly that other version would have looked like. Staying true to the original story meant that the beginning of the play is narrated by a male character who has very little stage time and while this works in the story by drawing attention to this man's misconceptions of Johanna, it doesn't translate successfully to the play. There is little reason for the audience to adopt a perspective other than the narrator's. In the archival recording of the production, the director's blocking and scene transitions also chop up the show's movement, making the first scenes somewhat difficult to follow as a result.

Despite these minor early issues, the play is saved by Johnson's adept scenework and the lovely relationship between Sabitha and Edith. There is an appealing closeness and sense of fun in the relationship between these girls as they enjoy exploring the limits of societal expectations. They swear and push the boundaries of what it means to be a "good girl" by writing fake love letters to Johanna from a man for whom she ends up leaving her position and home. It is in these complications of the representation of rural girls that Johnson's play shines.

Another play certainly worth noting is *If Truth Be Told* by Beverley Cooper which was produced at the Blyth Festival Theatre in 2016. It is not an adaptation of Munro's work, but rather examines the debate of banning books including Munro's book *Lives of Girls and Women* by

Christian communities in the late 1970s. While I firmly believe all books should be freely accessible to everyone, I was happy to see that Cooper's play presents a well-balanced debate. I agree with Lynn Slotkin's review which ends by stating, "I loved the play and was glad of the chance to hear such compelling arguments on both sides" (Slotkin, "From the BLYTH FESTIVAL").

The Blyth Festival itself, like the region more broadly, has been both influential for Munro and influenced by Munro. Munro can trace her ancestors back to some of the first settlers of Blyth in the 1850s as she conveys through her fictional accounts in *The View from Castle Rock*. As a child in the 1930s and 1940s, Munro regularly visited her paternal grandparents who lived on Drummond Street in Blyth (Thacker 31), a short walk from the theatre. Before the Blyth Festival Theatre was founded in 1975, Blyth Memorial Hall was used for travelling performances, especially because it was on the train route through Huron County which was unfortunately lost in the 1980s. Reportedly Munro says of her own memories of Blyth:

> I always spent part of the summer in Blyth, staying with my grandparents.... whenever I went past the Hall, I had a sense of extravagance and excitement of some formal spectacle that lit up the spacious eventful days before I was born. (Munro as qtd. in Tomasek)

While it's unclear which specific shows Munro saw in that time, if any, she may have been one of the last generations to see so-called Chautauqua travelling entertainments and other pieces created by local amateur artists.

After returning to Huron County in the mid-1970s, Munro also became invested in the social aspect of the Blyth Festival, often participating in the large country dinners the theatre provided by making a pie or serving drinks to playgoers. Living in the area, I have heard many stories from people meeting Munro at Blyth. One lawyer friend of mine excitedly met Munro in the theatre gallery before a show one afternoon. Another friend and her father met Munro in the theatre's front courtyard. This friend loves poking fun at her father for telling what she describes as dry and unnecessarily long stories about his boat, only later learning whom he had been addressing. The only time I ever met Alice Munro was not in Blyth, but on the streets of another Huron County town called Bayfield. Her assistant at the time, the mid-2010s, had gone to high school with me and introduced me to Munro as a writer before I could stop her. I remember Munro smiling at me and saying, "Well, good luck with that!" before heading into a nearby shop. I still laugh thinking about my awkward and confused "Thank you" in response as she disappeared from view.

The Alice Munro Book Club

In 2020, when the pandemic came along and we were all forced to stay inside our residences and communicate via screens, I wormed my way into a weekly on-line reading community started by scholars Paul Barrett and Ryan Porter and Sarah Roger. The group is full of prominent scholars and other Munro enthusiasts who began by reading Munro's final collection, *Dear Life*. The idea was to start with this text and work backwards throughout her books.

As I joined in week after week, this group reminded me of everything I loved about Munro's writing and got me thinking of her work in new ways. I looked forward to our Zoom chats every Wednesday evening and made many important friendships throughout the process. At the end of the summer we had completed discussing *Dear Life*, finishing with the title story where Munro grapples with the newspaper poet's version of her home. I found myself grappling with my own versions of home reflected in and contrasted with Munro's.

One of the young scholars in the group, Jessica McDonald, had some of us join her on a new podcast about teaching books where we talked about the book club. I enjoyed myself so much talking about the process of reading through Munro and found that this exchange, coupled with the questions prompted by "Dear Life," got my creative juices flowing. I remember waking up in the middle of that night after the podcast and running to my keyboard to start to write a new play.

Post Alice

Fiona Mongillo, the artistic director of the Here For Now Festival in Stratford, Ontario reached out not long after I had started writing my new play to see what I was working on. After chatting with me, Fiona and her associate artistic director Siobhan O'Malley commissioned me to write a new play which I decided to call *Post Alice*, to draw on the decidedly postmodern approach I was taking with this piece. *Post Alice* is inspired by four short stories by Munro. Probably to nobody's surprise two of the stories, "Pride" and "Train," are from *Dear Life*. The others are "Wenlock Edge" from *Too Much Happiness* and "How I Met My Husband" from *Something I've Been Meaning To Tell You*.

Essentially what I did was create four characters inspired by the four protagonists from each story and place them into a new narrative, a new story, something that resembled both Munro's and my own version of Huron County. In my play set in 2018, the protagonists came together as childhood friends reunited after a long spell apart. Edie rather than her love interest from "How I Met My Husband" became a pilot herself. She was much older than the character in the story too and married to another pilot. I reimagined the character as having a life of freedom in the skies with many adventures. Belle from "Train" and the unnamed narrator from "Wenlock Edge" became sisters in my play. Like Belle from the original story, my Belle was facing surgery and had recently been abandoned by someone she relied on closely. My Belle, whom the other characters nicknamed *Cow*belle, had a few other similarities with Munro's Belle. She owned a rundown farm property and had a complicated relationship with the property's previous owner, Cowbelle's now deceased father. The play took place over the course of one night around a fire on this property. Cowbelle's sister whom I eventually named Wenlock was home to visit, prompted by Belle's illness, after a long time being away due to an event similar to the bizarre and traumatic incident in "Wenlock Edge." In *Post Alice* this event is left unresolved and each character is affected by it in their own ways to be revealed throughout the evening.

Because I was so fascinated with questions of the real and the unreal at the time, inspired by Munro's final four stories in *Dear Life*, I also decided to grapple with a true story in the middle of this fiction. Included among these stories is the true story of Mistie Murray, a teenager who went missing from Goderich in 1995. I am deeply indebted to Anne Murray, Mistie's mother, who shared stories with me about Mistie from the moment she adopted her until the day she never came home. From Anne Murray, I also learned that Mistie's biological mother is Mi'kmaq, a fact which connects her with a long and deeply difficult history of missing and murdered Indigenous women, girls, and two spirit people in Canada. The gifted Terre Chartrand, a non-status Indigenous artist and writer, worked with me as a cultural consultant on the piece, specifically focusing on the Indigenous content in the play. Actor Heather Marie Annis, who is Mi'kmaq, French, and Scottish, played the character Oneida inspired by her namesake in Munro's "Pride" who in my play is at the beginning of a journey to learn more about her own Indigenous heritage and history. Like Munro's, my Oneida had a prosperous father and was often unable to express her true feelings to those closest to her, but in *Post Alice* these barriers are the result of colonial injustices facing many people living across Turtle Island today.

Munro's short fiction featuring complex Huron County women and girls, and Mistie's tragic tale likely the result of sex trafficking, loomed large for me throughout my childhood and early adulthood. It was important to me that the play was complex, like life, including moments of comedy. Women and girls in Huron County that I grew up around are some of the funniest people I know. This culture was important to capture for me and as we all know humour is a great mask for trauma. Throughout the night at the fire, truths are revealed including unseen or unacknowledged sexual violence felt by all the women and the affect of Mistie's tragic story on their lives.

Upon reflection, I realize that *Open Secrets* was also deeply influential on *Post Alice*'s development. I perhaps didn't grasp this as I was writing because I haven't reread this collection for many years, but looking through the stories again I see that they are an unavoidable precursor for *Post Alice.* Without romanticizing the writing process too much, because sometimes the act of playwriting can be anything but romantic, there's a strong possibility that I started to imagine versions of this play in my head the day I put *Open Secrets* down after reading it for the first time sometime in the late Nineties. The awful facts of lost women and sexual violence are certainly present throughout both texts. As well, the title story in Munro's collection includes bits of songs which are also vital to the structure of my play. If only at an unconscious level, I think I was compelled to continue to respond to these stories in my own play, plus continue the work of Johnson, Cooper, and Munro herself in the dramatic transformation of Munro's fiction into theatre.

I lucked out with an extraordinarily talented team of women working on *Post Alice* including the show's director, Here For Now Festival's fearless Artistic Director, Fiona Mongillo. I couldn't have asked for a better cast: Heather Marie Annis, Ellen Denny, Aubree Erickson. and Siobhan O'Malley. Their ensemble work was exemplary. They worked to find the rich history among the characters which was essential for the play's final success.

Post Alice *Reception*

I'm certainly happy to report *Post Alice*'s premiere run in the summer of 2021 in Stratford sold out and was a critical success – a true honour for a playwright let me tell you! Lynn Slotkin called my play "arresting and funny" (Slotkin, "Reviews"), and Joe Szekeres described it as "Powerful, powerful, and courageous." It even made Christopher Hoile's *Stage Door Review* end-of-year list which called *Post Alice* "one of the best new Canadian plays I've seen in a long time." In Hoile's overwhelmingly positive five-star review from earlier in the year, he recognizes much of what I was trying to achieve while writing. Specifically a line from the review reminiscent of Ozick's praise of Munro was particularly validating. "The result," writes Hoile, "is a lyric, Chekhovian meditation on the loss of the past and the loss of the people we once thought we were."

While I am sincerely over the moon with the critical praise of *Post Alice*, I do find myself wondering what Munro herself would have thought of this play. As with the newspaper poet, would she have had any pointers for me? Did I get the trees right? I wonder what parts of my version of Huron County wouldn't fit with Munro's. Are there moments in the play that perhaps connect with her autobiographical feelings about Huron County? In many ways *Post Alice* is a conversation with her stories much like Munro's conversation with Netterfield's poem describing a previous version of her childhood home. While I likely won't ever learn if Munro knew about the play and what she may have thought about it, I would hope to hear from other writers or artists from Huron County, ones creating their own versions of a childhood growing up in Alice Munro Country. Here's hoping that our stories will keep merging and diverging along the shorelines of Lake Huron for years to come.

Acknowledgements

Many thanks to all the members of The Alice Munro Book Club who each taught me a great deal including prominent Munro scholars J.R. (Tim) Struthers, Robert Thacker, and Tracy Ware. I am forever grateful for the remarkable artistry and insight of the Here For Now Theatre creative teams behind the premiere of *Post Alice* at a local venue in Stratford, Ontario in the summer of 2021 and the remount at The Alice Munro Festival of the Short Story in Blyth, Ontario in June 2024. I am extremely thankful to the editorial team at Talonbooks for helping get the script ready for publication as part of the collection of my work entitled *Cottage Radio & Other Plays* (2024). The first draft of this essay was written while I was at an international playwright residency in summer 2022 at the Lyth Arts Centre in Caithness, Scotland. Thank you to Charlotte Mountford, LAC's Artistic Director, and the Canada Council for the Arts for their support of this residency. This essay was first presented at a panel moderated by Jessica McDonald at the Where From Here Conference at the University of Guelph Arboretum on 16 September 2022. A very special thanks is owed to Paul Barrett and Sarah Roger for creating the Where From Here Conference. My sincere appreciation also extends to my PhD supervisors Ann Wilson and Mark Fortier for patiently guiding me through my studies and to J.R. (Tim) Struthers for his diligent attention to editing this essay.

Works Cited

Anderson, Benedict. *Imagined Communities: Reflections on the Origin and Spread of Nationalism*. Rev. ed. London: Verso, 1991.

Cooper, Beverley. *If Truth Be Told*. Winnipeg: Scirocco Drama, 2016.

Duern, Liz. "Treaties & Huron County." *Huron County Museum.* 6 Nov. 2017. <https://www.huroncountymuseum.ca/treaties-huron-county/>.

Filewod, Alan. *Performing Canada: The Nation Enacted in the Imagined Theatre. Textual Studies in Canada* 15 (2002).

Graham, Taylor Marie. *Post Alice.* Dir. Fiona Mongillo. Perf. Heather Marie Annis, Ellen Denny, Aubree Erickson, and Siobhan O'Malley. Here And Now Theatre, The Bruce Hotel Back Lawn, Stratford, ON, 27 July - 15 Aug. 2021. Dir. Fiona Mongillo. Perf. Heather Marie Annis, Aubree Erickson, Zara Jestadt, and Siobhan O'Malley. Alice Munro Festival of the Short Story, The Blyth Festival Theatre, Blyth, ON, 5 - 8 June 2024. Printed in *Cottage Radio & Other Plays: Cottage Radio, White Wedding & Post Alice.* By Taylor Marie Graham. Vancouver: Talonbooks, 2024. 189-261.

Hoile, Christopher. "2021: The Year in Review." *Stage Door Reviews* 1 Jan. 2022. <https://www.stage-door.com/3/2021-Reviews/Entries/2022/1/2021-the-year-in-review.html>.

---. "Stage Door Review 2021: *Post Alice.*" *Stage Door Reviews* 6 Aug. 2021. <https://www.stage-door.com/3/2021-Reviews/Entries/2021/8/post-alice-1.html>.

Johnson, Marcia. *Courting Johanna.* Winnipeg: Scirocco Drama, 2009.

Kahgee, Randall. "What Does It Mean To Be Treaty People?" Huron Country Museum On-line Webinar. 4 Nov. 2021.

Munro, Alice. "Dear Life." *Dear Life.* Toronto: McClelland & Stewart, 2012. 299-319.

---. "Hateship, Friendship, Courtship, Loveship, Marriage." *Hateship, Friendship, Courtship, Loveship, Marriage.* Toronto: McClelland & Stewart, 2001. 1-52.

---. *How I Met My Husband.* Dir. James Roy. Blyth Festival. 1976. XZ1 MS A753001 Blyth Festival Theatre Archives, L.W. Conolly Theatre Archives, Archival and Special Collections, McLaughlin Library, University of Guelph, Guelph, ON.

---. "How I Met My Husband." *The Play's the Thing: Four Original Television Dramas.* Ed. Tony Gifford. Toronto: Macmillan of Canada, 1976. 13-34.

---. "How I Met My Husband." *Something I've Been Meaning To Tell You.* Toronto: McGraw-Hill Ryerson, 1974. 45-66.

---. *Open Secrets.* Toronto: McClelland & Stewart, 1994.

---. "Pride." *Dear Life.* Toronto: McClelland & Stewart, 2012. 133-53.

---. *The Progress of Love.* Toronto: McClelland and Stewart, 1986.

---. "Train." *Dear Life.* Toronto: McClelland & Stewart, 2012. 175-216.

---. *The View from Castle Rock.* Toronto: McClelland & Stewart, 2006.

---. "Wenlock Edge." *Too Much Happiness.* Toronto: McClelland & Stewart, 2009. 62-92.

"Performance File, How I Met My Husband / by Alice Munro; directed by James Roy, 1976." XZ1 MS A753001 Blyth Festival Theatre Archives, L.W. Conolly Theatre Archives, Archival and Special Collections, McLaughlin Library, University of Guelph, Guelph, ON.

Scott, Shelley. "Courting Johanna: Adapting Alice Munro for the Stage." *Alice Munro: Reminiscence, Interpretation, Adaptation and Comparison.* Ed. Mirosława Buchholtz and Eugenia Sojka. Frankfurt am Main, Ger.: Peter Lang, 2015. 107-27.

Slotkin, Lynn. "From the BLYTH FESTIVAL: IF TRUTH BE TOLD." *The Slotkin Letter* 19 Aug. 2016. <https://slotkinletter.com/2016/08/from-the-blyth-festival-if-truth-be-told>.

---. "Reviews: *Janet and Louise* and *Post Alice*, at the Here for Now Theatre, 2021 New Works Festival, Stratford, Ont." *The Slotkin Letter* 28 July 2021. <https://slotkinletter.com/2021/07/reviews-janet-and-louise-and-post-alice-at-the-here-for-now-theatre-2021-new-works-festival>.

Struthers, J.R. (Tim), ed. *Alice Munro Country: Essays on Her Works I.* Toronto: Guernica Editions, 2020. Essential Writers Ser. 51.

Szekeres, Joe. "Review: 'Post Alice' as Part of Stratford Ontario's HERE FOR NOW NEW WORKS Festival." OnStage Blog. 28 July 2021. <https://www.onstageblog.com/reviews/2021/7/28/review-post-alice-as-part-of-stratford-ontarios-here-for-now-new-works-festival>.

Thacker, Robert. *Alice Munro: Writing Her Lives: A Biography.* Toronto: McClelland & Stewart, 2005.

Thien, Madeleine. "Alice Munro Country." *The Globe and Mail* 5 Oct. 2017. <https://www.theglobeandmail.com/news/national/canada-150/fiction-story-of-canada-madeleine-thien/article36364937/>.

Tomasek, Keith. "Rarely Seen Alice Munro Play at the Blyth Festival." *Stratford Festival Reviews* 26 Dec. 2019. <https://stratfordfestivalreviews.com/blog/2019/12/26/rarely-seen-alice-munro-play-at-the-blyth-festival/>.

Times Alice Munro Asked Me a Question

John Tyndall

First

And then smiling she appeared
in the lineup
at the library help desk
and while I wondered where
were her pencils, her fountain pen
why was she not writing
she asked me for help
with the pronunciation
of a native name

Search as I might
all I could do was suggest
equal stress on every syllable
Me - Ne - Se - Teung
and then smiling she disappeared

Later that night I stood in line
behind her for the cinema
she remembered me but
did she hear my thought

Come back, Alice, come
back and ask me another

Second

In the library queue
of babbling inquisitors
she reappeared to ask me
a second quiet question
this time for her husband
who wanted to know
whether Jorge Luis Borges'
A Universal History
of Infamy comprised
actual bibliographic entries
or secret fabrications
to confound his readers

Off to the lower system
of rectangular rooms
I took her to seek
answers in The N.U.C.
The National Union Catalog
Pre-1956 Imprints, where
looking up each author
we discovered entries so near
yet so far from fact
we both felt we were
looking for meaning
in impenetrable dreams

She gave me her phone
number in case any further
information turned up
so later I ascended the stairs
to the seemingly limitless
shelves of books
retrieved Borges' original
Historia universal
de la infamia

and, repeating my quest
in The N.U.C., found
again only fantasies

*

When she returned
my phone message
she said she and her husband
laughed when I revealed
that he was not alone
that graduate students
of many languages
had posted digital laments
on various internet sites
about Borges' intentions
their voices crying
in the wilderness

Third

And one time
in the reference hall
she stood still
with the exalted grace
of a white tiger
watching from a hill
the rushing river rapids
and observing the flow
of economic, sociologic
historic budding scholars
none of whom recognized
the eminence in their midst

She drew close to my desk
and the third time she asked
me a question it was personal

Are you a writer?

I answered her a-blush
that poetry was all
I plied with words
in winnowed form
releasing chaff
and planting seeds

So no stories?

Her follow-up query
unlocked a fantasy
I told her my idea
of an obsessive man
convinced in his head
that he himself was she
his jibber-jabber stream
of subconsciousness
I thought I might title
Alice in Undermind

Casting Sad Spells: Alice Munro's "Walker Brothers Cowboy"

John Metcalf

Most of the fifteen stories collected in *Dance of the Happy Shades* had been previously published in magazines. Two or three of the stories, however, were specially written to enlarge and complete the volume and among these later stories were "Images" and "Walker Brothers Cowboy."

Both stories are interestingly different from most of the other stories in the book and represent a stylistic change. These two stories are more highly wrought than previous stories, the rhetoric at a higher pitch, the images more intense, the painting of detail more vibrant.

While some of the stories in *Dance of the Happy Shades* were first published in such literary magazines as *The Fiddlehead* and *The Canadian Forum*, others were first published in *The Montrealer* and *Chatelaine*. None of the stories were 'commercial' but all were traditional in form and one or two might be criticized for being overly explicit. The stories written especially for the book, on the other hand, seem more consciously 'literary'; they are more complex than the other stories not only in language but in form and they make no concessions to popular expectation.

That one of these stories is *called* "Images" directs us to the nature of the change in Alice Munro's work at this time; she is beginning to relinquish conventional plot and is beginning to work in what is essentially a poetic manner letting images and the accumulation of detail carry the story's line and emotional weight. She withdraws in these stories far more than she usually does as commentator or explicator and allows the reader to come into more unmediated contact with the imagery.

Not surprisingly, "Images" and "Walker Brothers Cowboy" also exhibit a concomitant change in form. The structures of the stories are unlike anything she had attempted before and they emphasize and enhance the primacy of the image. "Walker Brothers Cowboy" is divided into three sections; the first is introductory, the second is amplification and extension of the essential melody heard in the first, and the third concludes and returns us to the opening section by way of allusion and repetition. The important thing to realize about the first section is that it is, in itself, an image. It cannot be read conventionally as an aspect of plot for read in that way it makes little sense. If we approach it looking for the 'story,' looking for the 'what happens,' we will prevent ourselves from seeing what *is* there; we must give ourselves up to language and to image. The first section is the whole story in miniature; it contains in essence all that is to come in sections two and three. It might not be entirely fanciful to suggest that there is about the story something almost sonata-like but however one wishes to think about the structure of "Walker Brothers Cowboy" some sort of analogy with music seems inevitable.

Before considering this opening section, however, it is important to pay attention to the narrating voice because the pleasure we should take in Alice Munro's skilled handling of the narrative conventions is a rich part of the story's larger pleasures. Both "Images" and "Walker Brothers Cowboy" are initiation stories, stories about the gaining of knowledge, and so the effectiveness of the stories depends to a certain extent on our sharing the child's innocence and on our growing with the child towards understanding. Although the narrator of "Walker Brothers Cowboy" is actually the Jordan girl grown up and looking back at her childhood, the writing is intended to suggest a young girl's voice and sensibility. The use of the present tense in narration – a device which in the hands of a lesser writer could have induced numbing monotony – is varied here with subtle craft and goes a long way in itself towards suggesting youth and simplicity.

Consider the following passage:

> He has a song about it, with these two lines:
>
> And have all liniments and oils,
> For everything from corns to boils....
>
> Not a very funny song, in my mother's opinion. A pedlar's song, and that is what he is, a pedlar knocking at backwoods kitchens. Up until last winter we had our own business, a fox farm. My father raised silver

> foxes and sold their pelts to the people who make them into capes and coats and muffs. Prices fell, my father hung on hoping they would get better next year, and they fell again, and he hung on one more year and one more and finally it was not possible to hang on any more, we owed everything to the feed company. I have heard my mother explain this, several times, to Mrs. Oliphant who is the only neighbour she talks to. (Mrs. Oliphant also has come down in the world, being a schoolteacher who married the janitor.) We poured all we had into it, my mother says, and we came out with nothing. Many people could say the same thing, these days, but my mother has no time for the national calamity, only ours. Fate has flung us onto a street of poor people (it does not matter that we were poor before, that was a different sort of poverty), and the only way to take this, as she sees it, is with dignity, with bitterness, with no reconciliation. No bathroom with a claw-footed tub and a flush toilet is going to comfort her, nor water on tap and sidewalks past the house and milk in bottles, not even the two movie theatres and the Venus Restaurant and Woolworths so marvellous it has live birds singing in its fan-cooled corners and fish as tiny as fingernails, as bright as moons, swimming in its green tanks. My mother does not care.

In the lines, "Not a very funny song, in my mother's opinion. A pedlar's song, and that is what he is, a pedlar knocking at backwoods kitchens," I think we are hearing in the repetition of "pedlar" and the implied 'that's what you are' the child echoing something of the mother – though sharing none of her bitterness.

The next two sentences present the girl's voice; notice how the voice is suggested by "the people who make them into capes and coats and muffs" instead of, say, 'furriers.' The sentence following these, however, with its succession of "and"s and its final comma-spliced conclusion represents not so much the girl's voice as the girl reproducing the oft-heard monotony of her mother's litany of complaint.

Next, the mother is quoted directly though without quotation marks – an omission perhaps meant to suggest that this remark is made often and always in the same words, a suggestion that the remark has become ritual. The words in the next sentence, "but my mother has no time for the national calamity, only ours," sound rather sophisticated for the girl but we are meant to take them, I think, as her perception because of the words "these days." Perhaps such a phrase as "national calamity" was current on the radio or in newspapers. Had Alice Munro intended us to read this sentence as if spoken by the adult – looking back – she would have used different tenses and 'those days' as opposed to "these."

Note in the following sentence that in "Fate has flung us" we are again intended to hear, at a remove, the mother's vocabulary and histrionics. The long concluding sentence which also suggests the mother's voice with its *No, nor, not* then modulates back into the simulation of the voice of the child, a voice suggested not merely by subject matter but by the rhythm of the "and"s and by the syntax of "Woolworths so marvellous" and by the sentence's rhythmically awkward conclusion.

It's important to remember that in a writer like Alice Munro we are reading prose which is more subtle than much of what now passes for poetry; it's necessary to be alert to the play of voice because it is only by paying close attention that we can savour the story's fullness.

The first paragraph of the first section is a beautifully compressed piece of writing which suggests the girl's voice, gives us information about the family's straitened circumstances, and sketches the relationships within the family. The particular love the girl has for her father is established.

The description of the walk down to the lake is the presentation of a physical and emotional landscape. Alice Munro has rightly always resisted symbol-seekers and reductive reading insisting that a spade is indeed and always a spade but the accumulation of physical detail in this opening section obviously functions as more than topographical survey.

The evening games of the children they pass "are ragged, dissolving." The children "draw apart, separate into islands of two or one..., occupying themselves in ... solitary ways."

The sidewalks are "cracked and heaved"; father and daughter walk past "a factory with boarded-up windows." And then "the town falls away in a defeated jumble of sheds and small junkyards.... We enter a vacant lot ... and there is one bench with a slat missing on the back...."

Father and daughter sit and look at the lake – "Which is generally grey in the evening, under a lightly overcast sky, no sunsets, the horizon dim." Further along is "a life guard's rickety throne" and further off still are the docks where the grain boats load, boats that are "ancient, rusty, wallowing."

This landscape, then, is a suitable background to the Jordans' descent into urban poverty and it suggests something of the defeat and bleakness of Ben Jordan's emotional life.

The third paragraph of this opening section is rather curious. Why is it there? What does it contribute? Tramps wander along "the dwindling beach" and climb up "the shifting, precarious path." Such meetings are, we learn, not infrequent but they always frighten the girl. The paragraph tells us directly that the father is "hard up" and his actions suggest that he has sympathy for the tramps, perhaps even a fellow-feeling for he, too, has come down in the world.

The incident described is obviously important. The paragraph contains only the third sentence of the section actually spoken. It concludes with a sentence whose rhythms and word placements are deliberate: "My father also rolls and lights and smokes one cigarette of his own."

The use of the word "one" suggests that the father does not smoke a great deal, perhaps cannot afford much tobacco. The deliberateness of the sentence echoes the deliberateness of the act; the rhythm tells us that it is a *rationed* ritual and pleasure. We are meant to assume that the manufacture and smoking of a cigarette are something of a performance, something done deliberately and at significant junctures.

The story will return us to this incident.

The final paragraph contains the fourth line of actual speech in this first section: "'Well, the old ice cap had a lot more power behind it than this hand has.'" There is, perhaps, in this a faint suggestion of the ineffectual, of the father's powerlessness against the indignities of poverty. The section concludes with the child trying to think about Time and Change and wishing that everything would always remain the same and safe. This passage obviously looks forward to the concluding two paragraphs of the entire story and thus links beginning and end.

The body of the story, the second section, now amplifies what we've already been given in concentrated form in the first section. We learn the history of the family's decline into poverty and we learn in greater detail how the girl feels about her parents.

The girl is humiliated by the mother's pretentions to gentility and resists recruitment to her views: "I pretend to remember far less than I do, wary of being trapped into sympathy or any unwanted emotion."

The mother uses her various ailments as a weapon against the father and as a means of holding onto him:

"He goes back once again, probably to say goodbye to my mother, to ask her if she is sure she doesn't want to come, and hear her say, 'No. No thanks, I'm better just to lie here with my eyes closed.'"

The girl doesn't actually hear these words spoken on this occasion; she doesn't have to; she's heard them many times before. The girl's sympathies and feelings are entirely for the father.

It's probably important at this point to say something about those sympathies and feelings and about Alice Munro's young female narrators in general. At the end of "Walker Brothers Cowboy," the girl has begun to grasp something of the complexities of her father's life, about its sadness, about paths not taken; she has sensed the meaning of mysteries and has begun to learn things about herself as a female. Exactly *what* she has learned is neither described nor articulated but "Walker Brothers Cowboy" is charged with a sexuality we should not ignore.

The same is true of "Images." Too many readers, I think, have assumed too firmly that "Images" is concerned with the child's learning simply about death; they seem to have given insufficient weight to the story's sexual concerns. They seem to have overlooked the fact that Mary McQuade, Death's harbinger, has come to the house to deliver the girl's mother of another baby, that the girl is making a connection between death and birth and sex and being female, that Mary McQuade is always being teased about possible husbands. The child watches the shadows cast by her father and the flirtatious Mary McQuade and tries "to understand the danger, to read the signs of invasion."

The narrator in "Images" is slightly younger than the narrator in "Walker Brothers Cowboy" but in both cases the stories are richer for us if we realize that they are narrated by a girl who is very sensitive to the sexual currents around her, who is hungry for sexual knowledge, and who is eager to learn how this sexuality will affect *her* life. Both stories are in a way as much about sexuality and the female role as is the far more explicit "Boys and Girls."

(Adolescent sexuality is, of course, the main subject and focus of *Lives of Girls and Women*, the next book Alice Munro was to write.)

The girl, then, rejects her mother's embittered gentility and cleaves to her father. The father deals with their poverty and with their having come down in the world by maintaining a façade of jollity. He amuses the children with his improvised songs, with his patter, jokes, and comic self-mockery. There is even a suggestion of the father as artist turning his trials into the song. Father knows the short cut out of town; he represents for his children the "hope of adventure."

He bears the weight of the family on his shoulders.

He attempts to coax his wife into laughter by performing for her amusingly "rude" sales-routines. The daughter says: "and she would laugh finally, unwillingly."

The father's territory is a desolate landscape, "flat, scorched, empty" with dust hanging over the dirt roads and with "falling-down sheds and unturning windmills" on the decaying farms; all this forms the background for, and is the counterpart of, the father's emotional life.

The event which is the turning-point of the story is the emptying of the chamber-pot out of the window. He is not actually hit: "The window is not directly above my father's head, so only a stray splash would catch him."

But splashed or not, the event is the final degradation, the final straw. "He picks up his suitcases with no particular hurry" then walks back to the car "no longer whistling." He sits in the car which is raucous with the laughter of his son and daughter exulting in the naughtiness of *pee* and in the exquisite pleasure of pee having been poured out of a window. He sits there and does not start the car until he has rolled and lighted a cigarette. And it is this at the pivotal point of the story which should return us, if only for a moment in memory, to the scene in section one with the tramp.

Sitting there, smoking that deliberate cigarette, Ben Jordan reaches a decision. He starts to drive. He tells his son not to tell his mother about the pee because she wouldn't see the joke. In other words, her sympathies would not be for Ben's humiliation; her anger would be directed against him for working at such an 'ungentlemanly' job. The boy wants to know if the incident is in the song. Ben says that he'll try to work it in. But he isn't singing.

The conversation with the daughter is both naturalistic and yet full of significance: "'Are we still in your territory?' He shakes his head."

He is heading *out* of his territory, both physical and emotional, and he is neither singing nor being amusing. He is heading towards the house of a woman he *might* have married, a woman who would not have suffered headaches. He is driving so fast over the pot-holed roads that all the bottles clink and gurgle and are in danger of being broken, the bottles that are the source of his livelihood. He is driving in full flight both away from the scene of his humiliation and towards someone who can offer comfort.

Nora, not recognizing him at first, says: "'Have you lost your way?'"

It's a poignant question for us as readers, for by now we've realized that he'd lost it years before. This sudden appearance of Ben Jordan is an immense shock to Nora. "'Oh, my Lord God,'" she says harshly, "'it's you.'"

The heavy stresses fall on every word.

When asked if she has got a husband hiding in the woodshed, her laugh is "abrupt and somewhat angry." (Though we get the impression that Ben knows full well that she's unmarried.) When she is reintroducing Ben to her mother and explaining that he is now married, she speaks "cheerfully and aggressively" as though challenging her mother to comment. The blind old mother has not spoken to Ben for many years yet recognizes his voice instantly. We are to assume, then, that at one time Ben and Nora were extremely close.

We are told little about their past relationship. Like the daughter, we must try to piece things together. It would not be unseemly to guess that one strong reason for the failure of their relationship was that Ben Jordan was Protestant and Nora Catholic. The bigotry in Ontario in the twenties and thirties was virulent. Nora *digs with the wrong foot* – a Protestant Irish expression meaning 'She's a Catholic – she's not one of us,' 'She's not our sort.'

Whatever the reasons for the collapse of the relationship, Nora is the sister who has remained unmarried at home to care for her blind mother. One sister is married with children, the other is a teacher in western Canada, financially independent, who hasn't been back to the farm in five years. The "faint sour smell" that the girl smells in the kitchen is metaphorically the smell of frustration and disappointment.

When Nora reappears, washed, scented, changed into a flowered dress and "more sociable and youthful," Ben says of the flowers on the material that he'd never known there were green poppies. Nora's reply is both flirtatious and blunt: "You would be surprised all the things you never knew."

Nora and Ben drink whisky together. Nora's having a bottle other than for 'medicinal purposes' marks her as a woman out of the ordinary, a woman morally suspect. The girl is fascinated by the fact that her father is drinking because her mother has gone out of her way to tell the girl that he never does. We are to assume from this, I think, that Ben once drank more than the occasional nip but has been weaned from it – and from other enjoyable bad habits. His drinking days were those he spent with Nora. The implied background here is the puritanical connection between nonconformist Protestantism and the temperance movement. Ben's wife in her "good dress, navy blue with little flowers, sheer, worn over a navy-blue slip. Also a summer hat of white straw, pushed down on the side of the head, and white shoes I have just whitened on a newspaper on the back steps" is the embodiment of arid responsibility and Protestant religiosity.

It is at this point that Alice Munro starts to tinge Nora's speech with Irish syntax and rhythms.

(Implied social, religious, and historical backgrounds are precisely what give Alice Munro's stories their dense, textured feel. A single line of dialogue such as Ben's "'Keep it in case of sickness?'" vibrates with meanings that soon will have to be explained to a young and urban readership.

How should we read Ben's enquiry? Is it serious? Is it seeking an answer to questions not being directly asked? Is it jocular?)

Ben next performs for Nora a version of the chamber-pot incident. His daughter remarks on the discrepancy between what she'd seen happen and his account of it. As usual, Ben is turning his disappointments and humiliations into entertainment for others. There is a sense, too, that it is only by refashioning reality that he is able to bear it; in his created version of the incident he emerges as one of the "'heroes in the ranks of Walker Brothers'" even if his heroism is Chaplinesque.

Nora laughs "almost as hard as my brother did at the time" – the brother who has been told not to mention the incident at home because his mother wouldn't be "'liable to see the joke'." Ben then entertains Nora with his sales spiel and his song.

We are reading a scene which is parallel to the scenes alluded to earlier where Ben tries to coax his disapproving wife into laughter, where her laughter finally is unwilling; in this scene, then, she and Nora are being compared and contrasted. Ben's clowning is, in both cases, a kind of offering, a kind of courtship.

The scene immediately following, the scene where Nora dances with Ben's daughter, is curious; this, we feel, is no ordinary dancing-lesson; it is uncomfortable, fairly disquieting. The girl is aware of sexual currents even if she doesn't understand them; we the readers, however, understand the girl as a surrogate.

What is faintly disturbing about this scene – and the child's presence in it – is Nora's unladylike heat and arousal, an excitement which is conveyed through the child's registering of "her strange gaiety, her smell of whisky, cologne, and sweat. Under the arms her dress is damp, and little drops form along her upper lip, hang in the soft black hairs at the corners of her mouth."

Nora waltzes the girl to a stop in front of Ben and says:

"'Dance with me, Ben.'"

He replies: "'I'm the world's worst dancer, Nora, and you know it.'"

She stands there in front of him, "her breasts ... rising and falling under her loose flowered dress, her face shining with the exercise, and delight."

She asks him again.

"'Ben.'

"My father drops his head and says quietly, 'Not me, Nora.'"

The whole of this dancing passage is a masterly piece of writing. The second time that Nora asks Ben she is not asking him to dance. She does not say 'Ben?' She says, "'Ben.'" She is both offering and claiming.

(And is Ben's "'Not me, Nora.'" simply negative or does "'Not me'" imply someone else perhaps? Another or others who helped Nora drink half the whisky because she doesn't care for drinking alone? Or are we to accept her statement, "'I can drink alone but I can't dance alone'"?)

Ben's declining the invitation is a sad acceptance on his part of duty, of the choices he has made in life. The scene peters out in painful conversational small-change and ends in silence. Nora stands close to the car in her "soft, brilliant dress," a dress which is flamboyant, possibly even slightly vulgar – and so very different from the dress described earlier, Ben's wife's dress, which is "navy blue with little flowers."

The third and last section of the story restates and returns us to the story's first section; the story's last sentence – a reference to the Lake – returns us to the story's opening sentence.

The father does not behave on this afternoon as he usually does. He does not buy the usual pop or ice cream. He buys licorice. We realize that this is to mask the smell of the whisky when he gets home but the girl does not. She does, however, feel and share her father's sadness although she is unable to articulate its nature. She has caught some of the heated sexuality and sadness in Nora's front room and, without understanding why, knows instinctively that these are matters not to be mentioned to her mother. Alice Munro – not, of course, for the first time in the story – uses the girl's innocence and naivety to twist the emotional screws. The daughter, utterly devoted to her father, resolves that the mother will learn nothing of the afternoon from *her*. She guesses that the most serious material to be kept from the mother must be the dancing lesson and the whisky. This loyal innocence on her part somehow intensifies the sadness of what it really is that her father wants kept secret – the desolation that his life has become.

The girl feels confident that her little brother won't betray anything because "he does not notice enough." The most he might remember would be "the blind lady, the picture of Mary." With these two references, Alice Munro turns us back into the story before opening the throttle, as it were, for the story's conclusion.

The two flat references suggest again the sadness of Nora's life and its mystery for the narrator. The picture of Mary would only be found in the homes of Roman Catholics, those who *dig with the wrong foot*, words which now "seem sad to me as never before, dark, perverse." The "blind lady," Nora's mother, is recalled for us sitting in the faintly sour-smelling kitchen with "a drop of silver liquid" welling from the sunken eye, "a medicine, or a miraculous tear."

This is an example of the command of odd detail which makes Alice Munro's prose so rich and persuasive. It is so *peculiar* yet so real that we are persuaded it could never have been invented. At the same time, it renders the scene almost iconic, as though the old lady's silver tear is a tear for all human sadness and suffering.

The penultimate paragraph of "Walker Brothers Cowboy" has always troubled me. It feels as if Alice Munro is straining for rhetorical effect and impact. While it is true that the girl's feeling about her father's life is expressed in terms of fairy tale and enchantment, the syntax seems far less the girl's than the author's. I have never been quite sure what Alice

Munro *meant* by this paragraph; usually she writes with precision and economy but the writing here is vague and ambiguous. I am tempted to say that it is slightly pretentious.

Clark Blaise in a brief essay titled "On Ending Stories" describes two basic kinds of endings in modern stories:

> There are only two kinds of endings: those that lead you back into the story, and those that lead you – gently, or violently – away. I associate the first kind of ending with de Maupassant and Chekhov, and with modernists who adapted those stories for their own purposes – Hemingway, Joyce, James. Of authors who lead away from the story, who wish to emphasize the artifice of the story, or wish to address the reader directly, I associate dozens of our contemporaries. Impatience with art is as old as faith in art; the choice of ending is the battlefield for those particular feelings. …
>
> Endings that lead us away from the story can do so gently or abruptly. The most traditional kind of ending is the one that serves as a prose equivalent to the theatrical last scene, the rising of music and receding of the camera, as lights go out, one-by-one, and characters fade off together in a figurative sunset. Such endings announce a faith in continuity, order, harmony – no matter what particular horrors may have been investigated in the story. They are sophisticated and traditional ways of updating the old "happily ever after" ending so familiar from fables. Even if the endings are thematically "sad," they are formally (or cosmically) "happy"; they lead us away from the specific exemplum (the story) to a generalized harmony. They are religious in form, if not in content.
>
> How can you detect such an ending? Well, they *sound* like endings.

Let's look more closely now at the penultimate paragraph of "Walker Brothers Cowboy." It is too 'literary,' too wrought. It strives for the second kind of ending that Blaise talks about, the symphonic ending. What Blaise doesn't mention in his essay but which is typical of symphonic endings is that the writers consciously or unconsciously heighten their language. Elevated rhythms and archaic syntax tend to creep in. We may well hear biblical echoes in grammatical constructions or in repetitions. Sense sometimes capitulates to incantation.

What is meant *exactly* by "my father's life"? What does the word "life" mean? Why would that life be "flowing back from our car"? Back to where? To Nora? Or is it "flowing" in the sense of, say, blood from a wound? Or are we to understand "flowing" as meaning something like 'diminishing, emptying' in the manner of a deflating balloon?

Is it "life" which is "darkening and turning strange" or is it "the last of the afternoon"? In what way can we really compare a "landscape" and a "life"?

Is this language believable in the girl's mouth? Are these apprehensions totally credible in this child?

These confusions are compounded because in the final paragraph Alice Munro produces a *second* ending – an ending of the *first* type described by Blaise, the "let-down" ending. Thus the story ends symphonically and then ends in deflation. The result is somewhat of a mess.

It is gross impertinence to rewrite a writer but I've often thought the story could be improved by cutting most of the last section so that with the necessary adjustments the story could have ended with the father saying: "'I don't know. I seem to be fresh out of songs. You watch the road and let me know if you see any rabbits.'"

Or – even better – it could well have ended with Nora in her brilliant dress making an unintelligible mark in the dust of the car.

I suspect that's precisely where the story *did* end and that the final four paragraphs were added later. On the other hand, it must be remembered that this story appeared in Alice Munro's first book. Her writing since then has grown ever more dazzling. Few short story writers in Canada even now would be capable of matching the opening paragraph of "Walker Brothers Cowboy" for precision, economy, and grace.

> After supper my father says, "Want to go down and see if the Lake's still there?" We leave my mother sewing under the dining-room light, making clothes for me against the opening of school. She has ripped up for this purpose an old suit and an old plaid wool dress of hers, and she has to cut and match very cleverly and also make me stand and turn for endless fittings, sweaty, itching from the hot wool, ungrateful. We leave my brother in bed in the little screened porch at the end of the front verandah, and sometimes he kneels on his bed and presses his face against the screen and calls mournfully, "Bring me back an ice cream cone!" but I call back, "You will be asleep," and do not even turn my head.

Story as Acknowledgement: Returning to Alice Munro's Southwestern Ontario Story "Walker Brothers Cowboy"

Stephen Michell

In memory of Lee Maracle (1950-2021)

I hope they fall in love with the land the way I have: fully, responsibly, and committed for life.
– Lee Maracle, *My Conversations with Canadians* (85)

To begin with a land acknowledgement. What does that really mean? It is something you might see and hear at the beginning of an academic PowerPoint presentation. You might even sign off your e-mails with one. But what is it really? A genuine statement of concern? An institutional recitation? How is it achieved truthfully? Can it be fulfilled in story?

In my understanding, a land acknowledgement involves considering who you are in relation to the history of where you live. It's an act of *historicizing* your identity. For Sherene H. Razack, that process "begins by asking about the relationship between identity and space" (128). It is an approach to thinking about self in relation to place. Who are *you*? How have you been *formed*? How do you act *in* and *in relation to* a certain space you might call home? I think Alice Munro's fiction resonates strongly with that process as a form of imaginative historicizing. Alec Follett's essay "The Region That I Know" offers a compelling consideration of Munro's writing, and particularly *The View from Castle Rock*, as "bioregional literature" (118-19). His analysis of the story "What Do You Want To Know For?" reveals how the story's narrator "writes herself and her surroundings in a way that exudes wonder and care for self, region, and story" (126). I see a mirroring here between Follett's idea of the "care for self, region, and story" and Razack's conception of "the relationship between identity and space," and it makes me wonder if together they might offer a way of looking at Munro's stories as acknowledgement.

For myself, land acknowledgement involves thinking about a river. This real and imagined river has been a great source of guidance and imaginative energy in my attempt to historicize my identity within the space of Southwestern Ontario, both as a human being here and as a fiction writer. That process necessarily confronts my identity as a white settler "Canadian" with the Indigenous history and stories of this region. And the process remains unfinished.

Not far from where I am sitting flows the Grand River, known in the Mohawk language as *Kahyonhatátye* to describe the geographic feature of a long river, a big river, as Brian Maracle (Owennatekha) informed me. There are willow trees on the banks of the river, which have led some people to attach the Mohawk word for willow, *Ose*, as a prefix to the name. There are more rivers nearby like the Speed, the Nith, and the Credit. Farther west there is the Maitland River or *Meneseteung* in the Ojibwe language. There are more rivers still.

Rivers are an everyday feature of the natural landscape of Southwestern Ontario, weaving through what some people consider a flat land, though James Reaney would heartily disagree (see Reaney, "Souwesto Anthem" qtd. in Struthers, "Imagining" 70-71). "Souwesto" is a land of gently rolling hills and valleys. As Alice Munro has noted, it's "a landscape that most people think is dull. It's not dramatic in any way[....] But if you know it intimately, there are all these small differences" (Munro in Struthers, "Remembrance Day 1988" 66). In hopes of knowing the land and the literature more intimately, I employ the image of the river to help shape how I am thinking about the short story form in Southwestern Ontario. Like the river, the history of the short story form flows forward, changing through time and place, as new writers reach back and draw fresh inspiration from old styles and currents.

The image of the river is also helpful in addressing my understanding of what Lee Maracle calls "an Indigenous responsibility" (82) to this land, an attitude which I believe is a necessary element of any meaningful act of land acknowledgement. Maracle argues for a responsibility that begins with a love for the land: "fully, responsibly, and committed for life" (85). The image of the river helps form my understanding of Maracle's call to action. The river connects the past, the present, and the future; the river provides travel, energy, and sustenance; the river *lives*. The river is not buried or forgotten; the river matters today and tomorrow as part of the living land. Leanne Betasamosake Simpson's thinking on Indigenous pedagogy is similarly instructive. Simpson writes, "we shouldn't be just striving for land-based pedagogies. The land must once again *become* the pedagogy" ("Land as Pedagogy" 14; emphasis in orig.). An understanding of the land as pedagogy is connected to Lee Maracle's Indigenous responsibility towards how we should be approaching land acknowledgement.

Here I am returning to Alice Munro's "Walker Brothers Cowboy" in her first collection *Dance of the Happy Shades* (1968) to reconsider how her story operates as acknowledgement in an imaginative movement towards elements of Maracle's notion of Indigenous responsibility, and to suggest that reading stories through such a lens could offer a way to reshape how we both read and write literature in this land. The reader should know that when I discuss the idea of "Indigenous responsibility," I am working without a full and clear understanding of what Indigenous responsibility *means*. In terms of appropriation, I am aware of the distinction between "speaking about" versus "speaking for." Attributed to Kathleen M. Donovan, author of *Feminist Readings of Native American Literature: Coming to Voice*, "speaking about" is an analytical approach, whereas "speaking for" is appropriative (Donovan qtd. in Strong-Boag and Gerson 5). As best as I can, I am trying to speak *about* the idea of Indigenous responsibility. Several writers and scholars have helped me form a preliminary approach.

In *My Conversations with Canadians*, Indigenous Sto:lo and North Vancouver-born author, storyteller, and teacher Lee Maracle writes, "I always say that everyone here belongs here, but non-Indigenous people have only one heritage: a Canadian one. They do, however, have a secondary responsibility: *an Indigenous responsibility*" (81-82; emphasis added). Maracle raises the problem of assigning this responsibility, as it would require Indigenous nations to consider themselves "nations with the power to assign citizenship" (82), which she argues they no longer maintain. Colonialism has erroneously denied them this belief in their own power. She writes, "You can no longer become one of our citizens, Canada said so, and now we are buying it" (81).

Maracle's notion of Indigenous responsibility exists on at least two levels. On a historical level, it is an essential characteristic that *should* have been conferred upon citizens as newcomers to this land and *would* have been if Indigenous nations had maintained the power to confer it. On a contemporary level, Maracle presents it as a form of responsibility that non-Indigenous people (Canadians) *do* have. But what is this responsibility? Where does it exist? If Maracle is correct, and non-Indigenous Canadians have this responsibility, where can we look to find traces of it? Could it perhaps be found in stories?

In trying to understand this responsibility, it is important to note that Maracle refers to very real "caretaking responsibilities" (109) and traditions of knowledge-sharing with regards to the role of human beings as custodians of the land. In *The Truth about Stories: A Native Narrative*, Thomas King writes that the Indigenous relationship to the land is "about the webs of *responsibilities* that bind all things" (114; emphasis added). In Mohawk scholar Gerald Taiaiake Alfred's writing about Indigenous essentialism and sovereignty, he notes that a "partnership principle" with the land "gives human beings special responsibilities within the areas they occupy, linking them in a natural and sacred way to their territories" (Alfred qtd. in Coleman 66). To presume to know what these responsibilities entail would be a misguided step towards appropriation. However, I am inclined to believe that these responsibilities are directed *toward* and *in relation to* the living land. The importance of responsibility is also central to Alec Follett's view of bioregional literature, as it promotes thinking of "our bioregion as our home," and therefore as a relationship between identity and place (119).

There is an inherent sense of movement in thinking about the land as a *living* thing. The earth is moving, and living things move. In a 2020 interview on YouTube, cultural theorist Frederick Moten speaks of an "ethical responsibility" that arises when we think about moving *in* movement. Moten says, "The earth is in motion. We inhabit that movement. And that places an ethical responsibility on us [...] you lightly step with it, in rhythm with it [...] you look with it, not at it, you move with it" (*YouTube* 2:09:00-2:09:40). Although Moten is speaking from the position of a scholar working in Black diaspora studies, I think that the ethical responsibility he locates in this process could be aligned with Alfred's special responsibilities, King's webs of responsibilities, and Maracle's idea of Indigenous responsibility. Altogether, they frame a resistance to Western colonial ideologies through a way of thinking about the land as living. Guiding my own reading with the image of the river is helpful here, as it aligns my approach with the constant flow and movement of the current. If we are in the river, we must move *with* it. My aim is to move forward with the knowledge available to me, which is to *listen*.

Lee Maracle writes, "I hope [Canadians] fall in love with the land the way I have: fully, responsibly, and committed for life" (85). These words form the basis of my understanding of Indigenous responsibility, such that the responsibility requires a foundational love for the land. The very real caretaking responsibilities that exist within Indigenous history and knowledge, of which I am insufficiently informed, would have been built, presumably, upon this primary love for the land. Love is a powerful but flimsy term. I would argue that this sense of love and responsibility could be understood as an alignment of deference towards the land as a *living* thing with an understanding, awareness, and concern for the history, the present, and the future life of the land. Returning to the possibilities of the short story, I hear an echo of Alice Munro's interest in knowing the landscape "intimately," and I believe readers can find elements of this responsibility, this acknowledgement, in her early Southwestern Ontario story "Walker Brothers Cowboy."

***

For many readers, Alice Munro's fiction is considered Can-Lit realism. It is crafted with a similar surface-level realism in treating the everyday as that of James Joyce or Sherwood Anderson. In a 1988 interview with J.R. (Tim) Struthers, Alice Munro commented that what impressed her most about Sherwood Anderson's *Winesburg, Ohio* was a gesture towards "the light in the room" (Munro in Struthers, "Remembrance Day 1988" 80). It's my feeling that Anderson's primary interest in *Winesburg, Ohio* was to portray the human underneath the grotesque, revealing each character as one might turn on a light inside a room. In my own reading, Alice Munro's work presents a similar interest in revealing the human.

No other story in Alice Munro's first collection, apart from "A Trip to the Coast," engages with an "Andersonian" style of realist narrative revelation through the grotesque more than "Walker Brothers Cowboy." However, Munro goes further than Anderson with her decision to write a first-person narrative, which creates a more intimate experience of the moment of revelation. In addition, the structure of the story creates an almost Joycean style of epiphanic ending that adds new meaning to the whole story. It is ultimately through Munro's narrative structure that the story reaches a movement towards Indigenous responsibility. Altogether, "Walker Brothers Cowboy" is exceptional in the sense of its play with the techniques and styles attributed to the formal development of the modern short story, while Munro's added interest and engagement with the land and the human beings of Southwestern Ontario makes it a provocative piece for a discussion of story as acknowledgement.

The main action or conflict of the story revolves around the character Ben Jordan, the narrator's father, and his visit to an old girlfriend named Nora. The story is told in present tense from the first-person perspective of Ben Jordan's unnamed young daughter. While Anderson, in *Winesburg, Ohio*, maintained a quasi-omniscient, semi-oral-storytelling narrative voice, Munro hands the narrative voice over to her character and brings readers closer into the story. It is through the viewpoint of Ben's daughter that readers both witness the grotesque and also experience the revelation of the truth below the surface. In this way, Munro's achievement with the grotesque is much more intimate than Anderson's ever was.

Anderson's use of an omniscient narrator outside the drama of the story places the moment of realization or revelation on the reader alone. For instance, in Anderson's "The Untold Lie," only the reader witnesses Ray forget "all about being a quiet old farm hand" as he throws off his overcoat "to run across the field" (207). Only the reader experiences the revelation that Ray has thrown off the grotesque. In "Walker Brothers Cowboy," however, the reader enters into the story through the first-person perspective of the daughter and is therefore *sharing* these moments of witnessing and realization with the character.

Munro establishes her engagement with the grotesque through the device of characters being seen. It is through the eyes of Ben's daughter that we first see Ben as a grotesque: "He wears a white shirt, brilliant in the sunlight, a tie, light trousers belonging to his summer suit (his other suit is black, for funerals, and belonged to my uncle before he died) and a creamy straw hat. His salesman's outfit, with pencils clipped in the shirt pocket" (6). The daughter is describing the "outfit" or the *costume* that her father puts on to play the role of the travelling salesman. He conforms to the expectations of his role in society and thereby becomes a grotesque. It's important that one's role is connected to being seen. The connection of the grotesque with being seen is punctuated through the daughter's consideration of her father addressing her mother: "He goes back once again, probably to say goodbye to my mother, to ask her if she is sure she doesn't want to come, and hear her say, 'No. No thanks, I'm better just to lie here with my eyes closed'" (6). The scene creates a symbolic sense that the narrator's mother would rather keep her "eyes closed" than to *see* her husband in his grotesqueness.

Conversely, the narrator recalls how her mother puts on her own costume when they go for walks through town: "She wears a good dress, navy blue with little flowers, sheer, worn over a navy-blue slip. Also a summer hat of white straw, pushed down on the side of the head, and white shoes I have just whitened on a newspaper on the back steps" (5). Again, the issue is about being seen and judged in society and the performance of roles. Her mother's role is to be a lady: "She walks serenely like a lady shopping, like a *lady* shopping" (5; emphasis in orig.). The narrator encapsulates her mother's grotesqueness as "all I do not want to be" (5), and consequently turns a benign eye to her father because he offers "the rising hope of adventure" (6). As readers become aligned with the narrator, Munro's play with the idea of the grotesque becomes more intimate than that of Anderson.

Similar to Anderson, however, Munro establishes economic conditions that underscore the grotesque, such as poverty. The family used to own their business, and now the father is likened to "a pedlar knocking at backwoods kitchens" (4). However, the images of poverty extend beyond the family (and beyond this particular story) to create a generally impoverished atmosphere for Munro's Southwestern Ontario setting that critics such as Christine Lorre-Johnston have noted to be a quality of Munro's "Gothic" style (Cox and Lorre-Johnston 35). In the opening of "Walker Brothers Cowboy," the narrator and her father walk out of town past "a factory with boarded-up windows" through "a defeated jumble of sheds and small junkyards" to a "bench with a slat missing on the back," where "[t]ramps hang around the docks" (2). An overall economic depression pervades the mood of the story. Indeed, how the characters conform to their economic surroundings is what dictates their form of the grotesque. And yet this setting is interrupted or challenged when Ben Jordan offers one of the tramps some tobacco, emphasizing the complex and elemental human relationships that can and do exist regardless of economic conditions. One might even regard Ben Jordan's actions as a gesture towards an Indigenous responsibility of sharing symbolized by the use of tobacco in First Nations ceremony.

Ben Jordan seems to move naturally against the grotesque. Munro portrays Ben's resistance through moments of his daughter's intimate, first-person perspective observing her father. To achieve the intimacy, the narrative voice is crafted with heightened attention to detail. When they first arrive at Nora's place, the narrator observes that Ben and Nora "both laugh, [Nora's] laugh abrupt and somewhat angry" (11). The small detail of Nora's laugh lends weight to every other description as a part of the daughter's keen observation. During the visit, Nora changes her clothes. Changing her outfit changes her role, from country gal preparing to "'clean the hen-house'" (11) to "something more sociable and youthful" with even "a change of voice to go with the dress" (13). The grandmother's blindness furthers the importance of *seeing* in the story and effectively begins the process of revealing Ben's true self, as she is unable to see his grotesqueness. The full revelation, however, follows in three stages.

The first stage involves the whisky. Nora offers Ben a glass of whisky and he accepts it. They drink together. The young character-narrator observes this exchange and reflects: "One of the things my mother has told me in our talks together is that my father never drinks whisky. But I *see* he does" (15; emphasis added). The first stage of the transformation from grotesque to human being is framed through the narrator *seeing* her father in a new light. The next stage is through dancing. Nora puts on music because she wants to dance, saying, "'Here, I'm going to put on a piece I used to dance to and even your daddy did, in his dancing days. You didn't know your daddy was a dancer, did you?'" (16). The narrator's own ignorance of her father's fuller life is made manifest, both to readers but more importantly to the character-narrator. There are things she "'didn't know'" about her father. Readers are learning this fact, but also experiencing the sense of revelation more emphatically through the daughter's perspective.

The third and final stage of the revelation is reached on the drive home as a secret knowledge is passed between father and daughter: "My father does not say anything to me about not mentioning things at home, but I know, just from the thoughtfulness, the pause when he passes the licorice, that there are things not to be mentioned" (17-18). The narrator has come into an unspoken knowledge of her father, his life, and the world. The scene is capped off with the comparison to her younger brother, whom no one needed to worry about because "he does not notice enough" (18). In contrast, the narrator noticed nearly everything and saw through her father's surface outfit to the true human being within, if only for a moment. She thinks of her father's life "like a landscape that has an enchantment on it" (18). And therein lies the story's final and finest movement, as all at once readers are returned to the opening of the story and a secondary realization occurs.

The ending offers new meaning to the whole. As John Metcalf notes, the opening "is the whole story in miniature" (507). It is the same story, told twice, but in differing magnitudes; and we realize the story was about something much more than one man's past. It was about time and change, an allegory as J.R. (Tim) Struthers might say (Struthers, "The Place of Wisdom" 295-98). I would argue that the story is also about circularity as its structure emphasizes. Munro is not *contrasting* the time of a single human being against some larger geological time; she is *aligning* them. In the end, the story becomes an invitation to question a linear conception of time and instead to envision time as "something you will never know, with all kinds of weathers, and distances you cannot imagine" (18). To achieve the allegorical significance, the story's structure circles back on itself.

The opening of the story is a set piece that readers may have forgotten about by the end. In the opening, Ben Jordan takes his daughter for a walk to Lake Huron and tells her "how the Great Lakes came to be" (3). His story agrees with a Western geological understanding of glacial formations; and yet his description of the ice takes on a mythic quality as he uses his own hand to depict the "fingers of ice" (3) that would become the Great Lakes. He explains that "They were *new*, as time went" (3; emphasis in orig.). He is reflecting on himself, though readers may easily overlook the reflection at the start of the story. The narrator, too, is reflecting on time: "Even my father, who sometimes seems to me to have been at home in the world as long as it has lasted, has really lived on this earth only a little longer than I have, in terms of all the time there has been to live in" (3). The father's life is a landscape. As Coral Ann Howells notes, drawing on Kathleen Kirby's analysis, Munro's fiction transposes boundaries between "geographical place and individual psychic space" (140-41). I would suggest that Howells is observing an element in Munro's work that John Metcalf calls "a physical and emotional landscape" (509). Munro is combining the human being and the land within the same movement. In doing so, she creates an image of time and change as universal. Even as the story provides a meditation on the forward progression of time, as John Metcalf and Ailsa Cox insist, the narrative structure causes readers to move backward in time from the story's end back to its beginning. Consequently the final achievement of the story is to invite a conception of time and even existence as circular.

In Tanya Talaga's Massey Lectures, *All Our Relations: Finding the Path Forward*, she explains the importance of the circle as a form in Indigenous knowledge and philosophy: "The circle is a fundamental concept of Indigenous Intelligence, underscoring how everything is interrelated and life operates in a circular pattern" (25). From this insight we could imagine a universal *continuum*. In his essay "Too Little Geography; Too Much History," Dennis Duffy argues that Munro's story "Meneseteung" is interested in achieving "the construction of a felt continuum and the retelling of how one got there" (91). I would submit that Munro is attempting a similar task in the narrative structure of "Walker Brothers Cowboy."

The ending of the story suggests a flowing of Ben Jordan's life. It is a flowing backward even as they, in the car, move forward. The ending is reconnected to the beginning. Ailsa Cox writes that in this story distances "are temporal, as well as spatial" (Cox and Lorre-Johnston 71), a quality which is, again, universal. We could hear an echo of Frederick Moten's theory of the inhabitation of movement. *We flow with it.* I would suggest that Alice Munro's alignment of the human being and the land together within the same structure of thought concerning time and change as a circular flow or continuum constitutes a movement towards Indigenous ways of thinking. The shape of the circle is integral to Indigenous knowledge and, therefore, the circular structure of the story could symbolically represent evidence of Indigenous responsibility in Munro's work.

***

Returning to the image of the river, Alice Munro's whole body of work might be better imagined as its own unique watercourse. Each individual story could then be imagined as an island within that river, which one can visit. Each story-island offers its own particular worldview. Rather than solely looking *at* the story, we can attempt to follow Frederick Moten's approach of trying to look *with* the story at the world. For me, the idea that a story could be imagined as an island derives from Leanne Betasamosake Simpson's *Islands of Decolonial Love: Stories and Songs.*

Conceptually, Simpson's songs and stories exist as islands within the framework or landscape of her book. Similarly, in his essay "In Search of the Perfect Metaphor," J.R. (Tim) Struthers suggests imagining "the form of the short story as a metaphoric island" (180). Alice Munro's "Meneseteung" utilizes the Ojibwe name of the river as the central identity of the fictional poem within the story and of the actual story itself. An Objiwe word, Meneseteung means "place of little islands" (Struthers, "Imagining" 72). Rather than an appropriation of the Meneseteung, which would involve the very real act of "theft" (Maracle 101), the process in which Munro and her readers are engaged represents an imaginative confrontation with the violent totality of Canadian history, myth-making, narratives, and ourselves within it all. As Munro's Almeda reflects, "All this can be borne only if it is channelled into a poem, and the word 'channelled' is appropriate, because the name of the poem will be—it *is*—'The Meneseteung'" ("Meneseteung" 70). In other words, this work must occur first in the world of the imagination. Imagining the story-island as a place readers inhabit allows for an imaginative shift from a looking at approach to a looking with approach.

An island is land surrounded by water. One must cross water to reach the island. Yet questions of intention arise, for there is something inherently colonial about desiring to reach an island in order to look *at* it. The action seems to mirror Western scientific knowledge structures of objectivity. Trish Monture argues that the Western mind, or, more precisely, "'the white man'," is obsessed with "'thingifying everything'"

(Monture qtd. in Maracle 54). The Western mind wants to locate, dissect, and classify the natural world into objective *things* or *truths*. However, if we shift the perspective to imagine that we are looking out *from* the island rather than *at* it, we begin to look *with* the island out at the rest of the world. We start to align our way of perceiving more with Frederick Moten's idea of looking *with* movement. If we imagine the short story as an island, we are then engaged in looking with or through the story's worldview. I think a new mental approach is reached in this movement that is perhaps less colonized and, importantly, less colonizing.

In his essay "Returning to the Source," Charles E. May notes Munro's view of a short story's form as resembling someone building a house with the purpose of revealing "'the feeling'" inside the house, since the feeling is "'the soul of the story'" (7). Thinking of the short story as a construction with an *internal feeling* demands an imagined space that readers enter to be *in* it. From there, however, what if we looked out? What if we peered from the windows, gazed from the open doorway, out at the world? Returning to my initial conception of the river as metaphor for the short story genre, and drawing together Simpson's conceptualization of her own work with how Struthers has envisioned Munro's, what if we imagine that short stories are islands *in* the river? They exist as separate constructions like geological formations over time, but they are all interconnected within the flow and history of the river.

Each story-island presents its own characteristics or ecosystem through which it creates a particular worldview. Similar to imagining readers who enter the story-house and feel the essence or message of its soul, so too can we imagine readers who stand on the shore of the island or walk among the trees and feel the environment of the story-island's soul. To draw from bioregional literature and criticism, can we imagine readers who are inspired to *dwell*, who attempt "to live mindfully and deeply in place" (Tom Lynch et al. qtd. in Follett 119). Most crucial, however, is that readers can position themselves with the island and can therefore look outwards, listening to the story, to understand the story's worldview. Looking through the story's eyes, if you will, how does the story view the world?

Thinking about the short story, or of literature in general, through an idea of looking *with* and listening rather than looking *at* and determining seems to suggest a movement towards an Indigenous pedagogy. In her essay "Meschachakanis, a Coyote Narrative," Shauneen Pete argues that a kind of "two-eyed seeing" occurs when you notice "the colonial constructions around you" and at the same time move towards "the decolonial possibilities offered by Indigenous ways of knowing" (177). Situating myself in relation to Indigenous ways of knowing becomes an act of listening. Maracle emphasizes the importance of "sharing" as an arrangement of responsible co-operation (107-10). The alignment of looking with a story feels inherently co-operative. It is a reciprocal relationship between the reader and the story. The nature of that co-operative positioning therefore reinforces an imaginative space that is better attuned to revealing relationships and connections in the study of literature and to the world.

Rereading Alice Munro's "Walker Brothers Cowboy" through the lens of Indigenous responsibility moved me towards trying to see the story's worldview. It was an attempt to go beyond classification towards interpreting how the story is revealing the world. Munro's "Walker Brothers Cowboy" provides a worldview in which the flow of time is a mystery and yet there exists an intuition of its cyclical nature and the sense that all things from individual human beings to the Great Lakes are part of the same continuum. Positioned in that flow, I am writing in Cambridge, Ontario, near the banks of the Grand River (Kahyonhatátye), the city where I was born and the place I call home, but which is a region of contested land rights and historical theft as part of the Haldimand Treaty of 1784.

It is a land that I share with many people in the sense of calling it home, but the history and knowledge of the land belongs to those before me like the Six Nations, the Mississauga, and others who have conducted their lives with a greater responsibility to the land. If this responsibility is about love, intimacy, and an attempt to understand the relationship between identity and space, could it be said appreciatively that "Walker Brothers Cowboy" exemplifies the idea of story as responsibility, as a movement towards Indigenous responsibility, and therefore as land acknowledgement in Southwestern Ontario literature? Could it be a bioregional *story-island* that invites readers to inhabit it and consequently to reflect on their own relationships to self, region, and story? Could the very act of reading, as well as writing, then become a form of acknowledgement?

Moreover, can we follow Frederick Moten to look *with* the story to see not what kind of *thing* the story is, but what the story is showing us? Can we follow Thomas King and Leanne Betasamosake Simpson to try to *listen* in order to hear what the story has to say? Can we remember Lee Maracle and try to let the story teach us about the world and ourselves?

I don't know, but when I read Alice Munro I like to think so.

Works Cited

Anderson, Sherwood. *Winesburg, Ohio.* 1919. Introd. Malcolm Cowley. New York: Viking, 1960. Viking Compass ed.

Coleman, Daniel. "Indigenous Place and Diaspora Space: Of Literalism and Abstraction." *Settler Colonial Studies* 6.1 (2016): 61-76. <https://doi.org/10.1080/2201473X.2014.1000913>.

Cox, Ailsa, and Christine Lorre-Johnston. *The Mind's Eye: Alice Munro's* Dance of the Happy Shades. Paris: Éditions Fahrenheit, 2015.

Duffy, Dennis. "Too Little Geography; Too Much History: Writing the Balance in Alice Munro." *Alice Munro Country: Essays on Her Works I.* Ed. J.R. (Tim) Struthers. Toronto: Guernica Editions, 2020. 87-113. Essential Writers Ser. 51.

Follett, Alec. "'The Region That I Know': The Bioregional View in Alice Munro's *The View from Castle Rock.*" *Alice Munro Country: Essays on Her Works I.* Ed. J.R. (Tim) Struthers. Toronto: Guernica Editions, 2020. 115-37. Essential Writers Ser. 51.

Howells, Coral Ann. "Intimate Dislocations: Buried History and Geography in Alice Munro's Souwesto Stories." *Alice Munro Country: Essays on Her Works I.* Ed. J.R. (Tim) Struthers. Toronto: Guernica Editions, 2020. 139-53. Essential Writers Ser. 51.

King, Thomas. *The Truth about Stories: A Native Narrative.* Toronto: House of Anansi, 2003. The Massey Lectures Ser.

Maracle, Brian (Owennatekha). "Re: Mohawk language research." Message to the author. 4 Oct. 2021. E-mail.

Maracle, Lee. *My Conversations with Canadians.* Toronto: Book*hug, 2020. Essais No. 4.

May, Charles E. "Returning to the Source: Alice Munro, Flannery O'Connor, and Eudora Welty." *Alice Munro Everlasting: Essays on Her Works II.* Ed. J.R. (Tim) Struthers. Toronto: Guernica Editions, 2020. 1-30. Essential Writers Ser. 52.

Metcalf, John. *The Canadian Short Story.* Windsor, ON: Biblioasis, 2018.

Moten, Frederick. "Two Books: 'Sentient Flesh' and 'All That Beauty'; Professor R.A. Judy in Conversation with Professor Frederick Moten on Their New Books." Hosted by Professor Sadia Abbas. *YouTube*, uploaded by Naya Daur TV, 21 Jan. 2021. <https://www.youtube.com/watch?v=tjapcDOfbFE>.

Munro, Alice. "Meneseteung." *Friend of My Youth.* Toronto: McClelland & Stewart, 1990. 50-73.

---. "A Trip to the Coast." *Dance of the Happy Shades.* Fwd. Hugh Garner. Toronto: Ryerson, 1968. 172-89.

---. "Walker Brothers Cowboy." *Dance of the Happy Shades.* Fwd. Hugh Garner. Toronto: Ryerson, 1968. 1-18.

Pete, Shauneen. "Meschachakanis, a Coyote Narrative: Decolonising Higher Education." *Decolonising the University.* Ed. Gurminder K. Bhambra, Dalial Gebrial, and Kerem Nişancıoğlu. London: Pluto, 2018. 173-89.

Razack, Sherene H. "Gendered Racial Violence and Spatialized Justice: The Murder of Pamela George." *Race, Space, and the Law: Unmapping a White Settler Society.* Ed. Sherene H. Razack. Toronto: Between the Lines, 2002. 121-56.

Simpson, Leanne Betasamosake. *Islands of Decolonial Love: Stories & Songs.* Winnipeg: ARP, 2015.

---. "Land as Pedagogy: Nishnaabeg Intelligence and Rebellious Transformation." *Decolonization: Indigeneity, Education & Society* 3.3 (2014): 1-25. <https://jps.library.utoronto.ca/index.php/des/article/view/22170>.

Strong-Boag, Veronica, and Carole Gerson. *Paddling Her Own Canoe: The Times and Texts of E. Pauline Johnson (Tekahionwake).* Toronto: U of Toronto P, 2000.

Struthers, J.R. (Tim). "Imagining Alice Munro's 'Meneseteung': The Dynamics of Co-Creation." *Alice Munro: A Souwesto Celebration.* Ed. J.R. (Tim) Struthers and John B. Lee. *The Windsor Review* 47.2 (2014): 68-91.

---. "In Search of the Perfect Metaphor: The Language of the Short Story and Alice Munro's 'Meneseteung'." *Critical Insights: Alice Munro.* Ed. Charles E. May. Ipswich, MA: Salem-EBSCO, 2013. 175-94.

---. "The Place of Wisdom, Divination, the Act of Reading, and Alice Munro's 'Powers'." *Alice Munro Everlasting: Essays on Her Works II.* Ed. J.R. (Tim) Struthers. Toronto: Guernica Editions, 2020. 293-343. Essential Writers Ser. 52.

---. "Remembrance Day 1988: An Interview with Alice Munro." *Alice Munro Country: Essays on Her Works I.* Ed. J.R. (Tim) Struthers. Toronto: Guernica Editions, 2020. 65-86. Essential Writers Ser. 51.

Talaga, Tanya. *All Our Relations: Finding the Path Forward.* Toronto: House of Anansi, 2018. The Massey Lectures Ser.

Answering the Call of the Wild: Poetry, Sex, and Living in Alice Munro's "Meneseteung"

Dennis Duffy

Call of the Wild? Alice Munro? Really?

Maybe if I start by telling you how I came up with this title, then I can show you my plan for what I want to do here. Back in that dream time before COVID hit, I was visiting the Jack London State Historic Park in the Sonoma Valley in northern California, near the town of Glen Ellen. I knew then that I was slated to give a talk in the Great Books Lecture Series hosted by the Toronto Public Library, and that the talk would be about Alice Munro's "Meneseteung." Yes, I knew it was labelled a short story, but Munro's later stories are as rich as any novel, well worth a lengthy reflection. The theme of the lecture series was "The Wild." How did Munro's story fit into that format?

When I got to the Visitors Center and gift shop, you can just imagine what Jack London novel occupied the focal point of the book display there. The same book that had enthralled me as a kid, the same book that I can recall scenes from now, seventy-plus years later. And *right there*, springing from that book's title, was not only the title of my talk, but the angle I had been in search of.

Consider:

- Jack London's novel first saw print as a pulpy serial in *The Saturday Evening Post*;
- the narrative remains accessible to younger readers;
- it assumes that an omniscient narrator can actually get inside an animal's mind;

- what we call anthropomorphism we now view as a mark of fable rather than of fiction.

Jack London crafted his tale as a narrative that upholds a kind of species-determined, Darwinian immutability. The protagonist, Buck, cannot escape what he is. Place this domesticated creature amid the wilderness and its brutality (dog eat dog???), strip away the human rules restricting him to domesticity, parachute him inescapably into his natural environment, and what happens? He grows into the leader of the pack, a wolf / one-time dog whose deepest comfort comes out of returning to the environment where his species started out.

London's tale is deterministic in its outlook. There is no escaping the facts of your origin. Your social role is a veneer over your actual self. Given sufficient switches in your environment, you will revert or evolve, or devolve – call it what you will – into what you inescapably are. Let me stop here, rather than follow this determinism as it wends its way into social regimentation and racial hierarchies. Instead, let's just admit that London's tale for kids is a repository of some fairly grown-up ideas.

Whoa!, you tell me, what has that got to do with Alice Munro's story which focuses upon a late-nineteenth-century Ontario small-town woman and her predicaments? How did I get from London's animal story to Munro's re-creation of a spinster poet? Canadian writers – Ernest Thompson Seton and Charles G.D. Roberts – may have excelled at such work, but the story's heroine, Almeda Joynt Roth, like her historical counterpart, Eloise A. Skimings, plays no role in their genetic code. Yet the turmoil of the call of the wild, the struggle between the tamed and the unruly, shapes Munro's narrative. That conflict I seek to explore.

Beneath all its sophistication and artfulness, "Meneseteung" is a story evoking a protagonist who gets done in by a series of primordial anti-societal forces. The call of that wild cannot go unanswered. Almeda's role in that variety of social drama transforms her into *our own* boreal Blanche Dubois. The frail vessel of personality cannot navigate the reefs of desire and the shoals formed by thwarting it. Almeda is broken by the wild. She is broken by the untameable, the uncivilized, even the unsocialized that dwells both without and within us. Those two unstoppable forces, the wild that is without and the wild that is within

Almeda Roth, join to destroy her. Taking a look at those drivers is what this piece is about.

We have a clue into Alice Munro's thinking as she assembled her material. Margaret Atwood's anthologizing "Meneseteung" in the 1989 *Best American Short Stories* gave Munro the space for a writer's afterword. Under the heading of Contributors' Notes, Munro set out the social perspective her story included: she wanted to portray "that town, that time, when so many sturdy notions were pushing up together – the boisterous commercialism and austere hard-hearted religion, the tenacious gentility hungering for class distinction." Let's linger over that town and that time, the early Ontario new town of Goderich in the late nineteenth century.

A few points ...

This is settler history, victors' history if you will. Not at all the kind of history we now invoke whenever we acknowledge the cultures that occupied this land before we did. Those previous occupants do not figure in this account of experience, except as the products of Almeda Roth's imagination and, as J.R. (Tim) Struthers has explained, in the story's title, which, translated from Ojibwe to English means "place of little islands."

To Almeda's culture, their surroundings are the wild, the forest from which the settled landscape has been wrested. Those sharing that culture – Almeda, Jarvis Poulter, the *Vidette* – are at once suspicious and fearful of the wild. They fear slipping back into its heart of darkness. They represent a colonial mentality, a garrison mentality, a mindset that we now find cringeworthy. Just hearing about it makes us yearn for some act of virtue-signalling.

The story's anonymous modern-day narrator can no more escape the limitations of this settler attitude than can we. The townscape and its agricultural hinterland form a rampart against the wilderness.

As Faulkner's Gavin Stevens reminds us in *Requiem for a Nun*, "The past is never dead. It's not even past" (73). Almeda is an oddity in her culture. One aspect of this lies in her attempt to integrate her imaginative vision of the past with her experience of the present. Almeda Joynt Roth is a poet, one of a tribe of misfits who refuse to live wholly in the present. The reality of the present, the hard colonial settler existence, is that the place itself resists poetic packaging: "It's true that you can gather wildflowers in spring in the woodlots, but you'd have to walk through herds of horned cows to get to them."

In Munro's contributor's note, she outlines the nature and the predicament of her protagonist. "So I thought, What about imagining one of these women and giving her some talent [in order to] stir her up? Then put her in one of these towns and see what will happen. ... I wanted to see what she would do about poetry, sex, and living, in that town, that time." Make no mistake, Eloise A. Skimings, Munro's historical model for Almeda Joynt Roth, proved the very model of the small-town literary lady of that period. Daughter of a tailor, Eloise A. Skimings filled the columns of the Goderich *Signal-Star* with her poetry, as Louis K. MacKendrick has discussed.

"The Poetess of Lake Huron," the newspaper noted, presented two copies of a volume of her verse to the visiting Lord Stanley, Governor General (and the man who has a sporting trophy and Vancouver's magnificent park named after him). Skimings was known as a musician, composer, artist, advocate, and, in the words of her obituary of May 8, 1919, "one of Goderich's best-known citizens." In celebration of her eightieth birthday, a proposal was considered to hold "a concert or a public entertainment of some sort ... doing honour to one who has for many years helped to keep Goderich before the world." She became enough of a local celebrity for the local photographer, Reuben R. Sallows, to snap her in a festive outfit for the Coronation of 1902. And he also shot her in other, more conventional poses.

Munro's narrative leaves Almeda a more marginalized figure than Skimings was in fact. What Almeda Joynt Roth does retain is a sense of the past, historical and pre-historic. And her sense of the past attempts to integrate the wild with the tamed. Thus Almeda's poem "Champlain at the Mouth of the Meneseteung" juxtaposes the Euro explorer / settler phenomenon with the aboriginal "host" culture. The pity of it lies in the failure of Almeda Joynt Roth to complete her visionary task. Almeda outlines her project during her opium-induced ruminations. But she never – in fiction or in fact – reached that goal.

> She has to think of so many things at once – Champlain and the naked Indians and the salt deep in the earth, but as well as the salt the money, the money-making intent brewing forever in heads like Jarvis Poulter's.

> Also the brutal storms of winter and the clumsy and benighted deeds on Pearl Street. The changes of climate are often violent, and if you think about it there is no peace even in the stars. All this can be borne only if it is channelled into a poem, and the word "channelled" is appropriate, because the name of the poem will be – it *is* – "The Meneseteung." The name of the poem is the name of the river. No, in fact it is the river, the Meneseteung, that is the poem – with its deep holes and rapids and blissful pools under the summer trees and its grinding blocks of ice thrown up at the end of winter and its desolating spring floods. (70)

Yet paradoxically, some version of that project is completed, but by Alice Munro rather than Almeda. Because Munro's story – whose title almost matches that of the epic Almeda longs to write – does complete the epic her character envisions. The whole interplay of fiction with fact recalls nothing less than the artistic registry that Virgil achieves in *The Aeneid*, Book I. There the newly-arrived Roman epic hero views a Carthaginian mural in a temple. The subject of the representation there? The Fall of Troy and its attendant suffering, the very event that has propelled Aeneas and his crew to these strange shores. Aeneas the hero beholds his own image of heroic defeat. This experience goads him into his cry that there are tears, tears at the heart of things, and that these sorrows touch all our hearts. It is a cry for recognition of the universality of suffering. Where does art and the emotions it arouses leave off and life begin? What has happened to the boundaries set so (seemingly) firmly between them?

But that experiential and imaginative unity we can find only in verse, and in a poem that has never *actually* existed. Even within the imaginative confines of Munro's story, Almeda Joynt Roth is torn by conflict. The basic conflict between the settled and the wild, the desert and the sown, the townsman and the nomad. It's that embedded conflict that Scripture figures forth in the rivalry between Isaac and Ishmael. The sensibility gap between Almeda and Jarvis Poulter gets portrayed in the language of gender. "Would she herself, knowing that there was salt in the earth, discover how to get it out and sell it? Not likely. She would be thinking about the ancient sea. That kind of speculation is what Jarvis Poulter has, quite properly, no time for." But male or female, the gap between pragmatic assessment of an environment and the imaginative embrace of it stands as an unplumbed, salt, estranging sea.

Like us readers, Almeda Joynt Roth cannot realize artistically this vision of reconciliation, this inclusion of wild and tamed within a single imaginative framework. The commonalities between her culture and ours render this an enduring conflict in our own imaginative life. But let us focus now on the way in which these wild / tame conflicts shape the experience, both inner and outer, of Almeda.

So we've looked at the role played by poetry in that trio of poetry, sex, and living that Munro set forth. Let's move on to sex now, before we conclude with a look at living.

First, consider for a moment the narrative structure of "Meneseteung." It resembles that of classical drama: a lengthy exposition about the setting and its characters, followed by a sudden, sharp, and decisive set of actions, followed by a summing-up in the epilogue. That summing-up is conveyed by our anonymous modern-day narrator, who has functioned throughout as a chorus. The decisive action – that is, the protagonist's response to the force of sexuality – occurs within a twenty-four-hour period. Those classical unities, the narrator-as-chorus: could it be that Munro was multi-tasking? Reading Euripides while all the while reviewing old photos?

I mention Euripides for a reason, because the surges of sexual passion – Medea, Phaedra, the Bacchae – so often swell over his characters. Jarvis Poulter, that wealthy salt miner, landowner, and town worthy, has his *anagnorisis*, his recognition moment of the power of sexuality. It happens in a glance, as Almeda, running around in her nightclothes, rouses him from his bed. A damsel in distress, she implores his protection against the riotous revels taking place on the edge of her property. Jarvis Poulter is "stirred by her loosened hair ... her flushed face, her light clothing, which nobody but a husband should see." On the spot, he declares that he'll be walking her to church in the morning (in their culture, the equivalent of a marriage proposal). A declaration which Almeda subsequently and passively spurns.

But I'm getting ahead of myself. Let's go back to the incident at the border of Almeda's property. A lower-class woman, surely a fallen woman as respectable folk would have termed her, brawls loudly and drunkenly with a lover or a client or a customer or all of the above. That struggle is then followed by the sounds of a brutal coupling which leaves the bruised female passed out and covered in her own vomit. Yes, this just might be the sort of thing to send The Poetess of Lake Huron to the shelter of some strong and respectable man. And it is in the rescue that the climactic moment occurs, in Poulter's display of his disgust with the (literally) fallen woman. He "nudges [her] leg with the toe of his boot, just as you'd nudge a dog or a sow." He dismisses the woman, sending her on her way to the rural slum where she lives. "'Gwan home, now.'" Does his almost casual command indicate a deeper familiarity? Has he known this woman in the past?

The encounter between the wrecked woman, the alpha male, and The Poetess of Lake Huron, this scene followed by Jarvis Poulter's gruff declaration that he'll be walking Almeda to church in a few hours, provokes a shocked revulsion from Almeda. Before the sounds in her backyard intruded upon her peace, Almeda had been calculating just what marital intimacy might entail. Everything seems to crystallize around the fact of a suit of long underwear, everywhere visible in the man's comings and goings. All this, we must assume, sends Almeda all a-tremble at the prospect of dwelling in this sort of intimacy. Jonathan Swift had put it shockingly well more than a century earlier in "The Lady's Dressing Room," when his parodically named lover realizes a basic fact about his love:

> Disgusted Strephon stole away
> Repeating in his amorous fits,
> Oh! Celia, Celia, Celia shits!

Bodily disgust and revulsion are not unknown in Munro's fiction. I've written about it in her story "The Love of a Good Woman." Our bodies and their inevitable physiological processes of elimination, change, and decay are ever-ready to trip us up in our romantic flights. When a character's consciousness can get no closer to this than a vision of soiled underwear, then the realization of our soiled corporeality hammers at us. Many embarrassments add up to all the mess that living entails. Almeda's shocked realization of the linkage between the prissily domestic and the brutally physiological provokes her into flight.

The narrative juxtaposes a homely domestic chore with the inexorable tide of sexual identity. Almeda has been preparing a mixture for grape jelly, and the juice of the crushed grapes has been dripping its way through the cheesecloth filter since the day's beginning. In another sort of culture, this play with grapes and must and the straining of it might appear as a prelude to wine-making. Not, dear reader, in the culture of late-nineteenth-century Ontario! Any Bacchanalia is going to be powered by grape juice, even as grape juice rather than full-blown wine serves as the medium for a Protestant Eucharist.

Yet this steady drip of the non-wine is paralleled by Almeda's inner processes of menstruation. Her period's onset follows her charged encounter with Poulter. With that onset, she pens a brief note to Poulter that declines on the grounds of illness his offer to accompany her to church. The narcotic forming the substance of the patent medicine that Almeda takes for her "female complaint" ensures that she passes the rest of the day in a haze of laudanum-induced dreaminess. At Sabbath Day's end, the facts of her bodily processes are inescapably before her, in "her escaping blood and the sweat of her body that has sat all day in the closed hot room." Join with me if you will in substituting one letter for another, and hear that she "set" rather than "sat" in the room. Almeda and her material surroundings are alike in their actions, in their process of setting. The pressed grapes drip; the blood in her body flows; the vagaries of her imagination push aside her intellect. That is when she comes up with the vision of the poem which she will never write (and which her creator Alice Munro *is* writing). All these currents flow together within and without her.

We are looking at Munro's enactment of the quest that her contributor's note declared she had set for herself in representing the actuality of such a woman in that town and in that time. In this scene of drugged reverie we locate the trinity of categories I listed in my tale's subtitle: Almeda Joynt Roth's encounter with *sex* in the scene with Poulter and the woman, her immersion in the flow of *living* in the interplay between the dripping grapes and her bodily flow, and her *poetic* vision. Small wonder that she leaves this setting for all these revelations in a post-coital-like indifference to the mess she leaves behind. "She knows that she will have to mop it up, but not yet," we are told. She has set her vision aside. The roses in the crocheted tablecloth that took on movement in her laudanum-induced trance are not real, she now understands. That's how, the narrator tells us, "she knows that she is sane." Like Max in Maurice Sendak's children's story, she has to come back from where the wild things are.

Can we go back for a minute and get a view of what we've been looking at? We've seen a tragic protagonist stuck in the wrong place at the wrong time when it comes to realizing her artistic aspirations. Almeda Joynt Roth is reminiscent of many Romantic heroines in nineteenth-century fiction. Madame Bovary and Dorothea Brooke are her kin: heroines of high ambition and idealist temperaments whose provincial cultures will not, cannot, support imaginative undertakings of the scope they – and Almeda Joynt Roth – dream of. And so are later literary heroines: I have already mentioned Blanche Dubois, one of many memorable female characters in the vast body of work by Southern writers that Munro reverences.

The "host" cultures are too materialist in their outlook, too cramped in their social *mores*, too limited in their preoccupations, and too suspicious of those who cannot conform to them. As if that were not enough, the protagonists themselves have internalized those outlooks. They want their dreams, but they are unwilling to pay the savage price such dreams exact. Even if Almeda Joynt Roth wanted to shift elsewhere and adopt some kind of outcast bohemian life (in Ontario in the late nineteenth century?) has she the sheer driving genius that would thrust her into the forefront of literary expression? These are extra-critical questions. Almeda is not an actual person; we are not in search of a happy sequel to this story. But I bring in a bit of other writing in order to acquaint us with the widespread nature of the dilemma that Munro treats here. She remarks in her contributor's note that she was aware of a number of other women provincial writers of that time, now scorned by metropolitan critics and present-day sensibilities. Nonetheless, she herself acknowledges a debt to these figures. She mentions one Barbara Mountcastle. Googling "Canada's Early Women Writers" will bring you to a website where you can encounter a slew of such figures, including Skimings and Mountcastle.

But I want to include this story within an even larger perspective. Of course, we should go ask Alice Laidlaw from Wingham, Ontario, the clever girl with the socially aspirant, bookish schoolteacher mom. We should ask *that* Alice just "Who Do You Think You Are?" and put her in her place. It isn't a bad place to be.

In writing "Meneseteung," *that* Alice carried on the High Modernist quest begun by Joyce in *Ulysses*. She launches an imaginative project in which the struggles of an isolated individual against his social *milieu* are viewed through a mythological framework. The adventures of Leopold

Bloom, Stephen Daedalus, and Molly Bloom can't measure up to their Homeric counterparts. They aren't meant to. But Almeda Joynt Roth's grape juice that isn't the wine of Bacchus is part of a general perspective on diminishment that the High Modernist imagination deals in. Robert Frost's injunction in "The Oven Bird," that our job lies in "what to make of a diminished thing," is a mainstay of our imaginative experience. Yet that diminishment – that failure in the realms of poetry, sex, and living – touches us in the way that the Punic temple painting touched Virgil's hero. You mean our griefs resonate elsewhere? is Aeneas' stunned response. Well, yes, and we have to imagine Munro's stoned heroine Almeda happy. Like Virginia Woolf's Lily Briscoe in *To the Lighthouse*, she has had her vision, make of it whatever you will.

What is a narrator to do with such a protagonist, especially if her treatment has progressed within the boundaries of the tragic mode? So of course the author kills off her heroine and the narrator/chorus steps forward for an ironic bow. Even Almeda Joynt Roth's death has to follow a stance of diminishment. Here's what I mean when I talk of this posture. Eloise A. Skimings' father was a tailor, not a manufacturer. His poetess daughter was earning her living as a housekeeper when she died in her eighties, or so one historical entry assures us. Almeda Joynt Roth, however, dies more dramatically and with lesser dignity. The *Vidette* speculates whether she died through a chill suffered when the feral boys of the town – the lads who enforce the town's suspicion of the Other – chased the crazy lady in the funny clothes into the swamp.

No, Almeda Joynt Roth wasn't actually Ophelia, any more than Prufrock was Prince Hamlet or was meant to be. But in bringing Almeda under the sway of what the *Vidette* terms "*the boldness and cruelty of some of our youth*," the narrator offers a blend of tragedy and farce that fully suits the ambience that she has created. The wild – the wild of the swamp, the wild of the hooligans – has triumphed over the lady seeking to control it, or at least contain it within the bounds of imaginative expression.

Maybe.

Because, the choric narrator reminds us, nothing is fixed, nothing definite, nothing really certain. Her epilogue recounting the death of Almeda is followed by another epilogue, this one on what Roland Barthes termed "the death of the author." The narrator in fact somewhat resembles – Robert Thacker's biography shows us – the actual Munro in her patrolling of obscure rural graveyards and uncovering the actualities of who lies buried there. That very narrator coolly assures us that she could likely as not be making stuff up. Maybe, the pert voice assures us, Almeda Joynt Roth never took the laudanum opiate that gave her the vision, and the voice even leaves the detail of making grape jelly in question. In other words, the chorus affirms, I don't know terribly much about the realistic underpinnings of the climactic symbolic scene that forms the linchpin of my story.

There lies the story's ultimate wildness: the anarchy, the randomness, the mystery of imaginative discourse itself. Coleridge's "Kubla Khan" says that he the poet once saw in a vision an Abyssinian damsel playing a dulcimer. We know the source of his visions; Almeda Joynt Roth and a host of other nineteenth-century dopers depended on that same source. Fragments are a specialty of Romantic verse, providing the subject of some works (Shelley's "Ozymandias") and the structure of others (Keats's "The Fall of Hyperion"). Coleridge also tells us that the vision – in which he wrote his marvellous poetic fragment – was interrupted by a persistent stranger from the village of Porlock who knocked on his door and interrupted the trance. No one has ever been able to trace that stranger. And in "Meneseteung" no narrator steps forward to assure us of the certainty of whatever happened to Almeda Joynt Roth. We are called, however, by the imaginative power of the wild.

Works Cited

Barthes, Roland. "The Death of the Author." *Image – Music – Text.* Selected and trans. Stephen Heath. New York: Hill and Wang, 1977. 142-48.

"Biographical Sketch." The Eloise A. Skimings Fonds, Huron County Museum. 2-3. <https://www.huroncountymuseum.ca/wp-content/uploads/2020/01/Eloise-Skimmings-Fonds.pdf>.

"Canada's Early Women Writers." <https://cwrc.ca/project/canadas-early-women-writers>.

Coleridge, Samuel Taylor. "Kubla Khan." *Poetical Works.* Ed. Ernest Hartley Coleridge. London: Oxford UP, 1967. 297-98.

Duffy, Dennis. "'A Dark Sort of Mirror': 'The Love of a Good Woman' as Pauline Poetic." *The Rest of the Story: Critical Essays on Alice Munro.* Ed. Robert Thacker. Toronto: ECW, 1999. 169-90.

Eliot, George. *Middlemarch.* 1872. Ed. and introd. Rosemary Ashton. London: Penguin, 2003. Penguin Classics.

Eliot, T.S. "The Love-Song of J. Alfred Prufrock." <https://www.poetryfoundation.org/poetrymagazine/poems/44212/the-love-song-of-j-alfred-prufrock>.

Euripides. "The Bacchae." Trans. and introd. William Arrowsmith. *Euripides.* Vol. 4 of *The Complete Greek Tragedies.* Ed. David Grene and Richmond Lattimore. Chicago: U of Chicago P, 1959. 529-610.

---. "Hippolytus." Trans. and introd. David Grene. *Euripides.* Vol. 3 of *The Complete Greek Tragedies.* Ed. David Grene and Richmond Lattimore. Chicago: U of Chicago P, 1959. 157-221.

---. "The Medea." Trans. and introd. Rex Warner. *Euripides.* Vol. 3 of *The Complete Greek Tragedies.* Ed. David Grene and Richmond Lattimore. Chicago: U of Chicago P, 1959. 55-108.

Faulkner, William. *Requiem for a Nun.* 1951. New York: Vintage International, 2011.

Flaubert, Gustave. *Madame Bovary: Backgrounds and Sources; Essays in Criticism.* Ed and trans. Paul de Man. New York: W.W. Norton, 1965. A Norton Critical Edition.

Frost, Robert. "The Oven Bird." <https://www.poetryfoundation.org/poems/44269/the-oven-bird>.

Joyce, James. *Ulysses: The Corrected Text.* Ed. Hans Walter Gabler, Wolfhard Steppe, and Claus Melchior. Harmondsworth, Eng.: Penguin, 1986.

Keats. John. "The Fall of Hyperion: A Dream." *Poetical Works.* Ed. H.W. Garrod. London: Oxford UP, 1970. 401-16. Oxford Standard Authors.

London. Jack. *The Call of the Wild.* 1903. Rpt. in *The Call of the Wild, White Fang, and Other Stories.* By Jack London. Ed. Kenneth K. Brandt. Introd. Earle Labor. London, Penguin, 2019. 1-86. Penguin Classics.

MacKendrick, Louis K. "Giving Tongue: Scorings of Voice, Verse, and Flesh in Alice Munro's 'Meneseteung'." *Alice Munro Country: Essays on Her Works I.* Ed. J.R. (Tim) Struthers. Toronto: Guernica Editions, 2020. 303-22. Essential Writers Ser. 51.

Munro, Alice. "Contributors' Notes." *The Best American Short Stories 1989.* Selected by Margaret Atwood with Shannon Ravenel. Introd. Margaret Atwood. Boston: Houghton Mifflin, 1989. 322-23.

---. "Meneseteung." *Friend of My Youth.* Toronto: McClelland & Stewart, 1990. 50-73.

---. "Who Do You Think You Are?" *Who Do You Think You Are?* Toronto: MacMillan of Canada, 1978. 189-206.

Roberts, Charles G.D. *The Kindred of the Wild: A Book of Animal Life.* 1902. Introd. James Polk. Toronto: Dundurn, 2013. Voyageur Classics.

Sendak, Maurice. *Where the Wild Things Are.* Illus. Maurice Sendak. 50th anniversary ed. New York: HarperCollins, 2013.

Seton, Ernest Thompson. *Wild Animals I Have Known.* Illus. Ernest Thompson Seton. 1898. Afterword by David Arnason. Toronto: McClelland and Stewart, 1991. New Canadian Library.

Shakespeare, William. *The Tragedy of Hamlet, Prince of Denmark: The First Folio (1623).* Ed. Ann Thompson and Neil Taylor. *The Arden Shakespeare Third Series: Complete Works.* Ed. Richard Proudfoot, Ann Thompson, David Scott Kastan, and H.R. Woudhuysen. London: The Arden Shakespeare, 2021. 383-421.

Shelley, P.B. "Ozymandias." *Poetical Works.* Ed. Thomas Hutchinson. New ed. Rev. G.M. Matthews. London: Oxford UP, 1971. 550. Oxford Standard Authors.

Struthers, J.R. (Tim). "In Search of the Perfect Metaphor: The Language of the Short Story and Alice Munro's 'Meneseteung'." *Critical Insights: Alice Munro.* Ed. Charles E. May. Ipswich, MA: Salem-EBSCO, 2013. 175-94.

Swift, Jonathan. "The Lady's Dressing Room." <https://www.poetryfoundation.org/poems/50579/the-ladys-dressing-room>.

Thacker, Robert. *Alice Munro: Writing Her Lives: A Biography.* Toronto: McClelland & Stewart, 2005. Updated ed. Toronto: Emblem-McClelland & Stewart, 2011.

Virgil. *The Aeneid of Virgil.* Trans. C. Day-Lewis. 1952. New York: Doubleday Anchor, 1953.

Williams, Tennessee. *A Streetcar Named Desire.* 1947. Introd. Arthur Miller. New York: New Directions, 2004.

Woolf, Virginia. *To the Lighthouse.* 1927. Ed. Stella McNichol. Introd. Hermione Lee. London: Penguin, 2019. Penguin Classics.

Scottish Roots: Alice Munro's "Hold Me Fast, Don't Let Me Pass"

Ailsa Cox

In Alice Munro's collection *Friend of My Youth* (1990), the guise of the amateur historian is adopted by the narrators of both the opening title story and the third story, "Meneseteung." The story "Friend of My Youth" concludes with the factual background concerning the Cameronians, the sect that the narrator has heard about through her mother's anecdotes. No sources are mentioned, but even though the facts may be selective, the tone is informative. "Meneseteung" begins with the sources – Almeda's poetry collection, including her preface and a photograph; and the newspaper archives that will conclude Almeda's story with an obituary. The evidence is coolly evaluated by a narrator who is more covert than her counterpart in the title story, and about whose identity even less is established.

The similarity between the historian's guesswork and fictive reconstruction is explored further in "Hold Me Fast, Don't Let Me Pass," the story of a Canadian widow visiting her husband's wartime haunts in Scotland. This story is told in free indirect discourse throughout, enabling its protagonist, Hazel, to be more fully fleshed as a character than either of the narrators in "Friend of My Youth" or "Meneseteung." Like them, she undertakes a little historical detective work in search of a past that becomes increasingly elusive.

Many Canadians in Southwestern Ontario, including Munro herself, are of Scots Presbyterian heritage. Her later collection, *The View from Castle Rock* (2006), explores that heritage, including the figure of James Hogg, author of *The Private Memoirs and Confessions of a Justified Sinner*

(1824), to whom she is related through his mother, Margaret Laidlaw, who provided many of the border ballads collected by Sir Walter Scott.

Scott's name appears amongst Hazel's notes at the opening of "Hold Me Fast, Don't Let Me Pass": "*Courthouse where Sir Walter Scott dispensed judgment, 1799-1832*" (74; emphasis in orig.). The historical information is mixed with brief impressions, as if in preparation for a travelogue: "*One gravestone sunk deep, crooked, name, date, etc., all gone, just skull and crossbones. Girls with pink hair going by, smoking*" (74; emphasis in orig.). Hazel edits these notes for style, replacing "judgment" with "justice" and removing "lilac" from the colours of the landscape.

The title of this story is taken from the climactic verse of "Tam Lin," one of the best-known ballads in Scott's *Minstrelsy of the Scottish Border: Historical and Romantic Ballads* (1802). Héliane Ventura regards the story of Flora and Ellie in "Friend of My Youth" as a reworking of another traditional ballad, "The Cruel Sister," the tragic tale of rivalry between two sisters in love with the same man. In "Hold Me Fast, Don't Let Me Pass," the ballad is recited by Miss Dobie, the elderly relative who was visited by Hazel's husband during the war. Ventura says she "bears a striking resemblance to Margaret Laidlaw" (163), perhaps on account of what can only be called her performance of the ballad, "with every inflection, every gesture, rehearsed and ordained" as Munro writes (95). Extreme old age is conveyed by Miss Dobie's "heavy, warty, dark old face" (92); she sits "in a high-backed chair, against the light of the windows" (91) like a sibyl.

Hazel has come to see Miss Dobie in the hope of discovering more about her husband Jack's time in Scotland during the war. But like a true sibyl Miss Dobie is unable to answer a straight question. She speaks largely in non-sequiturs, without inhibition, sometimes giving the impression of being mentally confused. Hazel is in the company of Jack's wartime sweetheart, Antoinette, the owner of the hotel where Hazel is staying and now the lover of Dudley Brown, a local solicitor. It is in fact Dudley who has arranged this meeting, but he has apparently dropped out – or was left out – at the last minute. Initially Miss Dobie identifies Antoinette as the Canadian visitor she has heard about, later admitting "'I know who you are now[...]. You're the woman from the Royal Hotel. Did you and Dudley Brown ever get married?'" (92).

W.R. Martin and Warren U. Ober give a detailed account of how Munro inverts the "Tam Lin" story, which is the key to the revelations in the plot. Like "Friend of My Youth," this is a story that switches focus partway through. Hazel's quest to discover more about her husband's past is frustrated by those who might have known him. Antoinette claims to be even younger than the sixteen-year-old courted by Jack; she says she was born in 1940. A new and different story displaces Jack's anecdotes, the love triangle amongst Antoinette, Dudley, and Judy, who has been Miss Dobie's carer after falling pregnant. "Tam Lin" tells the story of a Jennet who conceives a child with a handsome knight who has been abducted by the Queen of the Fairies. To claim the knight for herself, she must seize him from his steed as the fairies troop by on horseback, keeping a tight hold no matter what terrifying shapes he changes into.

When Hazel describes the visit to Dudley, she mentions the poem, tentatively remembering some of the lines about Tam Lin's instructions to his rescuer. Dudley supplies the rest, with a passion and a warmth that was missing in Miss Dobie's incantation: "'But hold me fast, don't let me pass,' Dudley cried, very pleased. 'I'll be your bairn's father!'" (100). Dudley's performance is a moment of complicity between the two of them, and of emotional abandonment; the recitation allows Dudley "to parade [his] longing without fear of making a fool of [himself]" (101). The declaration, "'I'll be your bairn's father!'" draws attention to Judy's illegitimate daughter, who by implication is Dudley's child. But Dudley's attempt to reconnect with Judy, on the pretext of taking Hazel to visit Miss Dobie, has been thwarted. Unlike Tam Lin, he is not rescued by the maiden he has made pregnant. As Martin and Ober explain, "Dudley's dilemma is similar to Tam Lin's, but inside out: he is living in the humdrum world, entangled with a mundane paramour from whom he can't escape" (46).

Miss Dobie's realm is filled with references to folklore. Judy's long red hair and sparkling dress might belong to a fairy. Martin and Ober point out both the ironic significance of her surname, Armstrong, in the context of her failure to hold on to Dudley/Tam Lin and the resemblance between her child's name, Tania, and Titania, "a queen of the fairies" (Martin and Ober 45), as we recall from Shakespeare's *A Midsummer Night's Dream*. Antoinette becomes unwell after the visit; Dudley jokingly suggests the cake they were given might have been poisoned, "'The way it often is, in the stories'" (100). Munro's story is more complex than a re-appropriation of an ancient ballad, but the incorporation of such recognizable symbols invites the reader to search for more, for instance through the motorbike Jack borrowed from Margaret Dobie, which plays such an important role in his memories. It may be something of a stretch to identify this motorbike with Tam Lin's "*milk-white steed*" (96), but a man on a motorbike can appear as romantic as a medieval knight; see, for instance, Munro's story "Differently," also in *Friend of My Youth*, where Georgia admires Miles's "valiant profile" (231) as he is parking his bike. When Miss Dobie fails to remember Jack, Hazel tries to revive memories of him using the motorbike, but Miss Dobie does not respond to these promptings. Hazel reads the signs astutely, when it comes to working out the Dudley/Antoinette/Judy triangle, but it seems never to occur to her that Jack's relationship with the middle-aged Miss Dobie might have been anything other than platonic, or that there might be other reasons than senility for Miss Dobie not to recognize his name. Jack was fifteen years older than Hazel; and most young people struggle to imagine the sex lives of anyone outside their own age range.

Throughout the story, characters and places are misidentified or displaced. At their first meeting, Hazel mistakes Dudley for the barman, just as he assumes by her accent that she is American. He tells her that he lives in the hotel, yet Antoinette is at pains to explain that he lives with his invalid mother, despite the fact that she has two nurses, one for day and one for night (a clear danger signal, if these nurses are anything like the other home nurses in Munro). Antoinette's pointed assertion that "'He has his own home. He has a lovely home. He shares it with his mother'" (83) is echoed by Miss Dobie's later insistence that "'I lived at home with Mother and Father and then I lived with Mother and then I lived alone'" (93). Both Antoinette and Miss Dobie are sticking to the public version of domestic circumstances, concealing any private modifications that might be in place. Antoinette also apparently misidentifies a dreary and waterlogged field as the site of Carterhaugh, where "'the girl goes out and loses her maidenhead, and so on'" (98) – a mistake corrected later by Dudley. The true Carterhaugh is a more fittingly magical location high above the river. Antoinette's distaste for this place and its sexual connotations contrasts with Dudley's enthusiasm for the ballad.

These multiple confusions, duplications, and distractions disguise whatever may be really going on in the characters' lives. Dudley himself is a kind of trickster, a bachelor type, who, Hazel sees at once, would be "the kind who sits at the back of the class, smart and indolent, making remarks you can't quite be sure of" (79). The comparison is hardly flattering, yet she comes to enjoy the flirtation more than this private put-down might suggest. When Dudley talks about taking her to the true Carterhaugh "'If the moon were out'" (102), she feels a thrill of sexual excitement: "But the moon was not going to be out – that was the other thing his tone made clear" (102).

The final pages of the story explore the consolations offered by mundanity, as Hazel weighs up his situation and her own. Dudley's imprisonment in what Martin and Ober disparagingly refer to as "the humdrum world" (46) is hardly against his will. Much of the information in the tête-à-tête between Hazel and Dudley is conveyed by subtext and implication; the mutual decision not to have the affair that has never been explicitly on offer in the first place is one that is made by unspoken agreement. There is a strong contrast between the outspokenness and the strongly vocalized desires of minstrelsy and the silent accommodations of the real world. Hazel sees that, for Dudley, a quiet life with Antoinette could have its consolations, "And she didn't even ask for a man's whole heart. She might shut her eyes to a secret visit once in a while" (103). Judy, on the other hand, will "be bursting with ballad fervor, all vows and imprecations" (103).

Dudley's self-serving protestation, "'I can't make two women happy'" (103), reminds Hazel of something Jack once said: "*I could make you very happy*" (103; emphasis in orig.). He was being euphemistic about the female orgasm, but the younger Hazel failed to recognize the allusion, believing his promise to be "rash and sweeping[...], dazzling but presumptuous" (103), something that belongs, perhaps, with the unattainable fantasies conjured by "Tam Lin." The ballad's co-existing realms are summoned once again at the time she recalls seeing Jack (a fairy-tale name, if ever there was one) when he is unaware of being watched as he stands behind the window of his store, with a "stillness about him, a look you could have called ghostly" (104).

The story's penultimate line, "Meanwhile, what makes a man happy?" (105) reverses the less-than-adequate endeavours of the two male figures to make their woman happy. This, in its turn, recalls the unanswerable question, attributed to Freud: "How do you make a woman happy?" (Jones 421). Here it is men, not women, who are cast as the unfathomable other. The fight for mastery over an enchanted knight stands for the unreadability of the masculine subject. In day-to-day life Jack is unassuming, a man of modest habits, who only becomes animated on the subject of wartime combat. His tales of his experiences as a bomber pilot have worn thin, so far as Hazel is concerned. Yet those experiences were not only the crowning achievement of his life, but also transported him high above the ground to a mysterious place that, like the fairy realm at Carterhaugh, defies explanation.

The idea of passing, or of stopping passage, referred to in the quotation that provides the story's title, returns in the closing passages, ostensibly in relation to Dudley's situation, but also evoking the memory of Hazel's late husband: there is "A hard limit that you might someday get past in a man, a knot in his mind you might undo, a stillness in him you might jolt, or an absence you might make him regret – that sort of thing will make you pay attention, even when you think you've taught yourself not to" (105). Here again, the modal verb "might," also used effectively in "Friend of My Youth," establishes possibilities that are fragile and provisional.

Scottish balladry, folklore, and oral history all contribute to a fictional world that is simultaneously mundane and deeply mysterious. "Hazel" itself, a common enough name for a girl born in Munro's generation, is also the name of the druidic tree that furnishes magicians with their magic wands.

Works Cited

Hogg, James. *The Private Memoirs and Confessions of a Justified Sinner.* 1824. Introd. Ian Rankin. Edinburgh: Canongate, 2008.

Jones, Ernest. *The Life and Work of Sigmund Freud: Volume 2: Years of Maturity 1901-1919.* New York: Basic Books, 1955.

Martin, W.R., and Warren U. Ober. "Alice Munro's 'Hold Me Fast, Don't Let Me Pass' and 'Tam Lin'." *ANQ: A Quarterly Journal of Short Articles, Notes, and Reviews* 13.3 (2000): 44-48.

Munro, Alice. "Differently." *Friend of My Youth.* Toronto: McClelland & Stewart, 1990. 216-43.

---. "Friend of My Youth." *Friend of My Youth.* Toronto: McClelland & Stewart, 1990. 3-26.

---. "Hold Me Fast, Don't Let Me Pass." *Friend of My Youth.* Toronto: McClelland & Stewart, 1990. 74-105.

---. "Meneseteung." *The New Yorker* 11 Jan. 1988: 28-38. Rpt. (rev.) in *Friend of My Youth.* Toronto: McClelland & Stewart, 1990. 50-73.

---. *The View from Castle Rock.* Toronto: McClelland & Stewart, 2006.

Scott, Sir Walter. *Minstrelsy of the Scottish Border: Historical and Romantic Ballads.* 1802. Ed. Thomas Henderson. London: George G. Harrap, 1931.

Shakespeare, William. *A Midsummer Night's Dream.* Ed. Sukanta Chaudhuri. *The Arden Shakespeare: Third Series: Complete Works.* Ed. Richard Proudfoot, Ann Thompson, David Scott Kastan, and H.R. Woudhuysen. London: The Arden Shakespeare, 2021. 1007-30.

Ventura, Héliane. "The Female Bard: Retrieving Greek Myths, Celtic Ballads, Norse Sagas, and Popular Songs." *The Cambridge Companion to Alice Munro.* Ed. David Staines. Cambridge, Eng.: Cambridge UP, 2016. 154-77.

Alice Munro's "A Wilderness Station": Arachne in the Attic, Stitching Tales That Do Not Quite Add Up

Corinne Bigot

"A Wilderness Station" is a complex story that has fascinated such scholars as Ildikó de Papp Carrington, Isla Duncan, Christopher E. Gittings, and Adrian Hunter. It was also adapted into a feature film entitled *Edge of Madness* (2002) by the Canadian filmmaker Anne Wheeler. In my reading, "A Wilderness Station" is also essentially concerned with the process of interpreting and writing stories.

In a 1994 interview with Gittings, Munro explains how she came up with "A Wilderness Station": "it takes off from my ancestors coming up to Huron County, except that I have completely invented a dreadful macabre incident that takes place, and I have no justification for this at all" (Munro in Gittings, "The Scottish Ancestor" 87). Munro thus adapted a family account of pioneer life in Morris Township in the 1850s, including a brief account of the death of James Laidlaw, which Robert Laidlaw wrote in 1907. While Munro claims that she had "no justification ... at all" for her invention, I would argue that she saw the literary potential of an account that was written fifty years after the event but could not be challenged because the other witness was dead, and also identified and exploited silences in Laidlaw's narrative of pioneer life that mostly ignores women. Her choices exemplify the process of adaptation, that is to say the creative "appropriating" of a source, which is transformed, in order to "mak[e] the adapted material one's own" (Hutcheon 20). While "A Wilderness Station" incorporates some of the details from Robert Laidlaw's actual text (Sheila Munro 126) the various changes Munro introduced allowed her to turn the family narrative into a typical Munro mystery story – possibly a murder mystery. In a 1994 interview with Val Ross, Munro said that "I couldn't make it into a story until I brought a woman into it" (C1), but it would be more accurate to say that she replaced the four Laidlaw men (three brothers and a cousin) with two brothers, Simon and George Herron, and the four Laidlaw women (James Laidlaw's wife, mother, and sister and Robert's wife) with one woman, Simon's wife, Annie. This pared-down cast of characters allowed Munro to introduce a familiar triangle in world literature – two brothers and one woman – and a familiar motif: the death of the woman's husband.

Munro revisits Robert Laidlaw's male-centred account (he details the men's hard lives, and rarely mentions the women except as cooks) to create a narrative that "centers, predominantly, on the female experience of a hard, punishing pioneer life" (Duncan 62). Munro later included Robert Laidlaw's original account in "The Wilds of Morris Township," collected in *The View from Castle Rock* (2006), which allows us to see that women are not exactly absent in Laidlaw's narrative, but that they are only defined in relation to a male Laidlaw – as a wife, cousin, sister, aunt, or mother – and that Laidlaw does not name them. Munro highlighted and used Laidlaw's silence about the women, including his own wife; for instance, there is a curiously reticent mention of his wife that I believe must have struck Munro: In "the spring of 1857, [...] I *got* a wife to share my hardships, joys and sorrows" (Munro, "The Wilds" 116; emphasis added). In "A Wilderness Station" Munro explores the idea of "getting a wife" and the violence that the process implies. Munro modelled George Herron's fictional account on Laidlaw's, and she used and repeated the same verb in such a way as to turn Annie into an object. In his account George explains that although his brother could have "*got* a wife on his own" (194, emphasis added) Simon asked the Matron of an orphanage for help, and after he received word that "there was a girl that might fit the bill" (195), he "went off to Toronto and *got* her" (195; emphasis added).

As pointed out by Adrian Hunter, Munro opened "lines of enquiry into the past – mostly the eccentric, liminal, *unwritten* pasts of women's lives" (Hunter 118; emphasis added). In order to do so, she started with an accumulation of written texts that appear to bear the stamp of authority. Annie's character is depicted by the Matron of the orphanage, and then discussed, if not dissected, by the Reverend McBain in Carstairs and by the Clerk of the Peace and a doctor in Walley. McBain claims authority on Annie: "I think it my duty to tell you who and what she is and her history here since I have known her" (197). The Clerk of the Peace, James Mullen, soon refers to "*our* young woman's health" (204; emphasis added), and Annie becomes a "case" when Mullen tells McBain about the doctor's diagnosis: "You may be interested in hearing what the doctor who visited her had to say about her case" (205). The letters these men write clearly reveal a narrow-minded and prejudiced male point of view on women, which Munro exposes: "His belief is that she is subject to a sort of delusion peculiar to females, for which the motive is a desire for self-importance, also a wish to escape the monotony of life" (205). While Annie's story and confessions are dismissed, George's account of their lives and of Simon's accidental death, as well as his version of Annie's reaction, are reported by McBain, and validated as true.

The profusion of texts by these male authorities is contrasted to and opposed by Annie's verbal confessions of murder that no one believes and a letter she writes to a friend, which cannot reach the addressee. Munro plays with the epistolary genre, which always allows for various accounts of the same event to be given by different characters, by adding Annie's letter to the first pile of letters. Annie's final letter reveals that *she* chose to have men such as Mullen and the doctor assume that she is mad: "If they think I am crazy and I know the difference I am safe" (215). Annie thus implies that she knew that these men would assume that she was mad not a murderer and would keep her in jail, so that consequently she would not be hanged. Similarly her letter reveals her fears that George was turning into his brother after he killed him – "he looked at me for the first time in a bad way [...] the same bad way his brother used to look" (213), which contradicts George's description of their relationship (he only refers to her as his brother's wife) and provides an explanation for her flight. Given the fact that McBain reports George's explanations without questioning them, Annie's confession – she tells Mullen she killed her husband – could be motivated by her understanding that she would not be believed if she accused George. Annie kept silent about the physical and sexual abuse she endured, and her version of their relationship and Simon's death is confined to a secret letter.

"A Wilderness Station" is composed of written texts that do not "add up" (225), to quote one of the characters. There are many differences between Annie's letter and George's account. The layers of texts remind me of the heavy snow that covers the ground, covers facts, secrets, and lies. In both accounts of Simon's death – Annie's and George's, which is published in a local paper some fifty years after the event – there is a strong emphasis on snow. Munro's inspiration seems to have come from Robert Laidlaw's account which mentions a snowstorm in 1852, during which the Laidlaws almost got lost (Munro, "The Wilds" 115). However, Munro conflated two different dates, which indicates that snow was important to her: the Laidlaws almost got lost in a snowstorm in April 1852, as "the east wind caused the snow to cover up the blaze marks on the trees" (Munro, "The Wilds" 115), while James Laidlaw died a year later in 1853 when there was no blizzard and "the snow was very deep and soft" (Munro, "The Wilds" 116). At first sight snow seems to be part of the realistic background depicting pioneer life and the Herrons' trials. Snow hampers the Herron brothers' work as they clear their land, and almost prevents George from finding his way back when his footsteps disappeared under the layers of snow. Yet snow is instrumental to the narrative in that it is endowed with the power to conceal *and* to reveal monstrous secrets. As George brings his brother's body home, snow hides the body (196), and transforms it into a log (208). Annie claims that she used snow to destroy evidence: in her initial (oral) account of her husband's death, in which she said she killed Simon with a large rock, she said that she washed the blood off the rock with snow (201). However, if we believe her letter, snow is instrumental in revealing the way Simon died. As the snow that covered his body thawed and melted with blood, Annie, assisted by George, turned the body over to clean the liquid mess and discovered the gash left by George's axe (209). This, Annie claims, led George to confess he killed his brother.

Depending on whose account one believes, the snowstorm which prevented Annie and George from getting help either forced them or allowed them to bury Simon on their own, without any witnesses. The details both George and Annie provide demonstrate that snow was instrumental in making Simon's body disappear. George, who writes that he could dig the grave because "The ground was not frozen under the snow" (196), explains that he later put "a wooden marker" (196) for Simon's grave, adding that in the end he never moved Simon's body to the local cemetery although he erected a "stone" (196) for Simon there. The fact that the grave and the body are not found and the remains never examined is of crucial importance to the story, as it prevents the truth from being firmly established, forcing the readers to compare the conflicting versions to decide. In her letter, Annie provides a different version, insisting that she and George purposely erased all traces of the grave after they buried Simon: "George beat [the snow] down flat with the shovel as much as he could. Then we moved all the wood back searching where it was in the snow and we piled it up in the right way so it did not look as if anybody had been at it" (210).

Annie's letter contradicts George's account and accuses George, but its most interesting aspect is its elliptical quality, leaving room for (mis)interpretation and doubt. Annie describes what happened after George confessed to having killed Simon: she got him to lie down on the marital bed, partially undressed him, and then lay on the bed next to him having taken off her clothes. Sexual energy or tension surfaces via textual blanks:

> When I got him to sleep I laid down on the bed beside him. I took off my smock and I could see the black and blue marks on my arms. I pulled up my skirt to see if they were still there high on my legs, and they were. The back of my hand was dark too and sore still where I had bit it.
>
> Nothing bad happened after I laid down and I did not sleep all night but listened to him breathing and kept touching him to see if he was warmed up. (213)

Annie's letter does contain blanks that trigger readers' involvement, as the paratactic style forces them to puzzle out the connections between the elements and to imagine scenarios in which Annie would get these bruises and bite her hand. Carrington thinks that while the bite mark indicates that Annie used to muffle the sounds of sexual intercourse so that George would not hear them, it does not mean that she was raped (Carrington, "Double-Talking Devils" 84). Drawing attention to references to heat in the passage, to the fact that Annie undressed George after *she* carried *him* to the marital bed, and to her touching him, Carrington argues that Annie induced sex with George (Carrington, "Double-Talking Devils" 84). By contrast, Duncan argues that the bruises are evidence of Simon's habitual rough treatment in the marital bed (Duncan 69-70). I personally find the elliptical phrase "Nothing bad happened after I laid down" (213) magnificently ambiguous since it may mean that Annie expected something bad to happen, implying that she was used to enduring painful sex with Simon, as argued by Duncan. It may mean that Annie and George did not have sex, which their Presbyterian upbringing would have characterized as 'bad', or, on the contrary, it may indicate that something good – pleasurable sex with George – happened, which would support Carrington's vision of Annie.

Munro added yet another account to the pile of texts that document Annie's life. The final section is another written account, a letter which details James Mullen's granddaughter's memories of "Old Annie" and describes a visit she and Annie paid to the Herrons in 1907, fifty years after Simon's death and Annie's flight. Interestingly, Christena Mullen's letter itself was written fifty years after the visit. Although Christena Mullen cannot provide any explanation as to why Annie asked to go to Carstairs in 1907, the emphasis on dates allows us to see that Annie's request coincides with the publication of George's account, which is mentioned by his grandson, as Christena remembers it (221), prompting us to assume that Annie intended to set the record straight with George. The drive to Carstairs, with Annie sitting proudly in Christena's brand new car in a magnificent dress, reverses Annie's initial and horrendous journey on foot. Annie, who is sitting "up straight in the front seat as if the show were already on the road" (219), urges Christena to sound the horn, showing that she is no longer afraid to make a noise.

Yet Annie remains strangely reticent. For instance when they are about to arrive, she points at a "mound" (Christena's word) (220). I find the word "mound" particularly significant in its ambiguity. Annie might be pointing at the remains of the Herrons' shanty – yet she does not say anything about her life there – or she might be pointing at something even more personal and meaningful to her. A "mound" can also refer to a rise in the ground's surface indicating an ancient burial site, so Munro also suggests that Annie could be pointing at Simon's grave. It is up to Christena to interpret her silent message. Amusingly but not surprisingly, given the emphasis on mistakes in the collection, Christena first believes that Annie is pointing at a herd of cows, and does not show much interest.

Annie's somewhat "gloating" tone when they return is noted and interpreted by Christena, who assumes that it "probably referred to her dress and the vehicle" (225), which draws attention to the process of interpreting and its uncertainties. The ending preserves these uncertainties since Christena left Annie and George alone and did not hear her story and Annie did not tell her anything. Even when Annie speaks, she never tells much, so that her story always remains partly untold. As argued by Adrian Hunter, Munro does not speak for Annie (Hunter 118) and the question of whether there is a text or a voice that readers can trust is central. Annie's voice and words are recalled by other characters, including Christena. What she recalls is that her mother used to tell her not to believe a word "Old Annie" said and that Annie provided her with several versions of her life and marriage. In one version Annie said that "a man had come to the Home and had all the girls paraded in front of him and said, 'I'll take the one with the coal-black hair'" (217). Annie's phrasing actually exposes the dehumanizing process through which Simon "got a wife" (Munro, "The Wilds" 116) with the help of the Matron, and her words reflect her comprehension of what took place at the orphanage.

Yet the story departs from what actually happened to Annie: "she refused to go with him, even though he was rich and came in a carriage. Rather like Cinderella but with a different ending" (217). The wording here allows for different readings. It is unclear who said or thought "Rather like Cinderella but with a different ending." If the thought is Christena's, she alludes to a more general fate of Annie's – her ending in prison. But if we understand the words to be Annie's, her mentioning "a different ending" could also be a way for her to say that life with Simon was nothing like a fairy tale, being a life of constant hardship and probably domestic violence. Christena also recalls that Annie then "said a bear killed her husband, in the woods, and my grandfather had killed the bear, and wrapped her in its skin and taken her home from the Gaol" (217-18). Annie seems to resort to a fable to tell her story – it is easy to assume that George is the bear and that Mullen rescued her from George by admitting her to the county jail. The fable introduces yet more ambiguity and uncertainty as it seems to paint Mullen as a saviour, which makes the jail a safe haven rather than a prison.

This picture is somewhat mitigated by a mistake Annie used to make and which Christena recalls: "Sometimes Old Annie called the Gaol the Home" (217). I find Annie's supposed mistake quite telling: first she clearly equates the orphanage ("the Home") with jail, but she may also hint at a life of uninterrupted entrapment, from the orphanage to the Herron home to the Walley jail. Thus when she told Chistena "that a girl in the next bed screamed and screamed, and that was why she – Annie – ran away and lived in the woods" (217), it is unclear whether Annie meant the jail (a woman's screams were mentioned by Mullen) or the orphanage or, perhaps, the Herrons' shanty since she did run away and stayed in the woods after Simon's death. Finally, the impression of imprisonment expands, perhaps, to the Mullen home too. In Christena's memories, Annie had turned the third floor into her domain, a marginal space that could have been a safe haven or a prison. So it is no coincidence that the Mullens' house subsequently became "a Home for Young Offenders" (216).

Ultimately, Christena evokes yet another picture of Annie that one of Christena's sisters, Dolly, says that she saw "whenever she dreamed of home" (216), namely, "Old Annie up at the top of the third-floor stairs brandishing her measuring stick and wearing a black dress with long fuzzy black arms like a spider" (217). The picture itself conjures up the image of a widow in black too – calling to mind the spider called the black widow, which is supposed to kill the male when it mates. Christena's sister's dreams then make Annie seem a more dangerous woman. Another image, however, may also be suggested since Annie was a seamstress: depicting Annie as a spider evokes the myth of Arachne, the weaver that Athena turned into a spider because she had depicted some of the Gods' most outrageous actions, that is to say, had told a version that contradicted Athena's. We may recall that Annie's version of the Herrons' life that revealed domestic and sexual violence was very different from George's published account. Annie's tales also told a very different story about the orphanage as she told Christena a story about a girl who had a baby out of a boil, "the size of a rat" (225), that had to be put in the oven to make it come alive. Although her stories are dismissed as fibs (217) or dreams (225), they clearly bear a relation to what happened to her, and could be interpreted as indirect truths. The readers who choose to believe Annie's letter must acknowledge that telling lies and tales, as Annie did, is better than telling the truth: Annie's lies, the confession that Mullen refused to believe, saved her from George and from being hanged. It is only through telling fibs and stories or hiding a letter that may never be read that Annie can (partly) reveal her life story. Munro gives Annie the final word, albeit in an indirect way, since her words are reported by Christena Mullen. Annie's last words recall the dreams she mentioned in her letter, a response that does not dispel the ambiguity: "'I did used to have the terriblest dreams'" (225).

Works Consulted

Carrington, Ildikó de Papp. "Double-Talking Devils: Alice Munro's 'A Wilderness Station'." *Essays on Canadian Writing* 58 (1996): 71-92.

---. "Talking Dirty: Alice Munro's 'Open Secrets' and John Steinbeck's *Of Mice and Men*." *Studies in Short Fiction* 31 (1994): 595-606.

Duncan, Isla. *Alice Munro's Narrative Art.* New York: Palgrave Macmillan, 2011.

Gittings, Christopher E. "Constructing a Scots-Canadian Ground: Family History and Cultural Translation in Alice Munro." *Studies in Short Fiction* 34 (1997): 27-37.

---. "The Scottish Ancestor: A Conversation with Alice Munro." *Scotlands* 2 (1994): 83-96.

Hunter, Adrian. "Taking Possession: Alice Munro's 'A Wilderness Station' and James Hogg's *Justified Sinner*." *Studies in Canadian Literature* 35.2 (2010): 114-28.

Hutcheon, Linda. *A Theory of Adaptation.* New York: Routledge, 2006.

Munro, Alice. "A Wilderness Station." *Open Secrets.* Toronto: McClelland & Stewart, 1994. 190-225.

---. "The Wilds of Morris Township." *The View from Castle Rock.* Toronto: McClelland & Stewart, 2006. 111-26.

Munro, Sheila. *Lives of Mothers & Daughters: Growing Up with Alice Munro.* Toronto: McClelland & Stewart, 2001.

Ross, Val. "A Writer Called Alice." *The Globe and Mail* 1 Oct. 1994: C1, C21.

Wheeler, Anne, dir. *Edge of Madness.* Montreal, QC: CinéGroupe / Credo Entertainment / Gregorian Films, 2002.

Alice Munro's "Save the Reaper": Making "Its Live Noise after Dark"

Catherine Sheldrick Ross

The story "Save the Reaper" from Alice Munro's collection *The Love of a Good Woman* (1998) is dark and terrifying, said ConstantReader book club members. As happens in a successful horror story, you get lulled by everyday details and then you get whapped. A car carrying a grandmother, Eve, and her two young grandchildren, seven-year-old Philip and Daisy who is barely three, takes an off-road turn down a lane toward a creepy farmhouse, which they enter. And just when you think the worst is over, a new threat suddenly pops up that could be much, much worse. In fact, very little actual violence occurs – it's left to the reader to imagine what *might* happen to Eve and the grandchildren. "Save the Reaper" draws on familiarity with the horror genre, in which viewers / readers realize, "Oh, oh. This is going to be bad," and silently warn the clueless characters, "Don't do it." As we read Section 8 of "Save the Reaper" – in length almost half the story – we think, "Don't go down that lane / don't get out of the car / don't go into that scary farmhouse / don't get trapped inside that infernally hot inner room / get away home." What starts off as a family outing to return a movie turns into a perilous journey to the underworld. This journey involves an impulsive turn-in-the-road, entrapment in a stiflingly hot room in a Gothic farmhouse peopled with drunken, violent, menacing figures, an encounter with an alien, and a return home in time for dinner. Munro readers have seen a version of this perilous journey before in "Images" in *Dance of the Happy Shades* (1968) in which the narrator recalls being taken along as a young child by her father on a trip through the bush to check traplines. The narrator describes a terrifying encounter in which she meets a man with "a little axe, or hatchet" ("Images" 37), is taken into his underground house with its disorder, dirt, and "terrible smell" ("Images" 40), and then returns home "dazed and powerful with secrets ... [and] never said a word" ("Images" 43). The version of the perilous journey in "Save the Reaper" is much scarier for the reader because the subject of focalization is the grandmother, Eve, who is frightened on her own behalf but even more keenly for the young, threatened grandchildren, Philip and Daisy, in her care.

This building sense of menace developed in the perilous journey sequence shapes how readers experience a story that is simultaneously about a great many other things. "Save the Reaper" is about entrapments of various kinds, including multi-generational attempts to escape the culture of the family-of-origin by creating psychological and physical distance. It is a story about transformation that happens at all levels from individual shape-changing to upheavals in social norms to changes in the built environment of farms, villages, and highways. Like so many of Munro's narratives, this one is also, at its heart, about the painful relationship of mothers and daughters, in this case presented from the perspective of the mother, Eve, longing for her absent daughter, Sophie. "Save the Reaper" is about saving something precious – recovering a connection to a lost daughter, saving grandchildren from harm, and also preserving memories for the future. On the story's last page, the central character Eve looks at her seven-year-old grandson, Philip, and thinks that "he had begun the private work of storing and secreting, deciding on his own what should be preserved and how, and what these things were going to mean to him, in his unknown future" (180). And finally, and perhaps unexpectedly, this story is about the world of art and its relation to everyday life.

Quotidian events in this story are undergirded by the mythic pattern of the descent to the underworld and return. In her article "Where Are You, Mother?: Alice Munro's 'Save the Reaper'" Ildikó de Papp Carrington demonstrates how this story uses, expands, and subverts the underlying Greek myth of Demeter and Persephone. Persephone is the daughter of Demeter, the fertility goddess of corn, grain, and agriculture. While picking flowers, Persephone was abducted by Hades, the Lord of the Underworld, and annually is held there a prisoner for six months, a period that corresponds to the number of pomegranate seeds that she was tricked by Hades into eating. During this six-month period every year, when Demeter is separated from her lost daughter, the earth goes into deep freeze and vegetation dies. Readers, even those unfamiliar with vegetation myths, will note the repeated references in Munro's story to grain and harvest and the end of the growing season: the rented cottage in the middle of a corn field, the sounds of corn growing, big rolls of hay drying in the field, a field of barley, two dozen cobs of corn bought at a roadside stand, and, most noticeably, the reaper in the title.

Munro's story takes place over a single day, during which Eve's often painful memories of the near and distant past are interwoven into the ongoing story of a car ride. In some brief remarks on the story, Munro said that "When I wrote 'Save the Reaper' in my mind ... were the changes in the lives of people like me, who are now in their sixties," with their "choices mostly made and lived with by now" ("Contributors' Notes" 388). When she was five years old, Eve had been taken along by her mother on outings over these same roads in the car belonging to the woman who ran the village hotel. It was wartime then and Eve's family had come for a holiday in the Lake Huron village on the train – quite possibly on the CNR line that went between Wingham, Lucknow, and Kincardine. This line, which opened in 1887, was shut down in 1988, just one of the kinds of changes that Eve's son-in-law and urban geographer Ian refers to as "the breakup of older patterns of village and rural life" (180). Now sixty years later, with her two grandchildren in the backseat, she is driving along county roads somewhere off Highway 21 near Southampton or Kincardine on Lake Huron. In her review of *The Love of a Good Woman*, novelist A.S. Byatt says: "The story runs, completely naturally and constantly surprisingly, through the grandmother's anxieties on a car journey, backwards and forwards in time, in and out of boredom and disaster. Only another writer, perhaps, could know how difficult that pace was to direct and control." Time markers guide the reader through significant events of the last day of the visit, which is when the drive-gone-wrong occurs: "That morning, when Sophie was leaving to meet Ian at the Toronto airport" (148); "Last night she and Sophie had watched Meryl Streep" (149) in the movie *The Bridges of Madison County*; "'We have to get that movie back to the store.... Maybe we should do it before we go to the beach'" (157); "Eve had come home from the village the day before, laden with provisions" (157); "Plans had changed – they weren't leaving till morning" (178); "If the girl came looking for her, they would all still be here" (180).

In the story's opening paragraph, Eve has initiated a car-game to amuse her grandchildren, Philip and Daisy: "The game they played was almost the same one that Eve had played with Sophie, on long dull car trips when Sophie was a little girl. Then it was spies – now it was aliens" (146). In this game, newly-arrived space aliens are being taken to a secret headquarters. The trick is to follow the car containing the aliens and be able to spot the switch when, as described by Philip, the aliens "'go *schlup* through the air into another body in another car'" (147). The aliens "got their directions from the signals offered by plausible-looking people in other cars or from somebody standing by a mailbox ... or women pushing baby carriages or even the babies riding in the carriages" (146). Philip is in charge of interpreting the signals and knowing which car to follow. Because aliens can change shape, anybody could be an alien. Philip directs Eve to switch from following a white Mazda to following an old green pickup truck with a dog in the open back area. The first section ends with Philip's warning, "'The dog's one too'" (148). As in most stories about aliens, the alien represents our deepest fears and anxieties about our own human lives. And Eve, as we shall see, has more than her share of reasons for worry: her still-distant relationship with her daughter Sophie, her well-founded fears for the safety of her grandchildren on the central car ride, and her own bleak future alone when Sophie and family leave.

The patterning of repeated car rides – Eve driving on the back roads near Lake Huron with her mother and then with her grandchildren; Eve playing the spies / aliens game with her daughter Sophie and then with her grandchildren – brings the pressure of three generations of replicated, fraught relationships to bear on the story's central journey. Eve and her mother and Eve and her daughter Sophie have had complicated relationships, as do all mother-daughter pairings in a Munro story. When Eve was quite small, she used to enjoy such country expeditions with her mother but later "She began to hate trailing along with her mother and being identified as her mother's daughter": she was embarrassed by "her mother's habit of dressing up, wearing large hats and gloves in the country" (162). Like Rose and Jocelyn in "Mischief" from Munro's *Who Do You Think You Are?*, Eve plays a game with her friends during "her first years free of home" called "'What did you hate most about your mother?'" (162). Turning away from the traditional values and styles of home, Eve reinvented herself as an actress, choosing the financially precarious but creative life of the artist. In a similar reversal, Sophie has suppressed the impulsive, risk-taker side of herself for the sake of creating a financially secure life for herself and her children. She has turned herself into a supportive faculty wife for Ian and is "not keen on reminiscence" (154) about the life she shared with Eve. Deeply hidden is "the girl Eve used to know, the young Sophie with her plentiful risks and loves and dramas" (157). In a pattern of doubling through the generations, Eve and Sophie each conceived a first child through a fleeting encounter – Eve with a young doctor from Kerala whom she met on a Vancouver-to-Toronto train trip. Sophie once joked "about keeping up the family tradition of flyby fathers" (156), but has since given up jokes and embraced stability and rootedness. Talk of her life before marriage to Ian makes her face acquire "a look of gravity and concealment, of patiently withheld judgments" (154). Throughout Sophie's visit, Eve is walking on eggshells. She unguardedly mentions the parent-run, "ungraded alternative school" (154), Blackbird, that Sophie had gone to for a few years as a child. Sophie is indignant and responds "almost viciously": "'Oh, Blackbird. What a farce. ... I learned Greek myths and I didn't know where Greece was.... I didn't know *what* it was. We had to spend art period making antinuke signs. ... You *paid*'" (154; emphasis in orig.). Any talk of Sophie's childhood "was a positive minefield" (154).

The day of the car ride marks the end of Eve's time with Sophie and her children, the visit having been abruptly cut short. For the long-awaited reunion with her daughter, Eve has rented a cottage in the middle of a cornfield half a mile inland from Lake Huron, picking this general area because her parents had brought her and her brother to this same stretch of shoreline when they were children. Eve told her grandchildren what her father had once told her – "that at night you could hear the corn growing" (149). Near the beginning of section 2, Eve is alone in the cottage with Philip and Daisy, "clearing up the remains of breakfast and disciplining herself" (149). Why does she need self-discipline? Because without it, she would be howling. After five years of separation from her daughter and many reunions postponed, a visit was finally planned – three weeks in the lakeside cottage where Eve would be reunited with her lost daughter and perhaps be able to heal the breach between them. But then, while Eve was out at the village getting provisions for the next week, Ian called to say he has changed his plans. He will collect them the next day to take the family to visit Quebec City. "Twelve days, Eve thought. Twelve days had passed of the three weeks. ... No mention of Eve's going along" (158). An uncomfortable suspicion occurs to Eve: did Sophie call Ian while Eve was getting groceries and say, "'*I can't stand it here ... let's figure out some plan to get me away*'" (160; emphasis in orig.). Some of the ConstantReader book club members interpreted this "'*I can't stand it here*'" dialogue as Philip's report of the actual telephone conversation rather than as a product of Eve's worst fears. However this exchange, in which Eve tries to winkle out of Philip information about who actually made the phone call, is set apart from the rest of the text by both parentheses and italics – the same typographical marking used at the end of the story to indicate an imagined scenario of a home invasion cooked up in Eve's fertile brain: "(*I know where there's a place we can stay, if we can get rid of the old lady.*)" (180; emphasis in orig.).

When first encountered, the title, "Save the Reaper," is puzzling. Who is the reaper? Saved from what? The initial word "Save" will at the outset be read by most readers as an imperative verb. That meaning does not disappear when later the source of the title is revealed as a misquotation from Tennyson's "The Lady of Shalott." As often happens in Munro's stories, readers are lured into misreading a piece of text until some later textual passage prompts them to backtrack and reconsider. Near the end of the story, after Eve and her grandchildren escape from the menacing farmhouse and are driving past a field of barley, Eve begins to recite, """"But the reapers, reaping early, in among the bearded barley–"""" (177). Trying to remember, she recalls the correct text, """"Only reapers, reaping early"""," but then settles on "Save": "'Save' was what sounded best. Save the reapers" (178). Among the ConstantReader book club members, Ann (post #41) asks other readers for help: "What is the significance of the title, 'Save the Reaper.' The only reaper I can think of is the grim reaper, i.e. death." Another reader, Dick (post #46) identifies the source in "The Lady of Shalott" and supplies the verse that begins "Only reapers, reaping early" and continues "by the moon the reaper weary, / Piling sheaves in uplands airy, / Listening, whispers 'Tis the fairy / Lady of Shalott.'" Barbara (post #48) acknowledges that she's "loving these notes" without which she would "never have found the 'Save the Reaper' reference from Tennyson. Now I just have to figure out what she means."

And what *is* meant? Death is certainly part of it, threatened at different levels of experience. There is the danger posed during the perilous journey; the death of the solar year as late August turns from harvest toward shorter days; and, in the final section, Eve's winding down of energy as she imagines herself alone in "this hollowed-out house" (180) in the middle of the corn field. Anxiety about death is first signalled in section 4 by Eve's fear that "strong swimmer" (156) Sophie might keep on swimming out and out farther into the lake, suffering from "not a failure of strength but of the desire to return" (157). The danger of a failure-to-return approaches closer when, in section 8, Eve's car journey with her grandchildren takes them on that fateful turn-off. The farther they follow the green pick-up truck down the rutted lane, the more hostile the scene appears: first "the skeleton" of a collapsing barn; then "pieces of machinery, old cars or trucks," "rusting junk strewed about"; and then the yard of a decaying brick farmhouse with its "windows stuffed with dirty foam rubber" or blocked "with aluminum foil" (164). The green truck, which has parked ahead of her in the gravelled yard, bars the way, so that Eve can't turn her car around to leave. "'Don't get out,' said Philip. 'Stay in the car. Turn around. Drive away'" (165). But Eve says "'I can't'" (165) and allows herself and her grandchildren to be ushered step by step, by the little man with the truck and by his dog, through a succession of anterooms marked by "[m]assive disorder" (167). Seemingly helpless to resist, Eve and her grandchildren progress through two dark rooms with blocked off windows where sensory experience is reduced to the smell of stale beer, a plugged toilet, unremoved garbage, vomit, and semen. In the third room which is about ninety degrees, Eve sees three men playing cards and drinking at a table – the leader Harold, who is entirely naked, a fully-dressed older man with a shaved head, and, with his back to Eve, a young blond man who is wearing only jeans. Also wearing jeans, a fourth man with skin purple or bluish with tattoos, has got up to kick the dog.

The threat of violence against the children in this scene is visceral and real, but has been displaced on the dog Trixie, who is a stand-in for Philip and Daisy, equally young, harmless, and vulnerable. Trixie has been introduced at the outset of the visit as "'okay'," a dog that "'won't hurt you'" and that is still "'not no more than a pup'" (166). In her article "Barking (with)

Dogs: The Grammar System of Transitivity in Munro's 'Save the Reaper' and 'Floating Bridge'," Sabrina Francesconi has analyzed the role of dogs, paying close attention to dogs-as-subjects versus dogs-as-objects. Notably, all the examples of dogs-as-subjects identified by Francesconi occur *outside* the farmhouse: the "barking with a great deal of angry spirit" (165) before being released from the parked truck; "yelping and bounding around them" (167); "wagging her tail, roused ... to bark farewell and chase them partway down the lane" (171). In contrast, once *inside* the farmhouse Trixie is exclusively presented as object in what Francesconi terms "a discourse of physical violence" (Francesconi 79): "'Fuck. Get that dog out of here'"; "The fourth man had got up to kick the dog"; "The little man hauled Trixie out from under the table and threw her into the outer room" (168). A paragraph of odd and unsettling juxtapositions places side by side three major elements in the story – Eve's search for some mosaic pictures remembered from her childhood; purposeless violence causing pain directed against the powerless; and the question of the freedom of choice and the choices that get made: "'Lady here wants to see some pictures,' the little man said. Trixie whined in pain – somebody had kicked her. Eve had no choice but to go on into the room" (168).

Trapped in the inner room of the farmhouse, Eve, the actress, fantasist, and storyteller, is thinking how she would describe her sense of menace and impending disaster: "she'd say it was like finding yourself in the middle of a Pinter play" (169). But finally galvanized into action when the tattooed man turns his dangerous attention toward Philip, Eve succeeds in getting Philip and Daisy out of the farmhouse, into her car, and away down the lane. Then just when it seemed they had escaped, "a figure [rose] up out of the tall weeds" (171) and jumped into the passenger seat. "It was the blond man," wearing jeans, who had been seated inside with the others, "the one whose face she had never seen" (172). An alien, perhaps? But no, it was a girl, crumpled, dingy, drunk, and now also wearing Harold's filthy, vomit-smelling undershirt, who said, "'Jesus I'm glad to get out of there.... I didn't know nothing about what I was getting into. ... It wasn't no place for me'" (172). The girl had escaped out of the bathroom window, not waiting to collect her money – another young abused victim in a volume of stories containing many such vulnerable characters.

In her article, Carrington analyses how Munro uses and transforms the Demeter and Persephone story in "Save the Reaper." She sees the shape-changing escapee from Harold's / Hades' domain as a daughter surrogate for Eve: "the girl ... becomes the abducted Persephone, seeking a Demeter to rescue her from Hades" (45). The young sex-worker with dyed blond spiky hair is "pretty enough, if you disregarded her present dinginess" (173). Without money or any clothes but her jeans and Harold's oversized, smelly undershirt and with an intention to hitchhike south down the highway, this daughter-surrogate is clearly still very much at risk. But is she also a danger to Eve? Especially after the girl looks into the backseat and notices Philip and Daisy, Eve's imagination runs along lines of a car-jacking, "a knife against Eve's side or a child's throat" (175). In her relief when the girl voluntarily gets out of the car at the highway, Eve offers her twenty dollars and tells her where her house is, in case the girl gets "'stranded'" (176).

Eve's compulsion to remember and revisit the past and her affiliation with the world of art was what got her into this pickle. Isla Duncan points to small but significant revisions to the *New Yorker* text made for the book version that suggest that not only "A child of Philip's age" but Eve herself "could get too carried away" (165) (Duncan 83). Some of the ConstantReader book club members were strongly critical of Eve's impulsive decision to follow the truck. One, Ann (post #40), described Eve as "extremely careless" in taking "her grandchildren to a very scary place.... Then, at the end ... [Eve] tells the whacked out girl where she lives even though she is frightened of her. Is this woman self-destructive or what?" Eve is certainly a risk-taker, but I see her as one of the many Munro characters whose lodestone is the world of art – for example, the piano teacher Miss Marsalles in "Dance of the Happy Shades" or the violinist Jill in "My Mother's Dream." When the green pickup truck turned into the lane, Eve told Philip that she could no longer follow it and she was prepared to drive on. But then she noticed the gateposts, which are described in detail: "unusual, being shaped something like crude minarets and decorated with whitewashed pebbles and bits of colored glass" (162). Partly hidden by vegetation, "they had lost all reality as gateposts and looked instead like lost stage props from some gaudy operetta" (162). Eve didn't remember the gateposts, but they reminded her of – and could only have belonged to – a place visited on one of those back-road trips she had taken with her mother. She recalled "a whitewashed outdoor wall" in which were set pictures of "stiff, fantastic, childish scenes" made from "pieces of colored glass set into cement or plaster" (163). Eve's dangerous quest down the laneway to the farmhouse was undertaken so that she could see those scenes again.

The minareted gateposts mark a threshold that takes Eve from her everyday world and puts her in touch with two other levels of existence – the dark underworld of Harold's domain, to be sure, but with the promise of the vision of an upper world of art. The title's echo of "The Lady of Shalott" suggests both: Tennyson's poem about the death of the Lady of Shalott is about the tension between art and life. In the second half of "Save the Reaper," direct references to the world of art, as represented by the glass mosaic pictures, are threaded through the story in five separate places, each time with a slightly different shading and a different emphasis. Patterned repetition with variation is a signal to readers to pay special attention. In their first appearance, the scenes are described as they would have appeared to five-year-old Eve in shapes (squares and triangles), colours (yellow, red, blue), buildings (churches, castles, houses), and the natural world (Christmas trees, tropical-coloured birds, a fat horse, rivers, a moon and stars, sunflowers):

> Churches with spires, castles with towers, square houses with square, lopsided, yellow windows. Triangular Christmas trees and tropical-colored birds half as big as the trees, a fat horse with dinky legs and burning red eyes, curly blue rivers, like lengths of ribbon, a moon and drunken stars and fat sunflowers nodding over the roofs of houses. (163)

The second reference to the wall pictures occurs as part of Eve's disingenuous apology to the little man with the truck about why it might have seemed she was following him – "'I made a mistake. I thought this was somewhere else. ... It was a place where I came once when I was a little girl. There was a wall with pictures on it all made with pieces of broken glass'" (165). The third reference repeats the details of "'when I was a little girl'," "'pictures made of colored glass set in a wall'," and "'I made a mistake'" and reframes these as something Eve tells Philip: "'Philip, I was just telling this man ...'" (166). In the fourth account, Eve has arrived in the hot interior room of the farmhouse and offers an amplified apology to Harold, the ruler of this underworld, in which she elaborates on the entire context of her quest and its significance to her: "There seemed to be nothing to do but go into her spiel, enlarging it to include staying at the village hotel as a little girl, drives with her mother, the pictures in the wall, her memory of them today, the gateposts, her obvious mistake, her apologies" (169).

Later that same day, the fifth and final version was provided during the final dinner, consisting of two dozen cobs of corn plus gin and tonic. "Eve told her story" beginning sixty years in the past "with the checker-board on the beach, the vanished hotel, the drives into the country" and including "her mother's city-lady outfits" and what her mother and the hotel woman saw: among other things, "the marvellous pictures made of colored glass" (178). "'They were a little like Chagall?' Eve said" (178), the question mark here indicating Eve's uncertainty whether urban geographer Ian would be familiar with Chagall. Then comes an account of the day's car ride: "the gateposts, the sudden memory, the dark lane and ruined barn and rusted machinery, the house a shambles" (178). Eve's story ends anticlimactically, told as a good joke at her own expense: the owner, who is playing cards with friends, "'didn't know anything about it'" (179). In this fifth rendering, the mosaic pictures of colored glass have become "marvellous" and "'a little like Chagall?'" (178) and the narrative is framed as an amusing story of mild disappointment and mistaken memory. When Sophie heard it, "She was glowing with relief to see Ian and Eve getting on so well together" (179). But as the narrator observes, this story charms its audience by leaving out "so many things": the game of aliens; "nearly everything about Harold and his companions"; "every single thing about the girl who had jumped into the car" (179) including the way she had "slid her hand along Eve's bare thigh" (173); and especially "what [Eve] was afraid of" (179). And one more thing she wouldn't tell: that when she swung her car around to escape the gravelled yard of the farmhouse, she saw, almost hidden by bushes and junk, a white-washed wall and thought that "she could see pieces of glass embedded there, glinting" (171).

The story ends with Eve imagining disaster: "The girl wouldn't come. Unless ..." (180). And at the same time she is thinking about being left alone and bereft, after the family departs without her the next morning for Quebec City. She thinks of herself "Not tonight but tomorrow night ...

[lying] down in this hollowed-out house ... with nothing in her head but the rustle of the deep tall corn which might have stopped growing now but still made its live noise after dark" (180). This story is one of Munro's darkest, but for me brightened by the counterbalance of the art glinting on the walls.

***

And the art glints there still. Recently a friend and Munro-fan from the United Kingdom asked if I had ever come across a place with minareted gateposts and mosaic pictures in my drives in Souwesto. In fact, I *had* noticed a curious set of gateposts in Bruce County, but had never investigated. This time, however, on an extremely hot day in June, I did stop, parked on the road allowance, and took photographs of what can be seen from the road. There it was: two gateposts made of stone, minarets, a curved wall set with mosaic pictures of triangles and squares of glass, a long laneway lined with old Scotch pines, a two-storey yellow brick farmhouse, and a surrounding cornfield. From the road, the property looked well kept up. Hoping to find someone to ask about the unusual stonework and the pictures, I walked up the laneway. The farther I went, the more I was reminded of details from Munro's story: an outbuilding blocked with rusted machinery and broken-down trucks; a chained-up, medium-sized, husky-type dog that was cringing but still barking a spirited alarm at my approach; the yellow farmhouse looking derelict; and no one emerging to answer my hellos. I could hear the echo of Philip saying, "'Turn around. Drive away'" (165). Which I did, my perception of the place infused by the creepy atmosphere of "Save the Reaper." I didn't wait to ask permission to look at the stone walls and minarets visible beyond the house. But surely this was the place. For the sake of her story, Munro must have taken this farmhouse, which is about forty kilometres north and east of Wingham, and moved it west, closer to Lake Huron.

Then another detail emerged. In her memoir, *Lives of Mothers & Daughters* (2001), Sheila Munro reports that when her mother was in grade thirteen she wrote a story, "the theme of which was art" (Sheila Munro 174). This story, one of the first two that she managed to complete, featured mosaics of coloured glass set in a wall, which, as she told her daughter Sheila, she had seen on a drive with her own mother. Then decades later, when Munro had returned to Ontario after twenty years in British Columbia, the author and her second husband, Gerry Fremlin, "were driving through Bruce County when they accidentally stumbled upon this same farmstead with the mosaic pictures still there in the wall," stopped to look at it, and ended up talking to "a strange man" (Sheila Munro 174) standing there who insisted "against their better judgement" (Sheila Munro 175) that they come into the farmhouse. Inside "was a scene of the most terrible decrepitude" along with "a real sense of danger": "There were men sitting playing cards in a windowless room and they were terribly drunk. One of them was naked" (Sheila Munro 175).

Works Cited

Byatt, A.S. "Their Normal Daily Lives Punctuated by Disaster." Rev. of *The Love of a Good Woman*, by Alice Munro. *Literary Review* Dec. 1998. <https://literaryreview.co.uk/their-normal-daily-lives-punctuated-by-disaster>.

Carrington, Ildikó de Papp. "Where Are You, Mother?: Alice Munro's 'Save the Reaper'." *Canadian Literature* 173 (2002): 34-51.

ConstantReader. Discussion of "Save the Reaper." Dec. 1999. <http://www.constantreader.com/discussions/loveofagoodwoman.htm>.

Duncan, Isla. *Alice Munro's Narrative Art.* New York: Palgrave Macmillan, 2011.

Francesconi, Sabrina. "Barking (with) Dogs: The Grammar System of Transitivity in Munro's 'Save the Reaper' and 'Floating Bridge'." La question animale dans les nouvelles d'Alice Munro / *The Animal Question in Alice Munro's Stories.* Ed. Héliane Ventura. *Caliban: French Journal of English Studies* 57 (2017): 69-84.

Munro, Alice. "Contributors' Notes." *The Best American Short Stories 1999.* Ed. Amy Tan. Boston: Houghton Mifflin, 1999. 387-88.

---. "Dance of the Happy Shades." *Dance of the Happy Shades.* Fwd. Hugh Garner. Toronto: Ryerson, 1968. 211-24.

---. "Images." *Dance of the Happy Shades.* Fwd. Hugh Garner. Toronto: Ryerson, 1968. 30-43.

---. "Mischief." *Who Do You Think You Are?* Toronto: Macmillan of Canada, 1978. 98-132.

---. "My Mother's Dream." *The Love of a Good Woman.* Toronto: McClelland & Stewart, 1998. 293-340.

---. "Save the Reaper." *The Love of a Good Woman.* Toronto: McClelland & Stewart, 1998. 146-80.

Munro, Sheila. *Lives of Mothers & Daughters: Growing Up with Alice Munro.* Toronto: McClelland & Stewart, 2001.

Tennyson, Alfred, Lord. "The Lady of Shalott." *Poetical Works: Including the Plays.* London: Oxford UP, 1953. 26-28. <https://www.poetryfoundation.org/poems/45359/the-lady-of-shalott-1832>.

Nothing More True: Reading Alice Munro

Michael Trussler

It takes a very long time to learn who you need. Someone to listen, to talk to. And there's hardly any possibility that one can succeed in speaking with them (those living ghosts we've never met who've made us) in each of their separate and combined voices. Those presences from our own lives we can never remember well enough. Their beauty. For me, Don Coles and Alice Munro blurring into Eugene Meatyard's photographs. Haunting me as much as anything.

She wished she could tell somebody. Him. ("Tricks")

Nothing more true.

Our lives are a raga spun from the umbilical cord. Spun from a telescope composed of sheets of disintegrating time. A placenta whose travails are contemplated by the interactive evolution of pigment sprinkled across the egg of a heron, a long sliver of hectic genealogy + screen memories → these melancholy notations the result of brain shrink and the agoraphobic peregrinations of the heart: seeking—

When I looked in the mirror. When I looked at the window. ("Powers")

Nothing more true.

It never stops, this haunting never leaves, pareidolia, this tyrannical echo that insists that what's on either side of the psychogenic window is unfailingly personal and also as completely communal as a city sleeping through a night of rain. But who can really say what someone else is thinking as something (more vague than hidden) waits for each of our monsters to come? The power's just gone out. The city shivers and waits. Can you hand me the flashlight in the cupboard above the stove? There. It's done, Lear thanks me: resilient darkness makes us into mongrels and none of this has ever belonged ... to anyone

← but, here's the thing: we really must start to work damn hard to design a bot that can flag the *Thanatos* vs. *Eros* quotient of any given post, weather forecast, or what's inside a person's careening life-span—

What she had seen was final. ("Passion")

Nothing more true.

Although I've been on both sides of what's final—waking up in the ICU, utterly disoriented: *shit, it didn't work*—the dark body of water that stretches on and on remains. How could things be otherwise? Despite limited life experience, we make the journey almost alone. It's untenable, this toothless struggle to reach the bottom of the food chain, a target with room inside for everyone—

The thing that was your bright treasure. You don't think about it. A loss you could not contemplate at one time, and now it becomes something you can barely remember. ("Chance")

Nothing more true.

I don't know how widespread regret is, but I'm curious to see what it really holds. Let me get at this by listening to someone else: when he was seven, the youngest of my three children, Jakob, told me that he and his friends in their imaginary town had a fire in which they roasted souls and what this burning did, according to him, was take away what these souls "were good at." How could he know such a thing is possible? The words one does or doesn't write; the ones that never could be written. After gaining some experience with marriage, divorce, and remarriage, wandering with confusion and tenderness amidst the multiple lives our children give us, writing too rarely, dealing with changes in health, and having pretty much understood the fire Jakob imagined, I know that failure's close, but not really the right word for what's possible in a life. And there's nothing I can do to cut through the necessary accrual of events that both clog and dissipate the decades between my two selves—the one who first sensed that necessary treasure and what's living inside me now—

The Rock of Realism: Land and Settler Memory in Alice Munro's *The View from Castle Rock*

Paul Barrett

I grew up in the north end of Brampton, Ontario, on the border of Caledon, in the new suburb of Heart Lake. Named after the vaguely heart-shaped lake that sits on its edge, the "village" of Heart Lake is Brampton's northernmost suburb: a sapling-laden network of neighbourhoods where spacious new housing developments are situated alongside schools and strip malls. Subdivisions are linked by a series of two-lane roads and catwalks in an attempted marriage of bucolic calm and modern convenience.

My family immigrated from Newcastle-Upon-Tyne, in the United Kingdom. Largely working-class and with a population, known as Geordies, comprised of almost entirely Labour voters, Newcastle was particularly devastated by the effects of Thatcherism, neoliberalism, and the decline of the coal mines that had been the lifeblood of the northern English economy for over a century. The conflict between Thatcher's emerging brand of neoliberalism and the miners' trade unionism, combined with a derisive view of the northern English population by cultural tastemakers in London, led to unemployment in Newcastle being the second highest in the United Kingdom. Only Northern Ireland, an active warzone at the time, faced higher levels of unemployment.

My parents responded to these economic conditions by migrating to Niagara Falls, and eventually Brampton, where their Britishness made them welcome immigrants. The relative affordability of Brampton real estate and its proximity to Toronto resulted in a rapid explosion of population from the early 1970s onward. Brampton's population of 41,000 in 1971 had nearly quadrupled by 1981 to 149,000 and was over 190,000 by the time we arrived in 1986. What had begun as a small settlement at the corner of Main and Queen Streets – a Southern Ontario village dominated by vocal Protestants – has since transformed into a major metropolitan centre, with Brampton's current population of 656,000 making it the ninth largest city in Canada.

The suburban design, layout, topography, and nomenclature of Heart Lake render it a suitable place for settlers, particularly as it is imagined as a place with no history. Brampton's design and naming evokes a form of settler realism that combines the concept of *terra nullius* with multicultural politics in a manner that obscures the historical conditions that enabled my family, and others, to arrive, to settle, and to claim the place as our own. That claiming depends upon the production of the image of Brampton as a collection of upwardly-mobile middle-class families from a range of ethnic, religious, racial, and cultural backgrounds, an image that obscures the manner in which the freshly-paved spaces of the suburbs conceal a history of settler colonialism.

The naming of Brampton streets evokes a lexicon of local placelessness and historical amnesia that disconnects naming from geography, environment, or history. The plant life, animals, ecology, and histories of Heart Lake (talk about affect!) are immaterial to the terms used to describe them. Yet these names appealed to the desires of many immigrant families like my own for whom the images and iconography of *terra nullius* was well-suited to the development of a new life in a new country. Unlike earlier settler developments, which imported the signifiers of the colonizing society onto the colonized space (via street names such as King, Queen, Kensington, or buildings modelled after European colonial centres etc.), in the newer sections of Brampton the naming of streets has more to do with asserting this principle of *terra nullius*: there was nothing here before your arrival. Consequently, the suburban paving over of 'undeveloped' land to create modern housing developments and suburban neighbourhoods finds a symbolic corollary in the acts of naming that disavow the history of the place.

Street names like Royal Palm, Primrose, and Oleander, named after plants that will not grow in Brampton, demonstrate the disjunction between the idea of the place and the environment it is built atop. Similarly, names like Renier, Monte Vista, Rushmore, and Barrington gesture towards other locales through a kind of geographic referentiality, providing cultural cache to otherwise generic suburbs. Other streets, like Mondragon and Cassander, attempt to offer Brampton some mythological panache. A street with a name like Lawn View is, at least, accurate.

The design of the space of Brampton, the naming of streets, and the construction of Brampton as an exemplary of Canada's "multicultural reality" (*Canadian Multiculturalism Act* 4) all represent a particular mode of realism wherein the idea of a place is mapped onto that place's topography. Suburban development paves over any record of the past resulting in local signs such as Orenda Road, Chinguacousy Park, or Nottawasaga Boulevard that have no meaning in relation to the places they mark on the map. In this sense, Ian Watts's classical definition of formal realism as "the narrative embodiment of a premise" (32) finds a spatial analogue in the layout of Brampton streets and Brampton's disavowal of the historical realities that made possible those communities. For Frederic Jameson, "the realistic novelist has a vested interest, an ontological stake, in the solidity of social reality" (5) and realism can be described as making "an epistemological claim ... [that] masquerades as an aesthetic ideal" (5). The "epistemological claim," the "ontological stake," or the social "premise" of Brampton's suburban layout depicts the land as unencumbered by the histories of settler colonialism.

My experience in Brampton is not particularly novel but one instance of settler realism, the process whereby land is reimagined and narrated in order to disavow the political conditions of settler colonialism that make such reimagining possible. While Canadian literature is replete with novels, short stories, and poems that aim to map the land in this realist fashion, perhaps no writer has done more to conceive of a realist vision of the land of Southwestern Ontario than Alice Munro. Coral Ann Howells intuits this realist mapping in her observation that "Munro's stories provide the fictional equivalent of a Historical Atlas of Souwesto, tracing layers of its history and prehistory" (141). Bharati Mukherjee writes that Munro "has deepened the channel of realism" (31) and Ajay Heble argues that Munro's work "reveals itself to be maintaining and undoing reality..., operating as both an instance and a criticism of fictional representation" (4). Heble's reading of Munro's postmodern and metafictional tendencies emerges out of this sense of "the tension between her interest in delineating a surface reality ...

and her fascination with the very limits of representation" (4). Yet how does Munro's complex engagement with realism permit, and limit, her depiction of the land and its history? Munro's doubled realism simultaneously grasps for a complete account of what she has called "*Real Life*" (*Lives* 242) while dwelling on the ineffable and mysterious dimensions of existence that resist representation.

As J.R. (Tim) Struthers, Coral Ann Howells, Ryan Porter, and others have shown, Munro's stories are highly allusive, often allegorical, while also maintaining a distrust in, and fascination with, the act of narration itself. The task of narrative poses a problem to Munro's depiction of realism because she simultaneously aims to include, within her vision of the real, the desire to narrate, yet, in doing so, exposes her realist story as the narrative fabrication that it is.

Part of the "epistemological claim" of Munro's fiction is that fiction and the real world fold into one another in the act of representation. Furthermore, if life is filled with experiences, affects, memories, and desires that escape linguistic expression, those "moments ... bright and clear and also filled with density and mystery" as Munro describes them (Munro qtd. in May 44), then her work asks how one can write a realist account of one's life that neither ignores those ineffable aspects of life nor attempts to domesticate them within relatable, known language. She recognizes that realism is not mimesis and her work is replete with narrative strategies for coping with these tensions, including structural mirroring, images and themes of paradox, metafiction, and narratives that blur the lines amongst memoir, memory, and fiction.

One of Munro's standard strategies for addressing realism's limits is to thematize the act of narration itself in a number of ways in order both to energize and to undercut a story's verisimilitude. In her early work Munro tends towards metafiction as a means of resolving the problem of the limits of representation. This approach changes in her later writing, however, with Helen Hoy arguing that "In the collections after *Who Do You Think You Are?*, metafictional self-consciousness is less frequent and more buried; Munro looks less at the literal fictions to be made out of our lives and more at the extent to which lives are themselves already self-created fictions" (Hoy, "'Rose and Janet'" 79). While we may disagree with Hoy's general pattern, this shift towards new modes of grappling with the fiction of life continues in *The View from Castle Rock*, where the struggle over realism, autobiography, and metafiction is rendered even more complex by the text's explicit engagement with land, history, and settler colonialism.

The View from Castle Rock is unique within Munro's oeuvre because her concerns with realism and representation are complicated by the collection's attention to history and land. In *Castle Rock*, Munro addresses the history of her ancestors, their home in Scotland, their migration to Canada, and their eventual settlement in Southwestern Ontario. While she has grappled with history elsewhere, *Castle Rock* uniquely collects an approximately contiguous collection of 'stories' (Munro, herself, seems unsure about what to call these pieces) focused on a group of related historical figures informed by her research. Her efforts to frame the relationships amongst the historical figures, her interest in those histories, and her work on the pieces in the collection are explicated in the Foreword:

> About ten or twelve years ago I began to take more than a random interest in the history of one side of my family, whose name was Laidlaw. ...
>
> I put all this material together over the years, and almost without my noticing what was happening, it began to shape itself, here and there, into something like stories. Some of the characters gave themselves to me in their own words, others rose out of their situations. Their words and my words, a curious re-creation of lives, in a given setting that was as truthful as our notion of the past can ever be. ([ix-x])

Munro's reluctance to settle on either the veracity or the fictiveness of these stories is evident throughout the Foreword, particularly in the passive language of "it began to shape itself" and "the characters gave themselves to me in their own words." These historical figures are "characters" but ones that "gave themselves to me" in the historical documents, in words taken from surviving records, and in the interpretation of history's silences and gaps.

Like the histories that animate the text, land is also depicted as a deceptively complex symbol of both belonging and historical continuity. Indeed, despite the seeming stability of "rock," land figures throughout *Castle Rock* in a manner that supplements Munro's engagement with realism, irony, and metafiction. The opening story in the collection, "No Advantages," takes its title from disparaging comments about the

Ettrick Valley from the "Contribution by the Minister of Ettrick Parish, in the county of Selkirk, to the Statistical Account of Scotland, 1799" (3). Juxtaposing historical documents with her own impressions and literary imaginings allows Munro to construct her historical vision as always partial, interpretive, and a sort of fiction. The story begins with the narrator's account of her visit to the Valley, the home of her ancestors:

> The Ettrick Valley lies about fifty miles due south of Edinburgh, and thirty or so miles north of the English border, which runs close to the wall Hadrian built to keep out the wild people from the north. During the reign of Antoninus later Romans pushed farther, and built a line of fortification between the Firth of Clyde and the Firth of Forth, but that was not so lasting. The land between the two walls has been occupied for a long time by a mix of people – Celtic people, some of whom came from Ireland and were called Scots, also Anglo-Saxons from the south, Norse from across the North Sea, and possibly some leftover Picts as well.
>
> The high stony farm where my family lived for some time in the Ettrick Valley was called Far-Hope. The word *hope*, as used in the local geography, is an old word, a Norse word – Norse, Anglo-Saxon, and Gaelic words being all mixed up together in that part of the country.... *Hope* means a bay, not a bay filled with water but with land, partly enclosed by hills, which in this case are the high bare hills, the near mountains of the Southern Uplands. The Black Knowe, Bodesbeck Law, Ettrick Pen – there you have the three big hills, with the word *hill* in three languages. (3-4; emphasis in orig.)

Castle Rock opens with the narrator describing the space of the Ettrick valley, the land itself, the history of the land's settlement, the groups that have crossed and settled the land, as well as the languages used to describe the place. Significantly, the narrator envisions the land populated "by a mix of people," a mix produced by the ebb and flow of empires and migration. The narrator's tone mimics, and then undermines, the confident voice of history while also linking this sweeping historical account with the present day. Hope is both an inadvisable luxury for the budding genealogist and historian as well as a meeting of land and language. It is an old word that connects past and present such that the linguistic and imaginative construction of the materiality of place is front and centre in the collection. Perhaps the irony of Far-Hope indicates both the hope of her ancestors in migrating to Canada as well as her own far-off hope of being able to recover some of their story.

Yet this genealogy of the local region gives way to a general dissatisfaction when the narrator first visits the valley:

> Nevertheless the valley disappointed me the first time I saw it. Places are apt to do that when you've set them up in your imagination. The time of year was very early spring, and the hills were brown, or a kind of lilac brown, reminding me of the hills around Calgary. Ettrick Water was running fast and clear, but it was hardly as wide as the Maitland River, which flows past the farm where I grew up, in Ontario. The circles of stones which I had at first taken to be interesting remnants of Celtic worship were too numerous and well kept up to be anything but handy sheep pens. (5)

The far hope proves to be a false one when the narrator's imagined Ettrick Valley is dispelled by the real place. Where the imagination elevates place and past, offering a mythos informed by a historical vision, the experience of the place offers something else. The narrator is left unsatisfied in her search for symbolic and genealogical meaning: the stone circles that she hoped were "remnants of Celtic worship" are mere sheep enclosures. Similarly, her first impression of the valley is of Scotland as a lesser Canada, with the comparison to "the hills around Calgary" meant to be anything but complementary. She is "struck with a feeling familiar ... to many people whose long history goes back to a country far away from the place where they grew up. I was a naïve North American.... Past and present lumped together here made a reality that was commonplace and yet disturbing beyond anything I had imagined" (7). The lumping together of past and present suggests the geological formations that inform the book's vision of history and contribute to the view of "a reality that was commonplace and yet disturbing."

"No Advantages" sets the pattern for the rest of the collection where historical account and imaginative engagement are placed alongside one another (not quite in juxtaposition) to reveal the continuities, points of disjuncture, aporetic gaps, and disappointments in engaging history as narrative, all with the land serving as a polysemous symbol for that engagement. In some respects, this opening works as a corrective against the too easy desire to transform history into myth or story, to arrange discordant pieces of information into an intelligible and recognizable narrative. Ken Adachi, in his review of *The Moons of Jupiter*, describes Munro's world as offering "mysterious simultaneity, both on the hard, dry land of everyday reality and in the fluid realm of artifice and imagination" (Adachi qtd. in May 54). While Adachi's contrast is perhaps too clear a distinction between land (reality) and artifice (imagination), the opening to *Castle Rock* does contrast history and memory's understanding of the past via the linguistic and material reality of land.

This attention to land is one of the distinguishing features of the collection. In the "Epilogue," the narrator reflects on the land of her ancestors and her historical project more generally. While attempting to find the gravesites of her ancestors in Joliet, Illinois, the narrator wonders if the land has remained wild because it is, in fact, the location where her ancestors are buried. She reflects:

> I could pursue this. It's what people do. Once they get started they'll follow any lead. People who have done little reading in their whole lives will immerse themselves in documents.... We are beguiled. ... We can't resist this rifling around in the past, sifting the untrustworthy evidence, linking stray names and questionable dates and anecdotes together, hanging on to threads, insisting on being joined to dead people and therefore to life. (347)

At the close of the collection the narrator offers an ironic view of the text's project: reflecting on the beguiling aspects of the myth of the past, namely the stringing together of "untrustworthy evidence" and "questionable dates and anecdotes" in an effort to establish a coherent narrative. In place of this pursuit of historical truth, she offers both a metahistory as well as a series of strategies for engaging with history such that it is rendered "commonplace and yet disturbing." Hence the titular "view" of history is equal parts partial and untrustworthy while these visual, scopic metaphors render the partiality of historical vision explicit. Yet, in traditional Munro fashion, she renders this visual, surface view of history ironic by contrasting it with metaphors of depth and genealogy, notably via her engagement with the land of Southwestern Ontario. As such the title *The View from Castle Rock* indicates the interplay of surface, perspective, layer, and depth that will frame the narrative's engagement with historical realism and Canada's settler colonial past.

Critics imagine the stakes of realism in Munro's work to be concerned with the limits of representation, with the overlap between memoir and fiction, with *écriture féminine*, and with the fundamental instability of memory as a corrective to the purported truths of history. Yet the opening of "No Advantages" demonstrates Munro's engagement with settler realism, particularly as her construction of land naturalizes the settler communities she describes. Land figures in her work in a number of ways, including as the stage upon which the narratives unfold, as an archive of a particular form of memory, and as a signifier of belonging. Certainly Munro's enshrinement of small-town Ontario as a major site of Canadian literary significance has helped to shape the perception of the Ontario small town as autochthonous to the land itself. There is a striking difference between her depiction of the "mix of people" that lived in the Ettrick Valley and her comparatively monolithic vision of the inhabitants of Souwesto. The contrast between her use of visual and spatial metaphors allows Munro to offer a fixed and familiar vision of the land while also gesturing towards the fundamentally unknowable dimension of the past. Land in Munro's work is a signifier of belonging and of a certain kind of rootedness and community, the Souwesto that has become a hallmark of her work, as well as an inscrutable figure for a presence that resists complete representation or understanding. However, while working in this doubled register, her writing naturalizes her own construction of the land in a manner that excludes the political exigencies that shape her historical vision.

This complex relation to the past, and the limits of Munro's historical vision, are evident in the fifth story in the collection, "Working for a Living," which includes a lengthy description of the shaping of the land, her father's experience on the land, and the connection between Munro and her ancestors. She describes how

> There was no more wild country in Huron County then than there is now. Perhaps there was less. The farms had been cleared in the period between 1830 and 1860, when the Huron Tract was being opened up, and they were cleared thoroughly. ... The early farmers hated the very sight of

> a tree and admired the look of open land. And the masculine approach to the land was managerial, dictatorial. Only women were allowed to care about landscape and not to think always of its subjugation and productivity. My grandmother, for example, was famous for having saved a line of silver maples along the lane. (130)

Where the land is a symbol of continuity across generations, the narrator has no access to the "wild country" (130) that existed prior to settlement. Rather, she traces the 'masculine' and 'feminine' approaches to taming the land, either through subjugation and management or through care and admiration. She reflects on the land near the Maitland River, "that it was possible to follow it and be hardly aware of the farms, the cleared land, the straight-laid roads and fences – it was possible to imagine that you were out in the forest as it was a hundred years ago, and for hundreds of years before that" (131).

Of course, this imagined arcadian space, before the farms and the settlements, is illusory, and the narrator understands that it requires the self-deception of not straying from the river. Yet the limits of her own imagination are evident in the description of "the Huron Tract ... opened up," the farms being "cleared thoroughly," and her idea that the forest was "wild country" "for hundreds of years before" settlers arrived. The processes by which Huron County opened up, or how the land was cleared, as well as the existence of the indigenous people who lived on the land prior to Munro's family's arrival, and who continue to live on the land today, are beyond the scope of the narrative's representation. While land figures throughout this story in her father's and grandmother's relationships to the land, in references to Fenimore Cooper, and in her own imagining of the "wild country" of the past, Munro's vision of land, as both place and genealogy of belonging, remains limited to a settler vision. Although the narrator represents the land in a doubled fashion, palimpsestically layering her father's fantasy of the land atop her own perception of the land, that doubled vision, within its realist construction, excludes any sense of the settler colonial processes that make it possible.

The final story in *Castle Rock*, "What Do You Want To Know For?," gloriously complicates the settler realist account of the land. In this story, set in the present day, the narrator and her husband, a geographer, crisscross Huron County in search of a mysterious tomb that they had once discovered but could not find again. The tomb first appears as "A large, unnatural mound blanketed with grass," and the narrator envisions it as being "Like a big woolly animal – like some giant wombat, lolling around in a prehistoric landscape" (316). The tomb is an enigma for the narrator and her husband and they long to understand its place in the land they know so well. Where the collection begins with a discussion of the hills of the Ettrick Valley, it proceeds towards a geological and genealogical account with land serving as a metaphor for the past. As the narrator explains, she and her husband "are possessive about this country, and try not to let anything get by us" (316).

Possession of the land depends upon the particular kind of knowledge that the narrator and her husband have and they take great pleasure surveying their territory, identifying its geographical features and attributes. The couple travels the countryside with "maps sold to accompany a book called *The Physiography of Southern Ontario*" (319) which allow them to interpret the geography of the region. The narrator confesses her "naïve and particular pleasure from matching what I see on the map with what I can see through the car window" (321). A textual and visual understanding of the land proves simultaneously pleasurable and naïve because it offers a false sense of recognition and understanding. While the maps may provide the narrator with a key to recognizing the topography of the place, they cannot provide the depth of knowledge that she seeks.

Throughout the story land offers a view of a surface of the place that secures belonging through recognition, notably the kinds of recognition that *Castle Rock* is replete with, while also employing depth metaphors to suggest the inscrutable nature of that connection to the past. Land depicts a geological approach to history, with the narrator observing that "The landscape here is a record of ancient events. It was formed by the advancing, stationary, and retreating ice. The ice has staged its conquests and retreats here several times, withdrawing for the last time about fifteen thousand years ago" (318). She explains, "A glacial landscape such as this is vulnerable. Many of its various contours are made up of gravel, and gravel is easy to get at, easy to scoop out, and always in demand. That's the material that makes these back roads passable – gravel from the chewed-up hills, the plundered terraces, that have been turned into holes in the land" (318). If the collection can be conceived of as an imaginative mapping of both Munro's own history and the land of Huron County, then each piece in the collection works as a kind of back road, offering a roundabout, indirect, and unstable path to accessing some part of that history. The process of converting unknowable, unruly, deep history into the kinds of stories that pervade this collection is akin to the process of pulling gravel from the land, complete with all of the pitfalls that accompany such an extraction. Munro's dual images of surface and depth simultaneously gesture to the desire to plumb the depths of historical understanding and the impossibility of doing so satisfyingly.

Images of surface and depth run throughout "What Do You Want To Know For?" as a way of thinking about the fundamental mystery of the past, and the difficulty of mining that past as part of the desire to see oneself linked with history, all with clear implications for the collection as a whole and for Munro's broader realist vision. In keeping with her stated desire for "a lot of overlap. I want things to come in as many layers as possible" (Munro in Macfarlane 54), the story moves between the narrator's search for the history of the mysterious tomb and her visits to a doctor's office to determine if a vaguely-shaped lump is cancerous. The enigmatic hill, the aforementioned lumping together of past and present, the pattern of lumps and cells all promise both death and meaning.

As the narrator continues her search for the mysterious tomb, she uncovers a number of clues that she hopes will help explain the tomb's origins. She learns that there are two crypts in Mannerow Cemetery, connected to St. Peter's Lutheran Church, and that "the larger crypt ... is said to have been built in 1895 to receive the body of a three-year-old boy" (329). She learns about the church from a woman named Rachel (as the Christian allusions begin to accrue) and soon discovers that Rachel's father knew her father. She also learns that after a great fire in the church "there was a surprise underneath. A faint text in German in the Gothic German lettering.... // And there it is. They touched up the paint, and there it is" (333). The passage reads, "*I will lift up my eyes unto the hills, from whence cometh my help. // Thy word is a lamp unto my feet and a light unto my path*" (333). The text comes from Psalms 121 and 119 and unites the collection's historical themes with its geographic interests, with "*Thy word*" serving as a guiding light for a kind of understanding of one's relation to place and past.

Standing with Rachel in the church, the narrator reflects: "Being in the church with this woman as guide gives me a slightly lost feeling, or a feeling of bewilderment, of having got things the wrong way round. The words on the wall strike me to the heart, but I am not a believer and they do not make me a believer. ... she is the believer" (334). In what sense does the narrator feel she has got things the wrong way round? Has she experienced deliverance without belief? Has her fascination with the tomb meant that she has missed the illumination of her own life? Or is she simply aware that her own belief in the restorative power of the past is insufficient?

In the interplay between surface and depth, appearance and deeper meaning, Rachel believes in a stable and secure meaning and appoints herself the caretaker of the church and the message, despite the fact that "a bit of the paint – in the ornate 'L' of Licht – has faded or flaked off" (334). For the narrator, the relation between past and present is less sure and neither historical text, nor scripture, nor geological record offers anything but a kind of "naïve and particular pleasure." In place of finally resolving the mysteries of the past, the last story poses the titular question to the narration, and the collection as a whole: "What do you want to know for?" She is more interested in understanding her own desire to uncover this past and to connect her own life to the lives of her ancestors than developing any sure belief in the meaning of that past.

These images of light, language, and land accumulate throughout the story, symbolizing and ironizing the narrator's desire to see herself in relation to the history she is assembling. For instance, when the narrator learns that an oil lamp was placed in the child's tomb, the lamp recalls the inscription in the church, "*Thy word is a lamp*," and serves as another visual metaphor and enigmatic clue to her own past. Similarly, when she meets the elderly man who knew her father, he remarks, "'Well now. I can see it in you. Bob Laidlaw's girl. 'Round the eyes. That's a long time ago'" (331). As with the inscription on the wall, and the title of the book, it is the eyes, and the ways of seeing, that enable a certain "naïve and particular pleasure" in their connection with the past. The narrator reflects that this connection to the past makes them "both happy. He is happy to be reminded of himself as a young man, fresh in the country.... // ... I am happy to find somebody who can see me still as part of my family, who can remember my father and the place where my parents worked and lived for all of their married lives, first in hope and then in honorable persistence" (331). The repetition of "lived" and "lives" stresses the overlap of life and death (and recalls the missing "L" on the inscription) that shades the narrator's desire to know her own past. In what ways do the ineffable mystery of the tomb, the strange meaning of her tumour, and the hidden inscription on the church wall connect her simultaneously to the lives of the past as well as to her own mortality?

The answer to this question, like the meaning of what lies beneath the surface of the historical text, is less important than the act of searching for that meaning. Throughout *Castle Rock* Munro represents that search in her own desire to understand her familial history. Yet in her use of land as a figure for a connection to the past and for the inscrutable mystery of the past, Munro mythologizes her own family history on the land all while using irony, doubling, and the interrogatory of the title to undercut that mythos. In doing so, Munro maps her complex realist vision onto the Southwestern Ontario landscape.

The comingling of historical presence and absence works in a delicate, fleeting balance to offer a doubled vision of the real. *Castle Rock* is an historic account of how Southwestern Ontario came to be settled by her ancestors and neighbours yet her vision of the land remains confined within mythos and cannot attend to the histories that might disrupt the text's delicate balance. Returning to Howells's description of Munro's work as "the fictional equivalent of a Historical Atlas of Souwesto, tracing layers of its history" (Howells 141), we may say that Munro's vision of history is restricted to particular layers. Her equipoising of the surfaces of everyday life with its unstated and ephemeral other offers a vision that presents itself as real because her settler realist vision cannot account for how the land was settled and how the place was made. Between the two poles of her realist vision, the apparent surface and the unknowable depth, lies a series of layers that escapes Munro's vision and has everything to do with the political processes and subaltern histories by which Souwesto has been shaped and through which Munro, and her ancestors, became "possessive about this country."

Works Cited

Canadian Multiculturalism Act. Bill C-93. 21 July 1988. Print.

Heble, Ajay. *The Tumble of Reason: Alice Munro's Discourse of Absence.* Toronto: U of Toronto P, 1994.

Howells, Coral Ann. "Intimate Dislocations: Buried History and Geography in Alice Munro's Souwesto Stories." *Alice Munro Country: Essays on Her Works I.* Ed. J.R. (Tim) Struthers. Toronto: Guernica Editions, 2020. 139-53. Essential Writers Ser. 51.

Hoy, Helen. "'Rose and Janet': Alice Munro's Metafiction." *Canadian Literature* 121 (1989): 59-83.

Jameson, Frederic. *The Antinomies of Realism.* London: Verso, 2013.

Macfarlane, David. "Writer in Residence." *Saturday Night* Dec. 1986: 51-52, 54, 56.

Mukherjee, Bharati. "Hometown Horrors." Rev. of *Friend of My Youth,* by Alice Munro. *The New York Times Book Review* 18 Mar. 1990: 1, 31.

Munro, Alice. *The View from Castle Rock.* Toronto: McClelland & Stewart, 2006.

---. *Who Do You Think You Are?* Toronto: Macmillan of Canada, 1978.

Porter, Ryan. *You Can't Get There from Here: The Past as Present in Small-Town Ontario Fiction.* Toronto: U of Toronto P, 2019.

Struthers, J.R. (Tim). "The Place of Wisdom, Divination, the Act of Reading, and Alice Munro's 'Powers'." *Alice Munro Everlasting: Essays on Her Works II.* Toronto: Guernica Editions, 2020. 293-43. Essential Writers Ser. 52.

Watt, Ian. *The Rise of the Novel: Studies in Defoe, Richardson and Fielding.* London: Chatto and Windus, 1957.

Great Advantages: Alice Munro's Invocation of Her Ancestral History/Herstory in the Opening Story "No Advantages" of *The View from Castle Rock*

J.R. (Tim) Struthers

an essay written in honour of the great literary love of my life, Alice Munro, and presented to the great personal love of my life, Marianne Micros, the two of whom – the stars aligning for this very lucky guy – I had the good fortune to meet in the same month of the same year, September 1974, in my old hometown of London, Ontario

Very possibly the most wide-ranging and the most important question that we can ask ourselves of Alice Munro's twelfth (and, as it proved to be, third-last) volume, *The View from Castle Rock* (2006), is what kind or genre of book is it, what style or styles does it involve? Speaking generally, I choose to identify it as a family history/herstory (*Power in the Blood* was an early proposed title for the book), beginning with a record of a return visit by Munro to her three-centuries-distant ancestral home in the Ettrick Valley in Scotland. Then more specifically, to distinguish the book's first group of five pieces, gathered under the heading "No Advantages" (and the book's comparable twelfth part, the "Epilogue: Messenger") from the book's second group of six pieces, gathered under the heading "Home," I choose to call the initial group "story-memoirs" and the next group "memoir-stories." Here the first word in each term is employed as a descriptive adjective and the second word as a noun identifying the piece's essential genre. That is, by "story-memoirs" I mean story-like memoirs and by "memoir-stories" I mean memoir-like stories. Especially interesting for us to discover, then, upon reading the opening section of the book's first piece, "No Advantages," is the range in fictional modes that Munro employs. There's a striking shift from the documentary style, literally, of what opens the work, a long dreary excerpt from the 1799 *Statistical Account of Scotland*, through to the seemingly fantastic passage a couple of pages later where we learn that "there is a story of Merlin – *Merlin* – being hunted down and murdered in the old forest, by Ettrick shepherds" (5; emphasis in orig.). To this statement Munro adds, bringing the seemingly remote, seemingly far-fetched tale much closer, "As far as I know, my ancestors, generation after generation, were Ettrick shepherds" (5).

The documentary style, or more precisely the documentary poem (and here we need to recall that in many respects for Munro the short story represents, as critic Eileen Baldeshwiler established, a lyric form), is something that poet Dorothy Livesay memorably identified as "A Canadian Genre." Moreover, Ian Rae has made the case for considering work by Munro, including *The View from Castle Rock* but also the much-admired story "Walker Brothers Cowboy" that opens her first collection, partly in the context of early semi-fictional sketchbooks such as fellow Huron County writer William "Tiger" Dunlop's *Statistical Sketches of Upper Canada* (1832). "For Dunlop," Rae writes, "a statistical account was a mixture of geology, botany, demography, political economy, economic speculation, pastoral description, and musings on local customs and idioms that would help prospective settlers to integrate into Upper Canadian society" (192). Yet even more importantly, Rae remarks of "Walker Brothers Cowboy" that it "shifts from an empirical mode in its first half to a more mythical mode in its second half" (200). In making this statement Rae effectively outlines the adjustment in perception, be it slight or great, that I believe readers of all of Munro's work must make in order to comprehend her art properly, a shift that I believe Munro herself directs us towards in the way she handles the range in the style of her writing from documentary to mythopoeia in the initial four-page prefatory section of "No Advantages." Ultimately, we find ourselves called upon to read Munro's work not so much as involving something close to documentary or realism but more as involving something close to mythopoeia or allegory.

But a few remarks first about the narration of *The View from Castle Rock*. As easy as it is for us to speak of *Munro* saying such-and-such, I have instead elected to employ a variety of terms in order to suggest that at least in some pieces in *The View from Castle Rock* there are significant differences amongst the vantage points (and the respective levels of understanding) involved. First, the participant or protagonist or *alazon*; second, the witness or narrator or *eiron* (these two being sometimes separated, but sometimes fused as my occasionally using the term "protagonist-narrator" is meant to convey); and third, the supremely comprehending writer of this book, Alice Munro. In sum, we as readers need to be ever-alert to the possibility that Munro is at times not only fictionalizing profoundly in the way that she portrays herself as the protagonist of a given piece but also fictionalizing significantly in the way that she develops, or imposes limits on, the characterization of herself as the narrator of that same piece. It proves all too easy to think of the protagonist and the narrator and the writer as a near-uniform entity with a near-identical understanding of situations being described – in short, to collapse what Munro sometimes means us to regard as three different levels into one level, thereby missing out on critical differences in understanding and on artistic ironies that we are meant to relish.

To provide what is perhaps the most striking example of this technique from the whole of *The View from Castle Rock*, I'll cite an instance that occurs at the end of "Working for a Living," the fifth and final story-memoir comprising the first half of the book. Here, we're offered a documentary-style two-and-a-half-page portion from a piece called "Grandfathers" that was actually written and published, as the protagonist-narrator of "Working for a Living" explains, by Munro's own father, Robert Laidlaw. In it, he recalls the visit paid to his grandfather, Thomas Laidlaw, by a supposedly wealthy cousin from Toronto, the "namesake" (169) of Munro's father, and reports that "The two old men sat under the maples in front of our house and talked" (169). Yet only a few lines later, in the single two-sentence paragraph of narration that follows the documentary excerpt and concludes "Working for a Living," the protagonist-narrator speaks of choosing in her description of the scene to leave her father as "a little boy, not venturing too close, and the old men sitting through a summer afternoon on wooden chairs placed under one of the great benevolent elm trees that used to shelter my grandparents' farmhouse" (169). Amazingly, here, we witness the protagonist-narrator completely transforming the all-too-evident fact of sturdy maple trees into the less-than-evident fiction of subsequently-decimated elm trees, that is, into the stuff of elegy as Karen E. Smythe would no doubt note – an imaginative act that underlines the romantic needs of the protagonist-narrator in contrast to the realistic, even ironic, vision of the work's writer, Alice Munro.

In reading this opening portion of "No Advantages," we find ourselves made captive by Munro's own sensations as she re-creates her experiences, proceeding from expectation to disappointment, transported in the direction of the magical and nearly unfathomable and then back to the dismal and all too believable as the ever-present rain falls. Most compelling is the scene when, once the rain lets up somewhat, Munro explores the churchyard of Ettrick Church, a building which, she says, "disappointed me too" since it had been erected only in 1824 and therefore "did not compare, in historic appearance, or grim character, to the churches I had already seen in Scotland" (5). Nevertheless, the churchyard itself – the sort of site previously memorialized by Thomas Gray in his "Elegy Written in a Country Churchyard" – proves extraordinarily interesting. For, as Munro explains, "There I found, first, the gravestone of William Laidlaw, my director ancestor, born at the end of the seventeenth century, and known as Will O'Phaup" (6). Of him she declares: "This was a man who took on, at least locally, something of the radiance of myth, and he managed that at the very last time in history – that is, in the history of the people of the British Isles – when a man could do so" (6).

Instantly Munro establishes a link that stretches across seven generations. And she stresses how, uniquely, her distant relative, Will O'Phaup, acquired in his time and continues to convey in hers "something of the radiance of myth" (6). But even more interesting to me is the one qualification – or perhaps two qualifications – that Munro succeeds in subtly including through speaking of Will's accomplishment being "at the very last time in history – that is, in the history of the people of the British Isles – when a man could do so" (6). Could Munro be suggesting, I wonder, that it might be possible for someone else to take on such lustre at a later time in a different place, say, in Canada or, more specifically, the region of Ontario called "Souwesto" or, as many would now say,, "Alice Munro Country"? Could Munro be suggesting, I wonder, that while Will O'Phaup's achievement might never be replicated by "a man," that it might be possible for *a woman* – say, a direct descendent of his, namely Munro herself – to take on such lustre at a later time in a different place?

Having discovered and pointed out to us the gravestone belonging to William Laidlaw, that is, Will O'Phaup, Munro explains, importantly, that "The same stone bears the names of his daughter Margaret Laidlaw Hogg, who upbraided Sir Walter Scott, and of Robert Hogg, her husband, the tenant of Ettrickhall" (6). The reference to Margaret Laidlaw Hogg castigating Sir Walter Scott grew out of a meeting arranged by her son, the writer James Hogg. As Munro relates in the volume's Foreword, "he took Walter Scott to see her when Scott was collecting ballads for his *Minstrelsy of the Scottish Border*. (She supplied some, though she later took offense at their being printed.)" ([vii]). Having described the gravestone marking the graves of the larger-than-life William Laidlaw, his daughter Margaret, and her husband Robert Hogg, Munro adds, "Then right next to it I saw the stone of the writer James Hogg, who was their son and Will O'Phaup's grandson. He was known as The Ettrick Shepherd" (6), on account of Hogg's using that as a pen name in articles he published in *Blackwood's Magazine* and in the title of his late collection *Songs, by The Ettrick Shepherd* (1831). Munro continues on from discussing the two gravestones erected for her relatives to observe: "And not far from that was the stone of the Reverend Thomas Boston, at one time famous throughout Scotland for his books and preaching, though fame never took him to any more important ministry" (6). Thus Munro lays the ground for the three ensuing parts of this opening story-memoir, parts respectively entitled "*Will O'Phaup*" and "*Thomas Boston*" and "*James Hogg and James Laidlaw*" and grouped under the broader, and I believe wryly intended, title "MEN OF ETTRICK." For surely that last phrase is meant as a possibly first unnoticed but subsequently appreciated provocation for readers to ask "What about the women?" (figures for whom Munro provides, or, I should say, for whom Munro invents, key roles in the three sections that follow).

Yet as interested as Munro is in discovering the stories of the people in and connected to her family and in investigating the nature of the place where they resided centuries earlier, she conveys a special interest in language as a sign of cultural influences. Accordingly Munro explains that the names of the three big hills – "The Black Knowe, Bodesbeck Law, Ettrick Pen" – that are local landmarks in her ancestral region of

Scotland derive from "the word hill in three languages" representing a mix of influences, respectively Anglo-Saxon and Norse and Gaelic (4). Even more knowledgeably, but effectively balancing the learnedness of this insight with a deliberate casualness in expression, she then mentions bits of "early Brythonic thrown in to indicate an early Welsh presence" (4). Turning to her own particular ancestry, Munro states that "The high stony farm where my family lived for some time in the Ettrick Valley was called Far-Hope." The word *hope* in that name, she explains, represents "an old word, a Norse word" (4), a geographical term. She adds that "*Hope* means a bay, not a bay filled with water but with land, partly enclosed by hills" (4; emphasis in orig.). Such precise attention to language on Munro's part is not simply a matter of curiosity; it's the mark of her particular and extraordinary craft.

Similarly, something special about Munro's attention to language is conveyed when, in search of her three centuries' old ancestral home in the Ettrick Valley, she takes "the twice-a-week Shoppers' Bus" south from Edinburgh to the village of Ettrick Bridge and discovers, to her dismay, that "The chief thing to be seen ... was a sign on a closed shop, advertising Silk Cut" (5). The sign leaves her bewildered, it appears. Could it perhaps be advertising a special service offered by a dress-making shop, we may wonder, in which some artisan has the skill to cut fabric as delicate and as precious as silk? That interpretation seems intriguing: both realistically as a way of underlining Munro's career-long fascination with clothes and the representation of female identity as seen from "Red Dress – 1946" in her first collection through to "Voices" in her last collection, and metaphorically as a way of underlining Munro's own deftness as a short story writer. But no, that's not what is meant by the words at all, which the protagonist-narrator later learns represent the name of what Munro may all along have known to be "a well-known brand of cigarette" (5). The point, we realize, of Munro's wry depiction of the sign which reads "Silk Cut" is to reinforce, metafictively, the challenge word by word that language offers us as readers in our efforts to interpret single details, let alone larger patterns, within the subtle fictive material we're being offered.

At the end of the initial section of this first of the book's opening group of five "story-memoirs," Munro chooses to emphasize about her day-trip to Ettrick Bridge how "I was struck with a feeling familiar,

I suppose, to many people whose long history goes back to a country far away from the place where they grew up" (7). She then goes on to reflect movingly that "Past and present lumped together here made a reality that was commonplace and yet disturbing beyond anything I had imagined" (7). This awe-inspiring statement invites readers to circle back to the phrase "distances you cannot imagine" that concludes "Walker Brothers Cowboy," the opening piece in her first collection, *Dance of the Happy Shades*. One hears, too, in the wording "commonplace and yet disturbing" chosen by Munro something very close to what Thomas Hardy sought to evoke through the memorable subtitle that he chose to give to his first collection, *Wessex Tales: Strange, Lively, and Commonplace* (1888). Yet while Munro portrays her own ancestral history/herstory in ways that remind us, for example, of Hardy, she nevertheless writes in ways that speak most powerfully for herself.

As we recall, Munro begins this first section of "No Advantages" with an epigraph, the long quotation from the 1799 *Statistical Account of Scotland* that starts – shall we say fatalistically? or from Munro's and our viewpoint drolly? – with the line "This parish possesses no advantages" (3). The epigraph used in the succeeding section devoted to Will O'Phaup takes the form of an epitaph for Will written by his grandson, James Hogg, that appears on Will's tombstone in the churchyard at Ettrick. "Here lyeth William Laidlaw, the far-famed Will o'Phaup, who for feats of frolic, agility and strength, had no equal in his day ..." (7), it reads, suggesting the near-mythical stature attained by Will not just in his own time but now forever as a result of Munro's own intriguing portrait of him in the second section, for which she acknowledges a large debt to descriptions by Hogg of Will's adventures. The third section focuses on the local minister, Thomas Boston, who, as Munro has noted, was "at one time famous throughout Scotland" (6) for his books and his sermons. This section, concentrating in fact on both the minister and his wife, Catherine, begins with an epigraph that takes the form of a lengthy epitaph for Boston inscribed on his gravestone stating that "As a Testament of Esteem ... This monument" has been "erected by a religious and grateful public" (14). And the concluding section, which focuses on two first cousins, James Hogg and James Laidlaw, grandsons of Will O'Phaup, begins with a series of three epigraphs: the first quoting a passage written by Hogg about Laidlaw and the second quoting a passage written by Laidlaw about Hogg. The third epigraph, attributed by Munro to the innkeeper Tibbie Shiel, describes Hogg as a "sensible man, for a the nonsense he wrat" (19), thereby offering a merry commentary not only on Hogg's profession as a writer but also, self-reflexively, on Munro's.

Readers may as a consequence justly conclude that Munro herself in this opening story-memoir and indeed in the successive parts of *The View from Castle Rock* as a whole is producing a set of epitaphs, or an extended epitaph – something in the manner, we might say, of Wordsworth's "A Poet's Epitaph." Moreover, as Louis K. MacKendrick has demonstrated through an analysis of "The Ottawa Valley," the final story of Munro's *Something I've Been Meaning To Tell You*, as offering "a series of metaphorical epitaphs" (179), this device is one that Munro has long favoured. Yet for what purpose, we may ask, has Munro produced not only this opening piece of the book, but the set of epitaphs or, we may say, the extended epitaph that the totality of *The View from Castle Rock* represents? Historically, in ways that involve great advantages rather than none, to document and to honour the lives of her ancestors and their contemporaries – for their own sakes as they have come to be cherished by Munro herself and as she has allowed them to be understood by ourselves, her readers. But also autobiographically, and again to great advantages, for Munro both as a woman of her own time and place and as an artist: the receiver and the transmitter of the cultural and family inheritance which her ancestors have bequeathed from generation to generation – *seven* in total from Will O'Phaup to herself.

***

Munro situates the personal history of Will O'Phaup – allegorically, we might say – in the larger context of major events in the history of Scotland, though she suggests that there can be no way of knowing how he viewed these events: "He had been born in 1695, when Scotland was still a separate country, though it shared a monarch with England. He would have been twelve years old at the time of the controversial Union, a young man by the time of the bitter failed Jacobite Rebellion of 1715, a man deep into middle age by the time of Culloden" (8). And interestingly, too, Munro coins the term "story-name" (7) as a designation for "Will O'Phaup" – "Phaup being simply the local version of Far-Hope, the name of the farm he took over at the head of the Ettrick Valley" (7) – to emphasize the need to distinguish between an ethereal level signified by this "story-name" and an earthly level conveyed by his actual name, William Laidlaw. Will's early exploits, which Munro records first, feature his ability as a runner; as physical and hence more believable activities, they serve Munro's purposes in literally and metaphorically grounding as "realistic" anything of a less believable nature that will be related subsequently. Yet at the same time these stories are, as Munro notes, "classic" (9) – or, we could say, "mythic" in nature.

Of one of Will's exploits Munro remarks: "I heard versions of it – with different names, different feats – when I was a child growing up in Huron County, Ontario. A stranger arrives full of fame, bragging of his abilities, and is beaten by the local champion, a simple-hearted fellow who is not even interested in a reward" (9). And there's humour involved, humour to which the women are indispensable. Thus in a comparable story involving Will's success as a runner, he is invited unprepared to participate in a race and subsequently in the course of the race finds his breeches slipping down, so kicks them off and finishes the race victoriously yet wearing "nothing but a shirt" (9). Despite being fussed over for winning the race, he refuses to join the gentlemen and ladies afterwards for dinner, "claiming to be mortified in front of such *leddies*" (9). Having first used "gentlemen and ladies" but then having changed to "*leddies*," Munro catches for us in a single word of much more precise and therefore much greater vividness the exact mixture of Will's feelings of awe and chagrin. The language chosen makes the scene real and compelling and funny. As Munro points out, repeating for emphasis the Scottish word that has grounded the tale, "the leddies' appreciation of such a well-favored young athlete is the scandalous and enjoyable point of the story" (10). The question we have posed – "What about the women?" – has been decisively answered; the women are indispensable; "the leddies' appreciation ... is the ... point of the story" (10).

As a result of Will's extraordinary exploits, he is said by Munro to be "a man who took on, at least locally, something of the radiance of myth" (6). This stature is enhanced by Will's reputation for being "'the last man in Scotland to speak to the faeries'" (59), as his grandson James Laidlaw recounts in the stories he tells aboard ship in the next story-memoir, the book's title piece. On that occasion, James relates, "'three little lads'" (69) come to visit and ask Will, "'*And by the by, could you give us the key, too, the big silver key that you had of us?*'" (70; emphasis in orig.) – a question that dumbfounds him because he had never possessed such an item but a detail that intrigues us because we recognize it as functioning, for Munro and for us, as a metaphor for all that is mysterious in what we experience both in literature and in life itself. In time, however, Will "turns into a mortal man" (10), probably subsequent to the early death of his wife, Bessie Scott, of whom little is said here or later other than that she and Will were married probably by Thomas Boston (17), that they started a family, and that she died "fairly young" (10). Specifically, Will becomes "a casual bootlegger," hosting parties at his home that involved "not whisky, but French brandy" (10) – a feature that could be thought by some to be a factor in assessing the reality of extraordinary events in his future. More importantly, this shift in Will's stature conveys how everyday circumstances, everyday behaviour, and especially everyday thinking – and, by extension, a literary style limited simply to realism – can drain away the mythic, the magical, the mysterious. For now, "The hero's name still stands for honorable behavior, strength, and generosity, but no more for sobriety" (10).

Nevertheless, having established the definitely probable, Munro turns to relating the conceivably improbable, an event that occurs appropriately at dusk, during the in-between or liminal time "as the day turns to evening" (10). The in-between time of this incident is significant in that it is metaphorically suggestive of various oppositions or divisions or border zones that Munro takes delight in exploring throughout this opening memoir-story: between the natural and the supernatural, between Pagan beliefs and Christian beliefs, between fact and fiction. The event occurs on a day of the year that Will remembers is "All Hallows' Eve" – a time when certain devilishly magical creatures such as Will now encounters "can work their way however they please with any human being" (11). What Will sees is "a whole company of creatures all about as high as a two-year-old child, but none of them are children" (11). And appropriately in a work that we come to see not just as "history" but "herstory," what Will sees are "little women, all dainty-looking and dressed in green" (11). Yet "the little chirp-chirp song" that these women are making, Will recognizes fearfully, is a song comprised of his own name: "*Will O'Phaup, Will O'Phaup, Will O'Phaup*" (11; emphasis in orig.). Terrified, Will runs home, assembles his children, and commences to pray as loudly and as steadily as he can. On this occasion, paradoxically, in order to fight off the unconventional powers of the faeries, whose world Will to a large degree inhabits, he chooses through prayer to draw on the conventional powers of the Presbyterian religion, which, we learn in the next section of "No Advantages," he heard Thomas Boston preach about every Sunday. His fear unrelieved, Will continues to pray straight through to midnight when at last "there is no more heard of the creatures, not a peep" (12). Here we can note that in the next story-memoir Munro picks up on the word "peep" – using it to signify the purely invented half of a word, "sailor-peep" – meaning "sailor" and "bird" (35) – in the child language that Young James speaks. Consequently, "sailor-peep" is a word that serves as a metaphor for Munro's own unique mix here of the factual and the fictional.

Here we see Will himself positioned between a Pagan world or Pagan beliefs and a Christian world or Christian beliefs – what we may call an allegorical situation involving the ferocious conjunction of one world and another, of one religious system and another. The next magical episode recorded by Munro again takes place during the in-between time "around the darkening hour of the evening" (12). While proceeding homeward, Will believes that he sees a group of his neighbours in the distance and decides to follow in order to talk with them about the day they have presumably spent at a nearby town fair. All appear to be simple country folk attired "in their plaids and bonnets, both men and women, and normal-sized" (12). Yet while they appear to be proceeding leisurely, Will is unable to catch up with them even though he runs "faster and faster" (12). The group, Will realizes, is headed in the opposite direction from home, not down the valley but up – that is, in a direction that we associate symbolically with the unknown, indeed the unknowable. Moreover, while these figures understandably appear to be growing fainter because the light is fading, they also curiously seem to be increasing in number, definitely "a strange thing" (13). Comprehending at last that "These are no neighbor folk" (13), Will is struck with dread and turns and runs. Fortunately, because this is "an ordinary night and not All Hallows' Eve" (13), these creatures lack the supernatural powers that they sometimes exert and therefore cannot chase Will. Yet the fear that he now experiences, though different, is equally cold on account of what Munro portentously describes as "the notion he has that they are ghosts of humans bewitched into fairies" (13).

After recounting this adventure, Munro acknowledges that "It would be a mistake to think that everybody believed these stories. There was the brandy factor" (13). But in general, she observes, "people would feel some curiosity, and some skepticism, but mostly a large portion of plain dread" (13). Fairies were definitely not to be grouped together with ghosts and with religion under any sort of "benign designation" such as "*spiritual powers*" (14; emphasis in orig.). Rather, they represented truly threatening, truly malevolent forces. Nor were fairies to be thought of as originating at any point in recorded history – not even in "the old historical times of Flodden" (14), the famous battle in which England defeated Scotland in 1513, nearly two hundred years before the birth of Munro's near-mythical forefather Will O'Phaup in 1695. Rather, they belonged to what Munro, using calculatedly antiquated language, calls "the olden times," to what she describes as "the truly dark times, before the Antonine Wall and before the first Christian missionaries came across the sea from Ireland" (14) – that is, before the building of the Antonine Wall by the Romans in the second century A.D. and before the founding of the monastery at Iona in the sixth century A.D. by St. Columba. Again Munro draws attention to the profound division – yet the dramatic intersection – between the world and the belief system of Paganism and the world and the belief system of Christianity. And here her twice-used word "before" emphatically underlines that division. Of the darkly mysterious faeries of old she concludes forcefully, "They belonged to times of bad powers and evil confusion, and their attentions were oftener than not malicious, or even deadly" (13). Munro addresses us in the past tense, but, troublingly, terrifyingly, intimates prophetically that such conditions can readily revisit us in the present.

***

As a counterbalance to the attention that Munro gives in the preceding section to the world and the belief system of Paganism as represented through Will O'Phaup's encounters with the faeries, she focuses the third section on the world and the belief system of Christianity as represented through the experiences of the Presbyterian minister Thomas

Boston and his wife Catherine Boston. Boston himself became renowned throughout Scotland – in some ways favourably, in others unfavourably – both for his sermons and for his writing. Most controversially, at one point he grew "deeply interested in a treatise called *The Marrow of Modern Divinity*" (16) – the word "modern" being one to which Munro returns, notably, in the very last sentence of "No Advantages." The work in question, we learn upon investigation, was written by Edward Fisher, originally published in the mid-seventeenth-century, then republished with Boston's encouragement in 1718 and soon after that, in 1726, in a new edition with full notes by him. As a result of Boston's enthusiasm for the unconventional doctrines promoted in *The Marrow of Modern Divinity*, he was beset publicly with accusations that he had become "a marrow-man" and was at risk of advocating antinomianism, a belief, Munro explains, that "asks a simple, direct question – why, if you are from the beginning one of the elect, should you not be able to get away with anything you like" (16). Together, Boston's ardour and his line of thinking, this "stain" as Munro puts it, may have been what "kept him so long in remote Ettrick, never to have been 'translated' (as the word was then) to a moderately comfortable place" (19). So Munro notes, again calling attention to the importance of language and its transformative power for the minister as an orator and as a writer, for herself as a writer, and for us as readers.

Interestingly, Munro states that Thomas Boston himself wrote an autobiography (called *Memoirs of the Life, Times, and Writings of Thomas Boston, of Ettrick*, we can discover) in which he reveals that privately his life is even more troubled than it is publicly and in which he laments "his own recurring miseries, his dry spells, his sense of unworthiness and dullness" (14-15). Yet despite the desolation Boston experiences, he always finds the strength to "rise up filled with the Spirit and enter marathons of preaching" (15). And in addition to what the brief passage by Munro concerning Boston's autobiography tells us about him, her seemingly casual reference to Boston's composing such a work reinforces our sense of the number of genres informing *The View from Castle Rock*: autobiography, memoir, and essay, together with fiction, metafiction, and allegory. Of Thomas Boston and Catherine Boston themselves we also learn that each is distraught by the very early deaths of certain of their children, including Thomas's "own favorite" (16), a boy of only three. Munro characterizes the minister as reproaching himself with the thought, "How wicked of him, how weak, to love this sinful scrap of flesh and to question in any way his Lord's wisdom in taking him" (15). For us, Boston's response is so self-critical and so self-wounding that we are led to regard it not only as inhumane but finally as tragic.

Catherine Boston, described sadly as "once the beautiful Catherine Brown" (16), experiences unrelenting private travails like her husband, notably the very early death of their first-born child (a girl, we discover from research), an event that leaves Catherine especially distraught. Without any apparent relief she suffers an unabated succession of unnerving domestic circumstances, highly strenuous responsibilities, and painful personal tragedies involving "births and deaths and care of the remaining children and troubles with the roof and the continual cold rain" (16). The fierce weight of her individual conditions and challenges persists, causing her to succumb to "some nervous disorder" that appears to leave her bedridden from one year to the next except for a short stretch when the entire family becomes ill and "she rises from her bed and cares for them, tirelessly and tenderly" (16). Through Catherine's example, Munro provides evidence of the benevolent workings of a kind-hearted morality that we can apply when choosing how to lead our lives, and when passing judgments on ourselves, rather than inflicting the hard-hearted dictates of the Presbyterianism promoted in her husband's preaching and his writing and especially his innermost thoughts. Then, too, by not simply reporting but amplifying Catherine's story, Munro further shifts her attention, and therefore ours, away from a possible portrait of simply the "MEN OF ETTRICK" to include due emphasis as well on the WOMEN OF ETTRICK, thereby creating an altogether balanced social portrait that is not just what we have long called history (or his story) but both that and what we now call herstory (or her story).

Of Thomas Boston, Munro points out that he "is remembered now – if he is remembered at all – as the author of a book called *Human Nature in its Four-Fold State*" (14), a work which begins with *Primitive Integrity* as found in the lives of Adam and Eve in Eden, followed by *Entire Deprivation*, then *Begun Recovery*, and, in the afterlife, *Consummate Happiness or Misery*. In its time, significantly, this treatise "was said to stand next to the Bible on the shelf of every pious home in Scotland" (14). For some readers, Boston's "four-fold" division of human life would bring to mind the notion of allegory as "four-fold" that Dante proposed in his book entitled in English translation *The Banquet.* Certainly it is reasonable to assume that Munro would make that connection, given the closeness of her knowledge of Dante's *The Divine Comedy* evident in different works including "No Advantages" where she explains that "In the lower Ettrick Valley was Aikwood, the home of Michael Scott, the philosopher and wizard of the twelfth and thirteenth centuries, who appears in Dante's *Inferno*" (5). Moreover, the fact that Boston is the author of both an autobiographical work and an allegorical work perfectly mirrors the range in form and style that I believe Munro herself employs here in *The View from Castle Rock.* And in terms of the endurance of Boston's reputation, though Munro suggests that he may not be remembered at all, surely her partly researched and partly imagined rendition of him – and her depiction of his wife – will significantly extend and alter the way the two of them are remembered.

Of Catherine Boston, to complete this account, Munro notes that "when next heard from she is back in bed" following the family's illness and recovery but is "still alive when the minister himself is dying" (16). At this point, passing from fact to fiction because facts by themselves, especially the records of facts, have significant limitations, particularly in terms of the portrayal of not just history but herstory, Munro proceeds to enjoin readers in speculating with her about Catherine's later life. Here very interestingly she speaks of Catherine's future in a way that prophetically anticipates Munro's own move from Clinton, Ontario to Port Hope, Ontario, in the Fall of 2019 to live at least briefly in a home of her own near her daughter Jenny Munro a few years after the death of Munro's partner of almost forty years, Gerald Fremlin. Of Catherine, Munro contemplates that ideally "we can hope that she will get up then and go to live in a dry house with some agreeable relations in a civilized town. Keeping her faith but holding it at arm's length, perhaps, to enjoy a bit of secular happiness" (16-17).

Happily, too, despite all the torments Boston experiences from without and from within, he successfully "presides at solemn festivals of Communion in which he knows himself to be the Vessel of God and witnesses the transformation of many souls" (15). And here we can see that Munro may be thinking of how, after decades of research and reflection and creative effort, she has been able to summon all her skill and strength to deliver herself of this remarkable book. Similarly, in what Munro imagines to be Catherine's ultimate destiny, we can see, by extension, Munro anticipating the chance "to enjoy a bit of secular happiness" (17) for herself at life's end when she, like Prospero, chooses to relinquish her own "rough magic" (Shakespeare, *The Tempest* V.i.59). But not now, not yet, not until completing two other masterful books of stories following the publication at age seventy-five of this very deftly written family history/herstory, a volume that might well have served as a radiant career-concluding envoi.

***

The final section of "No Advantages" concentrates on two perhaps not so entirely different first cousins, "the naïve comedian" (20) and eventually renowned author of *The Private Memoirs and Confessions of a Justified Sinner* (1824), James Hogg, son of Margaret Laidlaw Hogg, along with the sometime "joker" (23) but later seriously driven emigrant to "the New World" (25), James Laidlaw, son of Robert Laidlaw. The pair are grandsons of William Laidlaw, the legendary Will O'Phaup, about whom Munro writes elegiacally here that by the time the two young men reached adulthood, "the world of Will O'Phaup was almost gone" (20). Munro says of James Hogg that "It is mostly his writings I have to thank for what I know of Will O'Phaup," adding, in a sentence that speaks as much metafictively of herself, "Hogg was both insider and outsider, industriously and – he hoped – profitably shaping and recording his people's stories" (21). Yet, Munro is quick to mention, Hogg "had a fine source in his mother" (21), Margaret Laidlaw Hogg, the eldest daughter of Will O'Phaup, who "was famous locally for the number of verses she carried in her head" (21). Margaret's Homeric trait led her son to arrange a meeting with Sir Walter Scott, who at the time was a lawyer and the Sheriff-Depute of Selkirkshire and was gathering ballads for his book *Minstrelsy of the Scottish Border* (1802; final ed. 1830).

Margaret Laidlaw Hogg recited a number of pieces to Scott, including one that Munro mentions specifically, "the newfound 'Ballad of Johnie Armstrong'" (21) that had been collected by Margaret and her brother, interestingly, from a servant of Thomas Boston. Notably, after Scott published various ballads that Margaret had performed for him, she came to regret her decision: "'They were meant for singin and no for prentin,' she is supposed to have said. 'And noo they'll never be sung mair'" (22). Based on this distinction, we can reasonably regard Margaret Laidlaw Hogg as an emblem of the oral tradition just as we can reasonably regard Sir Walter Scott (or Margaret's son, James Hogg) as an emblem of the written tradition – two elements, orality and writing, that I believe Alice Munro sees as operating extensively in her own everyday world and therefore seeks to honour consistently from "Walker Brothers Cowboy," with Ben Jordan's stories and jokes and title song and the narrator/daughter's presumed adult writing, forward through the rest of her work. Consider, for example, the haunting melodies of the young radio show host and singer Sadie in the first story, "The Eye," of the "Finale" to Munro's last book, *Dear Life*.

"Johnie Armstrang," as the three-and-a-third-page ballad is entitled in Scott's *Minstrelsy of the Scottish Border*, is a lament or an elegy consisting of thirty-three four-line stanzas traditionally rhymed A, B, C, B. It relates the story of how Johnie, a border raider by profession, is invited with his men to the court of the Scottish king, James V, to receive what Johnie is led to believe will be a commendation for his exploits against the English, but instead they find themselves threatened with execution, resist, and die in combat. Four stanzas spoken by Johnie to the Scottish king begin with the identical deferential supplication: "'Grant me my life, my liege, my King!'" (153-54) followed by offers of extraordinary services or splendid gifts that Johnie will provide the king if he spares Johnie and his men. In striking contrast, the four stanzas that contain the Scottish king's reply ruthlessly conclude: "'I grantit nevir a traitor's life, / And now I'll not begin with thee'" (153-54). Subsequently Johnie vehemently declares of the king: "'Ye lied, ye lied'" – and of himself he contends: "'I've luved naething in my life, / I weel dare say it, but honesty –'" (154). As Scott notes in his seven-page preface to the ballad, the Armstrongs from very early on controlled a substantial territory including "the Debateable Land" (145) and seem to have maintained their "power and strength" (149) long after; yet following the time of the execution of Johnie and his men "we find little mention of the Armstrongs in history" (150).

Considered historically, or we might say literally, the ballad's depiction of the fatal betrayal of Johnie and his men represents a lament for the injustice and the cruelty with which such bold individuals, though seen by Scotland's ordinary populace as its real heroes, were treated so tragically by the country's governing powers in the early sixteenth century. But in addition, interpreted allegorically in the context of Munro's book, the fatal betrayal of Johnie and his men can be seen as representing the replacement, again so tragically to many, of an old order by a new one – much as Margaret Laidlaw Hogg lamented. Munro conveys a similar notion about the change over time that she has witnessed in her own home place, expressed notably in the two-page meditation that opens the three-part six-page epilogue to *The View from Castle Rock*. There, Munro reflects on the destruction of all that originally marked and defined the place where her immediate Huron County forbears resided: "The removal of so many of the fences, and of orchards and houses and barns[,] seems to me to have had the effect of making the countryside look smaller instead of larger – the way the space once occupied by a house looks astonishingly small, once you see only the foundation" (346).

A last couple of points about James Hogg, starting, very interestingly, with one involving a possibly wholly original contribution by Alice Munro to literary criticism. To this end, Munro presents a scene one night at Far-Hope when Hogg and some male cousins were meant to assemble for the evening "not to get drunk and to tell stories but to *read essays*" (22; emphasis in orig.) – an important point in light of the essay-like remarks that she offers at different places in "No Advantages" and again provides, this time with startling effect, here. The young men's choice of not telling stories but reading essays reinforces the distinction Munro is making between the oral tradition and the written tradition. By way of explanation of their preference for reading essays, she notes that the time of this gathering coincided with the Age of Reason, an era regarded as spanning the years from the death of King Louis XIV in 1715 to the start of the French Revolution in 1789 and defined intellectually by "the ideas of Voltaire and Locke and of David Hume, their fellow Scot and Lowlander" (22-23). But what was special about this particular night, Munro emphasizes, was that it brought a ferocious snowstorm lasting three to four days, "a storm which turned out to be the worst in half a century" (23). The threat of the coming snowstorm prevented Hogg from completing his journey to the gathering at Far-Hope, set for Saturday 24 January 1794 he tells us (Hogg 4), and thus denied him the chance of reading to the group "the flaming bombastical essay" (Hogg 5) that he had prepared for the occasion. Nevertheless, he did write a piece about the snowstorm for *Blackwood's Magazine*, to which he was a frequent contributor. And much later, in 1995, Hogg's article was collected under the title "Storms" as the opening ten-page selection in the standard edition of his essays, issued under the title *The Shepherd's Calendar*. Leading into the description of the event that will occupy the final two-thirds of his piece, Hogg writes: "But of all the storms that Scotland ever witnessed, or I hope ever will again behold, there is none of them that can once be compared with the memorable 24th of Janr 1794, which fell with such peculiar [sic] violence on that division of the South of Scotland that lies between Crawford-Moor and the Border" (4).

As Munro explains, *Blackwood's Magazine* "was the favorite reading of the little Brontës" (24) – and when as children the Brontës "each chose a hero to impersonate in their games, Emily chose the Ettrick Shepherd, James Hogg" (24). Significantly, Munro then points out that "*Wuthering Heights*, Emily's great novel, begins with a description of a terrible storm" (24). Turning to Brontë's 1847 novel – a story set back in 1801 at the very beginning of the nineteenth century, just seven years after the storm described by Hogg – we learn in Chapter II and Chapter III of the snowstorm Lockwood encounters soon after his arrival at his new residence, Thrushcross Grange. As Lockwood starts off across the moor on a walk to the neighbouring house, Wuthering Heights, he tells us that "the whole hill-back was one billowy, white ocean, the swells and falls not indicating corresponding rises and depressions in the ground: many pits, at least, were filled to a level; and entire ranges of mounds, the refuse of the quarries, blotted from the chart which my yesterday's walk left pictured in my mind" (25-26). Of his return, Lockwood adds: "The distance from the gate to the Grange is two miles: I believe I managed to make it four, what with losing myself among the trees, and sinking up to the neck in snow, a predicament which only those who have experienced it can appreciate" (26). Reflecting on the similarity between the description in Hogg's essay and the scene in Brontë's novel, a great favourite of Munro's as Catherine Sheldrick Ross and Robert Thacker and I have all noted (Ross 43, 45; Thacker, *Alice Munro* 104; Struthers, "In Search of the Perfect Metaphor" 185), Munro observes: "I have often wondered if there is a connection" (24). Here she provides an insight that we would typically regard as a feature of literary criticism – more precisely, of the essay, as she herself emphasizes – not as a component of fiction, thereby expanding the range in genre that *The View from Castle Rock* embodies.

And finally about James Hogg – in particular about his book *The Private Memoirs and Confessions of a Justified Sinner*, which was so boldly experimental that it showed how greatly inadequate the term "novel" is for many full-length works of fiction. At this point I cannot help but suggest revisiting Northrop Frye's timeless 1950 essay "The Four Forms of Fiction," reproduced in his *Anatomy of Criticism* (1957) as the section "Specific Continuous Forms (Prose Fiction)." There Frye opposes using the term "novel" to describe all full-length fictions and instead recommends employing the following four very different designations: "the novel," "the romance," "the confession," and finally "the anatomy" (Frye, *Anatomy* 303-14). In the *Anatomy*, Frye proceeds from this discussion to consider another category, "Specific Encyclopaedic Forms," notably the Bible and in modern times Joyce's *Finnegans Wake* (Frye, *Anatomy* 315-26). Personally, I'd be interested in proposing equivalents for Frye's four longer forms of fiction in my own area of special interest – "the short story" one might say colloquially before dividing that term properly, like its longer counterpart "the novel," into four unique forms: "the short story," "the supernatural tale," "the autobiographical sketch," and let's say "the parody." (Why "the parody"? you may ask – If only to pick a word that like "anatomy" ends with a why, oh, sorry, I meant to type "ends with a y").

In its strikingly and delightedly inventive form, Hogg's *The Private Memoirs and Confessions of a Justified Sinner* can be seen as a prototype, a literary ancestor, for Munro's own genre-defying style in *The View from Castle Rock*, another work for which we struggle to find a single descriptive term. Hogg, by way of signalling to readers – including, eventually, Munro – the originality of the book they were opening, chose to add the intriguing subtitle *Written by Himself: With a Detail of Curious Traditionary Facts and Other Evidence by the Editor*. The presence in Hogg's book of multiple points of view including that of a fictitious protagonist-narrator, that of a fictitious Editor, and Hogg's own perspective suggests a parallel way of thinking of the different roles Munro devises for herself: as protagonist, as narrator, and, beyond both of these, as writer. Indeed, as explained in the truly remarkable essay

"Messengers and Messaging in Alice Munro's *The View from Castle Rock*" by William Butt, whose critical writing Northrop Frye once described as "brilliant," Hogg's *The Private Memoirs and Confessions of a Justified Sinner* stands as "the most important literary model" (360) for Munro's book. Precisely like *The View from Castle Rock*, Butt writes, Hogg's book is "a memoir mélange" consisting of documentary and historical material along with "apparent folk-traditions of the Scottish seventeenth century, localist fantasy and superstition, diligently detailed archival researches, recollections, re-tellings that by point-of-view definition cannot be recollections and must be re-creations" (360-61). Certainly Munro must have come to regard Hogg's book as a very strong encouragement for her to be equally adventurous in her own exploration of genres here in *The View from Castle Rock*. For myself, I believe that the first five-part sequence and the second six-part sequence can be seen as mirror images of one another in terms of genre and style, "story-memoirs" as I have called the first sequence and "memoir-stories" as I have called the second sequence (with the book's epilogue, "Messenger," resembling the first group). Munro herself, in the Preface to the volume, poetically describes the two sequences by means of a metaphor of "two streams" which she explains "came close enough together that they seemed to me to flow in one channel, as they do in this book" ([xiv]).

Turning from one first cousin, James Hogg, to another, Munro reproduces for our enjoyment the occasion when James Laidlaw, her great-great-great grandfather, at a point when "he was probably a widower, a fellow on the loose" (25), is seen "putting on a show" at Tibbie Shiel's inn that is described as "Blasphemous, risky, and funny" (25). In fact James's actions represent – to employ the term I just introduced as a possible name for one of four forms of short fiction – a calculated parody of the religious practices seriously performed by ministers such as Thomas Boston that in turn contributes to our sense of Munro's writing as often itself involving good-humoured parodic strokes. Hence, "Down on his knees he is offering up prayers for several of those present. He asks forgiveness and specifies the sins that are outstanding, prefacing each one with *an if it be true*" (24; emphasis in orig.) – another description that points in this case to the allegorical element in Munro's work. These dramatics and pronouncements are so convincing and so specific that friends of James's have to get him out of the way before people named can harm him. Such "Self-dramatization," Munro has already noted, "got short shrift in our family" (20). "Though now that I come to think of it," she adds, again underlining her own fervent concern, and what she believes should be our matching concern, with language, "it wasn't exactly that word they used" (20). Instead of referring to "Self-dramatization," they spoke of "*Calling attention to yourself*" (20; emphasis in orig.). Yet opposed to the general wish to suppress any desire for self-expression was the "need to turn your life into a story, either for other people or for yourself" (20). At this point Munro – employing a strongly self-referential "some of us" – adds, "And when I study the people I know about in the family, it does seem that some of us have that need in large and irresistible measure" (20) as she demonstrates so splendidly through her composition of this family history/herstory.

Subsequently, James sets his sights on moving to America – hoping to take with him, as he proposes in correspondence seeking to establish his desirability as an immigrant, his five sons. Not so bewilderingly given the fiercely patriarchal nature of the time and place, late seventeenth-century to early nineteenth-century Scotland, that Munro wishes to represent in this portion of her book, James ignores his first-born, a daughter named Mary (a name that, interpreted allegorically, suggests an alternative to any strictly male-centred Christian belief) though Munro makes sure to mention Mary here. Again perhaps not so bewilderingly James's wife is not even named at this point: we are told only that she had died at the birth of the last of their six children, as Munro lists them, beginning with a daughter and then five sons, "Mary, Robert, James, Andrew, William, Walter" (25). Mary receives significant attention from Munro in the next story-memoir, the title piece, "The View from Castle Rock." There, too, we learn more about James's wife: that she was "born Helen Scott, and buried in Ettrick in the year 1800" (85) and that the names of her husband and herself appear on two different stones in the graveyard of a church in Equesing in Halton County, Ontario, named Boston Church in honour of Thomas Boston. One stone including the names of James and Helen is for Andrew and his wife Agnes, but very interestingly there is also an older-looking stone for James and Helen alone, which Munro describes as "a darkened, blotchy slab such as you are more apt to see in the churchyards of the British Isles" and which she suggests would lead anyone who saw the aged stone to "wonder if they carried it across the ocean, with the mother's name on it, waiting for the father's to be added" (85).

But the list of sons whom James expects to accompany him to the New World is soon shortened by the fact that the oldest son, Robert, takes off "for the Highlands," by the fact that the second son, James, heads off to Nova Scotia, and by the fact that the second youngest, William, "a boy not yet out of his teens," is apparently now "settled in the Highlands" and resolved never to return "to live in the Ettrick Valley ever again" (26). The final paragraph of this first story-memoir notes that "The poverty and the ignorance distress him, apparently. The poverty which seems to him willful, and the ignorance which he judges to be ignorant even of its own existence" (26). For as Munro emphasizes about William, "He is a modern man" (26). We will learn more about William's intriguing life, death, and afterlife in the book's third story-memoir, "Illinois," a work which, like Joyce's *Ulysses*, is concerned I believe with "Metempsychosis" or "the transmigration of souls" (Joyce, *Ulysses* 52) and which I think portrays William's return to this life to watch over his family in a form resembling Reynard the Fox of medieval fable. Further, Munro's subsequent joke in the fifth story-memoir, "Working for a Living," about her school-age father's misunderstanding of "Science notepaper" as "Signs Snow Paper" (128) is surely a playful echo of Molly Bloom's misuse, as her husband, Leopold Bloom, explains to her, of a phrase beginning with "Met him" in place of the word "Metempsychosis" (Joyce, *Ulysses* 52). Section by section, over the course of "No Advantages," this signature piece maps a series of utterly different worlds and world views, from Munro's own to Will O'Phaup's to Thomas Boston's to those of James Hogg and James Laidlaw, then, finally, to that of the William Laidlaw who Munro notes "will be my great-great-grandfather" (26).

By means of her unique imagination Alice Munro is able to perceive in this material the extraordinary passage of men and women all the way from the mythic to the modern and to re-create that epic journey for us. While there may be "No Advantages" in the Ettrick Valley practically speaking for many of Munro's ancestors, there certainly are great advantages imaginatively speaking for her. And, as we discern throughout this opening story-memoir, when writing about earlier figures Munro can at the same time be saying something crucial about herself. Most definitely, when Munro remarks of Will O'Phaup that "I have a feeling that his life was lived in a world still remote and self-contained, still harboring its own mythology and local wonders. And he was one of them" (8-9), she could be commenting, equally, about her own world – and, we may add, about herself. Similarly, Munro characterizes Thomas Boston's sense of despair and unworthiness, "even in the act of preaching the Gospel" (15) or when praying privately, much as she at times has darkly described her own personal feelings and professional accomplishments. As Munro once told me about her ongoing attempts to write stories, "I sometimes feel just *tormented* by the inadequacy and impossibility and feel that maybe this is quite a mistaken way to spend one's life" (Munro in Struthers, "The Real Material" 28; emphasis in orig.). And in discussing the two cousins James Hogg and James Laidlaw, Munro not only speaks biographically of them but also very likely autobiographically of herself, in a way that conveys Munro's displeasure about the critical attitude towards her in her home place while she was first living there, after she departed for the West Coast at age 20, and when she returned in 1975 in her mid-40s. Of the two cousins, Munro remarks: "Both men were born and raised in the Ettrick Valley, a place which had not much use for their sort – that is, for the sort of men who do not take easily to anonymity and quiet lives" (20). Once again speaking from deeply felt personal experience, but here with greater humour, Munro adds, "If such a man becomes famous, of course, it is another story. Alive he is booted out, dead he is welcomed home. After a generation or two, it is another story" (20). Or indeed another story *now*, for those readers who are able to appreciate how fully and how brilliantly Munro has succeeded here in delivering herself of this uniquely personal, artful, memorable, and I would say God-given book.

Acknowledgements

I would like to extend my heartfelt thanks to the many supportive family members and friends who offered me such vital encouragement and inspiration during the time I was writing and rewriting this essay, but in particular Kelsey McCallum (some people have a personal trainer; I'm fortunate to have a personal editor).

Works Consulted

Anderson, Linda. *Autobiography.* 2001. 2nd ed. London: Routledge, 2011. The New Critical Idiom.

Baldeshwiler, Eileen. "The Lyric Short Story: The Sketch of a History." *Studies in Short Fiction* 6 (1969): 443-53. Rpt. in *Short Story Theories.* Ed. Charles E. May. Athens, OH: Ohio UP, 1976. 202-13. Rpt. in *The New Short Story Theories.* Ed. Charles E. May. Athens, OH: Ohio UP, 1994. 231-41.

Bloom, Harold. "Criticism, Canon-Formation, and Prophecy: The Sorrows of Facticity." *Poetics of Influence: New and Selected Criticism.* Ed. John Hollander. New Haven, CT: Henry R. Schwab, 1988. 405-24.

Boston, Reverend Thomas. *Human Nature in Its Four-Fold State of Primitive Integrity, Subsisting in the Parents of Mankind in Paradise; Entire Deprivation, in the Irregenerate; Begun Recovery, in the Regenerate; Consummate Happiness or Misery, in All Mankind in the Future State; in Several Practical Discourses.* 1720. Bungay, Eng.: C. Brightly, 1812.

---. *Memoirs of the Life, Times, and Writings of Thomas Boston, of Ettrick.* Glasgow, Scot.: John M'Neilage, 1899.

Brontë, Emily. *Wuthering Heights: The 1847 Text; Backgrounds and Contexts; Criticism.* 5th ed. Ed. Alexandra Lewis. New York: W.W. Norton, 2019. A Norton Critical Edition.

Butt, William. "Messengers and Messaging in Alice Munro's *The View from Castle Rock.*" *Alice Munro Everlasting: Essays on Her Works II.* Ed. J.R. (Tim) Struthers. Toronto: Guernica Editions, 2020. 345-66. Essential Writers Ser. 52.

Caudle, Daniel. "Acclaimed Writer Alice Munro Sells Home, Leaving Southwestern Ontario." *The London Free Press* 23 Oct. 2019. <https://lfpress.com/news/local-news/alice-munro-acclaimed-writer-sells-home-leaving-southwestern-ontario>.

Dante Alighieri. *The Banquet of Dante Alighieri.* Trans. Elizabeth Price Sayer. Introd. Henry Morley. London: George Routledge, 1887. n.p.: Book Jungle, 2008.

---. *The Divine Comedy.* Rendered into English Verse by John Ciardi. New York: W.W. Norton, 1970. Rpt. as *The Divine Comedy: The Inferno; The Purgatorio; The Paradiso.* Trans. John Ciardi. New York: New American Library-Penguin, 2003.

Dickens, Charles. *Great Expectations.* Illus. F.W. Pailthorpe. Introd. Frederick Page. Oxford, Eng.: Oxford UP, 1953. The Oxford Illustrated Dickens. 21 vols.

Duffy, Dennis. "Too Little Geography; Too Much History: Writing the Balance in Alice Munro." *Alice Munro Country: Essays on Her Works I.* Ed. J.R. (Tim) Struthers. Toronto: Guernica Editions, 2020. 87-113. Essential Writers Ser. 51.

Dunlop, William. *Statistical Sketches of Upper Canada, for the Use of Emigrants: By a Backwoodsman.* 1832. 3rd ed. London: John Murray, 1833.

Fisher, Edward. *The Marrow of Modern Divinity: Containing Both First and Second Parts, in Two Volumes.* 18th ed. Notes by Mr. Thomas Boston. 1781. n.p.: Ecco, n.d.

Follett, Alec. "'The Region That I Know': The Bioregional View in Alice Munro's *The View from Castle Rock.*" *Alice Munro Country: Essays on Her Works I.* Ed. J.R. (Tim) Struthers. Toronto: Guernica Editions, 2020. 115-37. Essential Writers Ser. 51.

Frye, Northrop. "The Expanding World of Metaphor." *Myth and Metaphor: Selected Essays, 1974-1988.* By Northrop Frye. Ed. Robert D. Denham. Charlottesville: UP of Virginia, 1990. 108-23.

---. "The Four Forms of Fiction." *The Hudson Review* 2 (1950): 582-95. Rpt. (rev.) as "Specific Continuous Forms: (Prose Fiction)." *Anatomy of Criticism: Four Essays.* Princeton, NJ: Princeton UP, 1957. 303-14.

---. "The Mythical Approach to Creation." *Myth and Metaphor: Selected Essays, 1974-1988.* By Northrop Frye. Ed. Robert D. Denham. Charlottesville: UP of Virginia, 1990. 238-54.

---. "Specific Encyclopaedic Forms." *Anatomy of Criticism: Four Essays.* Princeton, NJ: Princeton UP, 1957. 315-26.

Gibson, Douglas. "Alice Munro: Not Bad Short Story Writer." *Alice Munro Country: Essays on Her Works I.* Toronto: Guernica Editions, 2020. 1-22. Essential Writers Ser. 51.

Gray, Thomas. "Elegy Written in a Country Churchyard." *The Norton Anthology of English Literature: Sixth Edition: The Major Authors.* Gen. ed. M.H. Abrams. New York: W.W. Norton, 1996. 1253-55. Also available at <https://www.poetryfoundation.org/poems/44299/elegy-written-in-a-country-churchyard>.

Hardy, Thomas. *Wessex Tales: Strange, Lively, and Commonplace.* 1888. Ed. Kathryn R. King. Oxford, Eng.: Oxford UP, 1997. Oxford World's Classics.

"Hiberno-Scottish Mission." <https://en.wikipedia.org/wiki/Hiberno-Scottish_mission>.

Hogg, James. *The Private Memoirs and Confessions of a Justified Sinner.* 1824. Ed. and introd. Ian Duncan. Oxford, Eng.: Oxford UP, 2010. Oxford World's Classics.

---. *Songs by The Ettrick Shepherd.* 1831. Ed. Kirsteen McCue with Janette Currie. Edinburgh: Edinburgh UP, 2014. Vol. 28 of The Stirling/South Carolina Research Edition of The Collected Works of James Hogg.

---. "Storms." *The Shepherd's Calendar.* Ed. Douglas S. Mack. With a Chronology by Gillian Hughes. Edinburgh: Edinburgh UP, 1995. 1-11. Vol. 1 of The Stirling/South Carolina Research Edition of The Collected Works of James Hogg. Rpt. in *The Shepherd's Calendar.* Ed. Douglas S. Mack. With a Chronology by Gillian Hughes. Edinburgh: Edinburgh UP, 2002. 1-11.

The Holy Bible. Cambridge, Eng.: Cambridge UP, n.d. Authorized King James Vers.

Hood, Hugh. *Great Realizations. The New Age / Le nouveau siècle.* Vol. 11. Toronto: Anansi, 1997. 12 vols. 1975-2000.

"James V of Scotland." <https://en.wikipedia.org/wiki/James_V_of_Scotland>.

"Johnie Armstrang." *Minstrelsy of the Scottish Border: Historical and Romantic Ballads.* By Sir Walter Scott. 1802. Ed. Thomas Henderson. London: George G. Harrap, 1931. 145-57.

Joyce, James. *The Restored* Finnegans Wake. Ed. Danis Rose and John O'Hanlon. London: Penguin Classics, 2012.

---. *Ulysses: The Corrected Text.* Ed. Hans Walter Gabler, Wolfhard Steppe, and Claus Melchior. Student's Edition. Harmondsworth, Eng.: Penguin, 1986.

Laidlaw, Robert. "Robert Laidlaw Reflects on Grandparents, His and Others." *The Village Squire* [*The Citizen*] [Blyth, ON] (Nov. 1974): 7-11. [Cited by Alice Munro in *The View from Castle Rock* as "a piece called 'Grandfathers'" (167).]

Livesay, Dorothy. "The Documentary Poem: A Canadian Genre." *Contexts of Canadian Criticism.* Ed. and introd. Eli Mandel. Chicago: U of Chicago P, 1971. 267-81.

MacKendrick, Louis K. "A Series of Metaphorical Epitaphs: Alice Munro's 'The Ottawa Valley'." *Alice Munro Everlasting: Essays on Her Works II.* Ed. J.R. (Tim) Struthers. Toronto: Guernica Editions, 2020. 173-82. Essential Writers Ser. 52.

Markson, David. *This Is Not a Novel.* 2001. Rpt. in *This Is Not a Novel and Other Novels.* Introd. Ann Beattie. Berkeley, CA: Counterpoint, 2016. 9-148.

May, Charles E. *"I Am Your Brother": Short Story Studies.* Garden Grove, CA: Amayzing Editions, 2013.

Morris, Wright. *The Home Place.* 1948. Lincoln: U of Nebraska P, 1968.

Munro, Alice. *Dear Life.* Toronto: McClelland & Stewart, 2012.

---. "Epilogue: Messenger." *The View from Castle Rock.* Toronto: McClelland & Stewart, 2006. 343-49.

---. Foreword. *The View from Castle Rock.* Toronto: McClelland & Stewart, 2006. [xiii-xiv].

---. "Home." *The View from Castle Rock.* Toronto: McClelland & Stewart, 2006. 285-315.

---. "Illinois." *The View from Castle Rock.* Toronto: McClelland & Stewart, 2006. 88-110.

---. "No Advantages." *The View from Castle Rock.* Toronto: McClelland & Stewart, 2006. 3-26.

---. "Powers." *Runaway.* Toronto: McClelland & Stewart, 2004. 270-335.

---. "Red Dress – 1946." *Dance of the Happy Shades.* Fwd. Hugh Garner. Toronto: Ryerson, 1968. 147-60.

---. *Too Much Happiness.* Toronto: McClelland & Stewart, 2009.

---. *The View from Castle Rock.* Toronto: McClelland & Stewart, 2006.

---. "The View from Castle Rock." *The View from Castle Rock.* Toronto: McClelland & Stewart, 2006. 27-87.

---. "Voices." *Dear Life.* Toronto: McClelland & Stewart, 2012. 286-98.

---. "Walker Brothers Cowboy." *Dance of the Happy Shades.* Fwd. Hugh Garner. Toronto: Ryerson, 1968. 1-18.

---. "Working for a Living." *The View from Castle Rock.* Toronto: McClelland & Stewart, 2006. 127-70.

Ong, Walter J. *Orality and Literacy: The Technologizing of the Word.* 1982. London: Routledge, 1988.

Prose, Francine. *Reading Like a Writer: A Guide for People Who Love Books and for Those Who Want To Write Them.* 2006. New York: Harper Perennial, 2007.

Rae, Ian. "Alice Munro and the Huron Tract as a Literary Project." *The Inside of a Shell: Alice Munro's* Dance of the Happy Shades. Ed. Vanessa Guignery. Newcastle upon Tyne, Eng.: Cambridge Scholars, 2015. 46-64. Rpt. in *Alice Munro Country: Essays on Her Works I.* Ed. J.R. (Tim) Struthers. Toronto: Guernica Editions, 2020. 181-205. Essential Writers Ser. 51.

Redekop, Magdalene. "Alice Munro and the Scottish Nostalgic Grotesque." *Alice Munro Writing On....* Ed. Robert Thacker. *Essays on Canadian Writing* 66 (1998): 21-43. Rpt. in *The Rest of the Story: Critical Essays on Alice Munro.* Ed. Robert Thacker. Toronto: ECW, 1999. 21-43.

Ricou, Laurie. *Everyday Magic: Child Languages in Canadian Literature.* Vancouver, BC: UBC P, 1987.

Scholes, Robert. *Fabulation and Metafiction.* Urbana, IL: U of Illinois P, 1979.

Scobie, Stephen. "Amelia, or: Who Do You Think You Are? Documentary and Identity in Canadian Literature." *Canadian Literature* 100 (1984): 264-85.

Scott, Sir Walter. *Waverley; or, 'Tis Sixty Years Since.* Ed. Claire Lamont. Introd. Kathryn Sutherland. Rev. ed. Oxford, Eng.: Oxford UP, 2015. Oxford World's Classics.

Shakespeare, William. *The Tempest.* Ed. Virginia Mason Vaughan and Alden T. Vaughan. *The Arden Shakespeare: Third Series: Complete Works.* Ed. Richard Proudfoot, Ann Thompson, David Scott Kastan, and H.R. Woudhuysen. London: The Arden Shakespeare, 2021. 1219-42.

Simpson, James, trans. *Reynard the Fox: A New Translation.* Illus. Edith E. Newman. New York: Liveright-W.W. Norton, 2015.

Smythe, Karen E. *Figuring Grief: Gallant, Munro, and the Poetics of Elegy.* Montreal, QC and Kingston, ON: McGill-Queen's UP, 1992.

Struthers, J.R. (Tim). "In Search of the Perfect Metaphor: The Language of the Short Story and Alice Munro's 'Meneseteung'." *Critical Insights: Alice Munro.* Ed. Charles E. May. Ipswich, MA: Salem-EBSCO, 2013. 175-94.

---. "Learning To Read, Learning To Write: An Interview with Clark Blaise (2007)." *Clark Blaise: The Interviews.* Ed. J.R. (Tim) Struthers. Toronto: Guernica Editions, 2016. 333-65. Essential Writers Ser. 45.

---. "The Place of Wisdom, Divination, the Act of Reading, and Alice Munro's 'Powers'." *Alice Munro Everlasting: Essays on Her Works II.* Ed. J.R. (Tim) Struthers. Toronto: Guernica Editions, 2020. 293-343. Essential Writers Ser. 52.

---. "Souwesto Stories: An Interview with James Reaney." *Alice Munro and the Souwesto Story.* Ed. J.R. (Tim) Struthers. *Short Story* ns 21.1 (2013 [2015]): 111-36.

---. "Story and Allegory, the Cast and the Mold: Reading Clark Blaise's 'The Birth of the Blues'." *Clark Blaise: Essays on His Works.* Ed. J.R. (Tim) Struthers. Toronto: Guernica Editions, 2016. 205-34. Essential Writers Ser. 44.

---. "Traveling with Munro: Reading 'To Reach Japan'." *Alice Munro:* Hateship, Friendship, Courtship, Loveship, Marriage*;* Runaway*;* Dear Life. Ed. Robert Thacker. London: Bloomsbury Academic, 2016. 163-83, 231-44 passim.

Tambling, Jeremy. *Allegory.* London: Routledge, 2010. The New Critical Idiom.

Thacker, Robert. "Alice Munro: Biographical." <https://www.nobelprize.org/prizes/literature/2013/munro/biographical/>.

---. *Alice Munro: Writing Her Lives: A Biography.* Toronto: McClelland & Stewart, 2005. Updated ed. Toronto: Emblem-McClelland & Stewart, 2011.

---. *Reading Alice Munro: 1973-2013.* Calgary, AB: U of Calgary P, 2016.

Woolf, Virginia. *A Room of One's Own.* 1929. London: Penguin, 2020. Penguin Classics.

Wordsworth, William. "A Poet's Epitaph." *Lyrical Ballads.* By William Wordsworth and Samuel Taylor Coleridge. 2nd ed. 1800. Rpt. in *Poetical Works.* By William Wordsworth. Ed. Thomas Hutchinson. Rev. Ernest de Selincourt. London: Oxford UP, 1969. 380.

Going Back (to) "Home"

Ryan Porter

There is a series of low glacial kames just outside the village of Baden in Southwestern Ontario. While I say low, their elevation is significant for the surrounding rolling topography. I grew up on the edge of this village in a small house just across the road from the lowest of these hills. From my front window, I could see the highest hill and its communications tower, which is visible from anywhere in the surrounding township. At night, I would watch the lights of this tower flashing into the dark or pulsing through the low clouds, lights I found, though strange now to think of it, comforting. They made the country night seem less open, less empty, dark, and lonely. I now live on the other side of the province, but when I return it is these same hills that I crane my neck to see as we pass by in the evening, my family and I, our long journey from Ottawa nearing its end. When we get closer to our destination, the landscape, of course, should feel like *home*, but for some reason that notion is easier to maintain through the images in my memory of this place than when driving through it. Perhaps that is because my memories are now more familiar to me than the place itself.

Anyone who completes a similar journey, as my family and I do on holidays or long weekends, will recognize Alice Munro's[1] initial fascination with landscape in the opening paragraphs of "Home." As her evening bus journey to see her father and stepmother nears its end, Munro strains to see those increasingly familiar locales that, in her adulthood, she is surprised to discover she is drawn to. She states: "the countryside here is what I most want to see – the reddening fall woods and the dry fields of stubble and the cows crowding the barn porches. Such unremarkable scenes, in this part of the country, are what I have always thought would be the last thing I would care to see in my life" (286).

In her description of these seemingly mundane details, or in her other stories that describe the distant fields and hills on the horizon, Munro's tone approaches the nostalgic; perhaps the closest Munro's writing ever gets to that tone is in her description of the landscape that surrounds her hometown of Wingham. Yet here this nostalgia takes her by surprise and seems to reveal itself only as she approaches her destination. Place, here, temporarily feels like home, but a version of home that cannot endure.

As her journey continues, the harder it is for Munro to maintain this illusion of placidity those earlier scenes might conjure; the hint of wistfulness in her voice dissolves when she recalls the region's other realities, the often stark truths of what occurs within this landscape. The bus she is riding in approaches what she gauges to be "a reckless speed, bouncing and swerving, over the remaining twenty miles" and she is reminded that this place "is great country for accidents. Boys too young to have a license will come to grief driving at ninety miles an hour over gravel roads [...] and most grown males seem to have survived at least one smashed telephone pole and one roll in the ditch" (286). Memory, here, complicates place, which cannot be understood from the window of a bus.

And reading Munro's words, I'm startled by their veracity, at least to my own experience growing up in a similar place and being required to navigate the hazards of the local backroads. I think of my own accident: fifteen years old, riding in a car with friends on a warm May evening and driving at "reckless speed" down a recently graded and therefore loose gravel road. The driver, just sixteen, overcorrected after drifting onto a soft shoulder and lost control. The car flipped end-over-end multiple times and landed upside-down in a ditch. I don't remember how I got out of the car, but I dimly recall waiting for an ambulance, dazed and soaked in blood from a head injury, asking every few minutes where another friend had gone who had sought help at a nearby farmhouse. "'Idiots'," Munro calls "the gravel-runners" (287) with a lack of compassion designed to appease her stepmother. I'm inclined to agree. How close we came to dying in that ditch, how close we came to grief because of a wager we were too young to know we were making. This memory comes to me often when thinking about home and tempers any wistfulness I may have about the place. It is a painful recollection, perhaps even more so now that I have children of my own. This memory, too, recurs in my mind's eye, particularly as we pass by the newly green hills illuminated in the last golden moments of a May sunset.

I have a strong urge to draw links between my own experience, my own crepuscular contemplations on place and time, and Munro's story. The more I read "Home," though, the more I realize that it is not a story about memory, or perhaps not *just* about memory. Munro does not examine the shaping influence that place has on the self, nor does she simply gauge the distance between her memories of place and the changes that have occurred since her initial departure. When the first version of "Home" appeared in the mid-1970s, her stories at that time often used memory to engage in a type of deep emotional self-scrutiny and to draw clear links between past and present experience. These examinations often produced a type of "summing up" at the end of her stories that Robert Thacker suggests is indicative of her early work ("Introduction" 18); the results were clear epiphanies providing understanding of that past experience. In "Home," however, Munro explores the sense of dislocation and bewilderment that results when place has become unrecognizable, and she does so by leaving the personal past largely unexamined. Munro uses memory only indirectly, filtered through a twisting nexus of indefinite vantage points and temporal layers. The story remains ambiguous and structurally loose, offering no clear reflection of the relationships among memory, place, and the self. But that is likely the point.

"Home" seems like a departure for Munro's stories at the time of its first appearance because memory is so often the medium through which her narrators convey their stories. Her protagonists scour their personal pasts, scrutinizing their actions and interrogating their perceptions to reflect on, arrive at, or at least approach an understanding of the past's significance. Katherine J. Mayberry states that Munro's narrators seek "narrative truth" through storytelling, but this truth often remains uncertain owing to "the failure of memory, the failure of nerve, the discontinuity between past and present, the alienation of language from experience" (30). Critics have long recognized the degree to which Munro's narrators rely on memory to produce her stories' characteristic, even uncanny insights. Thacker discusses a narrative technique of Munro's by which, through memory, she establishes "a dialectic between present and past, between experience and understanding" ("Clear Jelly" 58).

The narrator synthesizes past childhood experience with present adult understanding so that the narrative voice becomes a type of hybrid of selves at different times. Ailsa Cox suggests that Munro's narrative voice, perhaps more so than any other author, illustrates Henri Bergson's observation that all perception is a combination of memory and observation: "[m]emories and perceptions infuse one another, and this permutation of past and present is one of the distinctive elements in Munro's fiction" (72). Munro's narrators both grasp and convey the significance of past experience while in the process of describing it.

In an interview conducted by Graeme Gibson in the early 1970s, about the time Munro was writing the first version of "Home," she said about her writing: "it may be a way of getting on top of experience [...] I think it's a way of getting control [...] control by hindsight in a way [... but] it doesn't mean you have control over what is happening now" (Munro in Gibson 245). Munro writes through memory as a way of controlling experience "by hindsight," to provide shape to the past or to synthesize experience and understanding so that the narrative immediately conveys some overall insight on, or truth about, past experience. However, if "what is happening now" is more difficult to control through narrative, "Home" represents Munro's attempt to capture the experience but not the understanding of the present moment.

***

During our evening journeys, we pass by the edge of my old village. My mother no longer lives in that small house near the hills, but has moved to a larger home in a nearby town. As I take my family by my old house, which I invariably do, I'm startled by the incongruity between my memory of the place and the place as it exists. The house is too small, that tree in the yard is too big, the windows now have decorative shutters, and the garden is far too well kept. The scene contains the shell of the home in which I grew up, but the details are altered and disorienting. The house offers only a strange and diminished outline that no longer has any real hold on me; it was my home, but is now just a house, and any attachment I may still feel for it exists only in my memory. As Munro says about her own indifference to the changes observed in "Home," "I am not sure now whether I love any place, and [...] it seems to me it was myself that I loved here – some self that I have finished with, and none too soon" (290). What propels me back to this house is more curiosity than longing, as I, too, am happy to have left the place and the self that existed here. Place and self may intertwine, but only temporarily, something reflected in Munro's deep ambivalence about her home and even uncertainty over how to capture it on the page. While the story charts Munro's own homecoming after a long time away, she remains aware of the apparent paradox that distance both in time and space elucidates place through memory. Representing the home place in the here and now, though, is a far more equivocal process.

***

Munro's homecoming occurs in stages. The journey out of the city begins comfortably enough on a modern bus gliding along the highway, but becomes more intimate, with the buses smaller and provisional as her evening journey continues. Despite Munro's own claim that she "was aware of Stephen Leacock, but he wasn't important to me" (Munro in Struthers 17), the similarities between Munro's journey described in "Home" and the final chapter of Stephen Leacock's *Sunshine Sketches of a Little Town* demand comparison. Both depict a journey up and out of the city towards one's childhood hometown; both are set during chilly autumn evenings; both feature locals of the area, the "German and Dutch settlers" (285) of "Home" and the "Mariposa people" (143) of *Sunshine Sketches* on bus or train; and both are written in the present tense, which marks a shift from the past tense used in the previous portions within each respective volume and sets these stories apart.

Acknowledged or not, "Home" appears to be in conversation with the "L'Envoi" chapter of *Sunshine Sketches.* Leacock's journey occurs by train and Munro's by bus. Her mode of transportation is significant as this story, set in the mid-1970s, alludes to the recent de-railing of Ontario. Robert McGill has stressed that the conspicuous presence of trains in Munro's stories in fact "reminds her readers that trains no longer run through [S]outhwestern Ontario as they did during her childhood" and that the remnants of and allusions to this infrastructure often found in Munro's stories depict "the rise and decline of industrialization in Ontario" (136). Ten or perhaps even five years earlier, Munro would have taken this journey by train, a mode of travel more congruent with notions of the past and a common means of transport in stories of small-town homecomings. Travel by bus anticipates further changes that await Munro once she arrives home. Whereas the Mariposa of the present dissolves before the reader is able to re-enter it, Munro revisits her childhood home in the present, only to find it unrecognizable. Home as we knew it, and as Leacock's final chapter intimates, can only be revisited in memory. Munro's story, however, examines home not as she knew it, but as it has become in her absence.

Munro's use of the present tense in this story marks a shift from the past tense used consistently throughout her other more autobiographical stories in *The View from Castle Rock*. Her narrative voice is not that of a retrospective narrator, but one in the midst of experiencing, and, therefore, the narrative depicts not a past shaped by memory, but an unfolding present: "I sit with my father and my stepmother – whose name is Irlma – at the kitchen table, drinking whiskey" (287). In form, the story consists of short sections that contain little reflection on or connecting commentary between those experiences. Munro herself might explain both the narrative voice and the formal progression of the story as being a result of an inability to get control of these experiences, for there is little "control by hindsight" (Munro in Gibson 245) here. Rather, the story charts Munro's apprehensive and uncertain steps through the home place of the present.

Via an overview of her childhood home, Munro focuses on the unfamiliar and catalogues the changes that emphasize how different the house has become: new kitchen table and chairs, a new ceiling, repapered front room, or new siding that will eventually be installed over the red brick. In the midst of this description, Munro states: "[n]ow that I am living only a hundred miles away I come home every couple of months or so. Before this, for a long time, I lived more than a thousand miles away and would go for years without seeing this house. I thought of it then as a place I might never see again and I was greatly moved by the memory of it" (288). Those familiar, affecting things are what she now avoids, particularly those prompts that may provide a sense of situatedness, or that imbue place with a sense of *home*: "I don't go into the front room now, to rummage in the piano bench for old photographs and sheet music. I don't go looking for my old high-school texts, my Latin poetry, *Maria*

Chapdelaine" (290). At this point, Munro offers a description of the current physicality of the house she grew up in, not a prolonged reflection on her attachment to that structure or its affect. She does not seek out whatever familiar remnants remain, perhaps because "the house does not mean as much to me as it once did" (290); she also reflects that it doesn't matter much to her how her father might change it. Here, Munro hints at some possible irony in the story's title, that this is her home no longer, but that suggestion dissolves when she considers her lingering and deep attachment to those who remain in this place. Munro must hide her indifference from her father, who "wants some objections, some foolishness from me" (290), since to reveal her ambivalence to these changes might wound him.

Munro's childhood house is no longer her home; its physical structure has become a home for others but no longer for her: "it seems that this peculiar house [...] can be dissolved, in a way, and lost, inside an ordinary comfortable house of the present time" (289). The structure has become "*modern*" (emphasis in orig.), a word that her father and stepmother use "without quotation marks, quite simply and positively" (290); it has been swept along by the tide of currency upon which eventually all things must be carried or become decayed. For them, a rustic house is uncomfortable, impractical, and a chore to maintain. Their embrace of the modern in an unselfconscious way may seem artless to Munro's sophisticated city friends, but here the past is best left in the past (if one has the money to leave it there, that is). "'I know how you love this place'" her father says to her "apologetically yet with satisfaction" (290) as a way to explain the recent changes. Her father presumes her disappointment over these changes, which never materializes, and this presumption hints at his own sentimental affection for the house, his own connection to it through memory, and even his own unease at the changes catalyzed by his new wife. These changes and perhaps more fundamentally Irlma's presence itself result in Munro's distancing from this place. Irlma treats Munro as a guest, which, now, she is. Irlma's proprietorship is a *fait accompli* as she simultaneously serves Munro a late-evening meal while recounting her dog's revolting bowel issues in sickening detail. While the unacknowledged incongruity of Irlma's actions is hilarious, it signals that her claim on the place is now full and complete, and Munro can only ever be a visitor in this house.

Her father, once a great reader, hardly picks up a book anymore in part because Irlma has "corralled" all the books, which have been "chased and squeezed into this front-room bookcase, glass doors shut upon them" (291). This change of habit seems characteristic of her father who adapts himself to those around him and is described as having "trimmed himself" (312) to fit this life. He is "agreeable" to a fault, and advises that "the need to *fit in*" (298; emphasis in orig.) is a requirement of life in this place. While Irlma's influence on home and father may be most conspicuous, other internal changes have occurred as a result of illness; however, Munro does not notice at first until Irlma points them out. These become undeniable after an uncharacteristic encounter with a neighbour when she sees "that my father's face is not as usual, that it is not agreeable (that has been its most constant expression) and not ill-humored either. [...] Something has shut down in him, ground to a halt" (298). For Munro, her father's presence maintains a connection for her to this place, yet the illness that reveals itself during her brief stay anticipates a further, final loss of home.

What Munro also measures here is the dissolution of her mother's imprints on the house. These have been removed or papered over and as a result, "[r]eminders of my mother in this house are not so easy to locate, although she dominated it for so long with what seemed to us her embarrassing ambitions" (290). It was through her mother's presence or rather the remnants of her mother's presence that the place remained familiar. Instead of providing a straightforward comparison of then and now, of her childhood home and the home as it is currently arranged, Munro offers only indirect memories, really memories of memories: "[i]n my mind, when I was far away, I would also see the kitchen ceiling, made of narrow, smoke-stained, tongue-in-groove boards, and the frame of the kitchen window gnawed by some dog that had been locked in before my time. The wallpaper was palely splotched by a leaking chimney, and the linoleum was repainted by my mother every spring, as long as she was able" (288). Her mother's arrangements are part of how Munro *remembers* remembering the home; this displacement of memory suggests that now she is home, memory has nothing meaningful to tell her about it.

Herein lies the complexity of Munro's engagement with her material in this story. Not only is it told in an unfolding present tense, but also her characteristic synthesis of what Thacker calls "experience and understanding" ("Clear Jelly" 58) is absent. Memory, when it is finally shared, is indirect and its place in the overall shape of the story remains ambiguous, even uncertain; the ability to synthesize through memory seems to have eluded her here, as if this illuminated interchange between past and present was only manageable when she lived far away and what she remembered could be held at a distance. Now she avoids memory, as it seems irrelevant to the changing reality of place. In the Foreword to this book, Munro acknowledges the difference possessed by the stories collected in the second section of *Castle Rock*: "they were closer to my own life than the other stories I had written, even in the first person. In other first-person stories I had drawn on personal material, but then I did anything I wanted to with this material. Because the chief thing I was doing was making a story. In the stories I hadn't collected [...] I was doing something closer to what a memoir does – exploring a life, my own life" (Foreword [x]). As she frames it, "Home" is an exploration and, often, an open-ended one. When it was first published in 1974, "Home" appeared in the form of diary entries with metafictional commentary through which Munro questioned or even doubted the veracity or fairness of her depictions. These metafictional asides have been removed in the version that appears in *Castle Rock*, but the episodic structure remains. Here, her chief concern is not to fashion the material of memoir into a story, which, regardless of how much Munro might stretch the conventions of fiction elsewhere, typically has shape and resolution requiring the author to exert control over her material. "Home" lacks that sense of "control by hindsight" (Munro in Gibson 245) characterizing her other early stories, and explores present experience without the understanding that the distance of retrospect can provide.

Only in the closing section of the story does Munro finally offer a clear, sustained memory of home. After her father checks into the hospital and Irlma goes to visit him, Munro finds herself doing chores out in the barn. The mnemonic prompts that Munro earlier avoided inside the house cannot be avoided now since the corner of the barn in which she is standing represents "the scene of the first clear memory of my life" (314). Even here, though, Munro conveys memory only indirectly, as she again *remembers* remembering: "When I think about all this later, I will recognize that the very corner of the stable where I was standing [...] is the scene of the first clear memory of my life" (314). Munro keeps this memory in the present tense: "I am sitting on the first or second step watching my father milk the black-and-white cow" (314). The final section offers a clear recollection of being at home or rather the feeling of situatedness in time and place. Yet the recalled experience is immediate and barely distinguishable from the present-tense description in the rest of the narrative: "I am wearing warm clothes, a woolen coat and leggings [....] My father sits on the three-legged milking stool, in the cow's shadow. I can recall the rhythm of the two streams of milk going into the pail, but not quite the sound. Something hard and light, like tiny hailstones?" (314-15).

This image, interprets Howells, represents Munro's "true homecoming ... [but is] a fragile epiphany born out of panic and fraught with dread at the prospect of her father's death" (84). This "homecoming" is also overshadowed by where the memory travels to next: "[o]utside the small area of the stable lit by the lantern are the mangers filled with shaggy hay, the water tank where a kitten of mine will drown some years into the future; the cobwebbed windows, the large brutal tools [...] hanging out of my reach. Outside of that, the dark of the country nights when few cars came down our road and there were no outdoor lights" (315). That momentary image of comfort and safety, or "'home' restored" (84) as Howells puts it, is threatened by the uncertainty and menace of what looms in the darkness just out of sight beyond this brief moment of concord among place, memory, and self.

The story concludes with the following: "[a]nd the cold which even then must have been gathering, building into the cold of that extraordinary winter which killed all the chestnut trees, and many orchards" (315). There are various ways to interpret these enigmatic final lines: the looming cold that decimates the trees is a symbol of the impending death of her father, who, even in the memory, carries the seed of his own demise within himself; the lines could also suggest the mutability of home, that change and death are the only constants, that memories of the past must acknowledge its variability. Any of these interpretations would resolve a story that evades resolution, something that can perhaps best be explained by Munro herself when she discusses her writing method. What takes priority in her writing is not meaning but feeling: "when I write a story I want to make a certain kind of structure, and I know the feeling I want to get from being inside that structure" ("What

Is Real?" 332). Here that feeling could be described as not only menace, which is evoked by the impending descent of a killing cold, but also bewilderment and uncertainty.

The feeling induced by these perplexing, haunting final lines may reflect a writer's uncertainty over how to control the material of memoir and bewilderment about how to tie together these fragments of experience, to divine a connection between the strands of memory and the present. Howells would argue against that reading, as she sees the version of "Home" collected in *Castle Rock* as more "formally and emotionally controlled" (84) than the original version. That is, Munro displays greater certainty in her treatment of this overtly personal material and has largely eliminated those metafictional passages that questioned both her writing's fairness and its accuracy. Yet perhaps this certainty rests now in how to evoke uncertainty, how to convey that sense of pressing menace and deep ambivalence she feels through both memories and experience of this place.

By maintaining the present tense, Munro stresses memory's continuity with the present; memory cannot be held at a distance while standing in this place because sensation and feeling experienced in the past flow into the present. The rejection of the past tense here suggests her inability to apprehend or enclose both her feelings and her memories of this place and its people, and to understand their truth from a distance. The story's final section does not indicate a failure of reflection, and may not even be described as reflection itself, but rather a grasp at describing a physical contiguity she feels through time with her past self, a contiguity which language can adumbrate but provide little understanding of: this past cannot be examined from a distance because it is, emotionally, too close. The ending is also an honest admission of when the shape of story, or rather narrative's tendency towards resolution, cannot provide what is sought. And yet narrative is the only tool at one's disposal; the irresolution of the final lines may be the only form of "narrative truth" (Mayberry 30) for such an ambivalent experience.

Munro's return to the city at the end of the story is assured. Irlma's niece, Connie, visits while Munro is out in the barnyard, and says that she and her sons can do what's required for Irlma while Munro's father remains in the hospital: "'You must be wanting to get back to your own life'" (313), Connie says to Munro, absolving her of that sense of obligation that keeps her tied here. The return to the city and to her own life will return her not only to her current home, but also to her creative life, her life as an artist. Munro feels relief since the longer she stays in this place, the more she feels like "one of those misfits, captives," like one of those people "who should have left but didn't, couldn't, and are now unfit for any place. [...] I can see myself as a middle-aged daughter who did her duty, stayed at home, thinking that someday her chance would come, until she woke up and knew it wouldn't" (312). This vision precipitates Munro's later sense of panic, and is one in which choice and control have evaporated; place has ensnared her.

The fear is also an artistic one. Without that distance between home and self, Munro wonders if the locus of control will shift: no longer would she have control of home-as-subject, she worries, but home has the potential to render her voiceless, "useless, celibate, rusting" (312). A move away from this place back to the city and her own life promises that the requisite remove or artistic distance will be restored to allow her to look back at this place, both in time and space, and again exert control. "Home" documents the uncertainty and ambivalence we might experience when returning to a place left long ago, a place no longer wanted or needed as home, a place that holds a past entwined with our own, but a place whose present threatens the one we have created for ourselves.

***

As we travel back to Ottawa at the end of our most recent visit home, I notice a gravel pit newly scraped into the shoulder of the highest of the Baden Hills. Initially, I am dismayed: so much of my attachment to this area is tied to its topography, and I am cheered each time we drive by and this place aligns with my memory of it. Still, I must acknowledge that it is only the memory of these hills that remains mine. I have little claim on this place any more, for place changes whether we are there to witness it or not. Back in Ottawa, though, I will close my eyes and see the shadow of the dark hills outlined against the night sky. And I will even make the lights of the tower atop the highest hill flash, however briefly, into the black of the lonely country night.

Note

1. I will refer to the narrative voice here as Munro's rather than Munro's narrator's, since others (Coral Ann Howells, Robert Thacker) have argued persuasively that "Home" is autobiographical, essentially a memoir. See Howells, "Alice Munro and Her Life Writing" and Thacker, "Introduction: Alice Munro, Writing 'Home': 'Seeing This Trickle in Time'."

Works Cited

Cox, Ailsa. *Alice Munro*. Tavistock, Eng.: Northcote, 2004.

Gibson, Graeme. "Alice Munro." *Eleven Canadian Novelists*. Toronto: Anansi, 1973. 237-64.

Howells, Coral Ann. "Alice Munro and Her Life Writing." *The Cambridge Companion to Alice Munro*. Ed. David Staines. Cambridge, Eng.: Cambridge UP, 2016. 79-95.

Leacock, Stephen. *Sunshine Sketches of a Little Town*. Ed. Gerald Lynch. 1912. Ottawa: Tecumseh, 1996. Canadian Critical Editions.

Mayberry, Katherine J. "'Every Last Thing … Everlasting': Alice Munro and the Limits of Narrative." *Alice Munro*. Ed. Harold Bloom. New York: Infobase, 2009. 29-39. Bloom's Modern Critical Views.

McGill, Robert. "Alice Munro and Personal Development." *The Cambridge Companion to Alice Munro*. Ed. David Staines. Cambridge, Eng.: Cambridge UP, 2016. 136-53.

Munro, Alice. "Home." *74: New Canadian Stories*. Ed. David Helwig and Joan Harcourt. Ottawa: Oberon, 1974. 133-53.

---. *The View from Castle Rock*. 2006. Toronto: Penguin, 2010.

---. "What Is Real?" *How Stories Mean*. Ed. John Metcalf and J.R. (Tim) Struthers. Erin, ON: The Porcupine's Quill, 1993. 331-35. Critical Directions 3.

Struthers, J.R. (Tim). "The Real Material: An Interview with Alice Munro." *Probable Fictions: Alice Munro's Narrative Acts*. Ed. Louis K. MacKendrick. Downsview, ON: ECW, 1983. 5-36.

Thacker, Robert. "'Clear Jelly': Alice Munro's Narrative Dialectics." *Probable Fictions: Alice Munro's Narrative Acts*. Ed. Louis K. MacKendrick. Downsview, ON: ECW, 1983. 37-60.

---. "Introduction: Alice Munro, Writing 'Home': 'Seeing This Trickle in Time'." *The Rest of the Story: Critical Essays on Alice Munro*. Ed. Robert Thacker. Toronto: ECW, 1999. 1-20.

Searching for an Unknown God: Alice Munro's "What Do You Want To Know For?"

Alyda Faber

Could there be God not contained in the churches' net at all,
not made manageable by any spells and crosses, God real,
and really in the world, and alien and unacceptable as death?
Could there be God amazing, indifferent, beyond faith?
– Alice Munro, *Lives of Girls and Women* (115)

On the question of God, the narrative "I" in Alice Munro's autofiction story "What Do You Want To Know For?" could not, in one sense, be clearer: "I am not a believer" (334), the reader is told. And yet the story's overriding fixation with religious sites (a burial mound, cemetery, and church) tempers the fictive Munro's denial of belief, evoking something elusive and not reportable "behind" (334) the investigations of these surfaces. In this regard, despite her explicit denial of belief, the restless, energetic syntactical play of Munro's prose resembles a mystical religious language that participates in desire for a named and unnameable God. Paradoxes of this kind abound in Munro's fiction of indirection, a method that "is far more lying than it is speaking the truth" (147), as the thirteenth-century mystic Margaret Porette writes in her book *The Mirror of Simple Souls*. Porette says she is nothing and she is everything, that falling is rising: "I could not ... raise myself up ... or come to my own help; and it was then that my better was born" (169). Note that I am not calling Alice Munro a believer. As a believer myself, I have difficulty understanding what it means to be, or not to be, a believer. But declaring oneself an unbeliever is also not the same as being insensible to intimations of divinity, and in Munro's case I contend that the overt swerve away from orthodox belief-structures clears imaginative space for what is a fresh (if indirect) approach to the idea (or even the *reality*) of God. The uniqueness of Munro's approach is to create a story that, with its precise attention to "surface" detail, draws the reader almost imperceptibly into the ineffable *more*, the ever shifting spiritual resonance of "what is behind" (334) these surfaces.

"What Do You Want To Know For?" is the penultimate narrative in *The View from Castle Rock*, followed only by a brief epilogue. The opening story, "No Advantages," ponders the conflicting religious forces at play in Munro's great-great-great-great-great grandfather, William Laidlaw, who lived and died in the Ettrick Valley in Scotland. Known as Will O'Phaup, he's described as "a near pagan," a believer in sinister fairies, and "bound to have listened to, and believed in, the strictures and hard hopes of [a] punishing Calvinist faith" (17). Munro aligns herself with the "canny lying" (21) of those ancestors who feel an irresistible urge to turn their lives into stories, despite relations who "cringe with embarrassment and apprehension" in response to those stories and warn the storyteller not to "[*call*] *attention to yourself*" (20; emphasis in orig.). By contrast, she characterizes the restraint exercised by those who refuse the storytelling impulse as "not exactly modesty but a strenuous dignity and control, a sort of refusal" (20). Considering the narrative "I" of "What Do You Want To Know For?," Munro appears to be heir to both impulses, the imaginative exuberance of the "near pagan" storyteller and the restraint of the Calvinist naysayer. A jubilant curiosity (bordering on a child-like naïveté) strains with and against a "strenuous" unflinching ancestral eye on the world. The searcher delights in "impractical knowledge" (337) like glacial geography or the origins of strange burial mounds, but contends with internal voices that call her "an idler ... a person at loose ends, with ... *nothing better to do*" (326; emphasis in orig.), unconcerned with "Real things" and "Real work" (337). The jammed syntax of the title, "What Do You Want To Know For?," ending with that exposed preposition "For," gives a visceral jolt of a crash, a grinding metal stop. A person at risk of being stopped from doing what she most wants (to do). A voice often navigating those tensions with ironic wit.

Although I left Bruce County, Ontario when I was nineteen, and have lived on the east coast of Canada for decades, the geography that figures so centrally in "What Do You Want To Know For?" remains close to my heart. It's home. The Calvinism of Munro's early forebears was the reason for our hour-long car trips to Owen Sound most Sunday mornings (unless prevented by snowstorms), from a farm northeast of Walkerton, through the countryside of the story, Scone and Desboro in Sullivan Township. We always walked up the left aisle to the front of First Christian Reformed church, always late, heads down, the minister already in the pulpit, all the way to the second or third pew, the middle and back rows packed with on-time Calvinists. On good Sundays, we entered as people stood for the opening hymn, a forest of limbs and bodies hiding all but my father's tall walk to the front. These names – Scone, Desboro – ignited a burn trail of memories: changing out of my Sunday dress into my 'barn' clothes (most importantly, pants) during the drive home from church; my father's Frisian cutting into my brothers and me talking – "Why are you speaking that verotte Engels?" (rotted English); other times, he would drive with one hand on the steering wheel, the other hand a blind fist jabbed into sibling squabbles in the back seat.

Tucked in the midst of this very personal milieu, "What Do You Want To Know For?" opens with a surprise discovery by Munro and her husband on a drive to visit friends on Georgian Bay: "[a] large, unnatural mound blanketed with grass" (316) in the middle of a country cemetery. The mound's stone and brick wall has only a crudely etched "skinny cross" in the keystone of an upper arch, no other clues to indicate what this "'strange'" (316) thing is. Munro's investigation into the origins and purpose of this mound, in libraries, a church, in homes with local people, is the spine of the story. The playfully ironic description of the mound as "a big woolly animal – like some giant wombat, lolling around in a prehistoric landscape" (316) creates nearness ("woolly" and "lolling") and distance ("in a prehistoric landscape"). "[T]he FarNear" (Anne Carson notes that this is the equivalent in English of the term *le Loing-prés* in Old French that Porette invents in order to name/unname God [176]) of the mixed images of the mound relates to the etymology of the word God itself. That word's derivation can be traced back to the Proto-Indo-European *ghu-to-m*, usually related to the root *gheu*[ə]-, meaning 'to invoke,' a prayer, an invocation, that which is invoked, or, alternatively, related to the root *gheu-* 'to pour' (in the sense of pouring a libation, as in the Greek *khutē gaia* 'poured earth,' leading some to infer that the Germanic form refers to "the spirit immanent in a burial mound" [Watkins 31]).

Already charged with physical, historical, and religious connotations, the burial mound also takes on an intimate threat of death. The narrative "I" is confronted with "a lump deep in my left breast" (317), found during a routine mammogram, and requiring a biopsy. Her family doctor, a friend, places his hand on Munro's shoulder: "I knew that his first wife's death had begun in just this way" (317). This narrative strand expresses "a strenuous dignity and control" (20): understated emotion emerges through details. Munro preoccupies herself with mundane tasks: housekeeping, answering letters, hosting dinner parties, rather than "thinking about what you might call deeper matters" (317). She relates that she read very little, didn't listen to music or "go into a muddled trance as I so often do, looking out the big window in the early morning as the sunlight creeps into the cedars" (317), nor did she take any walks by herself, though she still goes for walks and drives with her husband. The threat of death cannot be remedied or helped or forced, it thwarts thinking and will-less drifting, it lies deep in the flesh. But there are still things that can be done nevertheless; plain sense work. Later in the story this contrast between the everyday and "deeper matters" (317), or "what is behind" (334), used to describe Gothic German words on two church walls, relates, in my reading, to an understanding of Munro's craft enacted through the distancing of the fictive Munro.

The restrained narrative "I" is textured with a changeful narrative voice in scenes where Munro and her second husband, a geographer, travel the countryside, unable to find the cemetery with the mound again. He has taught her to see the landscape in a new way: "I came back to where I never expected to be, in the countryside where I had grown up. So my knowledge is untainted, fresh" (321). Matching what she sees through the car window with their special maps, colour coded to show soil types and glacial landforms, like drumlins and moraines, gives her "a naïve and particular pleasure" (321). Matching territory and map, she acts *as if* they are commensurable, aware they are not: it's a "naïve" pleasure. Munro and her husband also claim a feeling of ownership: "we are possessive about this country, and try not to let anything get by us" (316). The voice here implies the possibility of trickery, but also a faith in the ability of surfaces (empirical observation of physicality) to create some clarity. Failing to find the cemetery again, their relationship to the landscape shifts; they're "puzzled and disconcerted" though still pleased while "looking at the countryside that we think we know so well and that is always springing some sort of surprise on us" (318). The glacial landscape is a trickster. It's also "vulnerable" (318) to extractive mining for gravel. "[T]he chewed-up hills, the plundered terraces" (318) result when farmers, in need of cash, sell the gravel on their land, as her father did with the river flats. She recalls her excitement, as a child, with the landscape made by the mining, "the novelty of pits and hollows" (319) filled with water, and later overgrown with weeds, bushes. Large gravel pits left little lakes in the hollows, their steep sides "bumpy with greenery" (319). Vegetation hides the plunder, "[b]ut the tracks of the glacier are gone for good" (319). A tectonic history has vanished. Pleasure and plunder – the narrator and her husband travel on convenient gravel roads made by a "haphazard" turning of part of the landscape "inside out" (319) so that hills become hollows.

The landscape's vulnerability to mutilation and change demands another kind of relation: "you have to keep checking, taking in the changes, seeing things while they last" (319). Throughout these paragraphs about the landscape, Munro accentuates "looking" (318), attentiveness expressed as "not to let anything get by us" (316), thereby evading trickery and deception, "seeing things while they last" (319), a sense of both cherishing and investigating, and the ever renewing possibility of surprise. The narrator attends to "the fact of these separate domains, each with its own history and reason, its favorite crops and trees and weeds ... each with its special expression, its pull on the imagination" (322). Attention creates distinction, "separate domains" and "*little countries* lying snug and unsuspected, like and unlike as siblings can be, in a landscape that's usually disregarded, or dismissed as drab agricultural counterpane. *It's the fact you cherish*" (322; emphasis added). What is "the fact you cherish"? Is it this shifting, ungovernable, irrepressible, receding, exuberant life in death, death in life – animated through the images of landscape and burial mound and breast – that is to be cherished? How hard is *that*? How hard is that cherishing? It likely calls upon all the powers of the straining differences at work in the narrative "I": the "near pagan" (17), the attunement to the sinister, the Calvinist restraint, the imaginative, the contemplative.

Cherishing might look like their search for the "surprising," "primitive" (323) burial mound (finding, losing, dogged looking, finding again), and their persistent interest in seeing land formations created by "ancient events," uneven movements of "advancing, stationary, and retreating ice" (318). What seems at a great distance in time, "about fifteen thousand years ago" (318), the narrator understands as quite recent (spatially near), having learned from her geographer husband "a certain way of reckoning history" (318). There's no stability to the landscape, just as there's no fixed point in the practical sense of Munro and her husband travelling through the landscape in a car, yet the mound gives a sense of purpose and a stopping spot on these travels. What you see, therefore, depends on how you reckon time, tell time, narrate time. "Reckon" comes from the Old English word *recenian*, "to narrate," suggesting a connection between Munro's glacial landscape and the telling of stories, a remembering of what has become hidden, what has been "plundered" (318), a telling that retains an ungovernable element of surprise. It's also intriguing with respect to the burial mound that navigation by dead reckoning requires a previously determined position, or fix, to reckon the current position of a moving object. It's as if each attempt at "saying" or "telling" – the burial mound, the breast, the landscape – becomes a temporary fixed point that opens a conduit for "unsaying," for what remains unsayable "behind" the saying.

Kame moraines, the narrator's favourite glacial formation, "are all wild and bumpy, unpredictable, with a look of chance and secrets" (321). They "show where a heap of dead ice sat, cut off from the rest of the moving glacier, earth-stuff pouring through all its holes and crevices," or "where two lobes of ice pulled apart, and the crevice filled in" (321). The glacial history of kame mounds is vulnerable to erasure by aggregate mining (gravel to boulders), and their surface stillness hides a past drama of grating, grinding movement, "earth-stuff pouring through" every opening. While restrained when talking about the biopsy, here the narrative "I" approaches death indirectly through image – as an outpouring of all that was once held in place, the risk of lost history, a strangely static point of "dead ice," isolated, "cut off from the rest of the moving glacier." I wonder if Munro's image of kame moraines represents the nature of her stories, their elements "of chance and secrets," together with characterizing the writer's situation, with the peculiarity that the writer is both subject to this grating and grinding movement, but also a perpetrator of extraction like the aggregate miner. John Metcalf cites the following from a commentary by Munro: "There is a sort of treachery to innocent objects – to houses, chairs, dressers, dishes, and to roads, fields, landscapes – which a writer *removes* from their natural, dignified obscurity, and sets down in print. There they lie, exposed, often shabbily treated, inadequately, badly, clumsily transformed" (498; emphasis added). Does particularity, a focus on the surface details of a specific thing, make the writing process extractive?

In the story "Nettles," collected only a few years earlier, the fictive narrative "I," Munro as a child, describes in general, indirect terms the nine-acre fox farm she lives on as a domain with personalities to be encountered: "every part had a particular look and character, which I could not have put into words" (156-57); "[e]ach of the trees on the place had likewise an attitude and a presence" (157). A boy, Mike, has changed her way of seeing, since he connects things with use (a rock for jumping off), but she still persists with her own way, "by its very nature incommunicable, so that it had to stay secret" (157). Does the adult narrative "I" in "What Do You Want To Know For?" have a similarly bicameral way of looking, her geographer husband's way and her own way? Does it have to do with the interplay of different ways of reckoning passing time, in eons (lyrical, geological) versus days (narrative: one year later, ten days later, two weeks, a few days, days with edges and others blunted by boredom)? And of eons grinding, percolating under days? There's also the intimation that secrecy is held somewhere between, rather than within, these different ways of seeing.

After we are presented with the images of gravel-mining and drastically altered landscapes, we are told that the narrator learned her appointment with the city doctor was not for a biopsy, but to determine if one should be done, and it will be, in two weeks. Biopsy, the extraction of tissue from a living body, in this case, cutting into the breast, intensifies the perception of extractive processes. Just as a breast through surgery might be turned inside out, a hill into a hollow. Just as writing extracts the visceral and fleshly life for the creation of fictional maps, at once a distancing through a made order, and an attempt to bring the reader close to the tumult "behind" the words on the page, a tombstone, the walls of a church. And just as time in a landscape changes with the point of view of the observer – the geographer's "FarNear" view of millennia that Munro has learned from her husband – the narrator, herself over sixty, considers that "[m]y death would not be a disaster"

(322) compared with the "young mother, a family wage-earner, a child" (323) seated in the doctor's waiting room. As with the greening of the excavated pits and hollows, she reconsiders: her death "would not be *apparent* as a disaster" (323; emphasis in orig.).

The hiddenness of mutability – in the glacial landscape, the burial mound, the narrator's breast – surges to the surface when Munro recalls the farm she grew up on, in near-proximity to the landscape of the story. The former farm "has changed, of course, it has changed utterly, becoming a car-wrecking operation" (332). Munro recollects the features of her childhood landscape, the heft of each thing accentuated by the definite article "the": "[t]he front yard and the side yard and the vegetable garden and the flower borders, the hayfield, the mock-orange bush, the lilac trees, the chestnut stump, the pasture and the ground once covered by the fox pens" which have all been "swept under a tide of car parts, gutted car bodies, smashed headlights, grilles, and fenders, overturned car seats with rotten bloated stuffing – heaps of painted, rusted, blackened, glittering, whole or twisted, defiant and surviving metal" (332). Here, just as the narrative dramatizes the glacier's "dead ice" (321), the violence of dying is indirectly exposed through the inanimate, insensible, man-made as it takes on aspects of flesh wrecked by death and "gutted," "smashed," "overturned," "rotten bloated," "painted, rusted, blackened, glittering, whole or twisted." The perversely "defiant and surviving metal" covers over, smothers, obscures a past life, as intimate, fleshly, as the lump deep within the breast, as complex as geological history. The narrative "I" lives only twenty miles away; if she wanted to, she could see the ruined farm every day, but this is too near for it to have meaning. "The past needs to be approached from a distance" (332). This sentence stopped me in my tracks on my first reading of the story, and it still feels elusive to me. Is distance created or imposed (or both)? Is the past the "dead ice" that pours "earth-stuff" into the present? Does the spatial metaphor suggest the physicality of time in whatever register it appears – personal, material, geologic, spiritual?

Images of gutted interiors introduced in the psalm-like lament of the farm turned into a car-wrecking yard, and the glacial landscape's mutations, carry over in quieter unsettling images that follow, when Munro learns more about the Mannerow family burial mound and sees the interior of St. Peter's Evangelical Lutheran, the church she thought was connected to the cemetery. The crypt "is said to have been built in 1895 to receive the body of a three-year-old boy, a son of the Mannerow family" (329). The visit to the church, with a woman named only as "Rachel's mother" (329), begins with attention to exterior detail, including the factions created in the church by adding a modern porch to the building. The focus of the visit becomes the surprising discovery of Gothic German lettering on the side walls, hidden under paint, possibly since the beginning of the First World War, and exposed after a large fire "gutted much of the inside but left the shell intact" (333). As elsewhere in the story, repetition accentuates wordlessness or excitement, as Rachel's mother presents the psalm texts with a repeated directive: "And there *it* is. They touched up the paint, and there *it* is" (333; emphasis added). The reference to "it" (singular) by Rachel's mother is disorienting: the narrator refers only to "[t]he words on the wall" (344), plural. The psalms, at the heart of the Lutheran (and Calvinist) liturgies, are represented on the walls by two verses. First, a verse from Psalm 121: "*Ich hebe meine Augen auf zu den Bergen, von welchen mir Hilfe Kommt.*" "*I will lift up my eyes unto the hills, from whence cometh my help*" (333). Munro has been looking at the hills with the help of special maps, identifying glacial landforms. Is the implication that the verse is a special map that some people – not Munro – use for seeing life? And second, a verse from Psalm 119: "*Dein Wort ist meines Fusses Leuchte und ein Licht auf meinem Wege.*" "*Thy word is a lamp unto my feet and a light unto my path*" (333). The relationship of the narrative "I" to "Thy word" and "[t]he words on the wall" returns the reader to the intense pressured relationship of the distinct yet coexisting voices, of the severe Calvinist and the pagan storyteller, propelling the narrative with their dynamic tension.

Guided through the church, the narrator feels "slightly lost," bewildered, a sense of getting "things the wrong way around" (334), as with the search for the burial mound. Following images of interiors becoming surface exposures, and breaking down, she says that "[t]he words on the wall strike me to the heart, but I am not a believer and they do not make me a believer" (334). She observes that Rachel's mother seems to view the church and the words as if she were their "vigilant housekeeper" (334): the "L" of Licht needs repair, she notes. The stranded "icht" of the word Licht is the dative form (the receiver of an action) of an obsolete pronoun in Middle High German meaning "something." Repairing the "L" would transform the word from the vagueness of the "something," into which it has deteriorated, to the inexhaustible play of religious meanings of "*light*." The inviting, bewildering significance deepens: "But she is the believer. It seems as if you must always take care of what's on the surface, and what is behind, so immense and disturbing, will take care of itself" (334). The narrator appears to make a fairly straightforward comment about a believer's habits, but with the ambiguous and intimate second person address, it redounds upon the narrator, and becomes a complex observation about Munro's methods as a writer. As if in this moment, the guided narrator becomes the guide. As if Munro is the vigilant housekeeper of words and sentences – which does not mean willed control, as any housekeeper knows, rather, an attempt to intervene into what always threatens disorder, undoing, and, like the landscape, regularly surprises us.

In the foregoing quotation, the narrative "I" characterizes Munro's art as a way of life, an approximation of faith that left me reeling with its intensity and suggestiveness, and touched me to the heart.

It seems as if
(double conditional, "it seems" and "as if")

you must always take care
(double imperative, "you must" [when: always, continuous present] "take care")

of what's on the surface,
(take care of what?)

and what is behind,
(take care of "what is behind" too? hidden, unseen?)

so immense and disturbing,
(immensity in the "behind"; disturbing the never-at-rest heart)

will take care of itself.
(No. Not your concern. What's "behind" will [future] take care of itself.)

As I've placed them here, the first two lines by Munro enact Michael Sells's "unsaying" (his translation of the Greek *apophasis*) of "saying" (Greek *kataphasis*). He uses this paradox to describe the effect of mystical writing: its affirmations about God live in a continuous dynamic tension with negations of those affirmations. Not only does Munro place the conditional in an "unsaying" relation with the imperative, she does the same with "you must always take care" of the surface and you never have to take care of what's "behind." How this works is inexplicable – how might "what is behind" take care of itself? It just does. The obscure "it" referred to by Rachel's mother ("there it is," another object or fact) seems to return here as some strange (implied) agency that "will take care of itself" ("it" has no need of our efforts, our will-full actions).

The unnameable "behind" is almost imperceptibly given a sense of will, a capacity for action, becomes a subject in some elusive sense. The movements in response to an unnameable agency – looking for it and addressing it – imply a trust in the possibility of always becoming a receiver in relation to whatever it is that "take[s] care of itself." If this sensibility can be said to characterize Munro's art, it resembles Richard Kearney's *anatheism*, "[t]he return of God after the disappearance of God," without any claim to know God, but searching, in wonder and bewilderment, and beginning "to recover the presence of holiness in the flesh of ordinary existence" (5). Munro's art circles around life in death and death in life, while a housekeeping of surfaces remains ever susceptible to "what is behind" taking care of itself, breaking out with its interior tumult. That susceptibility is figured in the "saying" and "unsaying" of Munro's writing, rhythmically conveyed through rapid and continuous shifts between voices and moods in the story. A pressured proximity and mutual resistance of the pagan storyteller (perceiver of the sinister) and the restrained Calvinist keeps both distinct but also merging, mirroring the strange unpredictability of the relation of "surface" and "behind." The "bumpy" shifts in voice between pleasure at the new and unexpected, and sober reckoning, are intensified and made realer by their proximity and rapid oscillation.

In the life of the Christian church, symbols are regarded as a physical sign of the largely incommunicable reality of God, and – I would argue not coincidentally – in the conclusion of the fictive Munro's visit to the church, there is a possible clue concerning her own attitude toward symbols. The narrative is broken with a list of symbols she sees in the panes of the church's stained glass windows, and ends with the only detailed description of a symbol: "The Mythical Pelican, with golden feathers, believed to feed its young on the blood of its own torn breast, as Christ the Church. (The Mythical Pelican as represented here resembles the real pelican only by way of being a bird ...)" (334-35). Munro's wit is evident in the poor rendering of the pelican (only recognizable as a generic bird) with a distortion of the "surface" reality she is accustomed to privileging, so that that the symbol distances her from rather than drawing her into the "behind" reality of Christ incarnate. And yet, despite Munro's overtly ironic pushback against the religious symbolism of the pelican, the reference to the "torn breast" brings the symbol – fascinatingly – into intense proximity with the narrative "I" awaiting a biopsy, a procedure haunted by shades of death. By indirectly associating the pelican with her own breast, she brings the symbolic Christ into the sphere of human helplessness and her possible imminent death, tensions between the theological/symbolic and historical/physical that also agitate the Christian doctrine of the incarnation. It seems to me that there are subtle similarities (and differences) here with Munro's *Lives of Girls and Women*, specifically, the young Del Jordan's opposing visions at her Uncle Craig's funeral: "To be made of flesh was humiliation. I was caught in a vision which was, in a way, the very opposite of the mystic's incommunicable vision of order and light; a vision, also incommunicable, of confusion and obscenity – of helplessness, which was revealed as the most obscene thing there could be" (57-58). Again in "What Do You Want To Know For?" death appears obscene, isolating, a supremely disordering human fact held in an unsettled and unsettling tension with the attempts people make, in the space of death, to create (and find?) order and light.

The fictive Munro learns about the details of the crypt's final opening just after receiving the ambiguous news that her biopsy operation has been cancelled, with an explanation from the radiologist to follow days later. During a visit to the Mannerow home in Scone, the last local relation of the family, Mrs. Mannerow, says she doesn't know why the family buried their people this way, it was just their way. The large vault was opened one last time "for Mrs. Lempke, ... born a Mannerow"; after that, "there was no room for anybody else" (338). Just as lump and lamp echo each other, Lempke – the last crypt occupant – resounds with both words. Inside the crypt there were coffins placed on shelves on both sides, and, at the back wall, a small table with a coal oil lamp and an open Bible: "'It gave me a strange feeling'" (338), Mrs. Mannerow explains. "'It did so. Because you get used to seeing the coffins when they're new, but not so much when they're old'" (338). She smiles at Munro "with a sociable sort of perplexity" and "gives a couple of tremulous nods. As if to say, it's beyond us, isn't it? A multitude of things, beyond us. Yes" (339). A living strangeness, not to be spoken of, even by a believer, a continuation of the revelatory unsaying throughout the story in Mrs. Mannerow's description of surfaces underneath surfaces. While the lamp in the grave is "just an ordinary old-fashioned lamp, the kind they used to burn coal oil in" (338), it is "ordinary" only in the way that the psalm verse on the church wall transforms the ordinary experience of lighting a lamp to see where a person is walking into the immense significance of being guided by God's words: "*Thy word is a lamp unto my feet and a light unto my path*." The lamp placed beside the Bible in the crypt suggests endless associations connected with Christ, particularly through John's gospel (Christ as *Logos* and light), or through Hans Holbein the Younger's great painting, *The Body of the Dead Christ in the Tomb* (1521). The lamp in the burial mound creates a jarring domesticity, suggesting the everydayness and strangeness of death, light in the sober reckoning of life, the tensions that disturb the underground of the narrative all the way through.

A reprieve (one never knows for how long) is granted to the fictive Munro's intimate, domestic relation to death, the final unsaying. The radiologist cancels the biopsy since the lump was the same size as in earlier mammograms from the country hospital, when it remained undetected. The narrative "I" observes that "[s]uch frights will come and go," knowing full well that "[t]hen there'll be one that won't. One that won't go" (339). It's late summer, "the corn in tassel ... time opening out with room again for tiffs and trivialities. No more hard edges on the days, no sense of fate buzzing around in your veins like a swarm of tiny and relentless insects" (339). The change of seasons the greatest change in the offing, room for the trivial, "[s]ome raggedness, carelessness, even a casual possibility of boredom again in the reaches of earth and sky" (340). In the end, it is left to the reader to consider what remains unsaid in Munro's parting gesture of curiosity about the lamp in the crypt, the final surface detail: she asks her husband on the way home from the city hospital, "'Do you think they put any oil in that lamp?'" (340).

***

"Bring your total self to it," Tim said, when describing his hopes for this essay/meditation, and I've attempted to do that here. If you know Tim, you can hear the tone of his e-mail response, "CARRY ON!" when I asked him for general comments on the essay's opening. (It reminded me of the first day I saw him, as he, with reddish curls agitating around his shoulders, bounced into our undergraduate classroom.) Usually I write at a snail's pace, but Tim's timeline didn't allow for that. I was greatly inspired by intense ongoing conversations with my friend, the poet Paul Merrimen, to whom I'm immensely grateful for his insights. Writing this essay has allowed me to cherish anew the landscapes, exterior and interior, conscious and unconscious, that Munro's writing invites the reader to inhabit. The sober Calvinist tone is familiar to me; I'm working on pagan jubilation. You may hear both voices in the poem I end with, "Portrait of My Mother as a Field," published in my book *Poisonous If Eaten Raw.*

Portrait of My Mother as a Field

A scrubby field the renters couldn't use.
The creek along the west fence has filled in,
a snaking strand of bulrushes.
The wooden bridge has collapsed;
its remains frame a bottomland pond
clotted with marsh marigolds.
Her children launched from the bridge,
surfers running the spring flood
on planks from the barn,
their clothes flung on fence posts,
underwear soaked on the first trip down
the gushing creek, grass stalks slicing past
their eyes, planks lugged upstream
again and again till blue fingers
took them back to the house,

and pneumonia in two children
closed spring surfing for good.
Pine seedlings grow in a clutch
as broad as the early morning shadows
of mangy trees that drop cones
along the east fence. Mole-sized
hawthorn trees have grown into sheep
scattered through the pasture.
Crows' late-night, barroom *aw aw aw*,
killdeers' shrieks, red-winged-blackbirds'
triple ripple-notes – the usual congregants
falling into an uncommon unison.

Works Cited

Carson, Anne. "Decreation: How Women Like Sappho, Marguerite Porete and Simone Weil Tell God." *Decreation: Poetry, Essays, Opera.* New York, NY: Alfred A. Knopf, 2005. 155-83.

Faber, Alyda. "Portrait of My Mother as a Field." *Poisonous If Eaten Raw.* Fredericton: icehouse poetry / Goose Lane Editions, 2021. 20.

Holbein the Younger, Hans. *The Body of the Dead Christ in the Tomb.* 1521. "The Dead Christ." *History Today* 71.4 (2021). <https://www.historytoday.com/archive/foundations/dead-christ>. Accessed 22 Aug. 2021.

Kearney, Richard. *Anatheism: Returning to God After God.* New York, NY: Columbia UP, 2010.

Metcalf, John. *The Canadian Short Story.* Windsor, ON: Biblioasis, 2018.

Munro, Alice. *Lives of Girls and Women.* Toronto: McGraw-Hill Ryerson, 1971.

---. "Nettles." *Hateship, Friendship, Courtship, Loveship, Marriage.* Toronto: McClelland & Stewart, 2001. 154-85.

---. "No Advantages." *The View from Castle Rock.* Toronto: McClelland & Stewart, 2006. 3-26.

---. "What Do You Want To Know For?" *The View from Castle Rock.* Toronto: McClelland & Stewart, 2006. 316-40.

Porette, Margaret. *The Mirror of Simple Souls.* Trans. and introd. Edmund Colledge, J.C. Marler, and Judith Grant. Fwd. Kent Emery, Jr. Notre Dame, IN: U of Notre Dame P, 1999. Notre Dame Texts in Medieval Culture 6.

Sells, Michael A. *Mystical Languages of Unsaying.* Chicago, IL: U of Chicago P, 1994.

Watkins, Calvert, ed. "*gheu-*: Language and Culture Note." *The American Heritage Dictionary of Indo-European Roots.* 2nd ed. Boston: Houghton Mifflin, 2000. 31.

Alice Munro's *The View from Castle Rock* as Epic

William Butt

We need more courageous people out front, whether they're women or men or young adults. We need their voices so that we can all be pushed to grow and open our eyes and our hearts.
– Louise Bernice Halfe – Sky Dancer,
Cree-Canadian Parliamentary Poet Laureate 2021-23,
in an interview by Robyn Bresnahan,
Ottawa Morning with Robyn Bresnahan,
CBC Radio, Ottawa, 15 Nov. 2021

May God us keep / From Single vision
– William Blake, "To Thomas Butts," 22 Nov. 1802 (818)

1. What Are You Looking At?

When I was young, living in Woodstock, Ontario, this was a local challenge, like Munro's "Who Do You Think You Are?," or "What Do You Want To Know For?." It could lead to tussles in playgrounds and tavern parking lots. Many readers may find *The View from Castle Rock* a challenge, and may not know what they're looking at. It may seem to be *sui generis.* For some forty years, when you opened a book by Alice Munro, you knew you'd be reading instances of that unmistakable genre, the Alice Munro short story. But picking up *Castle Rock,* for the first time in a book by Munro you're confronted with an author's *Foreword* (it's italicized in the table of contents; you could write a whole essay on the profligate, exuberant use of italics throughout *Castle Rock*) which seems to be less a helpful orientation/explanation than a sort of *avertissement* that you're heading into unfamiliar territory. In the first paragraph you're plunged in antiquarian specialties: the *Statistical Account of Scotland* (1799), *Blackwood's Magazine*, the *Minstrelsy of the Scottish Border*, John Knox. And, as the one-sentence second paragraph warns, "It didn't stop there" ([x]). Turn a page and you're into the first story, "No Advantages," which also starts out like a sort of garble of a lecture where you scramble to keep up: the Roman emperor Antoninus, jumbled guide-book geology of "Black Knowe, Bodesbeck Law, Ettrick Pen," snippets of "Norse, Anglo-Saxon, and Gaelic ... with some old Brythonic thrown in" – "words being all mixed up" (4). Initially the reader too may feel all mixed up. *Castle Rock* is indeed, as Dennis Duffy says, "Munro's most heterogeneous collection of narratives" (89).

What if that apparent miscellaneousness is by way of plunking the reader *in medias res*, into explicitly epic plenitude? The fairies taunt Old James by demanding "*the big silver key that you had of us*" (70; emphasis in orig.). Young James is perplexed. "'Key,' he says. 'Key?'" (70). Ten pages later he is still obsessed. "He chooses the same word every time. *Key*" (80; emphasis in orig.). What if Munro is nudging the perplexed reader to think key, and the key to *The View from Castle Rock* is to see it as epic?

2. Epic

We don't need to squint much to see that *Castle Rock* is slathered in signs of epic. For a start, the structure. *The View from Castle Rock* is comprised of twelve parts, like the twelve-book *Paradise Lost*, and Hugh Hood's twelve-book novel cycle *The New Age/Le nouveau siècle*, and like *The Odyssey* and *The Iliad* each of which has twenty-four. Also like *The Odyssey*, *Castle Rock* Part One is primarily journeys, quest patterns, and it's far-flung; Part Two (including the "Epilogue"), geographically less far-flung, focuses on the heroine-narrator's own life and times and immediate family, the way *Finnegans Wake* and the plays depicting the House of Atreus and the Book of Genesis are epics of family. Northrop Frye: "The first twelve books of *The Odyssey* deal with the wanderings of the hero.... The next twelve books never leave Ithaca" (*The Return of Eden* 13).

• At bottom *Castle Rock*, as ancestral history, is in large part and often a journey to the land of the dead, like every epic; to graveyards, where the dead find voice on tombstone epitaphs and the living are "insisting on being joined to dead people" (347). We think of Munro remembering herself entering the crypt at the Mannerow church, to find a lantern on a table, and we think of the frontispiece to Blake's epic *Jerusalem*, where Los who embodies Imagination enters a crypt through a Gothic arch, carrying a sun-shaped lantern (Blake, *Jerusalem: The Emanation of the Giant Albion* [18]).

• An epic also features an ascent to apocalyptic vision. We think of Dante at the end of the *Paradiso*. Or Wordsworth in his epic *The Prelude* climbing Mount Snowdon. In this context we think of Old James in the book's title story, climbing Castle Rock, and at the summit beholding in imagination – like Wordsworth – what he calls the Atlantic, and beyond to America in all its glory, where "'even the beggars is riding around in carriages'" (30). This perception seems delusional; we may see it as mock-epic; but the book's end, as we shall see, validates the idiosyncratic vision of Old James.

• There's the grand geographical scope: the view of Ettrick hills and villages expands to Edinburgh and the Atlantic Ocean; we visit the Mediterranean, New York state, Missouri Synod, Illinois, Nova Scotia, Pointe au Baril, Georgian Bay, Esquesing, on and on. The multi-coloured detail of *The Physiography of Southern Ontario*. The *Historical Atlas* with "rivers in Asia and ancient boundaries in the Middle East ... Alexander's route, and Napoleon's ... the Khazars had their capital city where the Volga flows into the Caspian Sea" (299).

• Think of the vast array of characters. On your behalf, Reader, I counted 222 named persons and animals – including a Homeric Nausicaa on an island (230). Consider the range of ages, from Mary's newborn, to toddlers and adolescents, to the narrator's father and others senile or on their deathbeds. The socio-economic range: in Scotland from peasants like Will O'Phaup to aristocratic Walter Scott, knighted in 1820 (long after his work on the *Minstrelsy of the Scottish Border*). In Southwestern Ontario, people in "the homes of the poor" (259) – Geordie who "delivered bread, but had to work in the Foundry at night to make extra money" (162), and Joe Thoms "who lives up the river in a trailer, with no telephone" (292); upward in the social scale to Henrietta Sharples in "the largest house I had ever been in ... its property ran right from one street to another" (263), to the Montjoys whose island house in Georgian Bay "was modern, with a flat roof and a deck extending over the water and a great many windows" (236), not to mention servants, including the "Hired Girl" who is daily aware that her employers perceive her as inferior.

• Consider the epic catalogues and their cumulative resonant breadth. We get a list of the heroine's wedding-trunk contents (256-57), a list of pioneers' food (97), a list of Irlma's cuisine (292). We get a list of back-road glimpses of Grey County:

> SPORTS CARDS GALORE, says a sign that is already weathering. TWO-DOOR DOGHOUSES FOR SALE. A place where chairs can be re-caned. TIRE SUPERYARD. Antiques and beauty treatments are offered. Brown eggs, maple syrup, bagpipe lessons, unisex haircuts. (327)

In grander epic style, sacred inscriptions in stained-glass windows:

> The Dove (over the altar).
> The letters Alpha and Omega (in the rear wall).
> The Holy Grail.
> The Sheaf of Wheat.
> The Cross in the Crown.
> The Ship at Anchor.
> The Lamb of God bearing the Cross.
> The Mythical Pelican.... (334)

• See the epically marvellous oceanic monsters, frightful as some Charybdis and Scylla – Here be dragons. A cow – *a cow!* – soars overhead, hey-diddle-diddle: Mary "hears the bawling in the sky and looking up sees the brown beast dangling" (37). James "*saw a cow and a pig fly through the air*" (38; emphasis in orig.). Walter "has seen drawings of fish as big as horses, fish with horns as well, and scores of teeth each like a skinner's knife" (40). Walter writes how he "saw several whales this day such creatures as I never saw in my life" (65). Old James fixates on "'*that leviathan*'" from Psalm 104, "'*That crooked serpent, the dragon that is in the sea*'" (76).

• See the supernatural machinery. Those ominous, ambiguous Ettrick fairies. Likewise in Illinois, Jamie's father's ghost "who was not under that stone but in the air or walking along the road invisibly" (103). In foundry small-talk "They argued about whether there were ghosts, and talked about who claimed to have seen one" (164). There's an Isak-Dinesen classical god: "Neptune, with a trident, steered his team of horses through high waves" (254). There are demons called up by a fundamentalist preacher, heir of Thomas Boston, on American radio in the year 2004: "Demons can possess animals and houses and features of the landscape as well as people. Sometimes whole congregations and denominations. The world is aswarm with them and the prophesies are proving true that they will proliferate during the Last Days" (345). And indeed in *Castle Rock* we do touch the Day of Judgment which Nettie's father invokes, when the dead will rise up (63).

• We might not expect in an epic of Southwestern Ontario anything like Agamemnon and his ritual arming – "he himself put the shining bronze upon him" (*The Iliad* XI.16; Lattimore trans. 234), the greaves, the corselet, the sword, the shield, the helmet crested and plumed, the two spears, for some thirty lines. Yet consider in *Castle Rock* the frequent descriptions of apparel, and the mood and mystique which apparel can enhance for the wearer and the audience. Every bit as much as a warrior's armour, stylish clothing builds self-confidence, and shabby clothing erodes it. There's Frances in her "child star's party dress," "an outfit that could have come out of one of those magazines" (188). There's Dahlia: "I remember a red V-necked sweater often worn by her, and a pleated Royal Stewart skirt" – she's the "pride of the family" (178). There's the heroine's wedding dress, devotedly hand-made by Aunt Charlie, "a knee-length dress of burgundy velvet, with a gathered skirt and tight waist and what was called a sweetheart neckline, and puffed sleeves" (281). Not until later in retrospect does she recognize the "artlessness" of it, "a soft droop, a lack of assertive style" (282), an irony all the tarter when we learn that this marital venture failed. She had pictured her lovers as torridly heroic, "bold-plumed" (281) like Agamemnon – though all that glorious apparel didn't save his marriage either.

• When we think of epic as a nation's defining story, *The View from Castle Rock* fits the bill for Canada. In "the far north" there are "Indian guides" (131). (This is the narrator's knowingly dated terminology. In *Castle Rock*, "'the way people talk about Indians'" (295) is decidedly politically incorrect, though of its time.) One of Old James's sons has gone to Nova Scotia. The Laidlaws pass through Quebec and even in Morris Township there's "A Frenchman from Quebec" (113). There's Canada's national theme of immigrants, like the Laidlaws of course but many others too, such as the German immigrants who built the Mannerow church and cemetery, and later Henry and Corrie who "had come to Canada from Holland" (233) in a mid-twentieth-century wave of immigration. There are the surveys and pioneer settlers' clearance of the forests, "the straight-laid roads and fences" (131), and Leo working on "a lumbering crew in Northern Ontario" and "a harvesters' excursion ... out west" (271). There's Southwestern Ontario agriculture, apples, "hundreds of thousands of bushels shipped out," and then "the orchards in British Columbia went into operation, with their advantage of a longer growing season" (344). There's capitalist industry: the local foundry and planing mill, and in Montreal Mr. Carbert who sells high-end wine, apparently to Montreal captains of commerce. There's the era of railroad building – the Canadian Pacific which made possible the development of western Canada; the "Grand Trunk, or the Butter and Eggs" (169), which serviced local farmers. As population grows and hub cities emerge there's the urban-rural, centre-versus-margin conflict: "people in town did generally look upon the people from the country as more apt to be slow-witted" (128). There's tourism and "the Pine Tree Hotel north of Gravenhurst" (140) – "They came up from Detroit and Chicago with money to spend" (146). We see the development of later technology – "My grandfather owned the first car on the Eighth Line of Morris. It was a Gray-Dorrit. And my father in his teens had a crystal set" (136). There's quite an assortment of religions – Scots Presbyterian of course; revival meetings where according to Old James "the Methodist prays as Loud as Ever He Can" (83); the heroine's father's mother is "a born Anglican who took on the Presbyterian righteousness-competition" (134); there are Roman Catholics, whom Protestants call "Papists" (133); the Craiks belong to the Salvation Army; Lutheran Germans have settled in parts of Grey County; the hometown doctor is "Hin-doo" (301); Joe and Peggy go to "the Tabernacle" (297); we hear of Leo's wife's "freak religion of the sort they had out west" (272); and even "some religion in India that held with all animals getting into Heaven" (154). There's politics with Uncle Cyril, "a notary public and the clerk of the township he lived in, and ... a force in the Liberal Party" (277). There's geology, long before history – the Pre-Cambrian Shield and the glaciation in Southwestern Ontario where "The landscape ... is a record of ancient events" (318).

• When we think of epic as in Wordsworth's sense, 'The Growth of a Poet's Mind,' that subtitle would describe *Castle Rock* literally and precisely. They are both books about writing, a writer, and learning to write. Dennis Duffy has a note that "Hugh Hood told me of a visit that Munro had made to his house, during which he read to her passages from *The Prelude* that moved them both to tears" (Duffy 106). Epic always self-reflexively celebrates language and narrative. Consider the *Castle Rock* sea-voyagers off to America, Odyssean story-tellers all – Old James presiding, and Walter with his careful journal, and stories and reactions to stories from Mary, Nettie, Nettie's father, and Andrew who writes a long letter and plans "to sum up in a small ledger" (79). Like Wordsworth who puts a whole book called "Books" in *The Prelude* (Book V), the heroine in *Castle Rock* recalls books she has read and loved, from *The Odyssey* to Dante to Lucy Maud Montgomery (230). She tells us of an early effort at writing. "*Softly, silently the yellow leaves fell – it was autumn*" – writing that she later can acknowledge is "foolish and self-consciously poetic" (261; emphasis in orig.). But she goes on struggling and learning, because she loves language and stories. Like *Finnegans Wake*, *Castle Rock* celebrates the world-profusion of tongues –Lowland Scot slang ("*Old shite-bag*" [45; emphasis in orig.]); low Souwesto slang ("'It's just a rabbit we got give for a present'" [297]); correct and plain English like the journal style of Walter; Latin ("Nova Scotia.... 'It's Latin, I think'" [65]); Portuguese (the sailors' word *rochas* corrupted by Nettie's father to "rotches" [63]); baby talk ("'Sailor-peep'" [35]; "*gruggin*" [38]); phonetic near-nonsense ("Lightoprasussciety. Pirazapenzanze" [186]); German ("*Ich hebe meine Augen auf zu den Bergen*" [333]); the childish English of the immigrant-Dutch Corrie to the senile Mrs. Foley ("'Bad. No. Spit out. Spit right out in Corrie's hand. Bad. You didn't do what Corrie say'" [234]); and much, much more.

• And speaking of Wordsworth, what can best be called Spots of Time thrust themselves forcefully and often into *Castle Rock*. Moments that "with distinct pre-eminence retain / A renovating virtue, whence ... / ... / ... our minds / Are nourished and invisibly repaired" (*The Prelude* XIV.208-15). For one, the heroine's experience of the German Gothic-script texts from Psalms 121 and 119 (333), uncovered beneath layers of paint: "The words on the wall strike me to the heart" (334). Another is the heroine's recovery in the family barn of "the first clear memory of my life" (314), which comes flooding back to her in present tense from 1935. You could do a whole essay on spots of time in *Castle Rock*, or on renovating moments in the entire Alice Munro canon.

• Albert B. Lord in *The Singer of Tales* encouraged us to understand epic as traditionally oral. This notion applies from Homer to Joyce and *Finnegans Wake* whose title and much of its structure we recall come from 19th-century Irish balladry. From her first page Munro cites Walter Scott's *Minstrelsy of the Scottish Border*, in which Scott assembled, edited, and annotated folk ballads, en route to constructing the Scottish national *epos*. In all three parts of the *Minstrelsy*, most poems come with an introduction and with explanatory notes at the end. Part I starts with seventy-eight pages of explanatory editorial introduction. Robert Chambers' *Life of Sir Walter Scott* devotes much of the eighty-eight pages of its appendix by Robert Carruthers, "*Abbotsford Notanda*," to reminiscences and explanations of the research into and interpretation of the ballads collected in the *Minstrelsy*. Like this: "Laidlaw had procured a version of another ballad, *The Demon Lover*, which he took down from the recitation of Mr. Walter Grieve, then in Craik, on Borthwick Water. Grieve sung it well to a singularly wild tune; and the song embodies a popular but striking superstition, such as Lewis introduced into his romance of *The Monk*" (Carruthers 122).

Castle Rock is composed largely of oral tales: from Scotland, such as the legends of Will O'Phaup (later written down, most notably by James Hogg), or from the heroine's hometown – Irlma is a font of local gossip-tales; chatty Aunt Charlie tells oral family history. Then follow the heroine's editorial comments on them. There are dozens of examples; it's the book's main texture and rhythm – stories told, or even just expressions, followed by the narrator's ruminations upon them. They may be very short, a single granular story-germ. "*Irlma's got the jump on you and me.* // What did my father mean by that?" (309; emphasis in orig.); right after that we get a paragraph of perplexed existential analysis not only of this local expression but of Irlma who has used it. The "*Abbotsford Notanda*," written notes on oral recitations, clearly is a model. So much is implicated in oral discourse that then requires the annotating written text. What is spoken, says Walter J. Ong, "never exists in a simply verbal context, as a written word does. Spoken words are always modifications of a total, existential situation" (67). The speakers never stop knowing that they work in collaboration with earlier others. Robin Wall Kimmerer says that oral tellers of indigenous North American legend "*begin by calling upon those who came before who passed the stories down to us, for we are only messengers*" (3; emphasis in orig.) – and already we know in part why the title of the *Castle Rock* "Epilogue" is "Messenger."

After the first page of the Foreword, the narrator returns twice more to her ancestor Margaret Laidlaw, a prime source for the ballads of Scott's *Minstrelsy*, and her "offense at their being printed" (Foreword [ix]); she "upbraided Sir Walter Scott" (6), and complained that "*noo they'll never be sung mair*" (22). Munro is fascinated by the way oral lore can influence, and be absorbed by, and colour written epic. Scott's methods in the *Minstrelsy* are a precedent for this process.

Because ballads are oral, not written, ballads must have characteristics that help their reciters remember them. The regular stanzas, often in 4- and 3-beat lines. The regular rhymes like *abcb*. Especially in our context, the short units of meaning – often two lines or so. Take "Sir Patrick Spens," the first ballad in Part I of the 1931 edition of Scott's *Minstrelsy* (after, that is, those seventy-eight pages of explanatory editorial introduction to the volume, and two pages of editorial preface to "Sir Patrick Spens" itself):

The King sits in Dunfermline town,
  Drinking the blude-red wine;
"O whare will I get a skeely skipper,
  To sail this new ship of mine?"

O up and spake an eldern knight,
  Sat at the King's right knee, –
"Sir Patrick Spens is the best sailor
  That ever sail'd the sea."

Our King has written a braid letter,
  And seal'd it with his hand,
And sent it to Sir Patrick Spens,
  Was walking on the strand. (98-99)

The excerpt proceeds via tiny blocks of narrative. It lacks connectives and exposition. Each small unit offers minimal development – because a small unit is all the reciter can handle in the moment. Often *Castle*

Rock proceeds this way, like a ballad, an elliptically-linked set of small discrete memes. Consider a sequence of "Home" (286-87): the heroine is headed home on "an old school bus" that is "driven at what seems a reckless speed"; she observes how "This is great country for accidents"; she inserts brief examples. We jump-cut to a scene at the kitchen table. "My father ... speaks of a terrible accident. My stepmother takes it further." Brief examples follow, images only. They are "drinking whiskey"; her late mother "made my father promise, before they were married, that he would never take a drink." We are spirited to something that is no longer there: "The wooden kitchen table that we always ate from, and the chairs we sat on, have been taken to the barn." And then we pass to the nineteenth century, and the now-vanished village of Sunshine, and "what was called the chair factory – it was probably just a workshop." Some of this progression you might call simply stream-of-consciousness association, or you might call it filmic, with its quick cuts. But it also draws on oral ballad structure, the way Lord's *The Singer of Tales* shows that Homer too turned oral tradition into written epic.

3. The Mighty Book

If you, the voyaging reader, persist *in medias res* for a few pages, in the Ettrick Valley you encounter "Aikwood, the home of Michael Scot, the philosopher and wizard of the twelfth and thirteenth centuries, who appears in Dante's *Inferno*" (5). Munro citing Dante is like Wordsworth citing Milton early in the first book of *The Prelude* – "some old / Romantic tale by Milton left unsung" (I.168-69): bold announcement to readers that the book they're starting into is very much meant to be in the epic tradition and succession. The *Castle Rock* narrator links Michael Scot with "Merlin– *Merlin*–" (5; again Munro's italics) and with the Scottish warrior-hero William Wallace. Michael Scot here isn't just local-colour garnish, some throwaway curiosity, but rather the narrator has dunked you the reader into epic, Dante's *Commedia* and Arthurian and Border-Scot saga. Here's a grand figure from Canto XX of Dante's *Inferno,* slyly laid in plain view by Munro, like Poe's Purloined Letter on the foyer table.

J. Wood Brown, the studious, assiduous late-Victorian biographer of Michael Scot (most commentators spell the name with one 't', deriving from the Latin "Scotus") tells us that from apparently 1200 to 1213 Scot served at the court of Frederick II, "King of Sicily, and afterwards Emperor of Germany: a Prince deservedly famous, not only for his own talent, but for the protection and encouragement he afforded to men of learning" (18). Man of learning for sure: Scot studied and wrote on mathematics, chemistry, physics, medicine, ornithology, philosophy, theology, and divination; Walter Scott in his "Appendix" to *The Lay of the Last Minstrel* adds "abstruse studies of judicial astrology, alchymy [sic], physiognomy, and chiromancy" (Scott, "Appendix," *Last Minstrel*, Note O, 312). Scot knew Arabic, Latin, Greek, Hebrew. He translated Aristotle on Natural History from the Greek, the Andalusian Averroes and the Persian Avicenna among others into Latin – becoming "the chief exponent of the Arabo-Aristotelic philosophy in the West" (Brown 46). Like Munro in *Castle Rock*, Scot wrote not only in his own but in other voices and other tongues. Parenthetically we can hereby understand why such a scholarly abstruse as Robertson Davies claimed to dote on Michael Scot, "my favourite bedside reading" (131). Davies' ghost story "The Perils of the Double Sign" invokes Scot as a canny wielder of the uncanny, and a mentor to those beset by astounding opponents – "I knew my Michael Scot, and I knew what tricky fellows these genies could be" (131).

Brown uncovers how Pope Gregory IX (Pope 1217-41) wrote to the Primate of England "desiring that Scot should be preferred to the first suitable place which might fall vacant in that country" (158). A holy man, then. However, "He spent his time upon Arabic texts, and, with the fanatical clergy, not to speak of the common people whom they taught, the Moors and all their works were accursed" (188). A Satanist too, then; tragic like Byron's Manfred and Cain; a Faustian character two hundred years or so before legends of Faust were first heard of; a fearsome Scottish folk-hero; yet a denizen of Dante's eighth circle of Hell (*Inferno* Canto XX; Cary trans.). Provokingly, Scot dressed in ostentatiously Moorish fashion, or like some magician – "flowing robes, the close-girt waist, the pointed cap" (139). Like most of those colourful characters we meet in *Castle Rock*, he's morally ambiguous, almost endearingly so, obscured in layers of legend and gossip.

Into the thick Scots Border brew in early *Castle Rock*, Munro in her Foreword already has tossed James Hogg and Sir Walter Scott. Both of them luxuriated in tales of Michael Scot. Hogg's novel *The Three Perils of*

Man: War, Women and Witchcraft starts with a siege of Roxburgh Castle, but Michael Scot usurps the book for hundreds of pages of digression coloured by what Hogg himself called "diablerie" ("Memoir" 55). In much the same way, readers persist in believing, with Blake in *The Marriage of Heaven and Hell* and with Shelley in "A Defence of Poetry," that Satan usurped *Paradise Lost*. Whatever John Milton thought of that matter, Alice Munro is of the Scot party, as we shall see. Eventually and eventfully in Hogg's novel, Scot meets his end in a duel with the Devil that's worthy of a Marvel superhero movie as much as of an epic: "[Satan] approached, and poured from his mouth and nostrils such a stream of liquid flame on the magician, that it appeared like a fiery rainbow between them ... and then the fiend threw trees and rocks at him, some of the latter of the weight of five tons" (*The Three Perils of Man* 458). Even that doesn't kill him, though he does eventually die. Hogg's novel ends with Scot solemnly and honourably buried clasping his book of black arts and his golden wand in the Eildon of Munro's Laidlaw ancestors, with solemn sentiments worthy for a hero in Shakespearean tragedy. "[L]et us all go and see his body reverendly [sic] deposited in the tomb" (*The Three Perils of Man* 463). Brown too is suitably elegiac: "The resting-place of Michael Scot will never now be accurately known, but there is every reason to suppose that it lies not far from that of his birth, in the sweet Borderland" (177). We might add that no evidence exists of Scot being buried there, or anywhere else for that matter.

Sir Walter Scott in *The Lay of the Last Minstrel* picks up the tale. The soldier William of Deloraine is sent by his Duchess to wrest from the tomb of Scot at Melrose his legendary book of spells. The *Lay* goes on for six stirring cantos, but in short Scot – wizard and writer, whose miraculously preserved corpse clutches his "Mighty Book" (Canto II, Stanza 21) – is, as Beth Lau says, "surely in part a figure for the inspired, immortal poet" (119-20). He's therefore of a piece with the Munro of *Castle Rock* who presents herself in the Foreword not only as diligent family historian but as a sort of Michael-Scot wizard/charlatan writing "not in an austere or rigorously factual way" ([x]). She describes herself spookily summoning the un-dead, transmogrified: "characters gave themselves to me in their own words, others rose out of their situations. Their words and my words, a curious re-creation of lives"; they "took on their own life and color and did things they had not done in reality. ... // These are *stories*" (emphasis in orig.) – or, more indefinably, "something like stories" ([ix]).

Therefore and thenceforth, *Castle Rock* is crammed with exuberant tellers of tales, with Scot as their avatar, battling the mono-mythopaths led by the Reverend Thomas Boston. Like the many who are simultaneously dreamers in *Finnegans Wake*, the hero(in)es in *Castle Rock* are multiple. Call them Team Scot – low-mims alongside the high-mimetic Scot. Odysseus is Scot's epic analogue, the rapscallion raconteur, whose variegated stories literally ensure his survival.

Like the crew of Odysseus, in *Castle Rock* many other figures together form a collegial storyteller hero.

• Will O'Phaup, and the stories told by and then about him, his meetings-up with fairies, a figure in and of an old world "still harboring its own mythology and local wonders. And he was one of them" (8-9).

• James Hogg, and there's always "some trimming and embroidering of material on Hogg's part. Some canny lying of the sort you can depend upon a writer to do" (21).

• Old James, a garrulous compulsive, always with an audience, whose voice, like the voice of Odysseus, "rises over all the hubbub of shipboard life" (43).

• Walter Laidlaw, who diligently inscribes his more scrupulous and unadorned journal of the trans-Atlantic voyage.

• Big Rob Laidlaw whose memoir, however false some of it may be, is Munro's prime source in "The Wilds of Morris Township."

• Munro's own father, Robert Laidlaw, at life's end writing his novel of pioneer days. Irlma puts it briefest and best: "'It keeps his head working,' she says" (291). It's like exercising muscles: doing what the heroic human head is built and meant to do.

• There are lots of other fanciful gossip-stories told via neighbours, newspaper items, comics, popular magazines, and movies. Creators of ephemeral pop-culture, each lining up on-side to offer a brief passing moment of story, no less exciting for being short-lived. Deanna Durbin and the Ziegfeld Girls (186); "old magazines – *Life* and *Look* and *Time* and *Colllier's*" (237); "books like *The Hucksters*" (245). These are foot-soldiers; spear-carriers; walk-ons; like Elpenor in *The Odyssey*, who appears just once and falls out a window, yet still is one of the Odyssean band.

• And then, there's the main narrator, Munro herself. "I am surely one of the liars.... [T]he story is full of my invention" (84).

Stories are what language does, and *Castle Rock* really is a festival of language. We have already noticed the linguistic variety. Consider too the word-play, the way words throughout tend to metamorphose. Far-Hope to Phaup to O'Phaup (7). Science Note Paper to "Signs Snow Paper" (166). Susie and Meggie "called somebody named George *Tom*, or somebody named Rachel *Edith*" (101; emphasis in orig.). Mr. Hammond repeatedly calls the narrator "Minnie," which she surmises must be "a special joke between us" (247). Mr. Montjoy's name devolves twice on the last page of "Hired Girl" to the sexualized "Mountjoy" (254). It's a mischievous and meaningful tinkering of the kind you expect in *Finnegans Wake*, which is also an epic in praise of languages, with its dozens of tongues referenced or utilized, portmanteau words, words neo-spelled, split, reversed, or combined with other words in a glorious polyglot reach for more meaning. In the *Wake* too, names change, like the dozens of echoings and re-referencings of the hero's name(s), Humphrey Chimpden Earwicker: "H.C.E." (198); "Honour commercio's energy" (264); "Hillcloud encompass" (480); there are many more.

As the *Castle Rock* story-telling language-wreaking other-siding heroes and heroines, "Incorrigibly plural" in the phrase from Louis MacNeice's "Snow," play intertextually on and with and against one another in the book's shifting and delighting rhythms, it's like a dance. "People are dancing ... all over the deck. They are grabbing anyone at all and twirling around. ... // ... In the thick of so many bodies ... [Mary] has to stamp and wheel to the music or be knocked down" (69). You could just swap 'story-telling' for 'dancing' and you'd be aptly describing *The View from Castle Rock*.

4. The Black Room

Who then in *Castle* Rock are our heroes' antagonists? Where or what is *Castle Rock*'s *Inferno*? In her biography of Alice Munro, Catherine Sheldrick Ross quotes from Munro's essay "What Is Real?": "Munro says that she thinks of a story not as a straight road, but as a house that you enter, move around inside of, and stay in for a while: 'So when I write a story ... I've got to make, I've got to build up, a house ...'" (Ross 65). She also quotes Munro on "'the black room at the centre of the house'" in the story "Royal Beatings" in *Who Do You Think You Are?* (Ross 81). You don't need to squint to see a black room at the centre of every Munro short story (see Struthers, "In Search" 187-89), or book of short stories, including *The View from Castle Rock*. In the *Castle Rock* architecture, surely the black room is the fierce, warped, fevered theology of the Reverend Thomas Boston. While most of the book is a marvellous riot of parti-coloured tales and voices, Boston's world is undeviatingly bleak and drear. Munro grapples at length with Boston. It's personal. Magdalene Redekop: "Munro has referred to the 'extremely crazy Calvinism' that she works with in herself" (24). She allots to Boston his own section of "Men of Ettrick" – the only Man of Ettrick presented centre-stage who is *not* a Laidlaw.

Munro quotes profusely from Thomas Boston's *Memoirs*, and from his vehemently, violently Calvinist *Human Nature in Its Fourfold State*. The last part of the book's title names these four states: *Primitive Integrity; Entire Depravity; Begun Recovery; and Consummate Happiness or Misery*. The book reads like some hideously debased version of *Paradise Lost* and of William Blake's epic mythology. "Now I a fourfold vision see" (Blake, "To Thomas Butts," 22 Nov. 1802, 818). But Boston is fanatically single-vision. In print and widely available for all of Blake's lifetime, Boston's writings were quite possibly known to Blake, who would have thought of his own four-fold epics as radically emending Boston's harsh Calvinist reductiveness. In any case, Boston's theology of disgust reads like a hysterical precursor's parody of Blake's fourfold vision, though conceived before Blake was even born. Northrop Frye: "If I were to see a small church labelled 'the foursquare gospel' I'd give it a wide berth, because I know I'd find nothing inside except what I'd call hysteria" (*Northrop Frye Unbuttoned* 155).

Boston's fourfold mono-myth is rancid with disgust at human depravity. There is one and only one story: humans are fundamentally corrupted by the Fall of Eve and Adam. "Let none wonder that such a horrible change could be brought on by one sin of our first parents; for thereby they turned away from God, as their chief end, which necessarily infers a universal depravation" (Boston, *Human Nature* 85). Struggle as you will not to sin, "A swine brought into a palace would soon get away again, to wallow in the mire; and corrupt nature tends ever to impurity" (Boston, *Human Nature* 86). Page follows frantic page, for frenzied compulsive stretches. It does sound like Dante's *Inferno*: "Innumerable sins compass thee about: mountains of guilt are lying upon thee; floods of impurities overwhelm thee, living lusts of all sorts roll up and down in the dead sea of thy soul.... Thy lips are unclean; the opening of thy mouth is as the opening of an unripe grave, full of stench and rottenness" (Boston, *Human Nature* 88). Try listening to that in your pew of a Sunday morning, or reading it in your cozy fireside chair of an evening; yet Munro tells us that Boston's book "was said to stand next to the Bible on the shelf of every pious home in Scotland" (14). No nuance, no context, no toleration for variance; it's the stark and absolute othering of all who are not of the Elect. "There shall be a separation made between the righteous and the wicked; the fair company of the elect sheep being set on Christ's right hand, and the reprobate goats on his left" (Boston, *Human Nature* 297).

Munro puts herself explicitly and entirely against Boston. "The bleakest, the most desperate life" (17). Near the end of the story "The View from Castle Rock" we see his namesake church, "Boston Church, in Esquesing, in Halton County, almost within sight, and well within sound, of Highway 401 north of Milton, which at that spot may be the busiest road in Canada" (84). The Church of Thomas Boston, strait and strong as ever, embedded by the 401, uncoincidentally at the suburban heart of our hectic culture which, like Boston's, lives by a single demoniacal myth: consumerism. Unsurprisingly the church has a false front, and an archway which may remind us of the one Dante passes through into Hell – "'All hope abandon, ye who enter here'" (*Inferno* Canto III; Cary trans.). Boston's church is limestone – not some lovely glowing grey but "blackened" (85). The Black Room indeed. Just as dark too are the views from "the freeways south of Chicago," views of an orthodoxy as absolute as Thomas Boston's, a kind of suburban parody of religion, relentlessly conformist:

> the restaurant that was built on an overpass and that is now empty and dark, a wonder of former times. And Joliet rimmed with new suburban houses, as every city is these days ... all alike. And even these are preferable, I think, to the grander sort of new houses which are here too ... with vast shelter for cars and windows high enough for a cathedral. (345)

And inside every one of those houses, no doubt, as in the summer home on the Montjoys' island, "a kitchen that followed with absolute correctness a current notion of what a kitchen ought to be" (240).

The most sustained gaze at the infernal in *Castle Rock* occurs in the foundry scene of "Working for a Living." It reads like the landscape of Browning's "'Childe Roland to the Dark Tower Came'," and Archibald Lampman's "The City of the End of Things," and the unrelentingly grotesque hell-panel of Bosch's "Garden of Earthly Delights." "The lights burning ... didn't light up the whole inside of the building, which was so large and high that I had the sense of being in a forest with thick dark trees" (160). "We came on an open area with a great heap of metal lumps on the floor, all disfigured with what looked like warts or barnacles" (160); "chunks of metal that were like grotesque stubby limbs" (161). "It was truly killing – around town, on the porches of small neat houses, there were always a few yellow-faced, stoical men set out to take the air. Everybody knew and accepted that they were dying of *the foundry disease*, the dust in their lungs" (162; emphasis in orig.). "'Like a tomb in here,' my father said" (161). Here again, as in Thomas Boston, we see human lives defined in their entirety by one demonic myth: men engaged in one degrading, repetitive, and self-destructive task, "Working for a Living," which ironically is Working for a Death.

Yet one more aspect of the mono-myth of conformist religion in *Castle Rock* is marriage: in Southwestern Ontario slang, "getting churched." To the young heroine, and to most folk in her culture – especially most women – marriage meant salvation; joining the capitalized Elect. In the language of one story's title, marriage is "The Ticket" out. In another story the narrator thinks of herself and Russell Craik "entered on the first stage of a life that would turn us, soon enough, into the Father and the Mother" (218). In the time before her own first marriage she envisions "Love and marriage. That was a lighted and agreeable room you went into, where you were safe" (281). The heroine imagines her own parents on the eve of their marriage, "kind and handsome and healthy and trusting their luck" (140), "as if ... life still bloomed with possibilities, as if they enjoyed all sorts of power" (139). "That can't be true of course" (139), she adds, sensibly enough; but the images pressing so insistently upon her show the marriage-myth's persuasive – even coercive – power.

5. Epic Battle: Other-Sidedness

Against the motley singers of tales whose roster *Castle Rock* has assembled, Boston boasts his own cohort of dogmatic mono-mythopaths who swoop and stamp through *Castle Rock* like the fallen-angel horde of Milton's Satan. You can easily spot them: this is the group, as the popular Fred Kaan hymn says, "that kills abundant living."

• The fundamentalist and intolerant Missouri Synod Lutherans who "could not stand the idea of a woman preaching" (333).

• The American preacher on the radio condemning "whole congregations and denominations" (345) as demonic.

• Joe Thoms, sinner in the hands of an angry God, who believes his God blinded him to stop his drinking – "'He struck me blind but I see his purpose in it'" (297). Souwesto taverns, like brothels in Blake's *The Marriage of Heaven and Hell*, are built from bricks of Religion.

• The Salvation-Army soldier willing to go to war and die believing it's the wish of his militaristic God, "a superior officer ... occasionally gracious but often inflexible and impatient" (212). "'I'll have to do what God wants me to'" (212). Munro's comment: "What terrible docility it took, to be such a believer" (212).

Dictators like Boston depend entirely on that docility in their believers. Usually in practice the question "Are you a believer?" means "Are you a believer exclusively in our one unquestionable dogma?" It is in that sense that Munro announces bluntly: "I am not a believer" (334). Munro would be with Blake in *Jerusalem*, speaking "To the Christians": "I know of no other Christianity and of no other Gospel than the liberty both of body & mind to exercise the Divine Arts of Imagination" (Plate 77; Blake, *Complete Writings* 716-17). Consistently subversive against mono-myth, she spots in the Bostonesque Salvationist household of the Craiks the breezy, under-cutting, pop-culture Mae-West and Tugboat-Annie and Daisy-Mae chickens (216). *Castle Rock* shows us a small town as conformist as ever suburban Joliet could be, a stunted culture that shuns creativity. "'My father and mother used to sing in the Light Opera Society,' [Frances] said. 'They sang in *The Pirates of Penzance*'" (186). If Frances had said these words "at school, in front of others, they would have been irresistible ammunition" (186). Instead *Castle Rock* honours many sides, many stories in many voices capable of being believed, a glorious medley of fundamental – as opposed to fundamentalist – energies zooming through the *Castle Rock* universe, penetrating and bouncing off and influencing one another in contact or at a distance like language quanta.

Given that *Castle Rock* enacts the epic battle of mono-myth Bostonites versus tale-tellers ebulliently plural, Munro pushes that logic faithfully to its limit: to the extent that even the anti-Boston cadre must not oppose Bostonism mono-mythically, so to speak. Other-sidedness is all. Even the episode of the foundry inferno does not become one-dimensional, anti-capitalist, anti-industrialist agit-prop. Any rebellious but monomaniacal Orc opposing each tyrant Urizen otherwise will eventually in turn become a Urizen. Therefore a key word on the side of the good is always the qualifier: 'But.' Always there must be receptivity to other facets of any truth. The foundry is hell, "But jokes were important" (164); "It was hard to explain," her father felt, "how you could be happy in such a situation, but sometimes he thought you were" (165). *Castle Rock* is thick with Keats's Negative Capability, and her father is one of its most ardent practitioners. From beginning to end the narrator too is what we may call a refuser of certainty; an adherent of ambiguity. "This might have had something to do with ..." (18). "I could be guessing wrong" (23). "There are always puzzles" (325). "I could pursue this" (347). "A multitude of things, beyond us. Yes" (339).

Supposing Thomas Boston to be a Urizen, we can see a figure like Will O'Phaup, who lives for and in imagination, as a breezy Los, and Munro acknowledges the puzzling fact that nevertheless he may sit in Boston's pews of a Sunday. In the current cliché, it's complicated. O'Phaup is not in any uniform way a revolutionary Orc. No one, certainly not O'Phaup, is entirely predictable. There's more to him than that. In Upper Canada James Laidlaw does dabble with his fellow Lowland Scot firebrand William Lyon MacKenzie – who fought the Urizenic Family Compact – penning letters to MacKenzie's newspaper *The Colonial Advocate*. But he doesn't march with the 1837 rebels, and his colourful letters are imaginative mainly for their own sake, not for publication: "Now Sir be so good as not put me in your News papers or I will stand a Chance of getting the Lake to keep where they put your Types" – as happened in the Types Riot of 1826 (Laidlaw quoted in MacKenzie, *Sketches* 470).

But then, on the other hand, why send the letters at all? We can call Old James Orc Lite. Nothing, not even or especially not genuine opposition to Bostonism, can be its own one-sided mono-myth. Munro: "'I get very excited about seeing the other side'" (Ross 85, quoting an unpublished 1975 interview with Munro by Barbara Martineau). The opposers of Bostonites are the Other-Siders.

If the Other-Siders are *Castle Rock's* composite epic hero, why are they heroes? Well, for a start, because they make the world more interesting, vivid, and diverse for both teller and listener. But the value of their heroism is much more than that – and this is of epic importance: the tales they tell help both teller and listener to understand and survive in the complicated world they live in. No one tale will do. "World is crazier and more of it than we think," says Louis MacNeice in "Snow," and so are the paths to explaining it. As our contemporary world grows steadily more globalized and various, our contemporary quest to understand it grows more urgent; and dependent more than ever on many voices, many books and guides in the plural. *The View from Castle Rock* is an epic for our globalized age. The publisher's pledge, from the medieval God-versus-Satan morality play, on the marble endpapers in the books – books plural – in the adolescent narrator's family bookcase, offers guidance – though not certainty: "*Everyman, I will go with thee, and be thy guide, in thy most need to go by thy side*" (290; emphasis in orig. – of course). In her adolescent Chamber of Maiden-Thought, as Keats termed it, stories are to the narrator as Virgil's tutelage is to Dante. She reads, and models, with a brave faith that she will spot the 'Words with Power,' in Northrop Frye's phrase, and gain strength to confront the world creatively, find or develop what Joseph Campbell called 'Myths To Live By,' so that "all my due would come to me, I thought, when I was full-blown" (226).

Not all stories are equally valid guides. In contra-distinction to the brutal one-sidedness of Boston, the stories of Other-Siders, in the Hippocratic phrase, Do No Harm. Trumpesque alternate-fact narratives don't count; they are just empty solipsism; not mental fight at all. They don't grapple with realities; they deny and distract from realities. They try to make you believe what isn't true, as Susie and Meggie do in "Illinois," using fake joke names, writing a cruel and harmful fake love-letter. "*A PRESENT from one of your SWEETHEARTS*" (108; emphasis and capitals in orig.). "How can we best make a joke, or fool somebody?" (103): that is the girls' only care. Their behaviour is a sort of demonic parody of religion: "secret rituals and special jokes and fanatical loyalty" (101). It is language as infernal weapon. What we can do in opposition is our own diligent mental fight, rooted in faith that fake tales can be fingered and then discarded through their own insubstantiality, like the love-letter "bit of paper which fell away" (107) unbeknownst to Andrew when he discovered Mary's missing baby, and which quite properly makes no sense to the stable boy Fergie.

6. *Paradiso*

If the world-view of Thomas Boston marks the *Inferno* in *Castle Rock*, and the valiant band of language-plyers are obviously living through *Purgatorio*, then where and what is the book's *Paradiso*?

In "What Do You Want to Know For?" the narrator meets a man who years ago had "worked with my father and my brother and sister preparing the Christmas turkeys" (331) – co-creators of festivity. The two continue in delighted conversation, exploring shared experiences, "and then we both say that it is a small world. We say this, as people usually do, with a sense of wonder and refreshment. ... We explore the connection as far as it will go, and ... we are both happy. ... // ... I am happy to find somebody who can see me still as part of my family" (331-32). 'Happy' is not a common word in *Castle Rock*, but its heroine has been engaged in a book-long, life-long struggle toward exactly this sense of connection: with other people, other places, other times, other memories. The world she portrays and inhabits is epic-huge, and yet through love and interrelationship distances may be collapsed, and anything can for moments seem near and therefore wonderfully small and charming.

Castle Rock continues in this vein towards its end at a cemetery in Blyth, with another Spot of Time, a sort of imaginative resurrection and a mystical recognition scene at a graveside:

> And here a live memory comes twitching through my mind. Jimmy Armour. *Jimmy Armour*. ... I know his name. And not only that – I think I saw him once or more than once, an old man come on a visit from wherever he lived then to the place where he had been born, an old

> man among other old people – my grandfather and grandmother, my grandfather's sisters. // ... Now all these names I have been recording are joined to the living people in my mind.... (348; emphasis in orig.)

Then the last of *Castle Rock*'s epic catalogues – "the lost kitchens, the polished nickel trim on the commodious presiding black stoves, the sour wooden drainboards that never quite dried, the yellow light of the coal-oil lamps ..." (348) – which springboards us via Huron County cattle to the world of *The Iliad*, "those cows whom you still spoke to in words common in the days of Troy. *So – boss. So – boss*" (348; emphasis in orig.). All the narrator's known progenitors and all their known associated objects stream into her ear and mind – as Milton at the all-defining moment enters Blake through his foot in the brief epic named after the earlier poet. Hearing in some one of those many houses *Castle Rock* has catalogued the "big mother-of-pearl seashell," she discovers – recovers – "the tremendous pounding of my own blood, and of the sea" (349). The sea has been always for humans the ultimate image of teeming life, fearsome power, mystery, that only God can claim to plumb – God who has engendered and tended it. "[W]ho shut up the sea with doors, when it burst forth, as if it had issued out of the womb? / When I made the cloud the garment thereof, and thick darkness a swaddling band for it" (Job 38.8-9). We recall that Milton in *The Reason of Church Government* called The Book of Job "a brief model" (668) of the epic.

The end of *Castle Rock* is genealogical apocalypse: distinctions of blood and ocean, inside and outside, hungry generations past and present vanish, and all becomes inside, in imagination unified, as by Noah in the Jay MacPherson poem "The Anagogic Man" who carries "between his nape and crown" "All us and our worlds" (56). Everything that has been in *Castle Rock*, "near and far" (349) – all those voices; context, intertext, relationship, interconnection; collaborative celebration of our world's variety, divergence, and indeterminacy – becomes for a moment in all abundance one gestalt, one rhythmic pulsing both of heart and all-encompassing sea. It's a vision directly in that epic tradition, the one that embraces us at the end of *Jerusalem*, "All Human Forms identified, even Tree, Metal, Earth & Stone" (Plate 99; Blake, *Complete Writings* 747). It's that same vision too at the end of *Finnegans Wake* where the river at last reaches the sea. We remember that in *Castle Rock* the heroine's father's own last word was "*wonder*" (307; emphasis in orig.). In Munro this wondrous union on epic scale is momentary, and then ends. In Dante the paradisal vision bears him "into the ray authentical / Of sovran light. Thenceforward, what I saw, / Was not for words to speak" (*Paradiso* Canto XXXIII; Cary trans.). So too *The View from Castle Rock* ends in an epic vision beyond words.

Works Consulted

Blake, William. *Jerusalem: The Emanation of the Giant Albion*. Ed. and introd. Morton D. Paley. Princeton, NJ: Princeton UP, 1991. Vol. 1 of *Blake's Illuminated Books*. David Bindman, gen. ed. 6 vols. 1991-95.

---. *Jerusalem: The Emanation of the Giant Albion. The Complete Writings of William Blake*. Ed. Geoffrey Keynes. London: Oxford UP, 1966. 620-747. Oxford Standard Authors.

---. *The Marriage of Heaven and Hell. The Complete Writings of William Blake*. Ed. Geoffrey Keynes. London: Oxford UP, 1966. 148-58. Oxford Standard Authors.

---. *Milton: A Poem in 2 Books*. Ed. Geoffrey Keynes. London: Oxford UP, 1966. 480-535. Oxford Standard Authors.

---. "To Thomas Butts." 22 Nov. 1802. *The Complete Writings of William Blake*. Ed. Geoffrey Keynes. London: Oxford UP, 1966. 816-19. Oxford Standard Authors.

The Book of Job. *The Holy Bible*. Cambridge, Eng.: Cambridge UP, n.d. 653-87. King James Vers.

Bosch, Hieronymus. *The Garden of Earthly Delights*. <https://www.museodelprado.es/en/the-collection/art-work/the-garden-of-earthly-delights-triptych/02388242-6d6a-4e9e-a992-e1311eab3609>.

Boston, Rev. Thomas. *Human Nature In Its Fourfold State, of Primitive Integrity; Entire Depravity; Begun Recovery; and Consummate Happiness or Misery*. Aberdeen, Scot.: George and Robert King, 1850. <http://www.digitalpuritan.net/Digital%20Puritan%20Resources/Boston,%20Thomas/Human%20Nature%20in%20its%20Fourfold%20State.pdf>.

---. *Memoirs of the Life, Times, and Writings, of the Rev. Thomas Boston, of Ettrick. Written by Himself. To Which Are Added, Original Papers and Letters.* Aberdeen, Scot.: George and Robert King, 1852. <https://archive.org/stream/memoirsofthelife00bostuoft/memoirsofthelife00bostuoft_djvu.txt>.

Brown, J. Wood. *An Enquiry into the Life and Legend of Michael Scot.* Edinburgh: David Douglas, 1897.

Browning, Robert. "'Childe Roland to the Dark Tower Came'." *Poetical Works: 1833-1864.* Ed. Ian Jack. London: Oxford UP, 1970. 614-21. Oxford Standard Authors.

Byron, Lord. *Cain: A Mystery. The Poetical Works of Lord Byron.* London: Oxford UP, 1945. 520-45.

---. *Manfred: A Dramatic Poem. The Poetical Works of Lord Byron.* London: Oxford UP, 1945. 390-406.

Campbell, Joseph. *Myths To Live By.* 1972. Fwd. Johnson E. Fairchild. New York: Penguin, 1993.

Carruthers, Robert, LL.D. "*Abbotsford Notanda*; or Sir Walter Scott and His Factor." *Life of Sir Walter Scott; With Abbotsford Notanda by Robert Carruthers, LL.D.* By Robert Chambers, LL.D. Ed. W. Chambers. London and Edinburgh: W. & R. Chambers, 1871. 109-96. <https://babel.hathitrust.org/cgi/pt?id=uc1.c051956237&seq=13>.

Chambers, Robert, LL.D. *Life of Sir Walter Scott; With Abbotsford Notanda by Robert Carruthers, LL.D.* Ed. W. Chambers. London and Edinburgh: W. & R. Chambers, 1871. <https://babel.hathitrust.org/cgi/pt?id=uc1.c051956237&seq=13>.

Dante Alighieri. *The Vision of Dante Alighieri or Hell Purgatory and Paradise.* Trans. H.F. Cary. London: J.M. Dent, 1908. Everyman's Library.

Davies, Robertson. "The Perils of the Double Sign." *High Spirits.* 1982. Markham, ON: Penguin, 1984. 127-38. Penguin Short Fiction.

Dinesen, Isak [Karen Blixen]. *Seven Gothic Tales.* 1934. New York: Vintage International, 1991.

Duffy, Dennis. "Too Little Geography; Too Much History." *Alice Munro Country: Essays on Her Works I.* Ed. J.R. (Tim) Struthers. Toronto: Guernica Editions, 2020. 87-113. Essential Writers Ser. 51.

Frye, Northrop. *Anatomy of Criticism: Four Essays.* 1957. New York: Atheneum, 1965.

---. *Northrop Frye Unbuttoned: Wit and Wisdom from the Notebooks and Diaries.* Selected by Robert D. Denham. Toronto: Anansi, 2004.

---. *The Return of Eden: Five Essays on Milton's Epics.* Toronto: U of Toronto P, 1965.

---. *Words with Power: Being a Second Study of "The Bible and Literature".* San Diego, CA: Harcourt Brace Jovanovich, 1990.

Goethe, Johann Wolfgang von. *Faust: The First Part of the Tragedy.* Trans. and introd. David Constantine. Pref. A.S. Byatt. London: Penguin, 2005.

---. *Faust: The Second Part of the Tragedy.* Trans. and introd. David Constantine. Pref. A.S. Byatt. London: Penguin, 2009.

Halfe, Louise Bernice – Sky Dancer. Interview by Robyn Bresnahan. *Ottawa Morning with Robyn Bresnahan.* CBC Radio, Ottawa. 15 Nov. 2021. <https://www.cbc.ca/listen/live-radio/1-100-ottawa-morning/clip/15878394-canadas-9th-parliamentary-poet-laureate>.

Hogg, James. *Contributions to Blackwood's Edinburgh Magazine; Vol. 1: 1817-1828.* Ed. Thomas C. Richardson. Edinburgh: Edinburgh UP, 2008. Vol. 23 of The Stirling / South Carolina Research Edition of The Collected Works of James Hogg.

---. *Contributions to Blackwood's Edinburgh Magazine; Vol. 2: 1829-1835.* Ed. Thomas C. Richardson. Edinburgh: Edinburgh UP, 2012. Vol. 26 of The Stirling / South Carolina Research Edition of The Collected Works of James Hogg.

---. "Memoir of the Author's Life." *Memoir of the Author's Life* and *Familiar Anecdotes of Sir Walter Scott.* Ed. Douglas Mack. Edinburgh: Scottish Academic, 1972. 1-81.

---. *The Three Perils of Man: War, Women and Witchcraft.* Introd. Douglas Gifford. Edinburgh: Scottish Academic, 1972.

Homer. *The Iliad of Homer.* Trans. and introd. Richmond Lattimore. Chicago: U of Chicago P, 1951.

---. *The Odyssey of Homer.* Trans. and introd. Richmond Lattimore. New York: Harper & Row, 1967.

Hood, Hugh. *The New Age / Le nouveau siècle.* Ottawa: Oberon, 1975, 1977, 1979; Downsview, ON: ECW, 1982; Toronto: Stoddart, 1984, 1986, 1988; Toronto: Anansi, 1990, 1993, 1995, 1997, 2000. 12 Vols.

Joyce, James. *Finnegans Wake.* Introd. John Bishop. New York: Penguin, 1999.

Kaan, Fred. "For the Healing of the Nations." "Hymns, Musical Responses, and Prayers 678." *Voices United: The Hymn and Worship Book of The United Church of Canada*. Etobicoke, ON: The United Church Publishing House, 1996.

Keats, John. "To George and Tom Keats." 21, 27 (?) Dec. 1817. *The Letters of John Keats 1814-1821*. Ed. Hyder Edward Rollins. Vol. 1. Cambridge, MA: Harvard UP, 1958. 191-94. 2 Vols.

---. "To J.H. Reynolds." 3 May 1818. *The Letters of John Keats 1814-1821*. Ed. Hyder Edward Rollins. Vol. 1. Cambridge, MA: Harvard UP, 1958. 275-83. 2 Vols.

Kimmerer, Robin Wall. *Braiding Sweetgrass: Indigenous Wisdom, Scientific Knowledge, and the Teachings of Plants*. 2013. Toronto: Penguin, 2020.

Lampman, Archibald. "The City of the End of Things." *The Poems of Archibald Lampman (including At the Long Sault)*. Introd. Margaret Coulby Whitridge. Toronto: U of Toronto P, 1974. 179-82. Literature of Canada: Poetry and Prose in Reprint.

Lau, Beth. "Authorial Disguise and Intertextuality: Scott's *The Lay of the Last Minstrel*, Coleridge, and Keats." *Studies in Scottish Literature* 40 (2014): 116-33.

Lord, Albert B. *The Singer of Tales*. 2nd ed. Ed. Stephen Mitchell and Gregory Nagy. Cambridge, MA: Harvard UP, 2000. Harvard Studies in Comparative Literature 24.

Mack, Douglas S. "James Hogg's Second Thoughts on *The Three Perils of Man*." *Studies in Scottish Literature* 21 (1986): 167-75.

MacKenzie, William L. *Sketches of Canada and the United States*. London: Effingham Wilson, 1833. <https://www.loc.gov/item/02010564/>.

MacNeice, Louis. "Snow." *Collected Poems*. By Louis MacNeice. Ed. Peter McDonald. London: Faber and Faber, 2007. 24. <https://www.poetryfoundation.org/poems/91395/snow-582b58513ffae>.

MacPherson, Jay. "The Anagogic Man." *The Boatman and Other Poems*. Toronto: Oxford UP, 1968. 56.

Milton, John. *Paradise Lost*. *Complete Poems and Major Prose*. Ed. Merritt Y. Hughes. New York: Odyssey, 1957. 173-469.

---. *The Reason of Church Government Urged Against Prelaty*. *Complete Poems and Major Prose*. Ed. Merritt Y. Hughes. New York: Odyssey, 1957. 640-89.

Munro, Alice. *The View from Castle Rock*. Toronto: McClelland & Stewart, 2006.

Ong, Walter J. *Orality and Literacy: The Technologizing of the Word*. 1982. London: Routledge, 2002.

Poe, Edgar Allan. "The Purloined Letter." *The Murders in the Rue Morgue: The Dupin Tales*. Ed. and introd. Matthew Pearl. New York: The Modern Library, 2006. 83-100.

Redekop, Magdalene. "Alice Munro and the Scottish Nostalgic Grotesque." *The Rest of the Story: Critical Essays on Alice Munro*. Ed. Robert Thacker. Toronto: ECW, 1999. 21-43.

Ross, Catherine Sheldrick. *Alice Munro: A Double Life*. Toronto: ECW, 1992. Canadian Biography Ser. 1.

Scott, Sir Walter. *The Lay of the Last Minstrel, a Poem*. 1805. Illus. Birket Foster and John Gilbert. Edinburgh: Adam and Charles Black, 1854. <https://babel.hathitrust.org/cgi/pt?id=hvd.hwp6zk&seq=2>.

---. *Minstrelsy of the Scottish Border: Historical and Romantic Ballads*. 1802. Ed. Thomas Henderson. London: George G. Harrap, 1931.

Shelley, Percy Bysshe. "A Defence of Poetry." <https://www.poetryfoundation.org/articles/69388/a-defence-of-poetry>.

"Sir Patrick Spens." *Minstrelsy of the Scottish Border*. By Sir Walter Scott. Ed. Thomas Henderson. London: George G. Harrap, 1931. 97-102.

Struthers, J.R. (Tim). "In Search of the Perfect Metaphor: The Language of the Short Story and Alice Munro's 'Meneseteung'." *Critical Insights: Alice Munro*. Ed. Charles E. May. Ipswich, Mass: Salem-EBSCO, 2013. 175-94.

Wordsworth, William. *The Prelude; or Growth of a Poet's Mind: An Autobiographical Poem. The Poetical Works of Wordsworth*. Ed. Thomas Hutchinson. Rev. Ernest de Selincourt. London: Oxford UP, 1950. 494-588.

"As Truthful As Our Notion of the Past Can Ever Be": William Maxwell, His *Ancestors*, and Alice Munro's *The View from Castle Rock*

Robert Thacker

According to Alice Munro, she and William Maxwell met "a few times" in Manhattan at *New Yorker* events. "The first time I met him I almost fell on the floor with admiration," Munro has recounted, "and he just sort of held me up, and started talking about very ordinary things, and got me through." In the same interview, Munro called Maxwell "my favourite writer in the world" (Thacker, Personal interview, 2010). When she said this, she had been referring to his work admiringly for some time: in 1985, for instance, Munro told an interviewer that Maxwell's fiction is "'orderly, deliberate, painstaking, traditional,' and also 'unsurprising – or so you think'" (qtd. in Martin 205). A few years later, in 1988, she published an essay, "The Novels of William Maxwell," in *Brick*. She allowed that magazine to republish it in 2000 as a tribute to Maxwell when he died that year, and she took it up again and expanded it while she was also shaping the family book she had long contemplated and would publish as *The View from Castle Rock* in 2006. When that book appeared, Munro mentioned the whole of Maxwell's work as an encouragement and, in particular, pointed to his *Ancestors* (1971) as an explicit model of what she was trying to do in her own book (Stoffman H10). Given these connections, this essay takes up as its subject the acknowledged influence of Maxwell's work on Munro's generally and, most particularly, the model his *Ancestors* provided her when she came finally to write her own long-contemplated book focused on her own ancestors in relation to her own life, *The View from Castle Rock*.

Beyond the explicit evidence of one writer's influence on another, and of one book's presence as model for the making of another, the Maxwell-Munro crux serves those interested in the dynamics of authorship as an important example of two compatible writers who, throughout their careers, created narrative rooted in the very stuff of their own experience in place and time – whether seen as fiction, memoir, or autobiography. Each did so in ways that accentuate, for the critic intent on analyzing authorship, the play of the past in shaping of any narrative (see Duffy).

One of the meetings of these two writers, an unusual one certainly, was well recorded in *The New Yorker*. It happened in May of 1994 at an event the magazine sponsored. Each was among the "fourteen fiction writers closely associated with *The New Yorker*" who had been gathered, according to then fiction editor Daniel Menaker, "to have their picture taken by our staff photographer, Richard Avedon, and then [the group] joined some of the magazine's editors for an on-location party" (110). The photographs may be seen in the 27 June and 4 July 1994 issue ("*The New Yorker* Celebrates Fiction" 2); the same issue first published Munro's "The Albanian Virgin." There Maxwell, flanked by Michael Chabon and Mavis Gallant, opens the photo portfolio and, four pages on, Munro stands between Harold Brodkey and Tom Drury, with Edna O'Brien rounding out the facing page (110-11, 114-15). In between Maxwell and Munro, for the layout gives the feeling of a line of people, stand such other persons as Ann Beattie, John Updike, and Jamaica Kincaid – it must have been some party. Likening the event, and especially the principals' delight in it and in their enjoyment of one another, to "the trope of the yearbook photo," Menaker asks, "what are writers of fiction if not people who can observe and respond to the world with youthful wonder and curiosity?" (117).

As it happened, Menaker was one of two fiction editors who brought Alice Munro to *The New Yorker* in late 1976. The other was Charles McGrath, who first edited her stories acquired by the magazine and did so into the mid-1980s until, owing to changed responsibilities, Menaker took over. Each was initially employed at *The New Yorker* in other capacities, but the two joined the fiction department to replace two other longtime fiction editors, Robert Henderson and William Maxwell, who were retired at the end of 1975. Before he left, Maxwell trained each young man in the new position, each of them sitting across a desk from him to see what was done as it was done (Menaker, "Gentle"; Thacker, *Alice Munro* 319).

Maxwell had been an editor at *The New Yorker* since 1936 when he was hired by Katherine White, working there three days a week while devoting the other four to his own writing. "To those he edited," one of them, John Updike, has written, Maxwell "gave a tenderness and an acuity of attention that could not but enhance their sense of vocation; his writers included John Cheever, Eudora Welty, Vladimir Nabokov, Frank O'Connor, Sylvia Townsend Warner, and Mavis Gallant" ("Maxwell's Touch"). A singular story often noted is that when J.D. Salinger finished *The Catcher in the Rye* he drove with the manuscript to Maxwell's house to read it to his editor.[1]

As a young writer himself, Maxwell had met and been mentored in Wisconsin by Zona Gale, who had recommended his first novel, *Bright Center of Heaven* (1934), to publishers. His second, *They Came Like Swallows* (1937), was published amid short stories in *The New Yorker* and a travel piece in *The Atlantic Monthly*. While he was established as a fiction editor at the magazine, most of Maxwell's novels (*The Folded Leaf* [1945], *Time Will Darken It* [1948], *The Chateau* [1961], and *So Long, See You Tomorrow* [1980]) were published, along with numerous stories and other pieces. As Shirley Hazzard once wrote, Maxwell "'stayed with the truth that was in him, developing it throughout his life'" (qtd. in Wilkinson 77).

For her part, Munro was aware of this prominence. She had been submitting stories to *The New Yorker*, without success, since the late 1950s. She began reading Maxwell's fiction "sometime in the early sixties," beginning with *They Came Like Swallows* (1937) and *The Folded Leaf* (1945), and "I knew right away that this was a good writer, but I don't think I knew how good" ("Maxwell" 34). She continues:

> Years later I read *So Long, See You Tomorrow* (published in 1980), and by that time I knew what I was reading. I went back and reread the novels I had read before, together with *Time Will Darken It* and all the short stories I could find. And I thought: So this is how it should be done. I thought: If only I could go back and write again every single thing that I have written. Not that my writing would, or should, imitate his, but that it might be informed with his spirit. ("Maxwell" 35)[2]

When Munro came to be edited by Menaker at *The New Yorker*, Maxwell was a presence in their relationship: he mentions him, for instance, when he writes Munro in March 1989 asking for changes to her story "Friend of My Youth" (1990); and as late as 2009, she wrote Menaker that "I have just this week been re-reading [Maxwell's] 'So Long, see you tomorrow.' It gives me enormous deep deep pleasure" (Letter to Daniel Menaker).

Without question, the influence Maxwell's writing exerted on Munro's was one of ongoing accretion, of shared similar circumstances and experience, and of an aesthetic recognition that each felt compelled to write of the people and place that were theirs. When Maxwell received the Gold Medal for Fiction from the American Academy of Arts and Letters in 1995, he said "'The novelist works with what life has given him. It was no small gift that I was allowed to lead my boyhood in a small town in Illinois where the elm trees cast a mixture of light and shade over the pavements. And also that, at a fairly early age, I was made aware of the fragility of human happiness'" (qtd. in Updike, "Maxwell's Touch"). This last reference is to his mother's death from Spanish flu in 1919 when Maxwell was ten and she had just delivered his baby brother. This death figures centrally throughout Maxwell's writing, "nowhere more movingly than in his second novel, 'They Came Like Swallows,'" as Updike wrote in that same piece and, as will be seen here, as *the* central moment in *Ancestors*. Munro's own mother – her remembered healthy presence, her long illness, and her eventual death – and the town they lived in are just as centrally at the core of Munro's work (see Ross; Thacker, "Finale"). As she writes at the end of "Face" (2008), such a place is resonant: "Something happened here. In your life there are a few places, or maybe only the one place, where something happened, and then there are all the other places" (162).[3] Writing to her Canadian editor Douglas Gibson on 13 October 1980, detailing the stories she then had available for a new book, Munro told him that she wanted to hold out her then finished memoir, "Working for a Living" (1981), saving it for "a kind of family book" she wanted to do someday (Letter to Douglas Gibson). Munro once spoke of Maxwell's influence on her as "especially and forever" and, as already noted, she recalled rereading him and realizing that "So this is how it should be done" ("A Conversation"; "Maxwell" 35; see Thacker, *Alice Munro* 527-29).

William Maxwell died at age 91 during the summer of 2000. In 2004, *A William Maxwell Portrait: Memories and Appreciations*, edited by Charles Baxter, Michael Collier, and Edward Hirsh, was published by Norton. It begins with a poem by Updike and its second essay is Munro's "Maxwell," a revised and expanded version of the 1988 essay. Throughout the book's essays, time and again, its writers recall Maxwell's own "youthful wonder and curiosity," in Menaker's phrase. He was a person who met and befriended others warmly, immediately asking about the details of their lives, especially their childhoods – interested, questioning, and eager to share his own recollections, his own remembered childhood, its textures, images, and being. And so Munro found him to be. She knew, along with Maxwell's other readers, that "he wrote mostly about his childhood," in a small town in Illinois, and knew too that the central event of that childhood was the death of his mother (Thacker, Personal interview, 2010).

Munro returned to her *Brick* essay at the instigation of Charles Baxter, who likely had seen its republication in 2000 and, along with his co-editors, thought an expansion would fit well into their volume. In an e-mail to me, Baxter recalls that, when they spoke about the possibility on the telephone, Munro "wasn't certain that she could write such an essay but said she would try – really, I think, out of her love for the man and his work." When the essay arrived, he says, "she struck a deprecatory note – she described herself as 'a nervous lady at the book club'" (Baxter). Munro has long expressed such doubts about her own critical facilities, but as Baxter and his colleagues decided, she had nothing to worry over in her revised and expanded essay. There she pays most attention to his great novel, *So Long, See You Tomorrow*, where, Munro writes, "Everything [is] given its due. Everything [is] arranged with such skill that there doesn't seem to be any skill to it at all. Nothing but easy, natural storytelling" (46-47). She quotes a long passage there from Maxwell's novel which she characterizes as having "Something to say about this matter of storytelling" (47). In part, the section reads:

> What we, or at any rate what I, refer to confidently as memory – meaning a moment, a scene, a fact that has been subjected to a fixative and thereby rescued from oblivion – is really a form of storytelling that goes on continually in the mind and often changes with the telling. Too many

> conflicting emotional interests are involved for life ever to be wholly acceptable, and possibly it is the work of the storyteller to rearrange things so that they conform to this end. In any case, in talking about the past we lie with every breath we draw. ("Maxwell" 47; Maxwell, *So Long* 27)[4]

Earlier in the essay, Munro describes Maxwell's *They Came Like Swallows* as being "about the life of a young family and the way in which that life is shattered by the death of the mother" (40). She continues, in a passage which is both sharply acute about Maxwell's work and, as well, speaks directly to its congruence with her own, and especially just then:

> This story is told again and again in Maxwell's fiction, in stories that seem autobiographical but may not be as autobiographical as they seem – and there is something new with each telling, some new action at the periphery or revelation near the centre, a different light or shading, a discovery, as there must be in the stories at the heart of our lives, stories that grow and change as we do and never go away. ("Maxwell" 40)

This passage did not appear in the original version of the essay, so it would appear to bear some relation to Munro's work during 2003-04. Just then she had produced the "Juliet Triptych": three connected stories – "Chance," "Soon," and "Silence" – first published together in a single issue of *The New Yorker* and then included in *Runaway* (2004); though not overtly so, they too have their autobiographical elements, especially "Soon." That story's penultimate paragraph, a single sentence and one Munro initially tried to use to end the story, is one that might be seen as a coda for Maxwell and Munro both; it reads "Because it's what happens at home that you try to protect, as best you can, for as long as you can" (125). During the time of her essay's revision too, Munro was finally shaping her next major project, her autobiographic family book, her own version of *Ancestors*, the book that would be called *The View from Castle Rock*.

In 2008 John Updike took up the Library of America's newly published Maxwell volumes and produced an essay, "Imperishable Maxwell," for *The New Yorker*. Reviewing and appreciating all of his former editor's writing, Updike comments at one point that "Maxwell did believe, ever more strongly, that reality was the best fiction" (74). Continuing, Updike remarks on how Maxwell "says in an aside that even when the author imposes the disguise of a name on characters, actual names 'are so much more convincing than the names he invents for them'" (74). He also cites an instance when Maxwell told an interviewer that "'For me, "fiction" lies not in whether a thing, the thing I am writing about, actually happened, but in the form of the writing ... a story, which has a shape, a controlled effect, a satisfying conclusion – something that is, or attempts to be, a work of art'" (74).

Just before this Updike makes a passing reference to Maxwell's *Ancestors* and calls it "his book-length essay about his family history" (74). That is so. Reading the book, which details the circumstances, assumptions, and histories of Maxwell's forebears at considerable length, its reader never forgets the presence of Maxwell shaping the story he is telling. It does read like a long essay. When there he again reaches the paradigmatic moment in his own life, the death of his mother in 1919, he closes the chapter with his aunt taking him in her lap, welling up, and telling him the news, writing "What had to be done she could be counted on to do" (267). The next chapter is a retrospective one, for Maxwell goes back to a series of memories of his family when they were together, all living, his mother among them. This interlude done, he returns to his chronology, to his essay. That is, as Updike quotes Maxwell, "a story, which has a shape, a controlled effect" though not in this instance nor, really, throughout Maxwell's numerous renderings of his mother's death, says Updike quoting Maxwell, "a satisfying conclusion." No question but that those renderings – *Ancestors* among them – are, again in Maxwell's words, "something that is, or attempts to be, a work of art."[5]

Toward the end of *Ancestors* Maxwell writes,

> It is not true that the dead desert the living. They go away for a very short time, and then they come back and stay as long as they are needed. But sooner or later a time comes when they are in the way; their presence is, for one reason or another, an embarrassment; there is no place for them in the lives of those they once meant everything to. Then they go away for good.
>
> When I was in college I was wakened out of a sound sleep by my own voice, answering my mother, who had called to me from the stairs. With my heart pounding, I waited for more and there wasn't any more. Nothing like it ever happened to me before, or since. (307-08)

Brendan Gill, one of the reviewers of *Ancestors* and Maxwell's colleague and friend at *The New Yorker*, asserted that the writer's "most successful feat of deception" in the book is "that at a certain, scarcely detectable point in his narrative the ancestors ... are made to slip away and we are left in the presence of a little boy who, all nakedly and touchingly, is about to lose his beloved mother by death, who is to suffer the ignominy of adolescence in a desolate household, and who is to spend years learning that the contest of love and suspicion between father and son can never be won by either and is not to be ended even after death" (90). Noting that however central the story of his mother's death is to Maxwell in *Ancestors*, Gill makes it clear that the passages regarding her are not about the father too. Citing a small contentious incident between father and son, which happened long after, but one described in the book, Gill comments that "We are all more or less uneasily descendants, and we are all imminently ancestral" (90). For Maxwell, a comment he later made about his methods in *Ancestors*, and we may say elsewhere, is salient: "'I came to feel that life is the most extraordinary storyteller of all, and the fewer changes you make [in facts and details] the better, provided you get to the heart of the matter'" (qtd. in Carduff 960). So Alice Munro saw and felt when she read *Ancestors* and *So Long, See You Tomorrow*: "the heart of the matter."[6]

Munro had been thinking about her own family book – the one which became *The View from Castle Rock* – since at least the late 1970s. As she wrote to Gibson on 13 October 1980, the foundational piece in that book was what she called in that letter "a long memoir I wrote about my father, which I think is pretty good, but I think it should be kept out for a kind of family book I want to do someday – maybe about the Laidlaws in Huron County and in Ettrick & James Hogg whose mother was a Laidlaw" (Letter to Douglas Gibson). That memoir was "Working for a Living," to be published the next year, 1981, in the inaugural issue of *Grand Street*. There, as with the preference for the mother's story over the father's that Gill notes in his review of *Ancestors*, Munro tells more about her father than her mother, although she is more balanced in her treatment of each of them at a key moment of their marriage. And she tells the story of that marriage too.

In some ways, though, such a family book from this writer now seems an inevitability: her own life and her family relations in Ontario were each at the core of the fiction she wrote and published during the over twenty years she lived in British Columbia (1952-73); her return there after she left her marriage to Jim Munro occasioned a new imaginative confrontation with the sights, surfaces, and culture of Ontario, and with her family. Especially with her father, Robert Eric Laidlaw, who had remarried after being widowed in 1959 and who still lived on the family farm in Lower Wingham. And when Munro moved back to Huron County, to Clinton in 1975 to live with Gerald Fremlin, her literal return home was complete. Imaginatively, it was a time of the rediscovery of her home place, of its mores, its textures, and of her ancestors; and it shows throughout the progress which was Munro's work from 1973 on: such memoir stories as "Home" (1974), "The Ottawa Valley" (1974), and "Winter Wind" (1974); her abandoned photo text, "Places at Home," much of it incorporated into *Who Do You Think You Are?* (1978) / *The Beggar Maid* (1979); and during this time too Munro researched and wrote about her mother's Irish heritage through "1847: The Irish" (1978), a Canadian Broadcasting Corporation television show (published as a story in 1979 as "A Better Place than Home"). Ancestral interests and this trajectory are evident into the 1980s with some of the stories in *The Moons of Jupiter* (1982) (the two-part "Chaddeleys and Flemings" and the title story), with "Working for a Living" (1981) and, in 1988, Munro published "Meneseteung," a complex story which has at its core a narrator deep in biographical research. In 1990 Munro spent three months in Scotland and, in 1995, six months in Ireland. "Home" and "Working for a Living" – each memoirs focused on Munro's parents – were destined for *The View from Castle Rock*, but the first overt evidence of the emergence of that book was "Changing Places" (1997), a narrative essay exploring her Laidlaw ancestors which Munro contributed to a PEN Canada anthology, *Writing Home* (see Thacker, *Alice Munro* passim; Thacker, "Alice Munro Country").[7]

But if it is fair to call Maxwell's *Ancestors* a "book-length essay," as Updike did, then what Munro offers in *The View from Castle Rock* is a structure more complex than a single, well-informed narrative in which the author may be seen shaping and responding to the historical and biographical facts at hand. Inspired by what Maxwell accomplished in *Ancestors*, Munro attempts and accomplishes a more ambitious structure in *The View from Castle Rock*, the family book that she had for so long envisaged. On 30 June 2005 – over a year prior to publication, when actually she was still shaping the book's structure – Munro drafted a foreword which carefully lays out the book's provenance. This draft is fundamentally what was published in the book but for one key added sentence, an emphatic paragraph. Of which more presently. Munro begins in the published version, "About ten or twelve years ago I began to take more than a random interest in the history of one side of my family, whose name was Laidlaw" ([ix]). She then explains some aspects of her research, that she "lived in Scotland for a few months, close to the Ettrick Valley, so I was able to find their names in the local histories in the Selkirk and Galashiels Public Libraries, and to find out what James Hogg had to say about them in *Blackwoods Magazine*" ([ix]). Hogg, "the Ettrick Shepherd," was one of Munro's own ancestors, the author of *The Private Memoirs and Confessions of a Justified Sinner* (1824), a novel, and friend of Sir Walter Scott. As Munro writes, Hogg took him to see Hogg's mother, "a Laidlaw," "when Scott was collecting ballads for the *Minstrelsy of the Scottish Border*" ([ix]; see Gilkison, Redekop). After offering this detail, she states that she

> put all this [historical] material together over the years, and almost without my noticing what was happening, it began to shape itself, here and there, into something like stories. Some of the characters gave themselves to me in their own words, others rose out of their situations. Their words and my words, a curious re-creation of lives, in a given setting that was as truthful as our notion of the past can ever be. ([ix-x])

Munro's foreword to this point addresses the first of the two parts of her book, the one called "No Advantages," the one based on family papers and her historical research and some scenes Munro imagined. She then shifts to the material in the second part, a section called "Home," and writes that

> During these years I was also writing a special set of stories. These stories were not included in the books of fiction I put together, at regular

> intervals. Why not? I felt they didn't belong. They were not memoirs but they were closer to my own life than the other stories I had written, even in the first person. In other first-person stories I had drawn on personal material, but then I did anything I wanted to with this material. Because the chief thing I was doing was making a story. In the stories I hadn't collected I was not doing exactly that. I was doing something closer to what a memoir does – exploring a life, my own life, but not in an austere or rigorously factual way. I put myself in the center and wrote about that self, as searchingly as I could. But the figures around this self took on their own life and color and did things they had not done in reality. ([x])

Munro then offers some detail from some of the second group of stories before, in a single-sentence paragraph added sometime after she wrote the 30 June 2005 draft, and clearly referring to both sets of narratives that she offers in *The View from Castle Rock*, "These are *stories*" ([x]; emphasis in orig.).[8] Yes, they are. Although, that having been said, it is perfectly reasonable to call two of the stories in the "Home" section – "Home" and "What Do You Want to Know For?" – memoirs. The same might be said of "Working for a Living," which ends the first section, "No Advantages," and of the book's epilogue, "Messenger."

At the closing of one of the 1974 memoir stories mentioned above, "The Ottawa Valley," Munro writes of her mother, maintaining that "she is the one of course that I am trying to get; it is to reach her that this whole journey has been undertaken" (246). This phrasing and the sentences that follow to finish both the story and the book have become a touchstone in Munro studies, defining her relation with her remembered mother, a relation which has vexed Munro in her published stories from first to last (see "Dear Life"; Ross; Thacker, "Finale"). Analogously, it seems that with the publication of "Changing Places" in 1997 Munro both continued her meditations on her ancestors and announced her movement toward *The View from Castle Rock*. Its account of the Laidlaws' 1818 emigration to Upper Canada, elaborated and also fictionalized, became the basis of "No Advantages" and "The View from Castle Rock," the first two pieces in the book. The story of her great-great grandparents, William and Mary Laidlaw, and their children became the focus, also elaborated and fictionalized, of "Illinois," which then follows. "The Wilds of Morris Township," the next story, takes up a 1907 memoir written by "Big Rob"

Laidlaw, one of the sons of her great-great uncle Andrew and his wife Agnes, and describes the circumstances of his pioneering an area of Huron County, Ontario, in November of 1851 with his cousins John and Thomas, Munro's great-grandfather (see Thacker, *Alice Munro* 26-32). She then follows the circumstances of some of Big Rob's children living in Huron County and, thereby, gets to "Working for a Living," connecting those children to her grandfather William Cole Laidlaw and to her grandmother Sarah Jane "Sadie" Code Laidlaw, and then to their only son, Robert Eric Laidlaw, her father. In this way she is able to reach, and to finish effectively, the first section of *The View from Castle Rock*, the predominately memoir section, "No Advantages."

John Updike maintained that Maxwell thought "'reality was the best fiction'" and in Munro's family book she can be seen taking the same path – quite literally. In the second section of the book, "Home," Munro places six predominantly fictional stories, all but one previously published; as she had gathered her collections over the years, she had held them back. These are the "special set of stories" Munro details in the foreword: not exactly memoirs, Munro asserted, but "closer to my own life than the other stories I had written, even in the first person" ([x]). In these stories – the earliest first published in 1974, the latest in 2002 – as she explained, "I was doing something closer to what a memoir does – exploring a life, my own life, but not in an austere or rigorously factual way" ([x]).

These stories may be variously characterized. The first, "Fathers" (2002), takes up the Second World War years, the time when eight-to-fourteen-year-old Alice Laidlaw was socialized; at its core is a comparison of two very different fathers. Neither looks at all like her own father, although the electrocution it features nearly happened to him in 1943. The second, "Lying under the Apple Tree" (2002), is a story of young love and was first published in *The New Yorker* as a memoir.[9] The third, "Hired Girl" (1994), was revised and deepened for *Castle Rock*; it focuses on a summer job Munro had in 1948 working for a Toronto family at their cottage on Georgian Bay. The last two stories in the "Home" section, the memoirs "Home" and "What Do You Want to Know For?" (1994), respectively feature Munro a forty-two-year-old writer returned to Ontario after many years living in British Columbia, and as that same writer long-lived in Huron County and now in her sixties, exploring her home place. The single story Munro wrote for *The View from Castle Rock*, "The Ticket" (2006), is the exception that proves the rule.[10] It returns to the circumstances surrounding twenty-year-old Alice Laidlaw's marriage to James Munro in December 1951, an action which both took her away from home – especially from her increasingly infirm mother suffering from Parkinson's Disease – and also probably made her the writer she became by distancing her from Lower Town Wingham, her core home-place subject. Munro knew this, and the structure for *Castle Rock* that she created was clearly one of integrating – connecting – her own life and experiences to those of her ancestors, whom she has worked to discover, write about, and connect to as forming a complex textual continuity.

In early March of 2005 Jennifer Rudolph Walsh, Munro's agent, submitted "The View from Castle Rock" to Deborah Treisman, fiction editor at *The New Yorker*. The manuscript was 140 double-spaced pages long; it contained almost all of what later appeared as the "No Advantages" first section of *The View from Castle Rock* plus the epilogue, and while the editors at the magazine were mostly enthusiastic about what they had, they knew it would have to be cut. Passing what she called "a very rough cut from Alice Munro's 150-page combination of family history and fiction (the characters' names are all true – the happenings on the boat trip imagined)" on to David Remnick, the magazine's chief editor, Treisman also wrote that the manuscript "could be made to work, and it has some real Munrovian highlights, which cutting would only accentuate" (Treisman). "The View from Castle Rock" – about thirteen pages of printed text there – was published as fiction in the 29 August 2005 issue. It focuses on the circumstances of the Laidlaw family's emigration to Canada in 1818, beginning with Andrew's visit to Edinburgh as in the book, describing the voyage over, and ending with young James Laidlaw's death "within a month of the family's landing at Quebec" (77).

I have in my possession a copy of the book manuscript of *The View from Castle Rock* as it was in late May 2005. (Munro was good enough to let me read it since, just then, I was in the final phases of completing my biography *Alice Munro: Writing Her Lives*, published that fall.) In Munro's manuscript, there is not yet the published foreword, the two-section structure with an epilogue, nor has "What Do You Want to Know For?" (1994) been included. Its place in the manuscript is held by "Wenlock

Edge," a story destined to appear in *The New Yorker* in December 2005 and one later omitted from *Castle Rock*. As indicated above Munro drafted the foreword in June 2005 and over that summer sought advice from her editors Ann Close and Douglas Gibson and her former agent, Virginia Barber, as to whether or not "Wenlock Edge" should be included in the book.[11] Having not yet decided upon the two-part structure in the published *Castle Rock*, Munro alternates historical narratives with the more memoir-like fictions. Thus the manuscript opens with a piece called "The View from Castle Rock" (in the published version it is retitled "No Advantages") followed by "Fathers"; then "Men of Ettrick" (the published "The View from Castle Rock") followed by "Lying under the Apple Tree"; then "Illinois" followed by "Hired Girl"; "The Wilds of Morris Township" followed by "Wenlock Edge"; "Working for a Living" followed by "The Ticket"; "Home" followed by "Remnants" ("Messenger") which ends the volume.

Munro obviously abandoned this arrangement, and it may well be that the replacement of "Wenlock Edge" by "What Do You Want to Know For?" occasioned the published sectional alignment of the two types of stories, but the existence of the interleaved manuscript does suggest in Munro what Updike characterized in Maxwell – that "reality was the best fiction" ("Imperishable Maxwell" 74). For her it is and, as she has written her lives throughout her long and very distinguished career, it always has been. At the heart of "Wenlock Edge" is a reality – Munro's recollections of her time at The University of Western Ontario, 1949-51 – grafted onto what is for her a fiction, the imagined dinner with the young narrator in the nude. And in "What Do You Want to Know For?" there appears an assertion that might be taken as coda for both Maxwell and Munro: "It's the fact you cherish" (322). Each writing their "stories at the heart of [their] lives," each has made their best fiction from their realities – Maxwell in *Ancestors* and most especially in *So Long, See You Tomorrow*. And so too Alice Munro, following his example but also her own deeply practised yet still developing aesthetic in *The View from Castle Rock*. Separately, though with Maxwell leading the way through the models of his *Ancestors* and *So Long, See You Tomorrow*, each fashioned narratives that should be seen, in the phrase used by Munro in 1980, as "a kind of family book," certainly, but more than that, as narratives which capture, in the words Munro used to describe Maxwell's fiction, "stories at the heart of our lives, stories that grow and change as we do and never go away" ("Maxwell" 40). Just as she wrote, "as truthful as our notion of the past can ever be" ([x]). William Maxwell and Alice Munro – as Munro said, connected "especially and forever."

Notes

1. Following on Updike's comment here, it is worth noting that three volumes of Maxwell's correspondence with his *New Yorker* authors have been published and that he, for his part, edited the letters of one of them, Sylvia Townsend Warner. (See Marrs, Steinman, Steinman.)
2. Munro's description of Maxwell's influence – "it might be informed with his spirit" ("Maxwell" 35) – is wholly consistent with her practice. (See my "Alice Munro's Willa Cather" and, for a broader discussion of influences on Munro, Martin and Ober.)
3. Throughout Munro's work, passages of poetry – usually recited by a character, although not always – are used to complement the narrative. In "Face," just before this quotation, Munro inserts Walter de la Mare's "Away" ("There is no sorrow / Time heals never") as part of a dream sequence between the narrator and an unidentified woman who recites poetry to him while he is in hospital with an eye injury, so that he is unable to see her. This may be a connection to Maxwell: during his sophomore year at the University of Illinois-Urbana, distraught over circumstances surrounding two intimate friendships, he attempted suicide. He used the friendships, and the suicide attempt, in *The Folded Leaf*. As Updike notes, Maxwell later "ascribed his suicide attempt to reading too much Walter de la Mare, which gave him a 'poetic idea of life after death,' a life in which he would be reunited with his mother" ("Imperishable Maxwell" 72; see Jamieson, Micros).
4. The reliability of memory is very much the subject of Munro's "The Progress of Love" (1985). This passage might serve as coda for that story, and perhaps for all of middle to late Munro (that is, from *The Progress of Love* [1986] on). For an extended discussion of Alice Munro's late style, one written after the initial analysis in this essay, see my critical study *Alice Munro's Late Style: "Writing is the Final Thing"*.

5. Paul John Eakin, in *Touching the World*, takes up *So Long, See You Tomorrow* as memoir, as autobiography. After reading it and so seeing it, Eakin then read *Ancestors* and, he writes, "I was not surprised to find the essential facts of the narrator's life in *So Long* repeated here" (46). He enumerates them and then asks "But so what? What if *Ancestors* did not exist? What then? Aping the narrator of *So Long*, I could have searched the files of the Lincoln *Courier-Herald* for details" (46-47) of the murder in the novel. Or he might have gone and tried to verify Maxwell's presence in the same Chicago high school mentioned there. He continues, "but I did not, unwilling, perhaps, to have my belief in *So Long* as an autobiography disconfirmed" (47). Eakin ultimately sees this as "an instinct to trust." "When the narrator speaks of *So Long* as 'this memoir – if that's the right name for it' ... I take him at his word" (47). This critic is writing of Maxwell here, but similar arguments might well be made about Munro's work, most especially *The View from Castle Rock*.
6. While beyond the scope of this article, and a subject on which I have already elaborated, Munro's "Finale" section in her last book, *Dear Life* (2012), is indebted to the pivotal point of the revelation of the mother's death in *Ancestors* (Thacker, "Finale"). The title story, "Dear Life" (2011), which ends the book, echoes that moment in Maxwell's. In a 2013 interview Munro responded to a question about it and the interviewer writes in a headnote that Munro works "by connecting her story or personal history to larger events or circumstances of the time in which it takes place – a technique she has said she admires in William Maxwell's *Ancestors: A Family History*" (Awano 180).
7. Munro published "What Do You Want to Know For?" in *Writing Away: The PEN Canada Travel Anthology* (1994) and, revised, it became the penultimate piece in *Castle Rock*. Because she decided on this inclusion late in the process of shaping the book, it makes more sense to see "Changing Places" as evidence of its emergence. Munro begins the foreword to *Castle Rock* writing, "About ten or twelve years ago I began to take more than a random interest in the history of one side of my family, whose name was Laidlaw" ([ix]). This would be 1994-96.

8. Munro italicized the word "stories" in the book manuscript. See Knopf copy-edited book manuscript, MsC 323 1.1: x, Alice Munro fonds, Archives and Special Collections, University of Calgary.
9. It is worth noting that "Lying under the Apple Tree" went through production at *The New Yorker* as a memoir. Deborah Treisman, Munro's editor, became sufficiently aware of its fictional elements that she requested – and wrote herself – a disclaimer that appeared at the "memoir's" opening in the magazine (88). The disclaimer was omitted from the version in *Castle Rock*.
10. The epilogue, "Messenger," which Munro initially called "Remnants," was also first published in *Castle Rock*, as was much of "Part One: No Advantages." But as the single unpublished fiction included in the "Home" section, "The Ticket" is indicative: Munro apparently decided that her marriage to James Munro had to be included along with these other stories "closer to [her] own life" ([x]), as she writes in the foreword.
11. Barber, Close, and Gibson were Munro's "literary triumvirate," as they co-ordinated her publication from magazines, most usually *The New Yorker*, through books – that is, with separate versions in the United States, Great Britain, and Canada – beginning with *Who Do You Think You Are?* (1978) / *The Beggar Maid* (1979). As such, each had a hand in shaping those collections in consultation with Munro. With "Wenlock Edge," Barber and Close counseled against including it since, published with the ancestral and memoir stories in the volume, readers would legitimately think that the central dinner in it, in which the narrator dines in the nude with a clothed older man, had actually occurred when Munro was at The University of Western Ontario in London. As it happened, early in 2004 Munro ascribed the practice of such dinners to a friend of hers (Thacker Interview, 2004). Also, in August 2005 Munro wrote to Barber, speaking of "What Do You Want to Know For?," "*I* think it could replace 'Wenlock'" (Letter to Virginia Barber). It did, and "Wenlock Edge" was included in her next book, *Too Much Happiness* (2009).

Works Cited

Awano, Lisa Dickler. "An Interview with Alice Munro." *Virginia Quarterly Review*, vol. 89, no. 2, Spring 2013, pp. 180-84.

Baxter, Charles. E-mail to author. 10 September 2010.

---, Michael Collier, and Edward Hirsch, editors. *A William Maxwell Portrait: Memories and Appreciations.* W.W. Norton, 2004.

Carduff, Christopher. "Chronology." *William Maxwell: Early Novels and Stories*, by Maxwell. Library of America, 2008, pp. 939-67.

de la Mare, Walter. "Away." *The Collected Poems of Walter de la Mare.* Faber and Faber, 1979, p. 281.

Duffy, Dennis. "Alice Munro's Narrative Historicism: 'Too Much Happiness'." 2015. Struthers, *Alice Munro Everlasting*, pp. 367-86.

Eakin, Paul John. *Touching the World: Reference in Autobiography.* Princeton UP, 1992.

Gilkison, Bruce. *Walking with James Hogg: The Ettrick Shepherd's Journeys through Scotland.* Edinburgh UP, 2016.

Gill, Brendan. "The Past Regained." Review of *Ancestors*, by William Maxwell. *The New Yorker*, 21 August 1971, pp. 88-91.

Jamieson, Sara. "'The stuff they put in the old readers': Remembered and Recited Poetry in the Stories of Alice Munro." *Alice Munro's Miraculous Art: Critical Essays*, edited by Janice Fiamengo and Gerald Lynch. U of Ottawa P, 2017, pp. 79-95.

Marrs, Suzanne, editor. *What There Is to Say We Have Said: The Correspondence of Eudora Welty and William Maxwell.* Houghton Mifflin Harcourt, 2011.

Martin, W.R. *Alice Munro: Paradox and Parallel.* U of Alberta P, 1987.

Martin, W.R., and Warren U. Ober. "Alice Munro as Small-Town Historian: 'Spaceships Have Landed'." Struthers, *Alice Munro Country*, pp. 237-54.

Maxwell, William. *Ancestors: A Family History.* 1971. Vintage International, 1995.

---. *So Long, See You Tomorrow.* 1980. Vintage, 1996.

Menaker, Daniel. "Authors! Authors!" Photographs by Richard Avedon. *The New Yorker*, 27 June and 4 July 1994, pp. 110-17.

---. "The Gentle Realist." *The New York Times*, 15 October 2000, p. 39.

---. Letter to Alice Munro, 15 March 1989. Virginia Barber Papers, Alice Munro fonds, Archives and Special Collections, University of Calgary.

Micros, Marianne. "'Pearl Street ... is another story': Poetry and Reality in Alice Munro's 'Meneseteung'." Struthers, *Alice Munro Country*, pp. 323-44.

Munro, Alice. "Changing Places." *Writing Home: A PEN Canada Anthology*, edited by Constance Rooke. McClelland & Stewart, 1997, pp. 190-206.

---. "A Conversation with Alice Munro." <https://knopfdoubleday.com/2010/01/08/alice-munro-interview/>.

---. "Dear Life." *Dear Life*. McClelland & Stewart, 2012, pp. 299-319.

---. "Face." *Too Much Happiness*. McClelland & Stewart, 2009, pp. 138-63.

---. Letter to Daniel Menaker, 5 August 2009. Author's private collection.

---. Letter to Douglas Gibson, 13 October 1980. 429.3, Macmillan Company of Canada fonds, William Ready Division of Archives and Research Collections, McMaster University.

---. Letter to Virginia Barber, 2 August 2005. Virginia Barber Papers, Alice Munro fonds, Archives and Special Collections, University of Calgary.

---. "Lying under the Apple Tree." *The New Yorker*, 17 and 24 June 2002, pp. 88-90, 92, 105-08, 110-14.

---. Manuscript draft foreword to *The View from Castle Rock*, 30 June 2005. Virginia Barber Papers, Alice Munro fonds, Archives and Special Collections, University of Calgary.

---. "Maxwell." Baxter, Collier, and Hirsch, pp. 34-47.

---. "The Novels of William Maxwell." *Brick*, no. 34, Fall 1988, pp. 28-31. Reprinted *Brick*, nos. 65-66, Fall 2000, pp. 23-29.

---. "The Ottawa Valley." *Something I've Been Meaning To Tell You*. McGraw-Hill Ryerson, 1974, pp. 227-46.

---. "Soon." *Runaway*. McClelland & Stewart, 2004, pp. 87-125.

---. "The View from Castle Rock." *The New Yorker*, 29 August 2005, pp. 64-77.

---. *The View from Castle Rock*. Manuscript version, May 2005. Author's private collection.

---. *The View from Castle Rock*. McClelland & Stewart, 2006.

Redekop, Magdalene. "Alice Munro and the Scottish Nostalgic Grotesque." *The Rest of the Story: Critical Essays on Alice Munro*, edited by Robert Thacker. ECW, 1999, pp. 21-43.

Ross, Catherine Sheldrick. "'At the End of a Long Road': Alice Munro's 'Dear Life'." Struthers, *Alice Munro Everlasting*, pp. 31-77.

Steinman, Michael, editor. *The Element of Lavishness: Letters of Sylvia Townsend Warner and William Maxwell 1938-1978*. Counterpoint, 2001.

---, editor. *The Happiness of Getting It Down Right: Letters of Frank O'Connor and William Maxwell 1945-1966*. Knopf, 1996.

Stoffman, Judy. "Making a Short Story Long." *Toronto Star*, 28 October 2006, pp. H1, H10.

Struthers, J.R. (Tim), editor. *Alice Munro Country: Essays on Her Works I*. Guernica Editions, 2020. Essential Writers Ser. 51.

---, editor. *Alice Munro Everlasting: Essays on Her Works II*. Guernica Editions, 2020. Essential Writers Ser. 52.

Thacker, Robert. *Alice Munro: Writing Her Lives: A Biography*. 2005. Updated ed. Emblem, 2011.

---. "Alice Munro Country." *The Dalhousie Review*, vol. 98, no. 3, Autumn 2018, pp. 412-18.

---. *Alice Munro's Late Style: "Writing is the Final Thing"*. Bloomsbury Academic, 2023.

---. "Alice Munro's Willa Cather (1992)." *Reading Alice Munro: 1973-2013*, by Thacker. U of Calgary P, 2016, pp. 115-31, 277-78.

---. Personal interview with Alice Munro. 24 April 2004, Comox, British Columbia.

---. Personal interview with Alice Munro. 14 June 2010, Goderich, Ontario.

---. "'Stabbed to the Heart ... By the Beauty of Our Lives Steaming By': Munro's Finale." Struthers, *Alice Munro Everlasting*, pp. 409-42.

Treisman, Deborah. Letter to David Remnick, 24 March 2005. Author's private collection.

Updike, John. "Imperishable Maxwell." *The New Yorker*, 8 September 2008, pp. 68-74.

---. "Maxwell's Touch." *The New Yorker*, 14 August 2000, p. 29.

Wilkinson, Alec. *My Mentor: A Young Man's Friendship with William Maxwell*. Houghton Mifflin, 2002.

Thank You for Visiting

Charles E. May

1. Alice Munro's "Dear Life"
Saturday 1 October 2011

I am currently editing a new book of criticism on the work of Alice Munro. The book includes fifteen original articles, especially commissioned for the collection, by noted scholars and critics from Canada, the United States, England, and Ireland. My own task, in addition to soliciting, compiling, and editing the essays, was to write a brief biographical sketch of Munro and a critical essay expressing my own approach to her work. I will talk more about the book as it gets nearer publication, but today I wanted to respond to a piece of "personal history" Munro published recently in *The New Yorker*, entitled "Dear Life: A Childhood Visitation" (19 September 2011).

My initial interest in the piece was to determine if Munro had included any "new" information about her life that I should add to my biographical sketch. I have read rather carefully the updated paperback edition of Robert Thacker's wonderful full-length (600 pages plus) biography, *Alice Munro: Writing Her Lives* (2005/2011). I have read all the interviews and occasional pieces in which Munro has talked about her life, as well as her daughter Sheila Munro's book *Lives of Mothers & Daughters: Growing Up with Alice Munro* (2001). I have also, of course, read Munro's *The View from Castle Rock* (2006), which is subtitled "Stories," but which includes several "personal history" or "memoir" pieces. She does not always make clear distinctions between them.

And that's what I would like to think a bit about in this post – the relationship between pieces that Munro calls "stories" and the works she calls "personal history," focusing particularly on her recent piece "Dear Life."

In the Foreword to *The View from Castle Rock* Munro says, "About ten or twelve years ago I began to take more than a random interest in the history of one side of my family, whose name was Laidlaw" ([vii]). After doing research and reading in the history of her Scottish family, Munro says she "put all this material together over the years, and almost without my noticing what was happening, it began to shape itself, here and there, into something like stories" ([vii]).

Not stories, mind you, but "something like stories." Munro also says that during these years she was "writing a special set of stories" ([viii]), which she did not include in the books of short stories she was publishing because she felt they did not belong. "They were not memoirs but they were closer to my own life than the other stories I had written, even in the first person" ([viii]). Munro explains that "In other first-person stories I had drawn on personal material, but then I did anything I wanted to do with this material. Because the chief thing I was doing was making a story" ([viii]).

However, she says that in this "special set of stories" (included in the second half of *Castle Rock*), "I was doing something closer to what a memoir does – exploring a life, my own life, but not in an austere or rigorously factual way. I put myself in the center and wrote about that self, as searchingly as I could. But the figures around this self took on their own life and color and did things they had not done in reality" ([viii]). Munro says that so many of these characters moved so far beyond their beginnings in real life that she could not remember who they were to start with. She concludes, "You could say that such stories pay more attention to the truth of a life than fiction usually does. But not enough to swear on" ([viii]).

"Dear Life" does not reveal anything about Alice Munro's childhood beyond what she and Robert Thacker have already disclosed. However, it does offer some insight into how Munro sees the relationship between "memoir" and fiction. Although "Dear Life" seems to fit into the category of memoir – "exploring a life" in a factual way, with the self at the center – given Munro's irresistible compulsion to write stories, this "personal history" often merges into the thematically rhetorical stuff of fiction.

I love the rhythm of Munro's sentences. Note this opening: "I lived when I was young at the end of a long road, or a road that seemed long to me" ("Dear Life" 40). She could have said, more directly: "When I was young I lived at the end of a road that seemed long to me." But the lilt would have been lost, don't you think? And she could have opened the memoir in many ways, but she chose to open it with her memory of the two bridges that separated her home from "the real town" ("Dear Life" 40). And with these bridges, we are made aware of her early sense of separation from the activity of town life.

We are also introduced in the first paragraph to the individuality of this little girl, for one of the bridges is "a wooden walkway, which occasionally had a plank missing, so that you could look right down into the bright, hurrying water. I liked that, but somebody always came and replaced the plank eventually" ("Dear Life" 40). I am glad that the little girl likes the gap made by the missing plank, for it does not frighten her as it might some children; it fascinates her.

If you have read Munro's fiction, you will recognize the source of some of her stories in this piece of "personal history," the most familiar being the whippings by her father for "'Talking back'" ("Dear Life" 42) converted to fiction in "Royal Beatings" in *The Beggar Maid.* At certain points in "Dear Life," Munro reminds us that what we are reading here is not fiction. For example, when she describes the house of a man named Roly Grain, which "was like a dwarf's house in a story" ("Dear Life" 42), she suggests that although he could be the stimulus for a story here he is not, for she says the man "does not have any further part in what I'm writing now, in spite of his troll's name, because this is not a story, only life" ("Dear Life" 42).

I like this little aside, for in it Munro indicates at least one way that remembered real life might mutate into a story. It is as if she finds it hard to resist the writer's urge to spin off from the "dwarf house" and the "troll's name" and start a story. The distinction she makes here between something that is "only life" and something that might be much more significant is a helpful one, it seems to me, for it suggests that real life is "only life" because it does not mean anything, whereas a story is more than real life because what makes it a story is some meaningful significance the author discovers in it.

Munro refers to the difference between real life and fiction again later when she describes the misfortunes her family faced – her father's loss of his business and her mother's Parkinson's disease – commenting, "You would think that this was all too much. … It wouldn't do in fiction" ("Dear Life" 44). It is as though Munro, and probably any writer, finds it difficult to think about life without thinking about the possibilities for fiction. It is as though writers like Munro experience almost a constant compulsion to convert everything into story, to see the world always in words and sentences and meaningful sequences.

In "Dear Life," Munro finally gives into the compulsion to convert events in the world into meaningful fiction when she recounts a story her mother told her about "a crazy old woman named Mrs. Netterfield" ("Dear Life" 44). The first story the mother tells focuses on a day when the grocer forgot to put butter into the old woman's order. When the delivery boy is opening the back of the truck, the old woman notices the butter is missing and goes after the boy with a hatchet, which made him drive away without closing the back door. Munro says that some things about the story puzzle her, though she did not think about them at the time, for example how the old woman knew the butter was missing and why she happened to have a hatchet with her. However, when Munro thinks about the story as a writer, she considers the issue of plausibility that governs fiction, but may have nothing to do with real life.

It is with the second story about old Mrs. Netterfield (which takes up roughly a third of "Dear Life") that Munro begins to transmute "only life" into a story. She begins in her writerly voice recalling not the experience (for she was too young to remember it), but her mother's telling of it. "It was a beautiful day in the fall. I had been set out to sleep in my baby carriage on the little patch of new lawn" ("Dear Life" 45). The mother is in the house washing baby clothes by hand. Since there is no window in the front, she has to cross the room to look out a window to check on baby Alice, a view which let her see the driveway. At this point, Munro the writer steps in with her inevitable questions: "Why did my mother decide to leave her washing and wringing out in order to look at the driveway?" ("Dear Life" 45). After considering possible reasons, including watching for her husband to come home with groceries for something she was making for supper (and an aside about how his family did not approve of her fancy cooking, or her fancy dress for that matter), Munro returns to what her mother saw – old Mrs. Netterfield coming down the lane. Then, thinking like a writer, she considers the possibilities – i.e., not what she knows, but what she thinks may be the case: "My mother must have seen Mrs. Netterfield at least a few times before she noticed her walking down our lane. Maybe they had never spoken. It's possible, though, that they had. My mother might have made a point of it, even if my father had told her that it was not necessary. It might even lead to trouble, was what he probably would have said" ("Dear Life" 45).

The mother runs out and grabs baby Alice out of the carriage and carries her into the house, locking the door behind her. "But there was a problem, wasn't there, with the kitchen door? As far as I know, it never had a proper lock. There was just a custom, at night, of pushing one of the kitchen chairs against that door, and tilting it with the chair back under the doorknob, in such a way that anybody pushing it to get in would have made a dreadful clatter" ("Dear Life" 45).

Then, writer that she is, Munro asks further questions about motivation, inner thoughts, background information that she does not know from "only life," but must invent if she were to write a story: "Did my mother think of any weapon, once she had got the doorknob wedged in place? Had she ever picked up a gun, or loaded one, in her life? // Did it cross her mind that the old woman might just be paying a neighborly visit? I don't think so. There would have been a difference in the walk, a determination in the approach of the woman coming down the lane. // It is possible that my mother prayed, but she did not mention it" ("Dear Life" 46).

The mother sees the old woman investigate the blanket in the carriage and fling it to the ground; she hides in the dumbwaiter, listening to the old woman walking around the house and stopping at every downstairs window. Then Munro as writer poses another question. After noting that the old woman did not have to stretch to see inside even though she was not very tall, Munro asks: "How did my mother know this? It was not as if she were running around with me in her arms, hiding behind one piece of furniture after another, peering out, distraught with terror, to see the staring eyes and maybe a wild grin" ("Dear Life" 46). Munro says her mother "stayed by the dumbwaiter" because "What else could she do?" ("Dear Life" 46). She thinks her mother would not have gone into the cellar because it would have been more horrible to be trapped down there in the dark, and she could not have gone upstairs because she would have had to cross the "big room where the beatings would take place in the future, but which was not so bad after the stairs were closed in" ("Dear Life" 46).

Munro says the earlier versions of her mother's story of old Mrs. Netterfield end here with the old woman peering in the windows, but that in later versions the old woman gets impatient and goes away. What the mother calls "The visitation of old Mrs. Netterfield" ("Dear Life" 46) actually seems to end for Munro when she asks her mother at some point what became of the old woman. Her mother's stark reply: "'They took her away.... She wasn't left to die alone'" ("Dear Life" 46).

But it is not the end of the story for Munro the writer. She tells about when she was married and living in Vancouver, but still getting the weekly paper from home, she sees the name Netterfield as that of the maiden name of a woman living in Portland, Oregon who has written a simple and sentimental poem about living in Munro's hometown. Munro realizes from reading the poem and the letter that she had lived in the same house Munro lived in. Munro, the writer, considers this: "Is it possible that my mother never knew this, never knew that our house was where the Netterfield family had lived and that the old woman was looking in the windows of what had been her own house?" ("Dear Life" 47). Munro then considers some of the perhapses that can convert a mere event into a story, thinking that the woman who wrote the poem was old Mrs. Netterfield's daughter who "perhaps" came to take her away. "Perhaps that daughter, grown and distant, was who she was looking for in the baby carriage. Just after my mother had grabbed me up, as she said, for dear life" ("Dear Life" 47). And this, of course, is where Munro the writer discovers just the right multi-layered title for her memoir.

Munro ends this "childhood visitation" by describing an event in her mother's life that she later converted into a fiction: "When my mother was dying, she got out of the hospital somehow, at night, and wandered around town until someone who didn't know her at all spotted her and took her in. If this were fiction, as I said, it would be too much, but it is true" ("Dear Life" 47).

But, of course, those who know Munro's fiction will know that this last event did become fiction; it concludes the story "The Peace of Utrecht" in her first book, *Dance of the Happy Shades* (1968). When the narrator of that story hears of her mother getting out of bed and putting on her dressing gown and slippers and going out into the January snow to make her flight from the hospital, she thinks this: "*The snow, the dressing gown and slippers, the board across the bed.* It was a picture I was much inclined to resist. Yet I had no doubt that this was true, all this was true and exactly as it happened. It was what she would do; all her life as long as I had known her led up to that flight" (Munro, "The Peace of Utrecht" 208).

"The Peace of Utrecht" is an important story in Munro's fiction. As Robert Thacker points out in his biography, it is the first of her stories to deal with the facts and memory of her mother. The story originally appeared in magazine form in 1960, a year after her mother's death; Munro says it is "my first really painful autobiographical story ... the first time I wrote a story that tore me up" (Metcalf 58). It is a story she says she did not want to write, but is "the first story I absolutely had to write" (Struthers 21). Thacker says the story "represents Munro's imaginative homecoming to Wingham after her years away in Vancouver, home to the personal material that would subsequently become her hallmark" (Thacker 150).

2. Memoir or Story? Munro, Moody, and Me
Monday 28 January 2013

I have been reading and rereading the four pieces in the "Finale" section of Alice Munro's new collection *Dear Life* (2012). Munro calls them "*not quite stories*," forming a unit that she calls "*autobiographical in feeling, though not, sometimes, entirely so in fact*" (Munro, "Finale" 255). She says she believes they are "*the first and last – and the closest – things I have to say about my own life*" (Munro, "Finale" 255).

I have already written about one of these memoirs – the concluding title piece that appeared earlier in *The New Yorker* as "Dear Life: A Childhood Visitation." The first three pieces – "The Eye," "Night," and "Voices"

– are interesting to me because they provide the opportunity to explore the differences between "memoir" and "short story."

As usual, I did a little research on this relationship between memoir and story by typing the following in Google: "memoir vs. short story." And the first thing that came up was a blog entry I wrote three years ago, and damn all, if it didn't focus on a story by Alice Munro ("Some Women")! I am not sure I have anything new to say about the issue of memoir vs. short story, vis-à-vis Alice Munro, but you never know until you start exploring.

Munro has said that she has based many of her stories on her own life. That is not unusual, of course. But the question I want to explore is: What is the difference between an anecdote of an actual event in one's life and a short story based on that anecdote?

If you do some research on the memoir/fiction topic, you primarily will find discussions on the issue of "truth," that is, did the event recounted "really happen"? This is a common question members of the audience often pose to writers at "readings." Indeed, it is probably one of the first questions children ask when you tell them a bedtime story. I used to tell my children a story about being chased by a huge bull while picking blackberries in a pasture near my childhood home. They were more impressed with the story when I told them it really happened; they would have been less engaged if I had told them it was "made-up."

This, of course, is one of the reasons why biographies and autobiographies are more popular than fiction; if the work is just a "story," it seems less important, less interesting, less "real." The flap about James Frey's *A Million Little Pieces* (2003) raised the ethical question about fictionalizing one's life experiences and calling it "memoir." However, more pressing than the ethical question is the profit question: Narratives billed as an account of what actually happened simply sell better than narratives labelled as fiction.

Although this issue is most often raised with long fictions, it does occasionally crop up with short fictions. For example, when Rick Moody's short piece "Demonology" was first published in magazine form, it was listed as a memoir. However, the following year, it was included in *Prize Stories 1997: The O. Henry Awards*. When asked to comment on the work for that collection, Moody said: "There are few things I've written that I would rather talk about less" (Moody, "Contributors' Notes" 442).

However, he once told an interviewer that he is always trying to muddy the surface of the nonfictional with fictional techniques by paying particular attention to form and structure. What makes "Demonology" so affecting are Moody's efforts to transform a powerful personal experience into something that has universal significance.

The title of the piece stems from the fact that the sister's death from arrhythmia takes place within the context of Halloween, her children dressed as demons and monsters, beating back the restless souls of the dead in search of sweets. This demon motif is repeated throughout the story until ultimately the sister is transformed into a "revenant" that compels Moody to find a way to use language to communicate his grief. The story ends with Moody, in a common self-referential tactic, considering how he should have constructed his memoir, telling himself he probably should have fictionalized it more, for example, conflating the sister's two children into one and making her boyfriend a husband. He says he should have let artifice create an elegant surface for the story, thus making his sister's death shapely and persuasive rather than blunt and disjunctive. However, it is precisely the blunt, barely restrained voice that makes the story so powerful.

As a student of the short story, what interests me most about the blurry line between story and memoir is not the ethical or the economical issue, but the aesthetic one: Is there a basic difference in technique and thematic significance between a short story and a short memoir?

We might ask, why did Alice Munro give us "The Eye" as a memoir rather than a story? Was it because she felt the event that she recalls from when she was six years old – her first encounter with death – would not have yielded a complex story, but only a cliché? Of course, it is unlikely that Munro can recall in such detail the events of something that happened when she was six; it is more likely that she recalls some of the events from what her mother has told her over the years, whereas other aspects of the recollection may have actually been invented over the years. But what difference does that make?

Munro might very well have made the event recounted in "The Eye" into a story, for the child's fascination with the romantic life of the hired girl Sadie and her own ambiguous relationship with her mother can be seen in a number of Munro's stories. The central thematic issue has something to do with the scene of the child looking down into the coffin and seeing the eyelid of the dead girl lifting just a tiny bit. This does not frighten the child, but rather it fits with everything that she knew about Sadie and also with "whatever special experience was owing to myself" (269). There is a sense of recognition here, a sense of identity, not the sense that a six-year-old would feel, but rather a sense that a woman would later remember as a mutual understanding.

The short piece "Night" is a much more discursive account, based largely on thinking about something rather than on seeing or doing something. We do not know the age of the child in this piece, but she is old enough, or young enough, to have some fantasies about strangling her younger sister during the night, and she loses sleep about it. Her brief talk with her father one night when she walks out of the house is enough to make her identify with him and to appreciate his wisdom. For when she tells him about her fantasies of strangling her sister, he says not to worry, for "'People have those kinds of thoughts sometimes'" (283). And she knows that he has given her just what she needed to hear.

In "Voices," Munro is ten years old and accompanies her mother to a dance in a home to which a prostitute has brought one of her girls. But it is not the girl that so fascinates the young Munro; rather it is the talk she overhears of some of the Air Force men stationed nearby who try to comfort the young woman, and she marvels at how they bow down and declare themselves in front of her. Later, she thinks of those men, and hears their voices directed to her: "Their hands blessed my own skinny thighs and their voices assured me that I, too, was worthy of love" (298). This fascination with mysterious sexuality and the risky business of becoming thought desirable to men is a common theme in many of Munro's stories. Of these three short memoir pieces, "Voices" is, because of this thematic echo, the closest to merging into the realm of fiction.

For me, the difference between the recounting of an actual event and a fictional event has nothing to do with whether the event actually occurred, but rather whether the event "means" anything. My own experience with writing fiction is minimal. Although I have several notebooks of observations, recollections, and descriptions, I have only published two stories. Both stories are based on actual events, although they did not all happen at the same time; rather they are disparate fragments that seemed to "go together" thematically. I think putting the various "real life" events together in the way I did by providing for them a "point of view" actually resulted in "stories." However, I still have many recollections in my notebooks that remain simply that – recollections. I will provide one example of what I think is a recollection that could, with the right point of view and the right context, become a story.

When I was young, my maternal grandmother lived in the country on a farm, and I recall her in that rural context. However, my father's mother was a "city girl," although the "city" where I lived was a small Kentucky mountain town of approximately 4,000 people. My "city grandmother" seemed more sophisticated than my country grandmother, although she only had a high school education. I have many memories of her, of course, but one image sticks in my mind, although I am not sure I ever actually saw it or whether I created it out of the "late show" 1940s movies that I stayed up and watched the whole summer the first year we got television.

Here is the image:

> The Paintsville Hotel is on the main street of town, just two doors down from the Greyhound bus station, which I remember as the center of exciting activity. Between the two is the Kentucky Cafe where I occasionally stopped to play the pinball machine and get a Cherry Coke. In front of the Hotel the sidewalk is made of glass brick. The barber shop, where my paternal grandfather, always dressed in a white shirt and black bowtie, cut my hair, was just below, and because he always kept a light on there all night, a glow came up through the glass bricks so that when you walked across them it was like something out of a Busby Berkeley musical. What I remember is my grandmother in a black dress and a long black coat with a high fur collar. The collar is pushed up on her neck so that it met her short white hair. She has on heels and I see her walking down the street toward me, past the bus station, past the Kentucky Cafe, and onto the glass bricks that give a radiance to her nyloned legs. Her head is high, and her pelvis is thrust forward a bit; she looks slightly amused at something. She walks fast, her arms across her breasts, and the breeze her motion makes stirs the fur around her neck.

That is only a memoir image, but placed in the right context with the right point of view, some meaningful narrative movement, and related thematic details, it could be a story, don't you think? Whether it happened or not is not important.

3. Alice Munro's Devotion to the Short Story
Thursday 10 October 2013

In honour of Alice Munro's wonderful win of the Nobel Prize in Literature, I post the following excerpt from the final chapter of my new book, *"I Am Your Brother": Short Story Studies* (2013).

Although in the last forty years the short story has been characterized first by experimentation and then by attenuation, Alice Munro has continued to go her own way, so confident of the nature of the short story and her control of the form that she needs to observe no trends nor imitate no precursors. Certainly she does not write in a vacuum, clearly aware of those short-story masters who have preceded her – Chekhov, Turgenev, Eudora Welty, Flannery O'Connor, Raymond Carver – but Munro has found her own unique rhythm and controls it consummately.

There is always something mysterious and unspeakable in Munro's stories, even though there is never the cryptic compression of much late twentieth-century short fiction. In an almost novelistic fashion, as if she had all the time in the world, Munro lovingly lingers on her characters and seldom misses the opportunity to register an arresting image. But a Munro story is deceptive; it lulls the reader into a false sense of security in which time seems to comfortably stretch out like everyday reality, only to suddenly turn and tighten so intensely that the reader is left breathless.

Book publishers usually consider short stories the work of the beginner – M.F.A. finger-exercises they reluctantly agree to publish only if they can promise on the flyleaf that the writer is "currently working on a novel." This commercial capitulation to the fact that most readers prefer novels to short stories – along with the assumption that a big work of fiction is more important than a collection of small ones – is so powerful and pervasive that few writers are able to resist it. That Alice Munro, who has been able to resist it for so many collections of short stories, has become one of the most highly praised writers of the last half of the twentieth century should therefore go a long way toward redeeming the neglected short form. When her one novel, *Lives of Girls & Women*, was called "only a collection of short stories," she wasn't bothered, saying she didn't feel that a novel was any step up from a short story. To her credit, she has never wavered from that judgment.

With remarkable unanimity, reviewers, critics, and fellow authors agree that Alice Munro is the best short-story writer in the world today, often justifying this assessment by arguing that the numerous characters and multiplicity of events in her stories make them somehow novelistic. However, Munro has always insisted that she does not write as a novelist does, that when she is writing a short story she gets a kind of tension she needs, like pulling on a rope attached to some definite place, whereas with a novel, everything goes flabby. Characters and events don't really matter in her stories, she says, for they are subordinated to an overall "climate" or "mood." In Munro's best work, the hidden story of emotion and secret life, communicated by atmosphere and tone, is always about something more enigmatic and unspeakable than the story generated by characters and what happens next. Her greatest stories simply do not communicate as novels do.

Alice Munro has probably been asked "Why do you write short stories?" so many times that she is tired of hearing it, especially since lurking behind the question is the corollary rebuke, "Why don't you write novels?" The most common reason she has given, the one that Raymond Carver noted in his essay "Fires," is the practical one of domestic duties. In a 1986 interview, after the publication of *The Progress of Love*, Munro replied to this increasingly impertinent question: "I never intended to be a short-story writer.... I started writing them because I didn't have time to write anything else" (Rothstein). Certainly, domestic duties may help explain why authors like Carver and Munro – two of the greatest short-story writers in the latter half of the twentieth century – initially wrote pieces of fiction that they could complete in stolen blocks of time. But it does not explain why they continued to write short stories when they had more time and when their publishers kept hounding them for a novel.

The pressure on writers by agents, editors, and critics to abandon the short story as soon as possible and do something serious with their lives, such as write a novel, is unrelenting. This narrative bias that bigger is better persists in spite of the fact that the faithful few who have ignored it are among the most critically acclaimed writers of the twentieth century: Anton Chekhov, Jorge Luis Borges, Flannery O'Connor, Grace Paley, Raymond Carver, Andre Dubus, and Alice Munro. Munro said back in 1986 that originally she planned to write a few stories to get some practice and then to write novels, but "I got used to writing stories, so I saw my material that way, and now I don't think I'll ever write a novel" (Rothstein).

The demand of household chores, although certainly not a trivial reason for choosing to write short stories, does not have enough explanatory power to satisfy the critic. On the other hand, Munro's notion that there is "a short-story way" of seeing reality is a genre issue with significant critical implications. And perhaps one way to try to understand some of the significant characteristics of the short-story form is to explore the beliefs and practices of one writer who has always seen her material in "a short-story way."

Munro once said, "I don't understand where the excitement is supposed to come in a novel, and I do in a story" (Rothstein). On another occasion, she used a metaphor of the tension you feel when pulling on a rope to describe this short-story excitement, whereas for her in trying to write a novel everything gets flabby. Munro says she doesn't seem to be able to write in any other way. "I guess that's why I can't write a novel. ... God knows I still keep trying. But there always comes a point where everything seems to be getting really flat. You don't feel the tension. ... I don't feel this pulling on the rope to get to the other side that I have to feel" (Struthers 15). Munro added, "People have suggested this is because I want to be able to manage everything and that I fear loss of control. ... I always say yes, yes, this is my training, I have to agree [laughter] that I may indeed fear loss of control. But I don't think it's anything as simple as that" (Struthers 15).

In "What Is Real?" Munro explained that when she reads a story she does not take it up at the beginning and follow it like a road "with views and neat diversions along the way" (Munro, "What" 224). Rather, for her, reading a story is like moving through a house, making connections between one enclosed space and another. Consequently, Munro declares, "when I write a story I want to make a certain kind of structure, and I know the feeling I want to get from being inside that structure" (Munro, "What" 224). She admits that the word "feeling" is not very precise, but that "if I try to be more intellectually respectable I will have to be dishonest" (Munro, "What" 224).

Munro used the term "feeling" again when Geoff Hancock asked her if the meaning of a story is more important to her than the event. "What happens as event doesn't really much matter," Munro replied. "When the event becomes the thing that matters, the story isn't working too well. There has to be a feeling in the story" (Hancock 81). Rather than being concerned with character or cause-and-effect consequence, Munro says she wants "the characters and what happens subordinated to a climate" (Hancock 82), by which, she says, she means something like "the mood" (Hancock 83). When Hancock asked Munro about meaning and intent in her stories, she said, "What I like is not to really know what the story is all about. And for me to keep trying to find out" (Hancock 84). What makes a story interesting, she says, is "The thing that I don't know and that I will discover as I go along" (Hancock 84). When Hancock says he thinks she gives "voice to our secret selves," she agrees emphatically, "That's absolutely what I think a short story can do" (Hancock 76).

I will try to illustrate in what follows that the aspects of Munro's "specific kind of creative activity" – "tension," "control," "mood," "emotion," "mystery," "secret self," and the refusal to explain – underlie the complexity of her short stories in particular and the short story in general. What I wish to argue is that the complexity of Alice Munro's short stories is not the result of the mere multiplicity of characters and the addition of a social, ideological, or historical context, but rather the result of seeing the world in a uniquely "short-story way."

As I have argued earlier in this book, the short story's "way of seeing" is like that which Ernst Cassirer says characterizes perceiving the world in a mythic way, for it means not distinguishing objective characters, but rather "physiognomic qualities" (Cassirer 77). When Munro says she is primarily interested in "emotion," she echoes Cassirer when he says that within mythical perception "Whatever is seen or felt is surrounded by a special atmosphere" (Cassirer 76). In this realm, says Cassirer, "we cannot speak of 'things' as ... dead or indifferent stuff," for "All objects are benign or malignant, friendly or inimical, familiar or uncanny, alluring and fascinating or repellent and threatening" (Cassirer 77).

Rather than plot or ideology, what unifies the short story is an atmosphere, a certain tone of significance. As Alberto Moravia has noted, when Chekhov tried his hand at a novel he was less gifted and convincing than he was with the short story. If you look at Chekhov's long stories, says Moravia, you feel a lack of something that makes a novel, even a bad novel, a novel, for in them "Chekhov dilutes his concentrated lyrical feeling with superfluous plots lacking intrinsic necessity" (Moravia 148).

The very qualities that make him a great short-story writer become defects when Chekhov tackles a novel. Characters in short stories are the product of "lyrical intuitions," says Moravia; short stories get their "complexity from life and not from the orchestration of some kind of ideology" (Moravia 150). The short story focuses on an experience under the influence of a particular mood, or, as Munro would say, "emotion," and therefore depends more on tone than on plot as a principle of unity.

The secret of Alice Munro's short stories is that she is able to suggest universal, unspoken human desires – preferring meaningful fantasy to the insignificant actual, aesthetic disengagement to physical entanglement, the memoried past to the simple present – by describing what seems to be ordinary everyday reality. Her stories are complex and powerful not so much because of what happens in them, but because of what cannot happen except in the mysterious human imagination. More polished and profound than she has ever been, Alice Munro is the preeminent practitioner of the short story – and one of the most brilliant writers in any genre – in the world today. If there is any justice and judgment in matters literary, she should redeem the short story from its second-class status single-handedly.

4. Happy Birthday, Alice Munro
Friday 10 July 2015

To celebrate Alice Munro's 84th birthday today, I am posting the first few paragraphs of my new essay on Munro, which will appear in a book to be published in Canada soon.

Living in the Story:
Fictional Reality in the Stories of Alice Munro
Charles E. May
Professor Emeritus
California State University, Long Beach

Throughout her distinguished career, Alice Munro has frequently been asked by reviewers and interviewers, "Why do you write short stories?" – behind which, of course, always lurked the reproach, "Why don't you write novels?" Although she is no longer nagged about her narrative choice of the much maligned short story, reviewers and interviewers have shifted to a new tactic. Instead of chiding Munro for not writing novels, they now try to account for the success of her stories by claiming that they are *like* novels, not like short stories at all. How else to account for how great they are? Two or three such claims should be sufficient to underline the point:

> No one else quite constructs stories that have the slow, rich emotional depth of novels. (Lockerbie)

> You get, in fact, all the complexity and nuance of a novel, concentrated within several dozen pages. (Springstubb)

> Each story reads like a novel; each is a vast canvas of complicated characters, tangled events and quietly turbulent revelations. (Changnon)

Munro definitively answered the impertinent "Why do you write short stories?" question back in 1986, when she said that originally she planned to write a few stories to get some practice and then to write novels, but shrugged, "I got used to writing stories, so I saw my material that way, and now I don't think I'll ever write a novel" (Rothstein). And now everyone, even, I dare say, her agent and her publishers, are glad she never did.

Given my long-time interest in the genre, I have always been very gratified by Alice Munro's suggestion that there is a "short-story way" of seeing reality and delighted with her persistent denial that her stories are *like* novels. She has said she is not drawn to writing novels because she doesn't see that people develop and arrive anywhere, but rather that they are "living in flashes. From time to time" (Hancock 89) – an image that echoes Nadine Gordimer's famous argument that the short story as a form may be better equipped than the novel to capture whatever can be grasped of human reality "where contact is more like the flash of fireflies, in and out, now here, now there, in darkness" (Gordimer 180).

Still, it seems that reviewers can find no other way to explain the complexity of Munro's works except by lumping them together with that flabby, or, as Henry James once called it, that "baggy" monster – the novel (James 84). Can we blame her then for not being able to resist a sly jab at short-story naysayers in a fairly recent story in *Too Much Happiness* entitled "Fiction" – in which the central character buys a book written by a woman she has met briefly at a party and is disappointed to find out it is only a collection of short stories, not a novel: "It seems to diminish the book's authority, making the author seem like somebody who is just hanging on to the gates of Literature, rather than safely settled inside" (52).

Jonathan Franzen scolded critics and judges for the international neglect of Munro a few years ago by chiding, "Evidently, the feeling in Stockholm is that too many Canadians and too many pure short-story writers have already been given the Nobel" (Franzen 14). We are all happy now that Alice Munro is safely inside the Nobel gates of Literature – even if she does *only* write short stories. In one of her first interviews after winning the prize, she graciously said that the award was not only a wonderful thing for her, but a wonderful thing for the short story in general, and she hoped it would bring new readers to the form (Smith).

Despite critics' insistence on the "novelistic" nature of Munro's stories, the qualities of her work that are so compelling are actually the very qualities that have always made great short stories so powerful: for example, the short story's transformation of seemingly trivial and unrelated material into a tight, thematically-significant pattern. Fellow short-story writer Deborah Eisenberg has said that one of the joys of Munro's writing is "the apparently casual narrative that turns out to have led inexorably to some inescapable juncture" (Eisenberg 129).

And another fellow short-story writer, Lorrie Moore, noted, "The particular and careful ways Munro's themes are laid into her narrative trajectories cause them to sneak up upon the reader" (Moore 41). As I have argued for many years, this has been one of the dominant characteristics of the short-story form since Gogol, Poe, Hawthorne, Maupassant, Chekhov. Like the stories of her predecessors, Munro's fictions build toward a tightly unified thematic pattern, not the construction of a mirror in the roadway.

5. Thank You for Visiting
Friday 17 September 2021

Today my blog "Reading the Short Story" marked two million page views. I know that is not a lot in the Internet world, but it pleases me that so many people are reading my thoughts on the short story, even though I have not posted any new essays for the past three years, when, without any notice or explanation, I just stopped writing.

However, today, I thought it might be a decent gesture to make a few remarks about my decision to stop. I have been reading stories since I first discovered Edgar Allan Poe when I was growing up in the mountains of eastern Kentucky. I have read thousands of stories and written about hundreds of stories in books, articles, essays, reviews, and blog posts. It amuses, rather than amazes me, to confess that as of today, I have not read a single short story in the past three years, much less written about any.

Why?

Even my doctor at my last physical exam a year ago asked me that question. No real reason. I just turned my attention to other things – more time with my wife, children, and grandchildren. And more time returning to my pre-reading roots on my grandfather's hardscrabble farm, in honor of which I tend a garden in my back yard (great tomatoes this year) and tend four healthy hens, who faithfully deliver a couple of dozen delicious eggs each week. I also bake bread, make soup, cook meals, and enjoy watching British detective television on Britbox with my wife Patricia, who beats me at gin rummy regularly.

In the past three years, I have been invited to contribute criticism and literary theory essays by several of my colleagues in Canada, Europe, and America. Although I much appreciate the honor of these invitations, I have respectfully declined them.

In short, as I sit here surrounded by hundreds of books and four filing cabinets of drafts, notes, and ideas about the short story, I just feel that I have said enough. I turned eighty a few months ago. Other than the typical glitches that the body experiences at this age, I am basically healthy, and my mind, with the exception of the usual lapses in memory, seems, if not keen, at least capable.

I will continue to read comments that readers of my blog make to my posts and to respond to them. However, I have no plans to post any more full-length essays – unless, of course, I get wind of something that gets my goat or piques my pleasure.

I hope that students and admirers of the short story continue to find my blog essays useful. Thank you all for your support over the years.

I remain, as always, the strongest cheerleader of the short story that I can possibly be.

Cheers,
Charles

Works Cited

Carver, Raymond. "Fires." *Call If You Need Me: The Uncollected Fiction and Other Prose.* Ed. William L. Stull. Fwd. Tess Gallagher. New York: Vintage, 2001. 93-106.

Cassirer, Ernst. *An Essay on Man: An Introduction to a Philosophy of Human Culture.* New Haven, CT: Yale UP, 1944.

Changnon, Greg. "Traditional Roles Hold Munro's Women in Thrall." Rev. of *The Love of a Good Woman,* by Alice Munro. *The Atlanta Journal and Constitution* 25 Apr. 1999: 11L.

Eisenberg, Deborah. "New Fiction." Rev. of *The View from Castle Rock,* by Alice Munro. *The Atlantic Monthly* Dec. 2006: 128-29.

Franzen, Jonathan. "Alice's Wonderland." Rev. of *Runaway,* by Alice Munro. *The New York Times Book Review* 14 Nov. 2004: 1, 14-16.

Frey, James. *A Million Little Pieces.* New York: Doubleday, 2003.

Gordimer, Nadine. "'The Flash of Fireflies'." *Short Story Theories.* Ed. Charles E. May. Athens, OH: Ohio UP, 1976. 178-81. Rpt. in *The New Short Story Theories.* Ed. Charles E. May. Athens, OH: Ohio UP, 1994. 263-67.

Hancock, Geoff. "An Interview with Alice Munro." *Canadian Fiction Magazine* 43 (1982): 74-114.

James, Henry. "Preface to 'The Tragic Muse'." *The Art of the Novel: Critical Prefaces.* Introd. Richard P. Blackmur. New York: Charles Scribner's Sons, 1934. 79-97.

Lockerbie, Catherine. "The Loving Literature of Alice Munro." Rev. of *Hateship, Friendship, Courtship, Loveship, Marriage*, by Alice Munro. *The Ottawa Citizen* 30 Sept. 2001: C11.

May, Charles E. *"I Am Your Brother": Short Story Studies*. Garden Grove, CA: Amayzing Editions, 2013.

---. "Living in the Story: Fictional Reality in the Stories of Alice Munro." *Alice Munro's Miraculous Art: Critical Essays*. Ed. Janice Fiamengo and Gerald Lynch. Ottawa: U of Ottawa P, 2017. 43-61. Reappraisals: Canadian Writers 38.

---, ed. *Critical Insights: Alice Munro*. Ipswich, MA: Salem-EBSCO, 2013.

Metcalf, John. "A Conversation with Alice Munro." *Journal of Canadian Fiction* 1.4 (1972): 54-62.

Moody, Rick. "Contributors' Notes." *Prize Stories, 1997: The O. Henry Awards*. Ed. Larry Dark. New York: Anchor Books, 1997. 442.

---. "Demonology." *Conjunctions* 26 (1996): 172-82. Rpt. in *Prize Stories, 1997: The O. Henry Awards*. Ed. Larry Dark. New York: Anchor Books, 1997. 424-35.

Moore, Lorrie. "Artship." Rev. of *Hateship, Friendship, Courtship, Loveship, Marriage*, by Alice Munro. *The New York Review of Books* 17 Jan. 2002: 41-42.

Moravia, Alberto. "The Short Story and the Novel." *Short Story Theories*. Ed. Charles E. May. Athens, OH: Ohio UP, 1976. 147-51.

Munro, Alice. *Dear Life*. New York: Alfred A. Knopf, 2012.

---. "Dear Life." *Dear Life*. New York: Alfred A. Knopf, 2012. 299-319.

---. "Dear Life: A Childhood Visitation." *The New Yorker* 19 Sept. 2011: 40-47.

---. "The Eye." *Dear Life*. New York: Alfred A. Knopf, 2012. 257-70.

---. "Fiction." *Too Much Happiness*. New York: Alfred A. Knopf, 2009. 34-63.

---. "Finale." *Dear Life*. New York: Alfred A. Knopf, 2012. 253-319.

---. *Lives of Girls & Women*. 1971. New York: McGraw-Hill, 1972.

---. "Night." *Dear Life*. New York: Alfred A. Knopf, 2012. 271-85.

---. "The Peace of Utrecht." *The Tamarack Review* 15 (1960): 5-21. *Dance of the Happy Shades*. 1968. New York: McGraw-Hill, 1973. 190-210.

---. "Royal Beatings." *The Beggar Maid: Stories of Flo and Rose*. New York: Alfred A. Knopf, 1979. 3-24.

---. "Some Women." *Too Much Happiness*. New York: Alfred A. Knopf, 2009. 165-88.

---. *The View from Castle Rock*. New York: Alfred A. Knopf, 2006.

---. "Voices." *Dear Life*. New York: Alfred A. Knopf, 2012. 286-98.

---. "What Is Real?" *Making It New: Contemporary Canadian Stories*. Ed. John Metcalf. Toronto: Methuen, 1982. 223-26. Rpt. in *How Stories Mean*. Ed. John Metcalf and J.R. (Tim) Struthers. Erin, ON: The Porcupine's Quill, 1993. 331-34. Critical Directions 3.

Munro, Sheila. *Lives of Mothers & Daughters: Growing Up with Alice Munro*. Toronto: McClelland & Stewart, 2001.

Rothstein, Mervyn. "Canada's Alice Munro Finds Excitement in Short-Story Form." *The New York Times* 10 Nov. 1986: C17.

Smith, Adam. Telephone interview with Alice Munro. 10 Oct. 2013. <https://www.nobelprize.org/prizes/literature/2013/munro/interview/>.

Springstubb, Tricia. "Short Story Collection Shows Munro in Top Form." Rev. of *The Love of a Good Woman*, by Alice Munro. *The Plain Dealer* [Cleveland] 22 Nov. 1998: 11-l.

Struthers, J.R. (Tim). "The Real Material: An Interview with Alice Munro." *Probable Fictions: Alice Munro's Narrative Acts*. Ed. Louis K. MacKendrick. Downsview, ON: ECW, 1983. 5-36.

Thacker, Robert. *Alice Munro: Writing Her Lives: A Biography*. Toronto: McClelland & Stewart, 2005. Updated ed. Toronto: Emblem-McClelland & Stewart, 2011.

Song for Alice Munro

J.R. (Tim) Struthers

On the first day of Christmas my true love gave to me Alice Munro's first three books: the story collection *Dance of the Happy Shades* (1968); what I believe publishers would now call 'a novel-in-stories' rather than "a novel," *Lives of Girls and Women* (1971); and the story collection *Something I've Been Meaning To Tell You* (1974).

♫

On the second day of Christmas my true love gave to me copies of the Canadian, American, and British editions, published in 1978, 1979, and 1980 respectively, of Alice Munro's fourth book, the story cycle *Who Do You Think You Are?* – or as it was entitled in the United States and Britain, *The Beggar Maid: Stories of Flo and Rose*. A volume to which I would devote a full chapter in my PhD dissertation, "Intersecting Orbits: The Canadian Story Cycle" (1981).

♫

On the third day of Christmas my true love gave to me Alice Munro's fifth book, the story collection *The Moons of Jupiter* (1982), along with the first two full-length critical studies of Munro (each by various hands), Louis K. MacKendrick's *Probable Fictions: Alice Munro's Narrative Acts* (1983) and Judith Miller's *The Art of Alice Munro: Saying the Unsayable* (1984), and to my special satisfaction the first biographical study of Munro, my good friend the now sadly-deceased Catherine Sheldrick Ross's concise and astute *Alice Munro: A Double Life* (1992).

♫

On the fourth day of Christmas my true love gave to me Alice Munro's next four books: the story collection *The Progress of Love* (1986), the story collection *Friend of My Youth* (1990), the story collection or, given the links among four of its eight stories, we could say the story cycle *Open Secrets* (1994), and the story collection *The Love of a Good Woman* (1998). The group that I and Ailsa Cox and Corinne Bigot and Catherine Sheldrick Ross would later examine with special care in the critical study that I envisaged and named *Reading Alice Munro's Breakthrough Books: A Suite in Four Voices* (2024).

♫

In the interview with Alice Munro that I conducted in 1981 at the invitation of Louis K. MacKendrick for his book *Probable Fictions: Alice Munro's Narrative Acts* (1983), Munro told me that she regarded the story "Royal Beatings" – the first story in *Who Do You Think You Are?* (or *The Beggar Maid*) and, prior to that, on 14 March 1977, her first story published in *The New Yorker* – as "a *big* breakthrough story" for her artistically speaking. In the same vein, although I don't think that Munro has ever identified an entire collection of hers as being highly important to her, I've long regarded her sixth book, *The Progress of Love* (1986), as her first big mid-career breakthrough book not simply commercially but most importantly artistically, as I argue in the four-author critical study *Reading Alice Munro's Breakthrough Books: A Suite in Four Voices* (2024).

I appreciate that my good friend here in Guelph Ajay Heble, author of the erudite study *The Tumble of Reason: Alice Munro's Discourse of Absence* (1994) – Ajay's a sophisticated metonymy man, I'm a simple metaphor man, sometimes a bit of a joker – would wish to make a strong case for Munro's next collection, *Friend of My Youth* (1990), though it *was* Ajay's chapter on *The Progress of Love* that Harold Bloom chose for his anthology of previously published Munro criticism *Alice Munro* (2009). And no doubt Ailsa Cox would also want to make a strong case for *Friend of My Youth*, as she does in *Reading Alice Munro's Breakthrough Books: A Suite in Four Voices* (2024).

And I appreciate that the distinguished American short story critic and theorist Charles E. May, editor of the collection of new studies of Munro (by various hands) *Critical Insights: Alice Munro* (2013), would wish to make a strong case for the succeeding volume by Munro, *Open Secrets* (1994), as Charles did in conversation with me during a short story conference at l'Université d'Angers in April 2011. And no doubt Corinne Bigot would also want to make a strong case for *Open Secrets*, as she does in *Reading Alice Munro's Breakthrough Books: A Suite in Four Voices* (2024).

I also assume that my good friend since our early years at The University of Western Ontario, my fellow Alice Munro enthusiast Catherine Sheldrick Ross, would want to add to this group Munro's next collection, *The Love of a Good Woman* (1998), based initially on Catherine's brilliant examination, published in the *University of Toronto Quarterly* (Summer 2002), of that book's opening title novella and subsequently on her superb re-examination of that same collection in *Reading Alice Munro's Breakthrough Books: A Suite in Four Voices* (2024).

Giving us what we might well agree to call Alice Munro's four big mid-career breakthrough books. Something that brings to mind the metaphor of "the four pillars," as the four major foundational books – *Fearful Symmetry*, *Anatomy of Criticism*, *The Great Code*, and *Words with Power* – of the late Canadian critic Northrop Frye's oeuvre can be viewed. A notion about Frye's work that Alvin A. Lee, general editor of the thirty-volume *Collected Works of Northrop Frye* (1996-2012), has observed in correspondence with me possesses "descriptive usefulness and connotative power." And a notion, I would suggest, that may be applied appropriately and effectively to characterizing the stature of Munro's four volumes *The Progress of Love* (1986), *Friend of My Youth* (1990), *Open Secrets* (1994), and *The Love of a Good Woman* (1998).

♫

It would be challenging, I think, to find a much bolder, much more complex, much more compelling book by Munro than *The Progress of Love* (1986) – though undoubtedly Ailsa and Corinne and Catherine would have something to say about that view! And it would be difficult, I think, to find a much bolder, much more complex, much more compelling story than the third-last piece in that collection, "A Queer Streak." Mind you, the subsequent novellas by Munro "The Love of a Good Woman," "Hateship, Friendship, Courtship, Loveship, Marriage," "Powers," "The View from Castle Rock," and "Too Much Happiness" do stand out. Especially mesmerizing in "A Queer Streak" is the moment near the end when the by then seemingly dementia-diminished main character Violet Thoms, after uttering the wholly incomprehensible and thoroughly terrifying noise "*Annhh*," offers the absolutely dumbfounding line "'There is a wild pig running through the corn.'"

A line which, as I stated in the essay on Munro that I contributed to Charles E. May's *Critical Insights: Alice Munro* (2013), initially seems like complete madness, thereby proving to be even more horrifying later when it finally registers clearly for us as pure metaphor, as a poetic revelation allowing us to look back on the story and interpret anew the very complex, sexually fraught, very dark web of family relationships portrayed therein.

A line which, I wish to argue here, can be connected in terms of both subject and phrasing to Sir James Frazer's chapter on "The Corn-Spirit as an Animal" in *The Golden Bough: A Study in Magic and Religion*. Indeed anyone who recalls Violet's statement that "'There is a wild pig running through the corn'" will note with interest in Frazer's chapter that it is the pig or boar or sow that he chooses to emphasize as the final type of manifestation of the corn-spirit in animal form. Moreover, to our considerable excitement, we encounter as Frazer's very first illustration of this phenomenon the eerily familiar statement that "In Thüringen, when the wind sets the young corn in motion, they sometimes say, 'The Boar is rushing through the corn.'"

Of course, from *Friend of My Youth* (1990), there's Munro's widely praised and widely studied story "Meneseteung." A story I like to call a "brief epic," as I termed it in the essay "In Search of the Perfect Metaphor: The Language of the Short Story and Alice Munro's 'Meneseteung'" that Charles E. May kindly included in his book *Critical Insights: Alice Munro* (2013). An essay that I was especially happy to see published, if only, though certainly not only, because it allowed me to identify for the first time in print the source of the first name, Almeda, of the fictional nineteenth-century Southwestern Ontario poetess Almeda Joynt Roth whose story is told in "Meneseteung": that source being one of the imaginary names chosen for herself by Emily Brontë, author of the mesmerizing poetic novel *Wuthering Heights* – one of Munro's lifetime favourite literary works and also, I believe, the greatest influence on the design, the narration, of her stories. "Meneseteung" also being the subject of my creative/critical essay "Imagining Alice Munro's 'Meneseteung': The Dynamics of Co-Creation" published in *Alice Munro: A Souwesto Celebration*, the special issue of *The Windsor Review* (Fall 2014) that I co-edited with poet John B. Lee.

Then in *Open Secrets* (1994) there's "Spaceships Have Landed," of which, when Munro and I spoke over the phone after I had reviewed that collection for *Books in Canada* and I stressed how much I had enjoyed that story, she said to me, "I wanted it to be like Mozart" – a comment which continues to amaze, mystify, uplift me in the way that "Spaceships Have Landed" does itself. As I remain fascinated by the same book's title story, "Open Secrets," about which I wonder if any critic besides me and George Elliott Clarke has ever speculated that this story very conceivably represents Munro's historiographic take on, that is, her fictional take-off from, the actual 1959 rape and murder in Clinton, Ontario (Munro's hometown for forty-five years from 1975 until 2019) of twelve-year-old Lynne Harper *supposedly* by her fourteen-year-old classmate Steven Truscott. A crime for which Truscott was originally found guilty, sentenced to be hanged but then given a life sentence, imprisoned from 1959 to 1969, and eventually, in 2007, after much more careful judicial deliberations, acquitted.

And turning to *The Love of a Good Woman* (1998), selections particularly worthy of attention, I would say, besides the opening title novella so effectively studied twice by Catherine Sheldrick Ross, include the unrelentingly fierce, horrifying, and yet extraordinarily beautiful story "Save the Reaper" also brilliantly examined in a separate essay by Catherine and the haunting and indeed haunted final story, "My Mother's Dream."

♫

Sometime, I reflect, I'd like to write an essay analyzing all four final stories of what I regard as Alice Munro's four big mid-career breakthrough books: namely, "White Dump" from *The Progress of Love* (1986),

"Wigtime" from *Friend of My Youth* (1990), "Vandals" from *Open Secrets* (1994), and "My Mother's Dream" from *The Love of a Good Woman* (1998). For the time being, I'll identify this imagined essay of mine by the title "'Last Things': Night and Delight in Four of Alice Munro's 'Last Stories'." I've got an even stronger title in mind, one based on an idea I have about the choice she made for the title of one of these 'Last Stories' I want to discuss, but I think I'd like to wait a while before disclosing that.

♫

On the fifth day of Christmas my true love gave to me a veritable shelf of critical and/or biographical and/or bibliographical studies of Alice Munro: Brenda Pfaus's monograph *Alice Munro* (1984); Hallvard Dahlie's monograph *Alice Munro and Her Works* (1985); The University of Calgary Press's *The Alice Munro Papers: First Accession* (1986); W.R. Martin's critical book *Alice Munro: Paradox and Parallel* (1987), the first single-author study of Munro; The University of Calgary Press's *The Alice Munro Papers: Second Accession* (1987); E.D. Blodgett's critical book *Alice Munro* (1988); Michelle Gadpaille's monograph *The Canadian Short Story* (1988); Lorraine M. York's critical book *The Other Side of Dailiness: Photography in the Works of Alice Munro, Timothy Findley, Michael Ondaatje, and Margaret Laurence* (1988); Ildikó de Papp Carrington's critical book *Controlling the Uncontrollable: The Fiction of Alice Munro* (1989); Neil K. Besner's monograph *Introducing Alice Munro's* Lives of Girls and Women*: A Reader's Guide* (1990); Beverly J. Rasporich's critical book *Dance of the Sexes: Art and Gender in the Fiction of Alice Munro* (1990); W.J. Keith's critical book *Literary Images of Ontario* (1992); Magdalene Redekop's critical book *Mothers and Other Clowns: The Stories of Alice Munro* (1992); Karen E. Smythe's critical book *Figuring Grief: Gallant, Munro and the Poetics of Elegy* (1992); James Carscallen's critical book *The Other Country: Patterns in the Writing of Alice Munro* (1993), the kind of book, I like to imagine, that Northrop Frye would have written had he given the same attention to Alice Munro that he devoted to the earlier visionary William Blake; Louis K. MacKendrick's monograph *Some Other Reality: Alice Munro's* Something I've Been Meaning To Tell You (1993); Ajay Heble's critical book *The Tumble of Reason: Alice Munro's Discourse of Absence* (1994); John Cooke's critical book *The Influence of Painting on Five Canadian*

Writers: Alice Munro, Hugh Hood, Timothy Findley, Margaret Atwood, and Michael Ondaatje (1996); McClelland & Stewart's pamphlet *ALICE MUNRO:* Selected Stories*: A Tribute* (1996); Coral Ann Howells' critical book *Alice Munro* (1998); and Robert Thacker's collection of new studies of Munro (by various hands) *Alice Munro Writing On ...*, a volume published as a special issue of the journal *Essays on Canadian Writing* (Winter 1998) and then republished in book form under the new title *The Rest of the Story: Critical Essays on Alice Munro* (1999).

♫

On the sixth day of Christmas my true love gave to me copies of Alice Munro's tenth and eleventh books: the story collection *Hateship, Friendship, Courtship, Loveship, Marriage* (2001), highlighted for me by such stories as "Floating Bridge" and "Family Furnishings," and, along with that volume, the story collection *Runaway* (2004), featuring, along with the novella "Powers" to which I was able to devote a long essay published in *Alice Munro Everlasting: Essays on Her Works II*, the stories "Chance" and "Soon" and "Silence." The last three representing linked stories or a "mini-cycle" – to employ the critical term invented by Allan Weiss and discussed by him in a notable series of essays and later in his critical book *The Mini-Cycle* (2021), a volume that Allan very kindly dedicated to me.

♫

On the seventh day of Christmas my true love gave to me copies of first, Munro's father's, Robert Laidlaw's, historical novel *The McGregors: A Novel of Pioneer Life* (1979), second, Munro's own twelfth book, *The View from Castle Rock* (2006), a volume that brings together works of fictional autobiography (or as I call the first group, "story-memoirs") and works of autobiographical fiction (or as I call the second group, "memoir-stories") – placing the emphasis on the second part of each term, with the first part modifying it – and, third, Munro's eldest daughter Sheila Munro's memoir / autobiography *Lives of Mothers & Daughters: Growing Up with Alice Munro* (2001). Three volumes edited by the renowned Douglas Gibson, who, at an event in Guelph promoting his own book *Stories about Storytellers: Publishing Alice Munro, Robertson Davies, Alistair*

MacLeod, Pierre Trudeau, and Others (2011) – a good twenty-five years into my well-paying career as an English professor at the University of Guelph; that is, many years after he rejected the application I had made, in my hour of need as I finished my PhD work, for a modestly-paying position as an editorial assistant to him – would wittily, and warmly, inscribe my copy of his book (on what I mentioned was the twentieth anniversary of the death of my father) "For Tim, An old friend, who owes me his salary! On a significant date – November 25, 2011 Doug."

The McGregors (1979), *The View from Castle Rock* (2006), *Lives of Mothers & Daughters* (2001). Three volumes that are so individually unique and yet so intriguingly related that I find myself wishing they could be issued anew together, and thus be read together, either as a boxed set or as an omnibus. Perhaps to be titled *The Munro Saga.* A good subject – and a good title – for another new essay, it occurs to me as I write.

♫

On the eighth day of Christmas my true love gave to me another shelf of studies of Alice Munro: including a copy of Sheila Munro's memoir / autobiography *Lives of Mothers & Daughters: Growing Up with Alice Munro* (2001) inscribed "For Tim With best wishes Sheila Munro April 25, 2001 Guelph"; Gerald Lynch's critical book *The One and the Many: English-Canadian Short Story Cycles* (2001); JoAnn McCaig's critical book *Reading in: Alice Munro's Archives* (2002); Héliane Ventura and Mary Condé's collection of new studies of Munro (by various hands) *Alice Munro: Writing Secrets*, a volume published as a double-issue of the journal *Open Letter* (Fall 2003-Winter 2004); Ailsa Cox's critical book *Alice Munro* (2004); Robert Thacker's comprehensive *Alice Munro: Writing Her Lives: A Biography* (2005); Charles W. Mayer's collection of new studies of Munro (by various hands) which I'll entitle, borrowing the wording that appears on the volume's specially commissioned cover, *Alice Munro*, this published as a special issue of the journal *Eureka Studies in Teaching Short Fiction* (Spring 2006); a copy of the issue of the *Virginia Quarterly Review* (Summer 2006) containing a special section, introduced by the journal's editor, Ted Genoways, called "Ordinary Outsiders: A Symposium on Alice Munro"; Carol Mazur and Cathy Moulder's authoritative bibliography *Alice Munro: An Annotated Bibliography of Works and Criticism*

(2007); Gianfranca Balestra, Laura Ferri, and Caterina Ricciardi's collection of new studies of Munro (by various hands) *Reading Alice Munro in Italy* (2008); Brad Hooper's critical book *The Fiction of Alice Munro: An Appreciation* (2008); Ulrica Skagert's critical book *Possibility-Space and Its Imaginative Variations in Alice Munro's Short Stories* (2008); Harold Bloom's collection of previously published Munro criticism *Alice Munro* (2009); Deborah Heller's monograph *Daughters and Mothers in Alice Munro's Later Stories* (2009); Jayasree Sukumaran's critical book *The Feminist Challenge: Alice Munro and Anita Desai* (2009); Daniel Deleanu's monograph *Imaginary Time-Space Continuum: Logosophistic Reader-Response Incursions Into the Fiction of Alice Munro and Margaret Atwood* (2010); and Héliane Ventura's collection of new studies of Munro (by various hands) *The Short Stories of Alice Munro*, a volume published as a special issue of the *Journal of the Short Story in English* (No. 55, Autumn 2010).

♫

On the ninth day of Christmas my true love gave to me a copy of Alice Munro's thirteenth book, the story collection *Too Much Happiness* (2009). While reading the final pages of its closing title novella, my eyes filled with tears – in part at experiencing the beauty and the emotion of what was being evoked, in part at appreciating the beauty and the emotion of the writing itself, in part also at feeling such sorrow because this book might be, as Munro had hinted upon its publication, the final volume she would ever write. Not that the connection with Munro that I have enjoyed both aesthetically through studying her work and personally through readings and interviews and conversations and correspondence would end, or even be reduced, with the publication of a final volume of new work. But, but, I thought and felt momentarily. Then again, I reminded myself, there are, there will always be, the stories – "radiant, everlasting," to borrow the words used by Munro's fictional alter ego Del Jordan in the end-piece, "Epilogue: The Photographer," to *Lives of Girls and Women.*

It was while reading or right after reading the final pages of the title novella "Too Much Happiness" that I realized what I thought had to be the source from which Alice Munro derived – consciously or half-consciously or unconsciously, be that as it may – the title phrase of the novella and of the book: Thomas Hardy's 1891 novel *Tess of the d'Urbervilles.* Specifically a passage from Chapter 58 of that novel, the overwhelmingly sad speech by the title character towards the close of the mythically sculpted, mythically charged, second-last chapter set at Stonehenge, where the soon to be imprisoned and executed Tess declares to her beloved, "'Angel, I am almost glad – yes, glad! This happiness could not have lasted. It was too much.'" A further case, I discovered later, could be made for a different source, a work by a favourite author from Munro's childhood, L.M. Montgomery's 1908 novel *Anne of Green Gables*. Specifically a passage from Chapter 21 of that novel, where we learn – about Anne's response upon seeing the pleasure of the minister and his wife, Mr. and Mrs. Allan, at Anne's decorating the family tea table for them – that "Anne felt that Mrs. Allan's approving smile was almost too much happiness for this world."

♫

On Thursday 10 October 2013 when I opened my first e-mail message of the day and learned from Will Wellington, my convivial and bright undergraduate research assistant over the preceding summer, the glorious news of Alice Munro's being named the winner of the Nobel Prize in Literature, I suddenly found myself, to my complete surprise, weeping: weeping uncontrollably for ten minutes or more. For delight *for Alice*, of course – the first person concentrating wholly on short story writing to receive this absolutely warranted yet still astonishing recognition, the first Canadian writer thus honoured, and only the thirteenth woman so honoured – but I was sure for some other reason besides.

That day I decided I wanted to hear two voices. One was that of my very good-humoured old friend, the now sadly-deceased University of Windsor English professor Louis K. MacKendrick, who more than thirty years earlier had asked me to do an interview with Alice for his book *Probable Fictions: Alice Munro's Narrative Acts* (1983), who subsequently wrote the monograph *Some Other Reality: Alice Munro's* Something I've Been Meaning To Tell You (1993), and who composed a number of very fine essays on contemporary Canadian fiction, including three for me: one on John Metcalf and Leon Rooke's anthology *81: Best Canadian Stories*, one on Jack Hodgins' novel *The Invention of the World*, and one on Alice Munro's story "Meneseteung." Kim was as delighted for Alice as I was. And when, during our phone conversation, I spoke of planning to write this piece, he encouraged me to emphasize that "Meneseteung" had been the *only* story by a Canadian to be selected for John Updike's historic anthology *The Best American Short Stories of the Century* (1999).

The other person whose voice I wanted to hear that day was Vancouver Island novelist, short story writer, and now-retired University of Victoria Creative Writing professor Jack Hodgins, subject of a book I edited under the title *On Coasts of Eternity: Jack Hodgins' Fictional Universe* (1996) and a very supportive mentor and good friend to many, myself included. Alice and Jack are old friends, from even before he published the first of his now more than a dozen books, the story cycle *Spit Delaney's Island* (1976) – ever since the time in the very late Sixties when Alice had only recently published her début collection *Dance of the Happy Shades* (1968), was living in Victoria, and accepted an invitation from Jack to visit his senior English class at the high school in Nanaimo where he taught for two decades. That pleasurable experience has now been recorded by Jack in his piece "Looking, Imagining" published under my editorship in *Alice Munro Country: Essays on Her Works I* (2020). Happily, I was able to visit over the phone with Jack the same day as the announcement about the award was made, at which time, after expressing his own delight for Alice, he observed, "What a blessing for us all!"

How exhilarating, too, it was for me that day and in the days following to receive messages, salutations, from family members, friends, writers here and in the rest of Southwestern Ontario, including my fellow Guelph, Ontario resident, the now sadly-deceased biographer of Northrop Frye and authority on Inuit art, John Ayre, including Woodstock, Ontario writer Robyn-Marie Butt, including London, Ontario writers William Butt and Jason Dickson. In addition to greatly-appreciated e-mails from several current or former University of Guelph students including, as previously mentioned, Will Wellington, along with Kayla Besse, Alec Follett, Graeme Northcote, Abigail Slinger, Tara Sutton, Christine Tavener, and Meredith Kemila (subsequently a high-school English teacher here in Guelph of my granddaughter Rowan) – as well as a very considerate phone call, on the day the award was announced, from Maša Torbica, who in 2023 successfully completed her PhD work in English at the University of Waterloo.

People wishing to express their amazement and pleasure at being a part of what I – as a life-long student of the pioneering Canadian literary historian Carl F. Klinck, for whom I did my initial research and essay-writing on Munro in the summer of 1974 at Western and with whom Alice Munro herself studied a quarter-century earlier there – consider fair to call "the greatest moment in Canada's literary history." People wishing to express their amazement and pleasure to someone whom they appreciate for striving to illustrate in every course he taught, and now for fifty years as a Munro scholar, how much can be gained from reading and rereading Munro's stories. A group that I believe can be seen as standing for their counterparts of all ages throughout what, by way of allusion to a line in our national anthem, I'd call "The True North strong and free!" – heroes, if you will, in the epic quest to achieve a genuine, rich, diverse Canadian education and culture and scholarship in whatever forms those need to develop.

And how gratifying it was for me to receive a thoughtful (in both senses of that word), hand-written letter from my former University of Guelph student Murray Tong, who at the time worked for the University of British Columbia Press and now works for Wilfrid Laurier University Press – a letter that began, very appropriately I thought, on the back of a postcard depicting the front cover of the first edition of E.V. Rieu's translation of Homer's epic *The Odyssey*, the first volume, published in 1945, in the Penguin Classics series. Reasons for the appropriateness of this postcard including the fact that various contemporary practitioners of short fiction, among them Canadian writer and editor Kent Thompson, have devoted a good part of their attention to developing the form of "the postcard story," along with the fact that one of the strongest stories in Munro's first collection, *Dance of the Happy Shades*, is called "Postcard." And the fact that a character in the final story, the title story, of her story cycle *Who Do You Think You Are?* (or *The Beggar Maid*) is called Milton Homer after not one but two writers of epic, along with the fact that there are further indications in other works by Munro – the creation story "Walker Brothers Cowboy" chosen to open *Dance of the Happy Shades*, the "brief epic" "Meneseteung" from *Friend of My Youth*, and, as my good friend William Butt has demonstrated, the twelve-part *The View from Castle Rock* – that she sees herself, at least in some fashion, as working out of the epic tradition, relocating it in Southwestern Ontario, balancing "history" and "herstory," making it her own: something ancient and modern, something oral and written.

♫

Reflecting back, I suppose that my deepest feeling about Alice Munro's being awarded the Nobel Prize in Literature – in addition to delight *for her* – involved some sense, not so much of "a blessing for us all," as Vancouver Island writer Jack Hodgins so graciously, and so characteristically of him, described it over the phone to me, but more of a vindication for us all, for devoted practitioners, readers, and scholars of the short story worldwide. Especially for those of us here at home: for Canadian writers, for Canadian readers, for those visionary and intrepid and diligent Canadian scholars who have chosen to specialize in their own literature, particularly those scholars who have chosen to focus on the short story, on Alice Munro and other Canadian story writers of the generation I call "The Canadian Renaissance."

Mavis Gallant, George Elliott, Norman Levine, Margaret Laurence, James Reaney, Hugh Hood, Alice Munro, Jane Rule, Leon Rooke, Rudy Wiebe, George Bowering, Carol Shields, Audrey Thomas, Elisabeth Harvor, Alistair MacLeod, Kent Thompson, Jack Hodgins, John Metcalf, Margaret Atwood, Clark Blaise, Raymond Fraser, Len Gasparini, Olive Senior, Ray Smith, Thomas King, Marianne Micros, Keath Fraser, Douglas Glover, Terry Griggs, Diane Schoemperlen. To catalogue for the benefit of non-Canadian readers (and librarians), and perhaps many Canadian readers (and librarians), a broad range of other story writers mainly of Alice Munro's generation whose writing, along with Munro's, has enriched – and to a very large extent *defined* – my imaginative life. Marianne Micros, my bride of now nearly fifty years, being the author of two story collections published by Guernica Editions, the Governor General's Award for Fiction short-listed collection *Eye* (2018), a book released exactly fifty years after Alice Munro published her first volume of stories, *Dance of the Happy Shades*, and then a second and I believe even stronger collection, *Statue* (2023).

And here I wonder, could certain critical essays, like certain short stories, be considered instances of "brief epic" involving epic subjects, epic catalogues, and other such devices?

♫

On the tenth day of Christmas my true love gave to me some further studies of Alice Munro: Isla Duncan's *Alice Munro's Narrative Art* (2011); the updated edition of Robert Thacker's *Alice Munro: Writing Her Lives: A Biography* (2011); Susan Lohafer's collection of new studies of Munro (by various hands) which I'll entitle, borrowing the name of the session of the short story conference at York University in Toronto from which the collection grew, *Theoretical Approaches to Alice Munro's "Passion"*, this published as a special issue of the journal *Narrative* (May 2012); Charles E. May's collection of new studies of Munro (by various hands) *Critical Insights: Alice Munro* (2013); and Charles E. May's own *magnum opus, "I Am Your Brother": Short Story Studies* (2013), which devotes its final chapter to Alice Munro.

Along with copies of the Canadian, American, and British editions of Munro's *Selected Stories* (1996), containing twenty-three works from seven of her first eight books, excluding *Lives of Girls and Women*, a volume later republished as *A Wilderness Station: Selected Stories, 1968-2014* (2014), along with Munro's *New Selected Stories* (2011), containing fifteen works from her next five books, a volume published first only in Britain but later republished in the United States as *Lying Under the Apple Tree: New Selected Stories* (2014), together with *Family Furnishings: Selected Stories 1995-2014* (2014) containing twenty-four stories from her final six books. As well as the New Canadian Library selection, *No Love Lost* (2003), with ten stories, and the Vintage selection, *Vintage Munro* (2004), with five stories. And, importantly, the Everyman's Library edition, *Carried Away: A Personal Selection of Stories* (2006), presenting seventeen stories chosen by Munro from the eight collections proceeding from *Who Do You Think You Are?* (or *The Beggar Maid*) through *Runaway*. And the Canadian counterpart to the Everyman's Library edition, published as *Alice Munro's Best: Selected Stories* (2006), and the paperback version of that, retitled *My Best Stories* (2009).

Yet exactly *which* stories, I find myself deliberating, would devoted readers of Alice Munro want to include in their own individual versions of a *Selected Stories* and a *New Selected Stories* or a one-volume best of the best by her? I do find myself imagining a collection consisting of – or at least a critical study discussing – each of the opening stories in Munro's fourteen books of new fiction. Wisest, however, not to narrow the choice but to read all of them. Wisest instead to adopt the view of

Munro's fellow Southwestern Ontario writer, the late James Reaney, who, when I praised a favourite early Munro story of mine and his during an interview with him, responded, "Oh, yes. Mmhm. Well, I don't know. I love them all."

♫

On the eleventh day of Christmas my true love gave to me a copy of Alice Munro's fourteenth book, the story collection *Dear Life*, inscribed – in Goderich, Ontario, on August 10, 2013, exactly one month after Munro's 82nd birthday and two months before she would win the Nobel Prize in Literature – "For Tim with all good wishes Alice Munro." I began reading and continued to read *Dear Life* while writing and revising the original version of this essay. "Still?" friends would ask me months later. "Oh, yes," I said. "How come?" they added – "I would have thought you'd have been one of the very first people to finish reading that book." "Not yet," I replied, then explained the method I'd devised to extend and to enhance the time spent reading it because this would greatly increase the satisfaction I gained.

"What I'm doing is, before I read a new story, I go back and reread whatever precedes it. So that before starting the second story, 'Amundsen,' I went back and read the first story, 'To Reach Japan,' for a second time. Then I moved on to 'Amundsen.' And before starting the third story, 'Leaving Maverley,' I went back and read the first story, 'To Reach Japan,' for a third time and the next story, 'Amundsen', for a second time. Then I moved on to 'Leaving Maverley.' See what I mean? By the time I get to read the last story, the title story, for the first time – I counted the stories and there are fourteen in all – I'll have read the first story, 'To Reach Japan,' fourteen times, the second story, 'Amundsen,' thirteen times, the third story, 'Leaving Maverley,' twelve times, and so on. It's a way of reading that is guaranteed to increase appreciation of all the stories in the book."

"Truth be told, though," I confessed months later, "I still haven't reached the four stories at the end headed 'Finale': 'The Eye,' 'Night,' 'Voices,' and 'Dear Life.' A group representing, in the words Munro herself uses introducing them, '*the first and last – and the closest – things I have to say about my own life.*'" "How can you stand it?" friends interjected.

I would pause to think. "Surely such a group is *worth* preparing myself for the very best that I can. I'll get to them, in good time."

I explained how I expected the rest of the process to unfold: "The first time, and each successive time, that I finish the last story and circle back to start through the collection again, I'm planning on dropping one story, then a second story, then another, beginning with the earliest, 'To Reach Japan,' then, the next time through, 'Amundsen,' and, the time after that, 'Leaving Maverley.' When I've read the last story for the last time, I'll have read every story in the book fourteen times. Probably no one else in the world, besides Alice Munro, will be able to claim that."

And how long should we have to wait, I wonder, how old do we have to be, before we allow ourselves that luxury? I was sixty-two years of age by the time *Dear Life* was published and sixty-three going on sixty-four when I first drafted this piece as 2013 rolled into 2014. But for the record, to the relief of my friends and to my own final satisfaction, I didn't keep to my original plan in the end: at some point after reading most of the stories multiple times, I skipped ahead and read the last stories in *Dear Life* including the "Finale" of four stories: "The Eye," "Night," "Voices," and the collection's powerful title story.

♫

"That's like the way we sing the old carol 'The Twelve Days of Christmas'," chimed in Alice Munro's friend, Goderich librarian, local historian *extraordinaire*, and all-round good guy Reg Thompson, when I told him how I was reading *Dear Life*. "Yes," I said, instead of "Thank you" – repeating the mistake that Munro's fictional alter ego Del Jordan initially made in response to the offering by Bobby Sherriff in Munro's "Epilogue: The Photographer" in *Lives of Girls and Women*. Now, however, recalling Reg's merry and inspiring reply, I find myself wanting to extend a heartfelt "Thank you" to him for providing an epiphanic insight that lingered potently in my mind until it needed to resurface to supply the structure and the impetus this essay required.

"The Twelve Days of Christmas" indeed, Reg! And would you believe that I started the first draft of this piece on the first day of Christmas and finished that draft on the twelfth?

♫

The late Canadian poet and story writer and critic Bronwen Wallace – author of a number of important essays including one on Munro called "Women's Lives: Alice Munro" and another called "Why I Don't (Always) Write Short Stories" – thought that ideally an essay ought to strive to be, or that at least it could choose to culminate in, a poem. I could try that here: say, reproducing the poem "Burning Land" by my good friend John B. Lee, the Southwestern Ontario writer whom I consider to be in many ways the very deserving heir, though he carries himself so humbly and warmly and generously, to James Reaney's and Alice Munro's massive creative mantles. But instead what I think I should probably insert would be something in a form that I myself am more experienced at creating, a bibliography.

My original thought when I began writing this piece was to conclude it with a list of recommended readings that – with an affectionate nod to my old friend the late Southwestern Ontario short story writer George Elliott's (and his friend the photographer John Reeves's) travel book *God's Big Acre: Life in 401 Country* (1986), and also with an admiring nod to the late Southwestern Ontario artist Jack Chambers' painting *401 Towards London No. 1* (1968-69) – would be comprised of 401 items and called "401 Ways of Looking at Souwesto." But I've subsequently researched and published a version of that imagined bibliography – it appears in *Alice Munro Country: Essays on Her Works I* under the title "A Bibliographical Tour of Alice Munro Country."

More appropriate, I then thought, while I continued to write this piece, would be for me to present at the end a reading guide, a critical guide, listing book by book, in the order in which each volume's contents have been arranged, the 148 stories collected by Alice Munro from *Dance of the Happy Shades* (1968) up to and including *Dear Life* (2012). That's a list we could all enjoy contemplating. But in fact I was able to compile that, too – for the special issue of *Short Story* that I edited under the title *Alice Munro and the Souwesto Story* (2013 [2015]). Now, therefore, some ten years having passed since I prepared and published the original version of this piece, I've decided, by way of an ending, to provide a bibliography of the critical books or special issues of journals published in honour of Alice Munro since she was awarded the Nobel

Prize in Literature on 10 October 2013 and since I drafted the original version of this essay.

♫

So here you go! A record of close to *thirty-five* critical books or special issues of journals published in honour of Alice Munro from 2014 to 2025!

Beginning in 2014 ... Corinne Bigot and Catherine Lanone's critical book *Sunlight and Shadows, Past and Present: Alice Munro's* Dance of the Happy Shades; a special issue of *Études Canadiennes / Canadian Studies* 77 edited by Françoise Le Jeune under the title *Alice Munro's Short Fiction Writing*; Mala Sharma's critical book *The Inner Voice: A Study of the Fiction of Alice Munro*; and the special issue of *The Windsor Review* 47.2 edited by J.R. (Tim) Struthers and John B. Lee under the title *Alice Munro: A Souwesto Celebration.*

Then in 2015 a host of volumes ... the special issue of *Commonwealth Essays and Studies* 37.2 edited by Corinne Bigot under the title *Alice Munro: Writing for Dear Life*; the collection *"With a Roar from Underground": Alice Munro's* Dance of the Happy Shades co-edited by Corinne Bigot and Catherine Lanone; the collection *Alice Munro: Reminiscence, Interpretation, Adaptation and Comparison* co-edited by Mirosława Buchholtz and Eugenia Sojka; Ailsa Cox and Christine Lorre-Johnston's critical book *The Mind's Eye: Alice Munro's* Dance of the Happy Shades; Sabrina Francesconi's critical book *Alice Munro, il piacere di raccontare*; the collection *The Inside of a Shell: Alice Munro's* Dance of the Happy Shades edited by Vanessa Guignery; the special issue of *Études de Stylistique Anglais* 8 edited by Manuel Jobert and Michael Toolan under the title *Stylistic Perspectives on Alice Munro's* Dance of the Happy Shades; the special issue of *Short Story* ns 21.1 (2013 [2015]) edited by J.R. (Tim) Struthers under the title *Alice Munro and the Souwesto Story*; the special section of an issue of *American Review of Canadian Studies* 45 edited by Robert Thacker under the title *The Genius of Alice Munro*; and Héliane Ventura's critical book *Alice Munro:* Dance of the Happy Shades.

And in 2016 ... the collection *Alice Munro: Understanding, Adapting and Teaching* edited by Mirosława Buchholtz; Jennifer Murray's critical book *Reading Alice Munro with Jacques Lacan*; the collection *The Cambridge Companion to Alice Munro* edited by David Staines; Robert

Thacker's critical book *Reading Alice Munro: 1973-2013*; and the collection *Alice Munro:* Hateship, Friendship, Courtship, Loveship, Marriage*;* Runaway*;* Dear Life edited by Robert Thacker.

Continuing with 2017 ... the collection *Alice Munro's Miraculous Art: Critical Essays* co-edited by Janice Fiamengo and Gerald Lynch; the collection *Alice Munro and the Anatomy of the Short Story* edited by Oriana Palusci; and the special issue of *Caliban: French Journal of English Studies* 57 edited by Héliane Ventura under the title *La question animale dans les nouvelles d'Alice Munro / The Animal Question in Alice Munro's Stories.*

Then in 2018 ... the collection *Ethics and Affects in the Fiction of Alice Munro* edited by Amelia DeFalco and Lorraine York and the collection *Space and Place in Alice Munro's Fiction: "A Book with Maps in It"* edited by Christine Lorre-Johnston and Eleanora Rao.

And in 2019 by no new titles.

Continuing with 2020 ... Mala Sharma's critical book *The Twilight Shades: A Study of* Dear Life *by Alice Munro*; the 40-piece pair of collections *Alice Munro Country: Essays on Her Works I* and *Alice Munro Everlasting: Essays on Her Works II* edited by J.R. (Tim) Struthers; and Héliane Ventura's critical book *Love-Sickness from Plato to Alice Munro.*

Then in 2021 by no new titles.

And in 2022 ... Li-Ping Geng's critical book *New Realism in Alice Munro's Fiction* and Eva Mendez's *"And Write She Did": Prerequisites for Women's Writing in the Writer Narratives of Virginia Woolf and Alice Munro.*

Continuing with 2023 ... Sabrina Francesconi's critical book *A Multimodal Stylistic Approach to Screen Adaptations of the Work of Alice Munro* and Robert Thacker's critical book *Alice Munro's Late Style: "Writing is the Final Thing".*

Then in 2024 ... J.R. (Tim) Struthers' and Ailsa Cox's and Corinne Bigot's and Catherine Sheldrick Ross's critical book *Reading Alice Munro's Breakthrough Books: A Suite in Four Voices.*

And now in 2025 ... the 24-piece collection *Thank You for Visiting: Essays on Alice Munro's Works III* edited by J.R. (Tim) Struthers.

♫

Yet recalling Bronwen Wallace's idea that ideally an essay ought to strive to be, or that at least it could choose to culminate in, a poem, I've decided after all, having recently written a poem of my own which I felt might be appropriate to use in this place (a choice that I'll say takes no little courage), to finish instead with it.

Not Just Another Birthday Poem

For Marianne Micros

On Her 80th Birthday

J.R. (Tim) Struthers

Can a person return
to writing poems
after long silence
as Yeats phrased it
but in this case after
forty-eight or more
years?

Back in September 1974
when as I like to say
the stars aligned
for this lucky guy
and I met both
my great literary love
Alice Munro
and my great
personal love
and bride of now
more than forty-six years
Marianne Micros

at the time me writing
a love poem for Marianne
about Ireland and Greece called
"To Us the Names Are Sacred"
a title that now brings to mind
the late poem
"Say the Names"
by the man described as
"the last Canadian poet"
Al Purdy

a bibliography of whose work
by Marianne
and here you have to laugh
she finished proofreading
while waiting to give birth
on 4 November 1978
to our younger daughter Joy
at St. Joseph's Hospital
in London, Ontario
where I had been born
some twenty-eight years earlier

the name Joy being chosen by me
from the lines by Coleridge
exclaiming "Joy, Lady!
is the spirit and the power,
Which wedding Nature to us
gives in dower A new Earth
and a new Heaven"
and of course also echoing
the title of Blake's poem
"Infant Joy" and
Beethoven's "Ode to Joy"

me saying younger daughter
in connection with Joy
because since getting to know
Marianne's first child Eleni
when she was not quite 5
upon their arrival from
Cuba, New York in Canada
I have always considered Eleni
to be my older very special
daughter for whom my
affection and admiration
have only grown with the years

Marianne having come to
The University of Western Ontario
in order to write her PhD dissertation
on Edmund Spenser while I
wrote mine on story cycles by
Hugh Hood and Jack Hodgins
and Clark Blaise and of course
Alice Munro about whose work
I believe that I can fairly claim
to have published in 1975
the first two scholarly articles
anywhere in the world

me continuing to be enthralled
by Munro's 148 stories
from first to last
as I am by my still-radiant bride
and our two daughters
and four grandchildren
ever more deeply
with the passing years

Can a person return
to writing poems
after long silence
as Yeats phrased it
but in this case
after forty-eight or more
years?
yes I said
to quote
another inimitable
Irish author
James Joyce
yes I said
and again
as in my wedding vow
yes

About the Editor

Highly respected throughout Canada and internationally by scholars and creative writers for his work as a bibliographer, an interviewer, a literary critic, an editor, and the publisher of Red Kite Press, J.R. (TIM) STRUTHERS has edited some thirty volumes of theory, criticism, autobiography, short stories, and poetry – including works in honour of, or by, such important writers as Clark Blaise, George Elliott, Jack Hodgins, Hugh Hood, John Metcalf, Alice Munro, and James Reaney. Among these titles are his earlier pair of Guernica Editions collections, *Clark Blaise: Essays on His Works* and *Clark Blaise: The Interviews*, published in 2016, and his more recent pair of Guernica Editions collections, *Alice Munro Country* and *Alice Munro Everlasting*, published in 2020. For now fifty years Tim has been writing about Canadian literature, particularly the short story, beginning in 1975 with the first two scholarly articles published worldwide on Alice Munro and including, in the past dozen years, a dozen other articles on Munro. Recently he contributed a substantial commentary on Munro's 1986 story collection *The Progress of Love* to *Reading Alice Munro's Breakthrough Books: A Suite in Four Voices* (2024), a volume conceived by Tim, co-authored by himself, Ailsa Cox, Corinne Bigot, and Catherine Sheldrick Ross, and published by Edinburgh University Press. Tim has conducted some forty interviews with Canadian writers, including two published interviews with Munro, and has been described by W.J. Keith, FRSC, as "probably the best literary interviewer in Canada." An enthusiastic teacher, he taught English full-time at the University of Guelph for thirty-seven years until his retirement from teaching on 31 August 2022. Tim lives in Guelph with his bride of now nearly fifty years, poet and short story writer and scholar Marianne Micros, inspired and delighted by the company of their two daughters, Eleni and Joy, and their four grandchildren, Matteo, Rowan, Asher, and Reed.

Contributor Biographies

MARGARET ATWOOD is the author of more than fifty books of fiction, poetry, and critical essays. Her latest novel *The Testaments* (2019), a joint winner of the Booker Prize, is a sequel to *The Handmaid's Tale* (1986). Her latest book of short stories is *Old Babes in the Wood* (2023). *Dearly* (2020) and *Paper Boat* (2024) are her latest volumes of poetry. Her most recent nonfiction books are *On Writers and Writing* (2015) and *Burning Questions: Essays & Occasional Pieces 2004-2021* (2022). Her other novels include *Cat's Eye* (1988), *The Robber Bride* (1993), *Alias Grace* (1996), which won the Giller Prize in Canada and the Premio Mondello in Italy, and *The Blind Assassin* (2000), winner of the Booker Prize. Her *MaddAddam* trilogy of novels is comprised of the Giller- and Booker-Prize-nominated *Oryx and Crake* (2003), *The Year of the Flood* (2009), and *MaddAddam* (2013). She has also worked as a cartoonist, illustrator, librettist, playwright, and puppeteer. Atwood has won various other awards, including the Arthur C. Clarke Award for Imagination in Service to Society, the Franz Kafka Prize, the Peace Prize of the German Book Trade, the PEN USA Lifetime Achievement Award, and the Dayton Literary Peace Prize. In 2019 she was made a member of the Order of the Companions of Honour for services to literature. Margaret Atwood lives in Toronto.

PAUL BARRETT is an Associate Professor in the School of English and Theatre Studies and in the Culture and Technology Studies program at the University of Guelph. He is the author of *Blackening Canada: Diaspora, Race, Multiculturalism* (2015) and the editor of *'Membering Austin Clarke* (2020) and the co-editor with Sarah Roger of *Future Horizons: Canadian Digital Humanities* (2023). His research is at the intersections of Canadian literature, digital humanities, diaspora, and critical race theory. His current research investigates discourses of humanism and the human in Canadian literature from the early nineteenth century to the present day.

CORINNE BIGOT has been publishing on Alice Munro's short stories for some fifteen years. She is currently Maîtresse de Conférences of postcolonial literatures at Université Toulouse Jean Jaurès in Toulouse, France, where she has been teaching full-time since 2016, having previously taught at Université Paris Nanterre for twelve years. She is the author of *Alice Munro, les silences de la nouvelle* (2014), and, with Catherine Lanone, *Sunlight and Shadow, Past and Present: Alice Munro's* Dance of the Happy Shades (2014). In addition, she has edited or co-edited two other volumes on Munro: *Alice Munro: Writing for Dear Life*, a special issue of *Commonwealth Essays and Studies* (2015), and, with Catherine Lanone, *"With a Roar from Underground": Alice Munro's* Dance of the Happy Shades (2015). Corinne has published work on Alice Munro's stories in a variety of books devoted to Munro and frequently in periodicals such as *Commonwealth Essays and Studies* and *The Journal of the Short Story in English* and *Short Fiction in Theory & Practice.* Recently she contributed a substantial commentary on Munro's 1994 story collection *Open Secrets* to *Reading Alice Munro's Breakthrough Books: A Suite in Four Voices* (2024), co-authored by J.R. (Tim) Struthers, Ailsa Cox, herself, and Catherine Sheldrick Ross and published by Edinburgh University Press. She has also been working on memory work in diasporic short fiction and life writing by women – including co-editing the two critical collections *Women's Life Writing and the Practice of Reading* (2019) and *Text and Image in Women's Life Writing: Picturing the Female Self* (2021).

WILLIAM BUTT has worked in seventeen different countries, and has published articles in Canada, the U.S.A., Europe, Africa, and Asia. He has written drama scripts produced for and broadcast on CBC television and other networks, and has had ten of his theatre scripts produced, all based on subjects from local histories. He was co-founder and for eight years artistic director of a music and video production studio in Quelimane, Mozambique, where he was based as communications consultant for the United Church of Canada. He has published criticism on individual Canadian writers including Margaret Avison, Clark Blaise, George Elliott, Robert Gourlay, Jack Hodgins, Eli Mandel, and Alice Munro, as well as *Behind Our Doors: A Memoir of Esther Warmerdam as Told to William Butt* (2011), reminiscences of World War Two in Holland by a woman who was then a teenage girl. He holds a PhD in English from The University of Western Ontario, where he wrote his dissertation under the supervision of James Reaney on the conflicts that resulted in the Donnelly mass murders and on the ensuing cultural legacy in legend, literature, and other popular art forms. He is based now in Southwestern Ontario.

ANN CLOSE was a senior editor at Alfred A. Knopf, where she began in 1970 and worked full-time until 2024. She was Alice Munro's editor there from 1977 to 2024, during which time she worked with Munro on her final eleven new books, of a total of fourteen produced by Munro over her entire career. The first was *The Beggar Maid: Stories of Flo and Rose* and the last was *Dear Life*, along with five volumes of selected stories. The final book that she edited while working full-time for Knopf was Jayne Anne Phillips' post-Civil War novel *Night Watch*, the 2024 winner of the Pulitzer Prize for Fiction. Also among her fiction writers are Sarah Bird, Jay Cantor, Stephen Harrigan, Gish Jen, Brad Leithauser, Jane Mendelsohn, Norman Rush, and Mona Simpson. Her nonfiction writers include Kai Bird, Tony Hiss, Alvin Josephy, Martin Sherwin, David Shields, and Lawrence Wright. She is the recipient of a Roger Klein Award for Editorial Excellence.

AILSA COX is Emerita Professor of Short Fiction at Edge Hill University in the United Kingdom. She is the author of *Alice Munro* (2004), *Writing Short Stories* (2005; 2nd ed., 2016), and, with Christine Lorre-Johnston, *The Mind's Eye: Alice Munro's* Dance of the Happy Shades (2015). In the past decade or so, she has published chapters on Munro in eight collections edited by short story specialists in Europe, Canada, and the United States, including volumes edited by Maggie Awadalla and Paul March-Russell (2013), Charles E. May (2013), Jochen Achilles and Ina Bergmann (2015), Robert Thacker (2016), Janice Fiamengo and Gerald Lynch (2017), Christine Lorre-Johnston and Eleanora Rao (2018), and J.R. (Tim) Struthers (2020 and 2025). Recently she contributed a substantial commentary on Munro's 1990 story collection *Friend of My Youth* to *Reading Alice Munro's Breakthrough Books: A Suite in Four Voices* (2024), co-authored by J.R. (Tim) Struthers, herself, Corinne Bigot, and Catherine Sheldrick Ross and published by Edinburgh University Press. Ailsa has also contributed essays to both *The Cambridge History of the English Short Story* (2016) and *The Edinburgh Companion to the Short Story in English* (2018). Along with her essay on "Katherine Mansfield and the Short

Story" in *The Bloomsbury Handbook to Katherine Mansfield* (2020), she has published two stories in the journal *Katherine Mansfield Studies* (2010, 2022). Additional short fiction has been widely published and collected as *The Real Louise and Other Stories* (2009) and *Precipitation* (2025). From its inception in 2011, she has been the editor of the peer-reviewed journal *Short Fiction in Theory & Practice* (Intellect Press). She has also edited the collections *The Short Story* (2008) and *Teaching the Short Story* (2011).

DENNIS DUFFY, now Professor Emeritus at the University of Toronto and formerly Principal of Innis College there, is the author of the monograph *Marshall McLuhan* (1969), the studies *Gardens, Covenants, Exiles: Loyalism in the Literature of Upper Canada/Ontario* (1982) and *Sounding the Iceberg: An Essay on Canadian Historical Novels* (1986), and three volumes focusing on nineteenth-century Southwestern Ontario writer Major John Richardson, including *A World Under Sentence: John Richardson and the Interior* (1996). He is the author, as well, of essays on numerous modern Canadian writers including Hugh Hood, Al Purdy, George Elliott, Timothy Findley, Robertson Davies, Rudy Wiebe (aka Ruby Weed, according to very young Jonathan Redekop, Dennis's beloved stepson), Michael Ondaatje, and, more recently, Alice Munro, along with articles on popular American writers such as L. Frank Baum and Annie Fellows Johnston and Edward Stratemeyer. He has also produced historical and cultural studies on topics ranging from the origins of Algonquin Park to the impact of the Vimy memorial to the preoccupations of William Lyon Mackenzie King. His reviews and commentaries have been appearing in various Toronto and national outlets over the last 50+ years. Dennis continues to live and write in Toronto.

ISLA DUNCAN is a Research Associate at the University of Chichester, West Sussex, England, where she worked for twelve years in the Department of English Studies. Before that, she taught language education at the University of Strathclyde, Glasgow. She has published essays on several female Canadian writers, among them Margaret Atwood, Joan Barfoot, Sandra Birdsell, Margaret Laurence, and Alice Munro. She is the author of *Alice Munro's Narrative Art* (2011). Her academic work is firmly rooted in the disciplines of literary linguistics and narratology. "Connections," here, represents the first personal essay she has published.

ALYDA FABER has earned degrees in English and French Literatures (Honours BA, University of Guelph), English & Creative Writing (MA, University of New Brunswick), Theology (BTh, McGill University; MDiv, United Theological College), and Christian Theology and Ethics (PhD, McGill University). In 2001 she began teaching Systematic Theology and Ethics at the Atlantic School of Theology, Halifax, Nova Scotia, where in 2023 she was appointed a Full Professor.

Faber has published essays on religious questions in film and literature appearing in journals such as *Studies in Religion*, *Literature and Theology*, and the *Journal for Religion, Film and Media*. She has also contributed essays on these subjects to various books including *The Performance Studies Reader*, *Woolfian Boundaries*, *Fascinatingly Disturbing: Michael Haneke and His Films*, and *Blessed Are the Eyes That Catch Divine Whispering: Silence and Religion in Film*. Her poetry has appeared in Canadian and Frisian literary magazines, including *Arc Poetry Magazine*, *Contemporary Verse 2*, *Ensafh*, *The Fiddlehead*, *The Malahat Review*. Along with a *Bitterzoet* chapbook, *Berlinale Erotik* (2015), Faber has published two poetry collections with icehouse poetry / Goose Lane Editions: *Dust or Fire* (2016) and *Poisonous If Eaten Raw* (2021, winner of the J.M. Abraham Atlantic Poetry Prize).

Originally introduced to Alice Munro's work by a librarian in public school, Faber grew up in "Alice Munro Country," not too far from the Gateway to Bruce (once proclaimed on an arch over Main Street in Mildmay, Ontario, now part of South Bruce), on a dairy farm equidistant from Walkerton and Hanover. As often as she's able, while cycling, she visits a "cottage" on Round Lake, Nova Scotia, a bench with hemlock branches reaching over it, on a fishing dock. No upkeep required!

DOUGLAS MAITLAND GIBSON was born in Scotland in 1943 and came to Canada in 1967, armed with degrees from St. Andrews and Yale. From 1968, until he "retired" in 2007, he worked as an Editor, and then as a Publisher. He first encountered Alice Munro when he was the Editorial Director at Macmillan of Canada, persuading her to continue writing short stories when the literary world was advising her to abandon stories in favour of "more saleable" novels. The first of the many story collections they published together was *Who Do You Think You Are?* (1978) with Macmillan of Canada. When, in 1986, he was given Canada's first editorial imprint, Alice Munro chose to follow him to McClelland & Stewart. He continued to edit all of her books, even after he became M&S's Publisher in 1988. He was among the Canadians who went to Stockholm to celebrate Alice Munro's Nobel Prize. He writes about her achievements in his books *Stories about Storytellers* (2011; 2nd ed., 2014) and *Across Canada by Story* (2015). His newest book, illustrated by Anthony Jenkins, is *Great Scots: Celebrating Canadian Writers with Links to Scotland* (2022).

TAYLOR MARIE GRAHAM is an award-winning playwright, librettist, director, theatre scholar, and educator who lives in Cambridge, Ontario / Haldimand Tract. She has an MFA in creative writing and a PhD in theatre from the University of Guelph. She works as a sessional theatre professor at universities in Southwestern Ontario and is the Community Engagement Officer at the International Institute for Critical Studies in Improvisation. Taylor has published in *Canadian Theatre Review*, *Intermission Magazine*, Routledge's *Journal of Applied Theatre and Performance*, *The Conversation*, and *Canadian Literature*. Critics have described her plays and operas as "arresting and funny" (*The Slotkin Letter*), "uncommonly cool" (*Mooney on Theatre*), "charmingly twisted" (*Toronto Star*), "powerful, and courageous" (*OnStage*), "meaningful to audiences of all ages" (*Intermission*), "darkly evocative" (*Istvan Reviews*), "psychological, theological, and ornithological" (*Our Theatre Voice*), "intriguingly oddball" (*Broadway World*), "skillfully blend[ing} dramatic and musical tones" (*NOW*), "magical" (*OntarioStage*), "searingly written" (Bill Mandel), and "profound, beautifully crafted" (*StageDoor*). Her play *Post Alice*, inspired by four short stories by Alice Munro, was produced at a local venue in Stratford, Ontario in the summer of 2021, then restaged at The Alice Munro Festival of the Short Story in Blyth, Ontario in June 2024. Her 2024 book *Cottage Radio & Other Plays*, including *Post Alice*, is published by Talonbooks.

NOAH KOZICKI was born and raised on a chicken farm in Ontario's Garden – Norfolk County. He left the farm to attend the University of Guelph where he further developed his interest in the literature and culture of Southwestern Ontario before receiving an Honours BA in English. It is this same interest which now informs poems, stories, and essays that are sporadically produced and typically unshared. The histories of Southwestern Ontario, its literature, and its inherited symbolic language are also explored in some of Noah's paintings. Will Donnelly's triumphant fiddle-playing (as animated by James Reaney) can be found alongside studies of shears and post-hole diggers on occasion at small galleries in the same geographic area that is his subject.

CHARLES E. MAY is Professor Emeritus at California State University, Long Beach, where he taught the short story for forty years. He is the author/editor of nine books on the short story, including *Short Story Theories* (1976), *Edgar Allan Poe: A Study of the Short Fiction* (1991), *The New Short Story Theories* (1994), *The Short Story: The Reality of Artifice* (1995), *Critical Insights: Flannery O'Connor* (2012), *Critical Insights: Alice Munro* (2013), and *"I Am Your Brother": Short Story Studies* (2013). He has published over three hundred articles, essays, and reviews on the form and has presented academic papers on the short story in the United States, Canada, Norway, Ireland, France, Italy, Portugal, and Spain. He was a Senior Fulbright Scholar on the Short Story in 1996-97 at University College, Dublin and Trinity College, Dublin. For many years, he maintained a blog on Reading the Short Story. The five-part composite essay published here represents his "Thank You for Visiting" assembled from his blog <may-on-the-short-story.blogspot.com> with gratitude for its reaching two million page views.

JOHN METCALF is the author of some twenty works of fiction, autobiography, and criticism, among them a collected novellas, *Vital Signs* (2016), a linked volume of stories and novellas about the writer Robert Forde and his wife Sheila, *The Museum at the End of the World* (2016), a career-spanning selected stories, *Finding Again the World* (2018), that includes "Gentle as Flowers Make the Stones," described by fellow Montreal Story Teller Ray Smith as "the most perfect short story in Canadian literature," along with the two autobiographical books *An Aesthetic Underground: A Literary Memoir* (2003; 2014) and *Shut Up He Explained: A Literary Memoir Volume II* (2007) and the monumentally important critical study *The Canadian Short Story* (2018). He has been one of the leading editors in Canada for more than five decades, editing well over two hundred books during this time, including numerous volumes of the acclaimed annual series *Best Canadian Stories*. Metcalf lives in Ottawa with his wife Myrna.

STEPHEN MICHELL is an author of novels, short stories, and children's books. He has an MA in English Literature from the University of Guelph, where his partly creative, partly critical thesis focused on short stories set in Southwestern Ontario. In 2020, his short story "As Worlds Collide" was featured on the storytelling podcast LeVar Burton Reads. His first novel, *Only the Devil Is Here* (2018, 2020) was long-listed for a 2018 ReLit Award. Most recently, he has partnered with his brother and illustrator Michael Michell to create the children's books *The Little Puppy Dragon* (2023) and *The Little Goblins* (2024).

RYAN PORTER completed his PhD at Queen's University in Kingston, Ontario, where his doctoral dissertation was awarded the A.C. Hamilton Prize for outstanding merit in 2010. His book *You Can't Get There from Here: The Past as Present in Small-Town Ontario Fiction* (2019) examines the literary myth of small-town Ontario as part of a larger "heritage industry" that reconstructs pasts according to the needs of the present. Porter's articles and reviews have appeared in *Studies in Canadian Literature*, *Canadian Literature*, *Topia*, *Excursions*, and *The Virginia Woolf Miscellany.* He lives in Ottawa and is a Professor of Technical Communication at Algonquin College, where he has also served as a General-Education Coordinator and Curriculum Consultant.

CATHERINE SHELDRICK ROSS was Emerita Professor in the Faculty of Information and Media Studies at Western University in London, Ontario, Canada. Her published work on Alice Munro includes seven critical articles, one interview, a television script for TVOntario, and a brief biography, *Alice Munro: A Double Life* (1992). Recently she contributed a substantial commentary on Munro's 1998 story collection *The Love of a Good Woman* to *Reading Alice Munro's Breakthrough Books: A Suite in Four Voices* (2024), co-authored by J.R. (Tim) Struthers, Ailsa Cox, Corinne Bigot, and herself and published by Edinburgh University Press. Her research expanded from a critical evaluation of literary works to studying the contexts of textual production and reception. Catherine and her graduate students conducted over 300 open-ended, qualitative interviews with pleasure readers on the reading experience. She drew on this corpus in numerous keynote speeches, presentations, and workshops given worldwide and in four books: the co-authored *Reading*

Matters (2006); the co-authored *Reading Still Matters* (2018); the chapter on "The Readers' Advisory Interview" in *Conducting the Reference Interview* (3rd ed., 2019); and her equally instructive and delightful *The Pleasures of Reading: A Booklover's Alphabet* (2014). She also wrote a trilogy of educational books for children, later collected as the single-volume *Shapes in Math, Science and Nature: Squares, Triangles and Circles* (2014).

Recognition of Ross's contributions includes: the Science Writers of Canada Award (1996) for best science book written for children in Canada for *Squares*; the Margaret E. Monroe Award (2013) presented annually by the American Library Association for "significant contributions to library adult services"; and Fellow of the Royal Society of Canada, Arts and Humanities (2018).

J.R. (TIM) STRUTHERS is highly respected throughout Canada and internationally by scholars and creative writers for his work as a bibliographer, an interviewer, a literary critic, an editor, and the publisher of Red Kite Press. To date he has edited some thirty volumes of theory, criticism, autobiography, short stories, and poetry over a period, it amuses him to say, of six different decades. Among these titles are his important pair of collections published by Guernica Editions in 2020, *Alice Munro Country* and *Alice Munro Everlasting*. Tim has been publishing on Canadian literature for some fifty years, beginning, in 1975, with the first two scholarly articles worldwide on Alice Munro and including, in the past dozen years, a dozen other articles on Munro. Recently he contributed a substantial commentary on Munro's 1986 story collection *The Progress of Love* to *Reading Alice Munro's Breakthrough Books: A Suite in Four Voices* (2024), a volume conceived by Tim, co-authored by himself, Ailsa Cox, Corinne Bigot, and Catherine Sheldrick Ross, and published by Edinburgh University Press. Tim has conducted some forty interviews with Canadian writers, including two published interviews with Munro, and has been described by W.J. Keith, FRSC, as "probably the best literary interviewer in Canada." Recognized for the delight he has taken in all of his publishing activities, and for the enthusiasm he has imparted as a university teacher, Tim also organized and hosted the largest celebration in history of Canadian literature and culture: the epic five-and-a-half-day and five-evening A Visionary Tradition: Canadian Literature and Culture at the Turn of the Millennium conference held in Guelph from 10 to 15 November 1999.

On 31 August 2022 Tim brought to a close a fifty-year university teaching career, including some thirty-seven years full-time at the University of Guelph commencing appropriately for a Canadianist on Canada Day, 1 July 1985. Tim lives in Guelph with his bride of now nearly fifty years, poet and short story writer and scholar Marianne Micros, inspired and delighted by the company of their two daughters, Eleni and Joy, and their four grandchildren, Matteo, Rowan, Asher, and Reed.

ROBERT THACKER is Charles A. Dana Professor of Canadian Studies and English Emeritus at St. Lawrence University in Canton, New York. The author of over seventy-five academic articles on Alice Munro, Willa Cather, the North American West, and Canadian Literature in English, his books include *The Great Prairie Fact and Literary Imagination* (1989), *Alice Munro: Writing Her Lives: A Biography* (2005; updated ed., 2011), *Reading Alice Munro, 1973-2013* (2016), and *Alice Munro's Late Style: 'Writing is the Final Thing'* (2023). His Munro biography was completed with Ms. Munro's co-operation and, at her request, he wrote the short Munro biography available on the Nobel Foundation website. Beyond his own writing, Thacker has been widely active. He was the Editor of the *American Review of Canadian Studies* (1994-2002), edited two volumes of critical essays on Munro (*The Rest of the Story* [1999], *Alice Munro* [2016]), co-edited two volumes comparing the Canadian and the U.S. West, and co-edited three volumes of *Cather Studies.* He edited a volume of Cather's poems in the Alfred A. Knopf Everyman series (2013) and is one of three editors of the *Willa Cather Review.*

Largely because of his Munro work, in November 2023 Thacker was awarded the Donner Medal in Canadian Studies by the Association for Canadian Studies in the United States. He now lives in Fort Collins, Colorado.

REG THOMPSON was for a long time friends with Alice Munro. They shared enthusiasm for rural landscape, history, and culture. They spent many hours rambling the back roads of their territory, investigating bypassed hamlets, remnants of ancient swamps, tiny pioneer cemeteries.

Thompson's focus on the intensely discovered local grows from over thirty years employment in the Huron County Library system. He has a reputation as the research specialist, helping countless researchers in history and genealogy, concentrating on the deep details, while always watching the shrubbery for overlooked clues. Appreciation for his research help has been expressed formally by authors in more books than he knows or remembers. One of the authors being Alice Munro.

He wrote the essay "All Things Considered: Alice Munro First and Last" published in the collection *Alice Munro Country* after Alice won the Nobel Prize. It was his personal consideration after reading many critical and literary assessments of her work, and the post-Nobel comments and coverage – much of which he thought missed the point. He contemplates producing a study of Munro's oeuvre, titled *Meadow Fescue; or, Goosefoot and Old Man's Beard: An Examination of Traditional Flora and Deracination in the Work of Alice Munro.*

MICHAEL TRUSSLER has published literary criticism, poetry, short stories, and creative nonfiction. His literary criticism has examined the work of Alice Munro, Mavis Gallant, Barry Callaghan, Gloria Sawai, Raymond Carver, Richard Ford, George Saunders, Rick Moody, Salman Rushdie, John Edgar Wideman, and Deborah Eisenberg. He has also written on film and photography. His short story collection *Encounters* won the Book of the Year Award from the Saskatchewan Book Awards in 2006. His collection of poetry *Accidental Animals* was short-listed for the same awards in 2007. JackPine Press published *A Homemade Life*, an experimental chapbook blending photographs and text, in 2009. The Alfred Gustav Press published the poetry chapbook *Light's Alibi* in 2018. Mansfield Press published *Rare Sighting of a Guillotine on the Savannah*, a poetry collection, in 2021. In 2022 he published his memoir about mental illness, *The Sunday Book*, with Palimpsest Press, this collection of essays winning the Saskatchewan Book Awards in the category of non-fiction and the City of Regina Award. The University of Regina Press published *The History Forest* in 2022, this book winning the Saskatchewan Book Awards in the poetry category. In 2024 Radiant Press published the poetry collection *Realia* and Goose Lane Editions published the poetry collection *10:10*. He teaches English at the University of Regina, where he was the Editor of *The Wascana Review* from 2002 to 2008.

JOHN TYNDALL lives in London, Ontario. His poems have appeared in print and on-line journals such as *The Fiddlehead*, *The Windsor Review*, and *Devour: Art & Lit Canada* and in print and on-line anthologies such as *Translating Horses: The Line, the Thread, the Underside* (2015) edited by Jessica Hiemstra and Gillian Sze, *Dénouement: A Poetry Anthology* (2021) edited by Andreas Gripp, and *True Identity: An Anthology of Writing, Poetry and Photography* (2021) edited by April Bulmer. His latest books include *Mangoes from the Seventh Dimension* (2023), first place winner of the 2022 Don Gutteridge Poetry Award, *Listen to People* (2020), and *The Fee for Exaltation* (2007). Before retiring in 2016, John worked for forty years at The D.B. Weldon Library at Western University, where Alice Munro would often ask questions of its research staff.

Acknowledgements

Margaret Atwood's "Alive to Herself: The Achievement of Alice Munro" was first published as the introduction to Alice Munro, *Carried Away: A Selection of Stories* (New York and Toronto: Everyman's Library / Alfred A. Knopf, 2006), ix-xx.

An earlier, shorter, untitled version of Ann Close's "Editing Alice Munro" appeared in "Ordinary Outsiders: A Symposium on Alice Munro," a special section of tributes to Munro published in the *Virginia Quarterly Review.*

The poem "Portrait of My Mother as a Field" by Alyda Faber that concludes her essay "Searching for an Unknown God: Alice Munro's 'What Do You Want To Know For?'" was originally published in *Poisonous If Eaten Raw* © 2021 by Alyda Faber. Reprinted by permission of Goose Lane Editions.

The five parts of Charles E. May's composite essay "Thank You for Visiting" first appeared on-line in his blog <may-on-the-short-story.blogspot.com>.

An earlier version of John Metcalf's "Casting Sad Spells: Alice Munro's 'Walker Brothers Cowboy'" was published in *Writers in Aspic.*

Earlier versions of J.R. (Tim) Struthers' "Celebrating Alice Munro" were first published on-line by Guernica Editions on its website under the title "Alice Munro: A Personal Tribute" on the occasions of her 90th birthday, 10 July 2021, and her 92nd birthday, 10 July 2023.

An earlier version of J.R. (Tim) Struthers' "Song for Alice Munro" appeared in *Alice Munro and the Souwesto Story*, a special issue of *Short Story* edited by J.R. (Tim) Struthers.

Robert Thacker's "'As Truthful As Our Notion of the Past Can Ever Be': William Maxwell, His *Ancestors*, and Alice Munro's *The View from Castle Rock*" first appeared on-line in the journal *Authorship*.

An earlier version of Reg Thompson's "The Change of Seasons: Once Upon a Time with Alice Munro" was published under the title "Cemetery Hunting with Alice Munro" in the magazine *The Rural Voice*.

An earlier version of the first poem in John Tyndall's "Times Alice Munro Asked Me a Question" was published in *Alice Munro: A Souwesto Celebration*, a special issue of *The Windsor Review* co-edited by J.R. (Tim) Struthers and John B. Lee, then in his book *Listen to People* (2020). An earlier version of the second poem was published in the on-line collection *Framed & Familiar, 101 Portraits: An International Anthology of Poetry and Photography* edited by Antony Di Nardo, then in his book *Mangoes from the Seventh Dimension* (2023).

The photograph reproduced on the cover of this volume was taken by Catherine Sheldrick Ross on an occasion that she describes in the coda to her essay published here, "Alice Munro's 'Save the Reaper': Making 'Its Live Noise after Dark'."

J.R. (Tim) Struthers wishes to offer his heart-felt appreciation to his editorial assistants Kelsey McCallum and Zariha Fatima and to his bride of nearly fifty years Marianne Micros for their generous, insightful, and good-humoured editorial assistance and personal support while he prepared *Thank You for Visiting: Essays on Alice Munro's Works III.* He would also like to offer his appreciation to the many other kind souls who provided him with such vital encouragement and inspiration during the time that he worked on this volume, including his good friends John Metcalf, Catherine Sheldrick Ross, Dennis Duffy, Robert Thacker, William Butt, Ron Shuebrook, Andrew McKague, Alec Follett, Paul Barrett, and good friend and researcher *extraordinaire* of local history Reg Thompson. And he would like to express his profound gratitude to each of the distinguished contributors to this volume, notably the many individuals who enthusiastically agreed to produce such bold new work in honour of Alice Munro. Finally, at the University of Guelph, Tim wishes to thank the ever-helpful InterLibrary Loan staff and the ever-courteous Circulation staff and the always generous, always cheerful Robin Sakowski, Manager, Access Services, at the McLaughlin Library.

MIX
Paper
FSC® C100212

Printed by Imprimerie Gauvin
Gatineau, Québec